Capitalism's Deadly Threat

Capitalism's Deadly Threat

Edited by
Walter Baier, Eric Canepa
and Haris Golemis

MERLIN PRESS

transform! Yearbook 2021
Capitalism's Deadly Threat

English edition published in the UK in 2021 by
The Merlin Press
Central Books Building
Freshwater Road
London RM8 1RX
www.merlinpress.co.uk

Editors: Walter Baier, Eric Canepa, Haris Golemis

Managing Editor: Vaggia Lyssikatou

Editorial Board: Walter Baier, Eric Canepa, Haris Golemis, Adoración Guamán Hernández, Dagmar Švendová, Andreas Thomsen

transform! europe EUPF, Square de Meeûs 25, 1000 Brussels, Belgium
Partially financed through a subsidy from the European Parliament.

Cover Illustration: Stavroula Drakopoulou

ISSN 1865-3480

ISBN 978-0-85036-770-6

Printed in the UK by Imprint Digital, Exeter

Contents

Preface
Walter Baier, Eric Canepa, Haris Golemis:
    Capitalism's Deadly Threat   9

In Memoriam
Ingar Solty: The Global Left, Marxism, and Democratic Socialism:
    Remembering Leo Panitch (1945-2020)   23

Europe
Walter Baier: The State of the Union:
    On the Eve of the Conference on the Future of Europe   35

Capitalism's Ecological Crisis and Radical Left Alternatives
John Bellamy Foster: The Planetary Rift
    Interviewed by Haris Golemis   57
Birgit Mahnkopf: On the Political Economy of the Ecological Crisis   73
Teppo Eskelinen: Climate Change and Capitalist Development   96
Nadja Charaby and Katja Voigt: The UN Climate Summits:
    Not a Solution to the Climate Crisis –
    But it is Important to be There   106
David Adler and Pawel Wargan: The EU's Green Deal and the
    Betrayal of a Generation: A Strategy to Fight Back   117
Kateřina Konečná: Sleepwalking from One Crisis to the Next   130
Oguz Turkyilmaz: Proposals for a Democratic Energy
    Programme in Turkey   142

Politics and Everyday Life Under the Pandemic
Maria Karamessini: The Covid-19 Crisis and Socio-Economic
    Disruption in Europe: Threats and Challenges for Labour   153

Adoración Guamán, Guillermo Murcia López, and José Miguel Sánchez Ocaña: The Coronavirus, Working People, and Precarity: Challenges for an Exit Based on Labour — 185

Roland Kulke: A Left Perspective on the Economics of the Corona Crisis — 200

Ursula Huws: Reaping the Whirlwind: Digitalisation, Restructuring, and Mobilisation in the Covid Crisis — 212

Amelia Martinez-Lobo and Andrea Peniche: The Pandemic Crisis and Its Impact on Women's Lives — 225

Joanna Bourke: Pandemics and Domestic Violence — 233

Sandro Mezzadra: Testing Borders: Covid-19 and the Management of (Im)mobility — 246

Monika Mokre: Covid and the Unequal Distribution of Vulnerability — 256

Fabian Fajnwaks: Contemporary Forms of the Death Drive in Pandemic Capitalism — 266

Kevin Biderman, Eleanor Dare, Laura Gordon, Eleni Ikoniadou, Matt Lewis, Joseph Pochodzaj, Cecilia Wee, and Dylan Yamada-Rice: Exercises in Exorcism – Ways of Healing (Through) Art Education — 277

Country Reports

Ethan Young: US Politics in Freefall — 297

Dimitris Psarras: Golden Dawn: The Rise and Fall of a Nazi Gang — 315

Asger Hougaard: Something Rotten in the State of Denmark? New Lessons and Old Problems for the Movements and Political Parties — 328

Michael Chessum: Corbynism's Demise: A Warning from the Brexit Moment — 339

Anniversaries

Luciana Castellina: 2021: 100 Years From the Founding of the Italian Communist Party – Ten Years After the Passing of Lucio Magri — 353

Walter Baier: The Constitution and Class Struggle: On the 100th Anniversary of Austria's Federal Constitutional Law — 378

Milena Gegios and Dimitris Kousouris: Histories of the Greek
      Revolution: The Political Framing of a National Anniversary 387

The Marxist-Christian Dialogue

Bernhard Callebaut: Catholics and the Economy:
      Pope Francis's Narrative and the Challenges
      for Today's Economy 399

Karl-Helmut Lechner: To Differ and Learn From Each Other –
      A Marxist Voice on the Social Encyclical 'Fratelli tutti' 416

Authors and Editors 428

Members and Observers of transform! europe 435

Capitalism's Deadly Threat

When was it going to happen? We knew that the capitalist valorisation of humanity's production of goods and services, that is, the trading in, competing for, and need for a continuous and exponential expansion of 'value' – the abstract accounting substance averaged out from all these concrete human creative activities – producing vast quantities of financial and fictitious capital desperate for higher rates of profit, now more important than its original sources in concrete products and their actual usefulness to people – would have to come up against its limits. But the astounding capacity of the system to ingest shocks and naturalise them, providing fragmentary solutions that dilute the impact of crises in the public's imagination – how long could this go on?

We knew that this stage of development of the capitalist mode of life had to lead to a crisis of the metabolism between humans and the rest of nature. But when would it happen? When would the crisis explode into people's lives and TV screens so that there would be no way to deny the immediacy and universality of the dilemma?

First, the effects of global warming became impossible not to see in the last two years. It was all over the media. No one living in California, Australia, the Amazon, or in flood zones could deny it any longer. But there were still many areas unaffected by dramatic climate phenomena.

Push finally came to shove with the combination of global warming, agribusiness and extractive industries' voracious deforestation programmes in Southeast Asia and the Amazon, and resultant migration of animal species, increased poverty and diseases associated with it, the international trade in wild animals, and simply the incredible intensity of continuous international air travel and tourism. In Mike Davis's phrase, the monster that had been at our door with avian flu had now finally entered. In his interview for the *transform!yearbook*, John Bellamy Foster grounds the Covid and climate crises in the capitalist crisis of the anthropocene, more particularly in the 'irreparable rift in the interdependent process of social metabolism, a metabolism prescribed by the natural laws of life itself' (Marx). Foster discusses his development of Marx's theory of an unsustainable rupturing of this metabolism under capitalism, violating the need to sustain the earth for 'the chain of human generations'.

The crisis has lifted the curtain on almost every contradiction in capitalist societies and their inherited patriarchal structures: under the lockdown the double oppression of women in reproductive, mainly care, and productive work, as outlined by Amelia Martínez-Lobo and Andrea Peniche, and the feudal inner-household power ecologies, with the violent displacement of male frustration and anger, in the face of unemployment and new or increased poverty, onto the female members of households (exactly as occurred during the Spanish Flu, as Joanna Bourke details, along with several consequences of lockdown, in this issue of the *yearbook*). And, notably in the US, the impossibility of continuing without a public health system. But also in Europe, with the EU's budgetary constraints imposed on the countries, which nevertheless bear responsibility for the healthcare systems that remain on the national level. The austerity measures levelled against the southern European countries, with the attendant enforced cuts to the healthcare systems – all this has come home to roost.

And so another gate has been broken through as well: austerity. Keynesian deficit spending is back. The contrast between Italy's two super-Marios could not be more stark. If Mario Monti's mission as the head of Italy's 'technical' government in 2011 was to administer austerity, Mario Draghi's mission as head of Italy's current 'technical' government is to administer deficit spending. By mid-2020, in Ursula Huws's reckoning, the belief in TINA was suspended among a critical mass of the population in the UK. The breakthrough is at least as dramatic in the US. Because of the organising and pressure exerted by Bernie Sanders's movement and the progressive 'squad' in Congress, and through the tailwind they had on their side due to the very absence of a national health service to this day, and, decisively, through the inevitable disaster of the pandemic, the new centrist-Democratic Biden leadership has found it politically feasible to push through the most ambitious Keynesian spending since the New Deal in the 1930s – and unlike in EU countries, there is no supranational financial governance to stop it. In this the left finds itself in the surprising position of punching above its own weight. Ethan Young, in this issue, lays out the contradictions and paradoxes behind this dynamic.

And meanwhile, even with these positive developments, assuming herd immunity is reached in the core countries by early 2022, even if western big pharma's monopoly of vaccine management was to be broken, and even with a return to the Paris climate goals, we will still be in a world that necessarily will generate other viral pandemics and catastrophic climate phenomena.

Walter Baier, in his overview of Europe's current position in the international balance of power and the dilemma it faces, points out that, unlike Biden's transfer-based stimulus in the US, in Europe, though there has been a breakthrough with important direct transfers, the stimulus, consisting mostly of loans, comes with the onus of placing countries even more at the mercy of the financial markets. Indeed, it hardly could be otherwise, seeing as the member countries want nothing but a very modest budget for the EU. Meanwhile, although this is ignored by the EU institutions, the cancellation of the public debt held by the ECB is increasingly being seen as both urgent and feasible by many economists. The pandemic has escalated the crisis of European integration to the boiling point. It has further made clearer that the global economic centre of gravity will shift away from the West to the Pacific area and particularly to China. Although the EU's public stance on China is ambiguous, there is increasing Chinese involvement in Europe. It is becoming clearer that, for the wellbeing of its population and leaving competitive ideology aside, the EU needs to adopt a Europe-wide industrial policy, which under current EU conditions is near impossible. Baier spells out what would be feasible demands for a progressive exit from Europe's crisis with incipient elements of post-capitalist transformation.

Maria Karamessini offers an in-depth synthesis of the impact of Covid-19 on European economies. Due to the various job-retention schemes (temporary layoffs and short-time work) adopted in EU-27 countries, the unemployment rate does not capture the size of the job crisis in the way that the underemployment and inactivity rates do. For all the shortcomings of the stimulus, and even though the exceptional NGEU and SURE measures are said to be temporary, they broke the two historic taboos of European integration: large-scale common debt issuance and fiscal transfers between countries.

Huws synthesises the pandemic's aggravation of the late neoliberal reshaping of work and the positive possibilities it simultaneously engenders. There has been an enormous increase in work within, or mediated by, digital platforms, which Philipp Lorig, Sarah Bormann, and others analysed in detail in the *transform! yearbook* 2020. Remote computer working has intensified pre-pandemic digital surveillance. The lockdown acted as a violent brake on many activities but an accelerator of others. Much of the casualisation and enormous expansion of outsourcing will be made permanent. Further de-skilling and still vaster data mining are additional results.

Adoración Guamán, Guillermo Murcia, and José Miguel Sánchez point out how several factors – chief of which was Unidas Podemos's presence in Spain's government – contributed to the participation of trade unions in settling on and regulating various job-retention schemes, including telework, and neo-Keynesian measures, a participation for which Spain stands out in Europe. The new popular appreciation of workers and the need for more, not less, human labour is particularly dramatic in Spain after the extreme neoliberal labour conditions that prevailed from 2006 to 2015 and the widespread discrediting of labour in the media. The importance of the measures adopted in Spain thus go beyond the concrete help they gave people: it was also about shifting the public's perception and appreciation of labour, including immigrant labour, and the world's interdependency through global production chains. In these months, the concept of work has already recovered some of its former value.

The double focus of this issue of the *transform!yearbook* is the pandemic and the ecological crisis that underlies it. 'With sober senses', Birgit Mahnkopf condenses considerable detail and analysis into a short space to convey what we are up against in the ecological crisis and indicates the extent to which official greening schemes are really adaptations to capitalism's destruction of the environment as well as the extraordinary capacity of the system to absorb and transform criticism. She points to the difficulty the left will face in telling the populations what would really be necessary for overcoming the climate threat to the extent still physically possible.

David Adler and Paweł Wargan, with equally sober senses, question the notion that pleas and the sheer numbers of protesting youth can catalyse political change, concluding that the 'pipeline from protest to policy does not work' – analogously to Jane McAlevey's observations about the limits of protest politics in the *transform! yearbook 2019*. Instead of dreaming of access to the decision-making process, what is needed is discovering the source's of one's own economic power and wielding it against the elites. They identify an immediate common enemy of climate activists and the everyday economic concerns of working populations, against which both can unite: austerity policy! Such a coalition targeted against this fiscal straitjacket could disable attempts to position labour as the enemy of just transition and, moreover, utilise the unique power of workers to threaten capital.

Teppo Eskelinen examines green capitalism strategies, concluding that decoupling growth from emissions can at best have effect in limited regions. On the other hand, the left can and should establish a dialectic of social transformation with Keynesian public investment. Moreover, government boosting of aggregate demand has always been intertwined with class politics, and workers' clout grows as full employment is approached. This state strategy does not, he points out, contradict the need for pre-figurative politics, that is, expanding and making the non-capitalist spaces – coops and commoning – within capitalist society visible.

Nadja Charaby and Katja Voigt trace the history of the UN Framework Convention on Climate Change and the COPs (Conferences of the Parties) and the impact climate activists have had on them, reviewing the important principles they established (e.g. the principle of common but differentiated responsibilities), their limited implementation, the problem with their market-based mechanisms, for example the Clean Development Mechanism, and others – tantamount to 'trade in indulgences'. Despite all the COPs' faults, no other global institution has brought together so many critical stakeholders, and abandoning them, they maintain, is not an option.

Kateřina Konečná has raised awareness in the European Parliament about a reality that contrasts with the EU's professions of saving the climate: the massive deforestation, resulting carbon sink destruction and release of CO_2 that lies behind palm-oil 'biofuel', which itself has three times the emissions of conventional fuel, and whose production requires the EU to look the other way on enormous labour- and human-rights violations outside Europe. And from Turkey, a country of key importance on Europe's periphery, Oguz Turkyilmaz projects what kind of initial energy policy measures need to be envisaged now that would be strategically appropriate in the event a left government comes to power at some point in the future.

Mobility, borders, and immigration have been directly affected by the pandemic, as Sandro Mezzadra points out, and this is true of 'boundaries' in several senses: the immobility and blocking of migrants in the informal economy of agriculture and care, the forced mobility from cities to the countryside, as in India, and the 'shock mobility' of essential workers such as delivery riders. Hygienic-sanitary border enforcement, with ports being declared unsafe, created vectors for the spread of the virus. And in ports, as on board ships and in warehouses, capitalism's logistics chain was particularly vulnerable – creating ever more friction between the network of 'seams', the hubs, of international capitalist logistics, and political space. Borders were aggravated around racialised minorities, and the home became a boundary, and a dangerous one for many women in heterosexual families, where, moreover, the gender division of labour was reinforced – but this has been confronted with a re-politicisation of domestic space. Mezzadra points out the strategic importance of the labour movements' contestation of border regimes.

While the pandemic led to recognition of one's own vulnerability and connection to the vulnerability of others along with the re-emergence of a sense of the social whole, Monika Mokre cautions that the community of reference tends, aside from local communities, to be the nation. Which is linked to a tendency, for example in Austria, to create mass collective quarantining of refugees, essentially as protection of the community from them, creating vectors of contagion that could easily have been avoided.

As Joanna Bourke points out, the vulnerability women have been experiencing in domestic households under the pandemic occurs within a pre-existing context of dependency. This vulnerability, she cautions, is in continuous danger of being seen as inherent to women rather than constituted by structural relations of domination. The result is that women's agency tends to drop out of sight, even among those sympathising with their plight.

The pandemic-induced recession has raised the issue not only of public investment but of macro planning. Roland Kulke draws the distinction between the 2008+ crisis and 2020-21: while in the former an appropriate left response would have been to boost the 'demand side', the current crisis is more complicated because this time there is a clear problem of supply and right now certain real-economy enterprises do need support. But in so far as private enterprise is to be supported, the left's orientation, he suggests, needs to be the expansion of government shares in companies and, crucially, a decisive government say in their management. This involves going beyond the localist participatory governance outlook that has constituted a kind of left communitarianism, whose necessary and welcome participatory decentralisation, while providing socio-psychological benefits, leaves the macro level to market price mechanisms. Models have been developed of left macro public planning, which has today become highly feasible technically due to computer capacities.

After discussing the positive side and negative aspect of the return of the state in response to the pandemic, Fabian Fajnwaks locates an important part of capitalism's legitimation in its ability to make the subjects feel responsible for their 'own' inscription into the discourse. For him, following Lacan, the relevance of psychoanalysis here has to do with the way in which every individual in capitalist society becomes a kind of proletarian in that worker and capitalist alike are objectified into impersonal functions in value creation and circulation, with whatever social bonds that do exist tending to disintegrate, e.g. with uberisation. In addition, every individual, including the unsuccessful capitalists, can at any moment become 'waste'. Fajnwaks points to the death drive in capitalism, which is essentially what Keynes called a 'morbid desire for liquidity', pushing it to destroy and destroy itself, something Keynes thought was inherent in the accumulation of capital. A way out of this, for Lacan, is a process of décharité, or 'wasting', that is, expending the enjoyment of accumulation.

Kevin Biderman, Eleanor Dare, Laura Gordon, Eleni Ikoniadou, Matt Lewis, Joseph Pochodzaj, Cecilia Wee, and Dylan Yamada-Rice take apart the business model, what Freire calls the 'banking' model of education, so widespread in art academies, with their creation of consumer-practitioners, according to a neoliberal 'employability' agenda. And they chronicle an experience of the self-organisation of faculty and students under the lockdown to mount a project to counter this ruling discourse.

In the face of the pandemic, economic crisis, and global warming, is hope rational? The very fragmentation and digitalised surveillance of work has spurred on successful movements by workers to use the same digital technology to organise and link internationally. Moreover, the pandemic has abruptly ended austerity policy, spectacularly so in the US, which has seen the growth of a significant socialist movement. Did we expect this ten years ago? And in the other 'Anglo-Saxon' core country, Britain, we have, notwithstanding Corbynism's electoral defeat, the largest party in Europe whose majority base is a counterpart to Sanderism. Both countries have seen an enormously increased attractiveness of labour unions. With the US' great cultural influence and history of exporting so many developments and fads, is it unreasonable to expect that some of these positive advances might spread to other Western countries too? In this situation, there is considerable room for the development of mass pressure that could spur re-publicisation and new publicisation of important economic sectors, more appropriate action against global warming, and the breakup of international big pharma's grip.

Kateřina Konečná points to something everyone experienced throughout last year: the extraordinary solidarity wave, for instance in the Czech Republic, the spontaneous, voluntary making of masks supplied to one's neighbours, old-age homes, and healthcare institutions, and a myriad other forms of cooperation based on a sense of being in this together, a wave that continues unabated and may constitute the first inkling of a new age of cooperation – a true human community.

In sum, with all due sobriety in the face of humanity's overwhelming crisis, a paralysing pessimism remains unjustified and unacceptable.

★ ★ ★

This year's country reports begin with Greece. Dimitris Psarras traces the early growth of Golden Dawn (GD) to its utility to the deep state in clashing with progressive demonstrators or provoking them to react – and to the extraordinary protection Greece's Constitution provided to political parties in reaction to the dictatorship. This, and the electoral boost it received when Laos, a non-Nazi extreme right party lost its anti-systemic appeal when it entered government in 2011 allowed GD to get so out of hand that the state had to act against it. And it surged because of the economic crisis; its new support was not primarily anti-immigrant but voters without hope for change and seeking revenge against the system. The decisive legal victory against GD, Psarras insists, was only possible through the left blocking with the centre, which, in so far as it is possible, is what is required in defeating fascism.

With the example of Denmark, Asger Hougaard warns of the powerful pull exerted on radical left parties, with significant presence in parliament, to become left flanks of liberalism. The climate law and recycling campaign in which the Red-Green Alliance has participated with the majority Social Democrats, have achieved some good results but, he points out, have accepted significant compromises on climate mitigation and a degree of privatisation in recycling. In Denmark, he warns there is a particular temptation to defend the welfare state in an exclusionary way in relation to immigrants.

While appreciating the Corbyn leadership's shattering of the neoliberal consensus inside and outside the Labour Party, Michael Chessum, who is critical of the historically Eurosceptical position of most of Britain's radical left, from Benn through the radical left parties, feels that the Labour left leadership's problems largely derived from its having won the party before it could create a movement, catching it in mostly still unreformed and undemocratic party process. With a substantial movement and democratic reform he feels that the base might have been able to bring its weight to bear, pulling the leadership away from a 'populist' tailgating of the 'will of the people' on Brexit and pressing it to act more quickly, with the possibility that Labour could have committed to a Norway-style arrangement and pushed for a second referendum very soon after 2016, with positive impact on voters.

★ ★ ★

In 2020 we are observing the bicentenary of the Greek Revolution and the centenaries of Austria's Federal Constitution and the Italian Communist Party, as well as the tenth anniversary of the passing of Lucio Magri.

Luciana Castellina recounts the history of Western Europe's largest and most modern post-war communist party, and the role Lucio Magri, played in it, particularly in arguing for a road that it tragically did not take. From Castellina's account the elements that contributed to this mass experience of post-war Italian communism come into focus: In Italy the rapid development and full impact of Fordism came very late, overlapping and nearly simultaneous with the emergence of the post-Fordist phenomena associated with the '68 youth rebellion in the core capitalist countries. It was a potent combination: the new, very young workers entering the automobile and appliance plants came from a mass communist culture in the cities and countryside in which the anti-fascist resistance was still hegemonic, and the university rebellions were overwhelmingly oriented to and intertwined with them. The result was the world's most modern version of a communist politics rooted in the working class and points of industrial production and the most significant attempt of the communist tradition to combine the principles of liberty and equality – all this coupled to the country's considerable left intellectual heritage.

Walter Baier takes the centenary of the Austrian Federal Constitution as an opportunity to reflect on the state and constitutions in socialist transition, referring to the rich history of debate on the subject among the Austro-Marxists. If socialists are to be more than a left within liberalism, Baier cautions, they will have to talk about socialism and transition again. The Austro-Marxist tradition posed the question of a democratic socialism different both from Bernsteinan reformism and Bolshevism. This is the background of Austro-Marxist thinking about what is possible with bourgeois social power still in place, what the state represents and how it functions, to what extent a constitution can be class-neutral and a working class achieve hegemony without severing the bourgeoisie from its economic power base, and the need for a power shift in the institutions of civil society outside the state to provide a solid and durable foundation for change in the state.

Milena Gegios and Dimitris Kousouris characterise the current Greek government's concept of the celebration of the 1821 Greek Revolution as a kind of 'branding' of the country's image projected abroad through a reaffirmation of a collective 'belonging to the West' with great emphasis placed on the future, digitalisation, etc. What is recounted from the past are the people and events that can be rebranded as attributes of this collective belonging, which echoes the Cold War conception of Greece as a 'frontline' state between the Civilised West and the Orient. But against the romantic notions of a continuous enlightened 'Hellenism' newer historians have counterposed the study of the collective ethnic identity of Christian Greek-speaking subjects of the Byzantine Empire and then within the Ottoman Empire – and a contextualising of Greek history within European social struggles. Although the commemoration committee has largely ignored the findings of scholarly research or the need for infrastructure for further research, it has made some interesting research available.

★ ★ ★

In a 2014 meeting at the Vatican between Pope Francis, Alexis Tsipras, and Walter Baier, the Pope proposed the establishment of a Christian-Marxist dialogue. Co-initiated by transform, the Transversal Dialogue Project DIALOP has been ongoing ever since. In this context, Karl-Helmut Lechner notes the increasing interest of left secular activists and Christian social activists in finding a common understanding and basis for action. Without slighting the major problem of entrenched conservative attitudes in the Catholic Church, he points out the astonishing advances. At the end of the nineteenth century the Church, although showing sympathy for workers, still fought against any attempt to convert private property to community property. Before the last encyclical, *Fratelli tutti*, Pope Francis had already counteracted some of this conservatism. But *Fratelli tutti* put him at loggerheads with representatives of capital almost everywhere. It places the principle of the common use of created goods above that of property and sees consistent solidarity with the poor as leading to social activism; it advocates 'Political Love' as love that organises and structures society, changing the conditions that cause suffering – and going beyond a policy *for* the poor, it calls for a policy *with* and *of* the poor that can reunite peoples – what Marxists would describe as the poor becoming subjects rather than objects of history.

Bernhard Callebaut offers a history of the relation between the left and the Church and the latter's relation to the social question, an introduction to the new methods and perspectives of dialogue among the churches and with the left – 'transversal dialogue', 'differentiated consensus'. He explains why the rapprochement between the left and the Church has occurred, and delineates the development of the Church's ideas on the economy. Previously occupying itself strictly with 'society' rather than 'economy', it has begun to develop, starting in the 1990s, the concept of 'civil economy' (the economy of redistribution and gift rather than contractual exchange), leading to a critique of economic 'laws' operating above human society – to the point that an appeal was made in a recent conference in Assisi by a noted Catholic economist for economic transformation rather than reform.

★ ★ ★

This year we mourn the passing on 19 December 2020 of our comrade Leo Panitch, one of the world's most respected socialist intellectuals and a touchstone for Britain's Labour left and the new generation of socialists in the US. Ingar Solty situates his remarkable red-blooded orthodox/unorthodox

Marxism and politics in precisely the decades whose reality made this kind of theory and politics highly unlikely.

★ ★ ★

The transform! europe network was established in 2001 during the World Social Forum in Porto Alegre by a small group of intellectuals from six different European countries, representing left research institutions or journals, who wanted to coordinate their research and educational work. Today transform! consists of 39 member organisations and observers from 23 countries.

The network is coordinated by a board of members, and its office is located in Vienna. transform! maintains a multilingual website and publishes a continuously growing number of reports, analyses, and discussion papers on issues related to the process of European integration.

We would like to thank all those who have collaborated in producing this volume: our authors, the members of our editorial board, our translators, and especially our publisher, The Merlin Press.

Walter Baier, Eric Canepa, and Haris Golemis

In Memoriam

The Austrian Revolution
by Otto Bauer,
Edited by Walter Baier
and Eric Canepa,
Introduction by
Walter Baier

Haymarket Books
(July 2021)
ISBN-10: 1642591629
ISBN-13: 978-1642591620

Otto Bauer's *The Austrian Revolution* is one of the now largely forgotten gems of the extraordinarily rich literature that Austro-Marxism produced. Thanks to an excellent new translation, this classic work is now available to English-speaking readers in a complete version for the first time. It is one of the classics of Marxist political analysis, only comparable to Marx's *The Eighteenth Brumaire of Louis Napoleon* or Trotsky's *History of the Russian Revolution*.

Michael R. Krätke, Lancaster University

The Global Left, Marxism, and Democratic Socialism: Remembering Leo Panitch[1]

Ingar Solty

I

I still cannot fathom and accept that Leo Panitch, Distinguished Research Professor at York University in Toronto and longstanding editor of the *Socialist Register* yearbook, has died. I am aware that we all are not immortal. Through his emails and Skype conversations I was aware that he had felt back pain since the summer of 2020 and was admitted to the hospital for a myeloma treatment in November. However, the last times I had met him in person and had dinner with him – in Montreal in May 2019 at the 'Organiser la resistance' conference and in November 2019 at the Historical Materialism conference in London – and the last time I was honoured to share a panel with him on 6 November 2020, covering the US presidential elections, he seemed unkillable. Throughout the summer he had been looking forward to tickling the newest family member, born to the wife of his son Maxim, and even in his emails from the hospital he expressed the most sincere 'la lotta continua' spirit, telling us that his life expectancy was beyond ten years. Right now, I am going through revisions of an article for the *Socialist Register* 2022 – revisions Leo requested, and I constantly hear his voice when reading a comment. It is hard to think that he is no longer where he always was, among his family and comrades in Toronto, thinking ahead. And I know how hard it is or must be for Melanie, his comrade of a lifetime, for Maxim and Vida, for Sam Gindin, Greg Albo, Donald Swartz and all the other relatives and closest friends.

In the days and weeks following Leo's death I had many video-calls with old colleagues, friends, and comrades from Canada. I realised once more how much Leo meant not only to me but to so many people. Angela Joya, one of his favourite students, called Leo 'an umbrella for working class kids', for kids like herself, her partner Geoff Kennedy, and many others.

For a long list of people, Leo was a moral and intellectual mentor. Leo was interested in, listened to, and remembered what his students had to say. This was visible in the way he taught his legendary Globalisation and the State graduate course – constructing the sessions around the unordered, occasionally incoherent, notes from, and questions raised by, his PhD students sent to him based on the required readings for his course. It was also reflected in the way that Leo would continue to read what his former students wrote, maybe not realising that whatever use value existed in pieces he welcomed with a 'bravo' or declared to be 'terrific', 'brilliant' or 'superb' was what we had learned from him and his colleagues and comrades in Toronto.

Leo's general interest in other human beings, especially if their class background made their career in academia unlikely, Leo's ability to listen and to remember had at least three origins. First, Leo was a real Marxist in the sense that he was fully aware that intellectual endeavours and knowledge production are a collective effort. With Bertolt Brecht he laughed at the solitary competitive intellectual entrepreneurs who 'boast in public that they are able to write great books all by themselves' who 'with only the scant material that anyone can carry in his hands […] erect their cottages! The largest buildings they know are those a single man is capable of constructing!' Secondly, Leo was a very un-'traditional intellectual', to use Gramsci's terminology, in the sense that he knew that he was always still in need of learning and that the relevance of his knowledge was connected to learning from 'organic intellectuals' in the engine shop of capitalist society. In fact, thirdly, Leo was an organic intellectual himself. And he could become one, because even though he was one of the most accomplished, distinguished, and most-cited intellectuals in the world, he was ultimately more interested in international socialist politics and advising socialist leaders like Jeremy Corbyn, trade unions like South Africa's Numsa, or the Syriza left government in Greece in its ill-fated fight against the European powers-that-be. But as Leo used to say: 'If Rosa Luxemburg and Lenin had had the ambition or chance of becoming university professors, then maybe there would never have been an October Revolution or German Revolution.'

Leo died prematurely on 19 December 2020 – Phil Ochs's birthday by the way – and at the age of 75. We are looking back at a long life in a lifelong struggle for socialism. His battle stretches across six, maybe – taking his family background in a socialist-Zionist working-class family in Winnipeg with roots in the Ukrainian shtetl into account – seven decades. As Brecht writes in his communist learning play *The Mother*: 'Those who are weak don't fight. Those who are stronger might fight for an hour. Those who are stronger still might fight for many years. The strongest fight for their whole life. They are the indispensable ones.'

II

So like Bertolt Brecht, Leo was a socialist revolutionary. In the past couple of weeks, however, I have been thinking about how unlikely and original Leo's scholarship and politics were; because Leo was a socialist revolutionary in non-, yes even counter-revolutionary times!

I would like to focus on this because as historical materialists we excel in historicising everything including ourselves and our own biographies and their class, gender, race, and ethnic underpinnings. We have learned to think our own historicity, including the fact that unlike past generations many of us are struggling for socialism, for communism, knowing that we are unlikely to reap the fruits of our struggle during our lifetime, knowing that we are not fighting for ourselves but for the generations to come. (Because, if we are honest with ourselves, the parole 'Socialism for Future'[2] means both that without socialism there is no future for humankind, at least not a very pleasant one, and that socialism is for future generations. As Leo himself said in Montreal in 2019, 'there are no shortcuts in history – we may have to build socialism in a world that looks like "Blade Runner".')

So we do excel in historicising everything and it was Marxists who will have given the time we live in its name, the name future historians will use: neoliberalism. I am convinced of this, because how else do you want to call it? (Let's just hope it won't be the Second 100 Year Peace.) And yet, because as Marxists we are situation-oriented thinkers, always aware that 'truth is always concrete' and always wanting to intervene in what are always historically concrete configurations of class and power relations, we sometimes lose sight of what the French historian Fernand Braudel called the *longue durée*. And maybe the passing of a moral and intellectual giant like Leo into the socialist Hall of Fame is a good moment to reflect on our longue durée, even if that is hard, because we know that, to use Hegel's famous phrase, 'the Owl of Minerva spreads its wings only with the falling of dusk'. In other words, it is hard to reflect on history still unfolding when we are like frogs in pots of boiling water not perceiving the rising temperature, and having to wait 'three or four decades' until the present moment 'is illumined from within', as Tony Kushner has put it. Trying to reflect on the longue durée and Leo's place in it, however, might help to clarify how Leo was possible and what a moral and intellectual giant he really was; because let us also remember that everything we loved about Leo did not fall from the sky.

As everything else, it had a history. Moreover, it was the result of concrete social relations. As Kushner once summarised the Marxist dialectical method: 'The smallest indivisible unit of a human being is always two.'

III

Up to the 2000s there were very few islands in academia that resisted the 'new' and modern ideas of the 'Third Way' 'beyond left and right' (Anthony Giddens), 'post-foundationalism', and Fukuyama's 'End of History' dressed up in the pseudo-radical chic of 'The End of the Grand Narratives' (Lyotard)… And do you remember the 'simulacrum' (Baudrillard) and the 'rhizom' (Deleuze) and how they revolutionised our thinking and inspired the masses?

Leo – but also Greg Albo, Sam Gindin, David McNally, and others at York University in Toronto – resisted this trend. (The only comparable centre at the time in Europe was 'Red' Marburg in Germany.) And Leo managed to sustain an uncompromising 'orthodox' Marxism that was at the same time unorthodox. It cannot be emphasised too strongly how unfashionable and unlikely this was in the 1990s and 2000s.

So Leo taught me and my fellow students an 'uncompromising Marxism' and helped us use the taboo word *class* in much more confident ways. And being able to do that helped me understand how much working class-ness permeates my whole family with 'hidden injuries of class' (Richard Sennett) of which I had been unaware even though they (should) have hit me in the face.

And yet, how was it possible to be an 'uncompromising Marxist' throughout the 1990s and the 2000s? For a long time we came and maybe even today still come to Marxism in very different ways when compared to say Brecht or Luxemburg and Lenin or even Marx and Engels themselves. Marx and Engels founded historical materialism during the 'Age of Revolution' (Eric Hobsbawm), with the memory and historical experience of revolutions as well as the class struggles they observed in France, which they linked theoretically to German philosophy and British political economy. Rosa Luxemburg and Lenin came to Marxism in the context of capitalist development, the intensification of its contradictions in the shape of class polarisation, open class struggle, and a working class which was growing into an organised political force and class-based party, moving from one electoral victory to the next, leading even Engels to believe in some sort of 'parliamentary socialism'. And Brecht came to Marxism through the barbarism of inter-imperialist world war and almost a decade of socialist revolution from Ireland to Central Asia, 1916-1923.

But what about left-leaning people today? The global left is still recovering from the historic defeat during the period of 1979 to 1989. Even if during that era left forces based in strong trade-union movements managed to overthrow Apartheid and authoritarian regimes from Brazil to South Africa, 1979-1989 really ended a global period of forward motion of socialist and anti-imperialist forces. The neoliberal turn was a counter-revolution eliminating the three pillars of working-class power: (1) the strength of labour unions in the West, (2) socialist anti-imperialism in the developing countries, and (3) real socialism in the East, despite all its flaws.

The Volcker Shock of 1979 essentially killed off the first two pillars, breaking the backbone of US trade unions domestically and forcing open, through debt imperialism, the countries of the Global South for the benefit of transnationalising corporations from the core capitalist countries. And the fall of the Berlin Wall and the collapse of the Soviet Union killed off the third pillar, further eroding what was left of the first two, insofar as it also increased capital mobility and its ability to exploit differences in wages, subsidies, and regulation and pit nationally organised working classes against each other, producing what Leo and Sam have called the 'never-ending corporate shakedown [of] subsidies and concessions'.

In other words, 1979-1989 was a counter-revolution insofar as it dramatically shifted the relationships of forces between capital and labour globally. The consequence was a deep political and ideological crisis for all tendencies of the broad left – whether or not they had harboured sympathies for real socialism: pro-Soviet communists, Trotskyists, Maoists, social democrats, social liberals, and greens alike.

Today we are still recovering from 40 years of neoliberal counter-revolution. Our reality is perhaps best captured by a term developed by Klaus Dörre: 'demobilised class society'. Capitalism does what it does best; class society weighs more heavily on the working class than ever in terms of union density, collective bargaining, the wage share, and wealth inequality, as well as social insecurity, downward mobility, and blocked upward mobility. At the same time, we are still working hard on the revitalisation and renewal of the labour movement. Meanwhile, segments of the actually existing working class have been turning right.

Unquestionably, we have learned the lesson from what Nancy Fraser calls 'progressive neoliberalism' and what ten years prior Mario Candeias and others analysed as the partial but perverted realisation of left-wing demands in neoliberalism. Precisely because the new social movements came to power at a moment of the most vicious pushing of organised labour (understood as the force trying to wrest material gains) into the defensive, we received essentially immaterial gains for the few instead of material gains for all. For instance, we received carbon emission trading instead of social-ecological transformation or gender-sensitive language on official documents and women's quotas on the boards of transnational corporations instead of equal pay, free day-care, and free care for the elderly. In other words, the experience of the late 1990s and early 2000s has taught us that no emancipation and social progress will come about without, not to mention against, organised labour and the working class. However, it is not surprising if a young leftist today sees more potential for change in the 'enlightened middle classes' than in the working class. It is not surprising when segments of the broader left, at best, pity the working class for being victimised by capitalism – as seen in how leftists address workers merely as victims instead of also as agents of self-emancipation – and if they, at worst, do not see the working class majority at all because of so much 'middle-classness' in radical left movements from anti-G7/8/20 Summit protests to pro-refugee, anti-fascist, and environmentalist struggles.

My thesis, in other words, therefore is: If Marxism is the theory and practice of the self-emancipation of the working class, then the new generations of socialists, whom Leo hailed and so greatly influenced, have been arriving at Marxism only in theory rather than through the concretely lived observation or one's own participation in intensifying economic and political class struggles from below. They experience the ravages of capitalism in their own precarious lives. Yet the working class movement capable of fending off these ravages and realistically challenging power is only beginning to re-emerge in a non-linear fashion.

IV

So, one thing is: How do you become a Marxist? The other is: How do you stay a Marxist in non- and even counter-revolutionary times?

This brings us back to the unlikeliness and sheer overwhelming achievement of Leo Panitch and his legacy vis-à-vis the new and especially North American generation of socialists and people interested in Marx's ideas. Beyond Leo's invaluable scholarly contributions, which I and others have focused on elsewhere, part of his legacy will have been his role in *allowing Marxism to both survive and to thrive*.

Leo helped Marxist thought to *survive a long period of counter-revolution*. Leo's theory and practice functioned like a global 'message in a bottle' for the 1980s until the 2010s, to be picked up by a new and global generation of socialists living through today's civilisational crisis which capitalism has produced. Just as much as the Frankfurt School functioned as a national 'message in a bottle' allowing Marxism to survive its organisational and physical extermination through the Nazis in the 1930s and early 1940s to be picked up by left-leaning generations in the West Germany of the 1960s; or just as much as Marx and Engels themselves helped social-revolutionary thought survive during the counter-revolutionary period following the defeat of continental Europe's 1848-1849 revolutions. And as Brecht wrote: 'One of the greatest deeds of the classics was that they gave up on immediate upheaval when they saw that conditions had changed. They predicted a time of another upsurge of the oppressors and exploiters and they modified their own actions accordingly. And neither their anger vis-à-vis the ruling class nor their efforts to overthrow it eased up.'

Furthermore, *Leo helped Marxist thought to thrive* because it is one thing to stick to principles. It is another thing entirely to not turn into a stubborn dogmatist. And we are all aware of Leo's theoretical contribution to the renewal of our understanding of capitalism and imperialism, how Leo and Sam have enabled us to think through the implications of the transnationalisation of capitalist social relations for state theory, the internationalisation of the state, and transnational class formation, and the special post-war role of the American state as what Leo once called the 'prototype of a global state', the American informal empire.

I cannot help but see a similarity between Leo and Rosa Luxemburg – thinking of Luxemburg's legacy regarding democratic socialism, the class-party question, and socialist politics in the triangle of workplace, parliament, and the street – even if Leo correctly pointed out the limits of our classical theories of imperialism, including Luxemburg's. Luxemburg, if you recall, was also a very unique figure and seemingly paradoxical: defending, in her day and age, Marxism against the revisionism of Bernstein, Konrad Schmidt, and all the others, but at the same time being one of the most prolific Marxist theorists renewing not only our understanding of the role of mass action for both the revolutionary path towards socialism and its sustainability but also our understanding of capitalism as an inherently globalising system in need of non-capitalist spaces, which, as we know today, can exist both outside as well as inside national boundaries, or, as Leo defined 'globalisation': just another word for 'the spread of capitalist social relations to every corner of the globe *and every facet of our lives*'.

V

To get a sense of how brightly the beacon of light, which was Leo, shone, we have to remember how long the relative darkness lasted – the period of counter-revolution and working-class defeat spanned more than just the 40 years of neoliberalism, lasting through roughly two thirds of Leo's intellectual development and career.

In effect, at least as far as Marxian debates are concerned: his lifespan seemed like a never ending series of defeats for many radical leftists. Let us remember that the post-war new left, which he grew up in, saw itself as new because it considered the working class to be fully integrated in what they erroneously called 'late capitalism'. It was because of this alleged full-scale integration of the working-class into capitalism that Stuart Hall and the 'First New Left' turned to culture, why the Frankfurt School also turned to culture (developing its culture industry thesis), why even self-avowed Marxists within French Structuralism like Louis Althusser developed a theory of the state which characterised trade unions as 'ideological state apparatuses' reproducing the status quo of capitalism. And it was this theoretical misconception of a permanent (social-imperialist) integration of the working class which led to conceptions of agency and practical change of either 'rien ne va plus' (the Frankfurt School) or fringe group strategies which, at least temporarily, replaced the working class and the socialist labour movement with either prisoners, the insane, or even Islamic fundamentalism (Michel Foucault), with counter-cultural drug addicts and sexual adventurers (Herbert Marcuse), or petty criminals and homosexuals (Pier Paolo Pasolini in his later life).

Some of these radical leftists eventually experienced the working class struggles of 1968, especially in France, as an eye-opening 'epiphany', as Clyde W. Barrow has analysed with regard to Nicos Poulantzas, one of Leo's inspirations concerning the theory of global capitalism. Diehard revolutionaries, especially Maoists, who had erroneously perceived 1968 as a world revolution, thought that a lack of connection to the working class was to blame for the defeat of this alleged world revolution. Some of them were so principled as to leave academia and join the ranks of the working class, with much disappointment. They threw themselves into the new, often ecological mass movements and also supported the massive strike waves against neoliberalism during the 1970s. But when '1979' broke the backbone of the labour movement and the 'new social movements' emerged as the most dynamic mass movements – at least visibly in the streets -, it was easy to believe in the new social movements and 'the middle classes' as the agents of change.

In short, Leo's uncompromising Marxism and the uncompromising Marxism of those who became Marxists and stayed Marxists during an era of counter-revolution was improbable in the context of a reality which, in some of its surface appearance, occluded older fundamental contradictions from view. Leo was a moral and intellectual giant because he stuck to his beliefs when it was highly unpopular to do so and when it destroyed careers, under the conditions of Cold War anti-communism and black lists in the 1970s and 1980s and neoliberal hegemony during the 1990s and early 2000s.

In Ken Loach's film *Looking for Eric* on working-class solidarity, the protagonist, none other than French football icon Eric Cantona himself, in one scene says: 'I'm not a man. I am Eric Cantona.' In his field, Leo Panitch also feels like a super-human being. But he was also a man. His humility, his lack of arrogance, and his real interest in what made his students – and people in general – tick seemed otherworldly in a world of professorial pretentiousness and intellectual mediocrity.

And still, his 'Haltung' developed not only from his origins but also because he himself had teachers from a working-class background, like the Polish-Jewish emigré Ralph Miliband, who taught him at the London School of Economics, including how to write in an accessible manner, and then went on to ask Leo to become his co-editor of *The Socialist Register*.

Leo's background and experience with the realities of working class life gave him a realistic and non-fetishising understanding of the working class and working-class life. Leo was not only always aware that the working class is not male and white, but, as his *Socialist Register* 2000 essay points out, that it is an ethnicised and feminised class. The Bernie Sanders activists strategising around the 'multi-racial working class' owe much to Leo's longstanding theorisation of class formation. Leo also always pointed out that the working class in and of itself is not a revolutionary class. In competition with one another, dependent on and deformed by capitalism, the working class cannot overthrow the capitalist system that exploits it, without organising itself into a mass party, without making itself into a class through a party. He was orthodox in his understanding that syndicalism was not enough.

It was Leo's realism in his understanding of the working class in capitalism, which enabled him to be a 'pessimist of the intellect' and simultaneously an 'optimist of the will' – realising the need for an alternative to capitalism, the potential of working-class self-organisation to replace capitalism through democratic socialism, and also the long-term struggle needed to get there, through the ups and downs, mostly downs which he experienced, and endured, with the pleasure of struggling for a new world together with tens of thousands of like-minded comrades and warm-hearted friends. And that struggle continues. And it is and will be fought by the tens of thousands of hearts Leo Panitch has touched.

NOTES

1. This essay is based on a paper delivered on 12 February 2021 at the 'Global Left, Marxism, and Democratic Socialism: Remembering Leo Panitch' conference at the University of the Witwatersrand in Johannesburg, South Africa. The other panelists were Sam Gindin (Toronto), Ana Garcia (Rio de Janeiro), Patrick Bond, Dinga Sikwebu, and Vishwas Satgar (all from Johannesburg).
2. See <https://www.rosalux.de/fileadmin/rls_uploads/pdfs/LUXEMBURG/RLS_LUX_Mini_SFF_SCREEN.pdf>.

Europe

The State of the Union: On the Eve of the Conference on the Future of Europe

Walter Baier

If the Conference on the Future of Europe were to introduce a radical new orientation to European integration, this would be the perfect time to do it. But the present political power relations being what they are we cannot expect this change to come from inside the institutions; and if the Conference turns out to be a propaganda show – a green-washing of the neoliberal integration model and a strengthening of its authoritarian tendencies – it will further undermine the hope for a social and ecological reform of the EU.

The situation is further complicated by the fact that the two most powerful countries in the EU, Germany and France, face crucial elections in the next year and a half, and in France the presidential election is in danger of becoming a showdown between Emmanuel Macron and Marine Le Pen – just at the moment when the debate on the future of Europe is due to reach its climax.

Is Europe at a tipping point?

European politics in a double bind

In February 2021, after one year of the pandemic, the situation has not improved in comparison to what was accomplished in countries such as China, Cuba, Vietnam, South Korea, or New Zealand. On the contrary, it has worsened, which should be occasion to open a discussion not only on the different strategies of dealing with the pandemic but also the institutional preconditions for coping with a crisis of such scope. This has become even more obvious during the second wave of the pandemic, which took hold in Europe toward the end of last year. Not only did the governments resort once again to uncoordinated lockdowns and closings of borders, but added to this there was chaos in the procurement and distribution of the vaccine.

If the virus can be contained through vaccinations – which at the time of this writing is not predictable – then the failure of the national and European authorities will nevertheless have cost tens of thousands of avoidable deaths.

Irrational as it already is to entrust the prevention of a global medical crisis to a handful of companies striving to maximise their profits, the coronavirus crisis has exposed the crass contradiction of the EU treaties assigning social and healthcare policy to the member countries while severely circumscribing their financial bases through EU legislation. The result is not only the notorious underfunding of national systems, which in some countries have been devastated by austerity policies, but also the lack of expertise and capacity of the EU Commission to coordinate the pan-European campaign against the pandemic, which became glaring in the contract negotiations with pharmaceutical companies. It is doubtful whether the damage this has done to the EU's prestige, especially in the states most affected by the epidemic, can still be repaired.

It is a good thing that the Growth and Stability Pact was suspended in spring of last year; however, its restoration is hanging like a sword of Damocles above post-pandemic economic recovery. Certainly, the compromise the European Council struck on the Multiannual Financial Framework of the EU (2021-2027) including the NextGenerationEU reconstruction plan, which provides for non-repayable transfers to the countries hit hardest by the crisis, brought desperately needed relief. And the decision to finance part of the fund through joint European borrowing is a step forward. But in view of the scope of the problems, the measures lag behind what would be necessary and possible (as has become particularly glaring when compared to the 1.9 trillion dollar package announced by US President Biden, which was added to the 900 billion stimulus relief passed by the Congress at the end of 2020.

Above all, however, in view of digitalisation and the environmental crisis, the capitalist economies are on the threshold of a comprehensive transformation that requires strategies other than those contained in neo-classical economics textbooks.

It seems that we are caught in a political double bind: On the one hand, the crisis is mercilessly revealing the structural flaws of the European treaties, which prioritise the unimpeded functioning of markets and establish an opaque interplay between the executive organs of the EU and the governments of the member countries, the effect of which is the systematic depletion and circumvention of parliaments on both levels. On the other hand, the international character of the crisis points up the absurdity of the nationalist hypothesis, which suggests that societies could cope with the upheavals and challenges in today's world by competing for scarce resources.

In the coming months, even mainstream economists will not tire of assuring us that they have never been neoliberals. The left can exploit the cracks that the crisis in public discourse has opened up. However, we have learned from the last financial crisis that this window of opportunity will remain open only until a new consensus forms within the ruling classes, mainly of the large European countries, on how to deal with the crisis.

We need to face the seriousness of the situation. The present form of capitalism is reaching its systemic limits. Yet, if this statement is to serve as anything more than ideological self-affirmation then we must conclude that strategies of reform only of individual sectors seen in isolation from each other are insufficient for formulating an independent eco-socialist position, and that it is the interdependencies between economy, ecology, welfare state, international relations, and culture that form the starting point from which an alternative policy must be conceived.

Therefore, we must not limit ourselves to just becoming the left Keynesian wing of the liberal mainstream. The crisis is posing the question of hegemony regarding the social interests that should prevail when dealing with it.

Distributional conflict and class politics

At the time of writing, the number of people infected globally is 100 million with more than 2 million deaths. The social and economic consequences are devastating. All forecasts of global economic recovery are dependent on overcoming the pandemic.

The consequences of the crisis are felt differently by the different classes.[1] Millions of unemployed, precarious workers, apprentices, single mothers, self-employed persons, low-skilled workers, and the large number of artists and cultural workers who do not belong to the narrow elite of the transnational entertainment industry are condemned to shoulder the costs not only of the pandemic but also of the 'creative destruction' which is to prepare the ground for the next cycle of capitalist accumulation.

According to the ILO, 2.7 billion workers have been affected by partial or full lockdown measures globally, with 17% of young people between 18 and 29 years of age having already lost their jobs in the first lockdown.[2] The social time bomb created by the millions of temporary labour contracts unprotected by labour laws and social rights is in danger of exploding, while at the same time the revenues and assets of the uppermost one percent are reaching astronomical heights.[3]

To pre-empt the immediate social and economic effects of the lockdown, governments passed special programmes last spring of an unimaginable scope, for example the German government decided to finance a package of measures decreed at the end of March 2020 amounting to 10 % of Germany's GDP.

These unorthodox fiscal decisions, which have increased the debt/GDP ratios by 10 to 15 percentage points, were reasonable in coping with an unprecedented crisis. However, they left the countries even more at the mercy of the financial markets and the European Central Bank.

Moreover, interest rates favour the financially powerful states and discriminate against the weaker ones. Germany, whose share in the EU economy is 26%, accounts for 50% of total expenditures so far by the member countries to deal with the consequences of the crisis. Thus, the indebtedness will further aggravate inequality between the deindustrialised regions in Southern and Eastern European and the economic power centres of the EU.[4]

Due to the historic low interest rates, social democratic and green politicians consider increased debt to be the single most effective way out of the crisis, since there would otherwise be conflicts over distribution they prefer to avoid. I consider this to be extremely short-sighted and fundamentally wrong from the point of view of politics in the interest of the subordinate classes.

Certainly, the rise in sovereign debt is socially much more acceptable than increased unemployment, but from an economic and political perspective, this takes us on a bumpy road, involving the risk of future debt rescheduling under conditions more disadvantageous than today's. Given the enormous sums involved in debt service, the effects of even slight increases in interest rates could have dramatic effects on national budgets and their possibilities of refinancing in the markets. That is why the cancellation of the public debt titles held by the European Central Bank, as demanded by 150 renowned economists from across Europe, is an urgent and at the same time feasible measure to 'reconquer Europe's destiny'.[5]

Moreover, the economic reconstruction after the end of the acute phase of the pandemic must be linked to the ecological transformation of the industrial and energy basis of the economies and will require unprecedented investments. In 2018, the European Commission calculated that 2.8 % of the EU's GDP will be necessary for decarbonising the economy.[6] Financing will therefore become the key problem of the post-corona period.

The financing of state debt through inflation would meet fierce political opposition in some of the EU member countries. The alternatives then are either to shift the burdens onto the populations through austerity and privatisation programmes, as happened in the last crisis, or to make the owners of great wealth, who hold the lion's share of loans, bear the burdens of public budgets through debt relief, confiscatory capital levies, and a capital gains tax. This means that it will be impossible to bypass distributional conflicts.

The implementation of this policy needs to be accompanied by capital controls and by guaranteeing the claims on capital-funded pension and health-insurance funds, accomplished through the public sector's takeover of these funds, not to mention closing the various tax havens inside and outside the EU, a policy that must be enacted by the member countries, but supported and coordinated on a supranational level.

The pandemic crisis is the moose test for the institutional structure of the EU. The only institution to actually pass the test was the European Central Bank, which increased its Pandemic Emergency Purchase Programme (PEPP) to 1.85 trillion euros through the end of 2020. In doing so, the ECB built a wall protecting the hitherto indebted countries from the greed of the financial industry.

However, when real interest rates move toward zero, monetary policy loses its effect, which is why the protection is only relative and may turn out to be transitory. Due to the pessimistic economic prognoses, the money from the Central Bank is not invested in the real economy to the extent expected but rather leads to a boom on the stock and asset markets. Since the second lockdown has destroyed the hope for a swift end to the recession it remains to be seen when and how the bizarre contradiction between an inflation of fictitious capital and a recessive real economy will erupt.

Moreover, the protection by the ECB is not irrevocable as the *ultra vires* judgement of the German Constitutional Court of 5 May 2020 shows, which considered the bond purchasing programme of the ECB incompatible with the German constitution.[7]

The judgement regarding the constitutional complaint lodged by an AfD politician was acclaimed by nationalist circles throughout the entire political spectrum of Germany as a 'victory of democracy and the rule of law'. The juridical controversy between, to put it in simple terms, 'German Europe' or 'European Germany' has a history. In 1993, the German Constitutional Court had rejected a complaint brought against the German Bundestag's ratification of the Maastricht Treaty, in line with the 'reasons of state' motivated by German reunification at the time, but also ruled that it would reserve the right to examine EU legal acts for their conformity with German constitutional law and to abrogate them if necessary. The court now considered the PEPP to be such a case and told the ECB that it 'exceeded its monetary policy mandate'.[8]

Although in practice the ruling remained without effect, since the

ECB preferred to bow to the German court's Gessler's hat[9] and provided explanatory documents,[10] the conflict with the constitutional jurisdiction of the German state, which with 18% of shares is the largest shareholder of the formally independent ECB, continues to smoulder and could be rekindled anytime by further complaints being lodged.

Apparently, in response to the demand of the 150 economists for debt relief mentioned above, the German Bundestag commissioned an internal report which was leaked to the conservative daily *Die Welt*; the report concluded that a cancellation by the ECB of public debt would be a violation of the European treaties.[11]

Compared to the ECB, the European Council reacted more awkwardly and could only with considerable delay and enormous political effort bring about an agreement on its Multiannual Financial Framework (MFF) for 2021-2027, which was increased to 1.85 trillion euros by the European Recovery Plan, NextGenerationEU. The 310 billion euros of non-repayable transfers to the countries hit hardest by the pandemic are burdened by a powerful caveat, as their scrutiny through the European Semester threatens to bind them to strict, neoliberal obligations supervised by the European Commission, something which would not contribute to lessen the industrialisation and social gap within the EU.

German Minister of Finance Olaf Scholz euphorically celebrated the first-time issuance of common bonds as 'the EU's Hamilton moment'. But while in 1790 Alexander Hamilton centralised the debts of all thirteen US states, thus laying the cornerstone for the monetary integration of the USA, we are dealing here with a small fraction of the current budget of the European Union, amounting to no more than 1.1 percent of the EU's GDP.

Dimensions matter here. The crucial question is whether the new financial instrument is sufficient to absorb the impact of previous austerity, if it can shield the working classes from further losses of income and prospects, and if it will be effective enough to cope with the global recession. The *Financial Times* spoke of 'smoke and mirrors' in the EU's recovery plan, deeming its € 310bn grants component not really sufficient to count as a discretionary fiscal stimulus, as it will account for only 0.7% of the EU's GDP over a period of three years.[12]

What about the Green Deal? A press release issued by the European Court of auditors warns that 37% of the green investment targeted in the recovery programme might be overestimated due to a biased and overoptimistic calculation method.[13]

From the inter-governmental institutional logic it follows that the EU will not finance European transnational projects in the member countries from its Recovery Plan fund but will be distributing the entire fund to the individual countries via their governments.

Therefore, Wolfgang Münchau, in the *Financial Times*, suspects that the grants will turn out to be 'a fiscal splurge crafted for the sole purpose of generating political support for those who spend it'.[14] In the end, this method of distributing funds will inevitably ignite nationalisms by pitting one nation against the other, especially 'donors' against 'receivers'. This will most of all please the nationalist autocrats in Hungary and Poland who have succeeded in negotiating away any stricter binding of the subsidies to the respect for the rule of law in their countries.

Yet, some important things remain unpredictable. The economic structural transformation will alter the position of industries, regions, and states within capitalist competition and change their financial clout, which is also expressed in the interest rate, and will add new contradictions and rivalries to the already existing East/West and North/South fault lines, which may even affect the core of European integration.

The experience of 2007 and subsequent years has shown that capitalist crises do not automatically trigger a development favourable to the left. In order to take advantage of this acute crisis the left has to offer an alternative by linking its solution to socio-ecological transformation. Its decisive criterion would not be to reach an agreement on general goals, which are obvious and widely recognised, but on the tools needed to implement them. The point at issue is the institutions and the balance of power between classes. Thus, an eco-socialist left must have the courage to go on the offensive and speak prominently about substantial haircuts, the socialisation of the pharmaceutical giants, a new role for the states in the recovery, about property, the socialisation of the financial sector, capital controls, economic democracy, and the strengthening of wage dependents at the level of enterprises, municipalities, countries, and the EU. This is the only way in which the left can take advantage of the available opportunities to expand social space for a new hegemony.

Strategic sovereignty, what for?

The coronavirus crisis – and its disastrous effects on Asia, Africa, and Latin America, too little noted in Europe – is further accentuating the unequal distribution of life opportunities on a worldwide scale.[15] This inequality is the principal truth, pointed to by the worldwide migratory movements that have reached Europe in recent years.

The conditions in Moria, Kara Tepe, at the Bosnian-Croatian border, and in other camps are the tragic proof of the moral and social failure of neoliberalism as a global civilisational model. The pushbacks at the EU's external border are not only violations of international law, but also of EU legislation. Thus, the shameful EU-Turkey statement on migration must be rescinded and replaced by a policy that implements the right to asylum guaranteed by the UN's Covenant on Civil and Political Rights. In January of this year, a report by the Hungarian Helsinki Committee documented the involvement of the European Border and Coast Guard Agency (Frontex) in these illegal actions, which is why the European Parliament established a Frontex monitoring group under the leadership of two left-wing MEPs, which will hopefully also lead to the dismantling of the agency.

Apologists of the inhumane border regime of the EU hypocritically argue that what must first be addressed is the social and economic causes of migration in the countries of origin. But if this were meant seriously, then the alleviation of the refugees' plight would have to be linked to an immediate reversal of the neoliberal trade and investment agreements that the EU has concluded with most countries of Africa, Asia, and Latin America.

It is still too early to know what the world will look like after corona. One thing is for certain, though: the global economic centre of gravity will shift away from Europe to the Pacific area. The major winner will be China, which was the first of the large countries to have returned to a growth path after the corona crisis. China also seems to have emerged strengthened from the economic war unleashed by Donald Trump.[16] Moreover, it has made significant progress in its international agenda, from President Xi Jinping promising that China will be carbon-neutral by 2060, to the signing of the 15-member Regional Comprehensive Economic Partnership and the conclusion of the China-EU Comprehensive Agreement on Investment.

The Trump administration's declaration of a Cold War against China has confronted the EU with a dilemma, which will continue to exist under the Biden administration. Should it stick to the concept of a strategic partnership with China that was decided already in 2016 or join in the confrontational course adopted by the US?[17] The EU's answers are still ambiguous. On the one hand, following the confrontational US/NATO rhetoric, the EU called China a 'strategic rival' in March 2019;[18] on the other hand, in December of last year it agreed with this 'rival' in signing an agreement for the foreseeable future: the Comprehensive Agreement on Investment.[19]

China's rise has more impact on European integration than is normally conceded in public. This is demonstrated by the official participation of Italy in the One Belt, One Road Initiative.[20] Since 2012, the Cooperation between China and Central and Eastern European Countries (abbreviated China-CEE, China-CEEC, as well as 17+1, formerly 16+1) has been gaining momentum, involving EU member and non-member countries in a dialogue with the Chinese government, which has progressed notwithstanding the increasingly hostile policy of the US towards China.

The required 'realpolitik approach' to China, whose increased imports have contributed 30% to the global economic recovery after the great financial crisis, should not be regarded as a love match, nor does it preclude political criticism; rather it rests on the knowledge that none of the immense problems we are facing on this planet, such as environmental protection, disarmament, and the overcoming of global inequality, can be solved without or against the People's Republic.

Of course, the same holds true for the US whose integration into a multilateral, international order based on international law must be a central goal of the EU and its member countries. The conditions for this might improve under the new US president. On the other hand, Joe Biden made clear that, although he will return to the Paris agreement and the WHO, and will even perhaps change Trump's Iran policy, China is another matter and here he will continue the last administration's approach, something that definitely runs counter to the EU's economic and political interests.

In recent years, the EU has had to acknowledge that there are limits to its strategic room for manoeuvre. This became obvious in the failed attempt to save the nuclear deal with Iran by creating the special bartering platform INSTEX.[21]

Remarkably enough, only a few days before Joe Biden's inauguration in January, the EU Commission in a draft policy paper called for measures 'to shield EU operators in the event a third country compels EU-based financial-market infrastructures to comply with its unilaterally adopted sanctions'. To reach this goal, the paper went on to say, the unilateral dependency of the global economy on the dollar needed to be curbed while the international importance of the euro had to be boosted.[22]

The keyword in this discourse is the EU's 'strategic sovereignty', ranging from autonomous decision-making in security issues within and beyond its borders to technological issues, in particular, digital sovereignty where the EU is indeed about to become the plaything of the rivalling super powers, the US and China. The term itself and the abundant funding of armament programmes provided in the EU budget indicate that military means are seen as playing an important role in the repositioning of Europe.

The fact that Europe is still in danger of becoming the theatre of a nuclear arms race triggered by the US' and Russia's abrogation of the INF Treaty demonstrates how hypothetical any talk of strategic sovereignty is.

From this, it should be obvious that Europe can achieve sovereignty not by military means but by creating a political architecture that provides equal and mutual security to all European countries. Shamefully, only two of 27 EU member countries (Austria and Ireland) joined the UN Treaty on the Prohibition of Nuclear Weapons, which came into force in January 2021 after its ratification by fifty states.

The UK's exit from the EU has reminded us that the EU is not a universal European entity and will not be one for the foreseeable future. It is therefore misleading to think of it as a republic *in statu nascendi*, a continuously expanding state based on the model of the US.

Because Europe is by no means identical with the EU, it needs to retain and activate those European forums, which have disappeared behind the European Union in the public's perception: the Council of Europe, to which all states on the continent belong, the Organization for Security and Co-operation in Europe, which includes the US and Canada, and the United Nations Economic Commission for Europe. Even seemingly unimportant institutions such as the European Danube Commission, which brings together the eleven riparian states of the Danube from the Black Forest to the Black Sea, need to play a part when it comes to tackling the environmental and traffic problems of the region. They should be seen as forms of cooperation/integration, with no less long-term importance for security on the European continent than economic and social cooperation/integration within the framework of the EU.

If the goal of the European Neighbourhood Policy (ENP) was to foster stabilisation, security, and prosperity in its Eastern and Southern neighbourhood, it has drastically failed.[23] The war in Libya seeing France and Germany supporting opposite sides, the tension in the Eastern Mediterranean caused by Turkey, the frozen conflicts in Ukraine and Moldova, and the critical relation with Russia forced the EU's foreign policy representative Josep Borell to admit last year that 'the European Union's neighbourhood is "engulfed in flames,"'[24] something which certainly does not showcase the quality of Ms von der Leyen's concept of a 'geopolitical commission' announced in 2019.

The general question of whether security policy should remain in the competence of the nation-states or be located at the EU level remains abstract and futile if it is not clear that its priority must be arms control and disarmament.

In any event, foreign and military policy must not be left to military experts and intergovernmental diplomacy in the EU – both insulated from the public; rather, it requires a debate in public space. Without the achievement of full parliamentarianism on the European level, there is no point in abolishing the principle of unanimity on military and foreign policy matters as proposed by the governments of Germany and France.

It would appear that the primary function of the prominence given to foreign policy in the reform debate is to detract attention from the EU's international position, which is essentially determined by its capacity to cope with its internal difficulties. Prognoses tell us that already by 2023, digitally transformed companies will contribute 50% of global GDP,[25] but of the ten globally most lucrative companies, only one is European . The picture is the same as regards hardware and digital infrastructure. If the EU and its member countries do not want to fall back further in the technological race with the US and China, what is required is a planned industrial policy and the mobilisation of enormous resources on a European scale. However, the requisite political will for this can, under the current shape of the EU, if ever, only form with increasing difficulties and frictional loss.

The fight for democracy in the EU

The Multiannual Financial Framework has had a policy trajectory worthy of note. The EU Commission had already finished the draft in May 2018 but the European Council needed almost three years to arrive at an agreement at the very last moment. This reluctance can be explained neither by the EU parliamentary elections in 2019 nor by the difficulties arising from the cancellation of British EU contributions but had to do with the resistance of the member countries to the increase of the EU budget. This political resistance was even exacerbated when in May the EU Commission presented its partly credit-financed coronavirus reconstruction plan – which called the 'Frugal Four' onto the scene.[26]

The mediatised meetings of the European Council, which are meant to showcase the 'bosses'' European problem-solving competences, turned into a scene of shameful populist intrigue, which questioned the system of the European Council altogether, the backbone of which is the permanent interaction between the bureaucracies in Brussels and the national governments in the frame of the weekly meetings of the Committee of Permanent Representatives (COREPER), and the General Secretariat of 3,500 persons, both of them shielded from public and parliamentary control.[27]

While the negotiations of the European Council were stuck, the European Parliament, in May 2020, made a remarkable move in passing a resolution demanding a substantially increased EU budget, a credible European Recovery and Transformation Fund of 2.0 trillion euros for which the European Parliament requested the creation of an autonomous funding basis for the EU. As possible sources for financing this budget a common consolidated corporate tax base, digital services taxation, a financial transaction tax, income from the emissions trading scheme, a plastics contribution, and a carbon border adjustment mechanism were proposed.[28]

This decision of the European Parliament of course has only symbolic meaning due to the lack of a legislative right of initiative and also due to the cowardly political behaviour of the majority parliamentary factions. Nevertheless, it became obvious that the alternative to the European Council, paralysed by nationalist populism, consisted in shifting the decision-making competence to the directly elected representative body.

The first half of 2021 will see the opening of the Conference on the Future of Europe jointly presided over by the European Council, the European Commission, and the European Parliament, which, it has been announced, is to come up with a groundbreaking reform agenda for the integration process.

Already in 2017, the European Commission, then headed by Jean-Claude Juncker, published the *White Paper on the Future of Europe*. In it, the fundamental alternative options for the future of the European Union are described in the following terms: a) The retreat to the nation state; b) deconstruction of the EU to become a free-trade zone without any further social or political integration; and c) triggering a public debate intended to lead to a quantum leap in integration.[29]

In September of the same year, in a keynote address at the Sorbonne, French President Emmanuel Macron announced the Initiative for Europe, indeed pointing to all of the EU's deficits in calling for a 'refoundation of Europe'![30] Yet only a short while later, when the heads of the German and French governments met in Paris for the 55th anniversary of the Élysée Treaty, symbol of the friendship between France and Germany, the closing statement contained nothing of Macron's ambitious proposals. And so the debate had already come to a standstill before the European Parliament elections.

Even the radical left parties, operating mostly in a nation-state framework, showed scant interest in a fundamental debate on European integration, which, at least partially, goes back to the disappointment of pro-European optimism by the defeat of Syriza in its confrontation with the Troika (or the 'institutions'). One result of the manifest indifference vis-à-vis European politics was the poor results of radical left parties in the European Parliament elections in almost all EU countries.

The EU's failure in social and climate policy does not really come as a surprise since the integration of capitalist states in a union cannot occur other than primarily through markets, which have no feel for society's needs. The only surprise might be that people are surprised at this.

The EU milestones – the Treaties of Rome, the Single European Act, the

Treaty of Maastricht, and the Treaty of Lisbon – have continuously deepened the EU's market-economy character. And even Emmanuel Macron, in contrast to his innovative gesture in the address at the Sorbonne, has called the Economic and Monetary Union 'the heart' of European integration.

However, integration via markets had, from the very beginning, been opposed by a social countertendency oriented to centrally planned political decisions taken by the European institutions – critically supported also by the Eurocommunists and their left tendency, the latter having opted for a democratic road to socialism, albeit with structural changes and ruptures, at the national and European level – to embed the economy within policy goals by means of state and supranational institutions.

The history of European integration consists of the clash of these two tendencies.

On the eve of the long expected Conference on the Future of Europe, it would be helpful to briefly summarise the history of this conflict. In 1951, Belgium, France, Italy, Luxembourg, and Germany founded the European Coal and Steel Community, replacing the International Authority for the Ruhr, which after the war had placed West Germany's heavy industry under Allied control. Alongside trade in the products of heavy industry without customs barriers, a High Authority was created with far-reaching dirigiste powers.

The 'politics and market' conflict reached a climax in 1984 when the first directly elected European Parliament accepted the Draft Treaty Establishing the European Union written under the guidance of Altiero Spinelli. It provided for the European market economy's subordination to social targets – explicitly named as full employment, the overcoming of inequality, protection of the environment, and cultural progress. Moreover, the initiative in the shaping and further development of the union was to be shifted to the European Parliament – and without restricting the rights of the national parliaments.

What followed was in complete contrast to Spinelli's aspirations. In 1985 the heads of states and governments passed the Single European Act, setting the goal of quickly realising an all-encompassing European internal market, which signified the victory of the market-economy tendency. In 1992, when the heads of states and governments met for the summit at Maastricht after the situation of the world economy and geopolitics had fundamentally changed following the triumph of neoliberalism and historic events of 1989, they felt confident in completing this victory through the creation of an economic and monetary union with the now (in)famous criteria of 'convergence'.

The conflict flared up again in 2005 when the heads of states presented their new construction, a draft of the Treaty for Establishing a Constitution for Europe, for ratification by all member countries and were rebuffed in three countries which held referenda on it. That the failed constitution was passed by an intergovernmental conference two years later as the Treaty of Lisbon, bypassing popular ratification, certainly did nothing to improve the EU's standing.

The most recent dramatic climax in the battle between market and democracy came in 2015 when Syriza, having come to government in Greece, sought to break out of the straitjacket of neoliberal austerity policy. The harshness with which the attempt to find an alternative way out of the crisis was quashed by the creditors and the brutality of the austerity programmes forced on Greece – much harder than those imposed on Ireland and Portugal – horrified many throughout Europe; but it also reanimated the differences in attitude towards the EU that had always existed within the radical left.

It is a fact that the longstanding disillusion with the European Union has evolved, in considerable parts of the radical left, into the conviction that the EU is not reformable. Europe's left, as well as the lefts of each country, has been wrestling for quite a long time with the question of what scale and form of European cooperation or integration, in contrast to the present EU, it sees as appropriate for confronting contemporary capitalism. The different, sometimes controversial answers they give diverge, less for ideological reasons than due to the concrete conditions of the individual countries.

There is no doubt that in all conceivable systems of European integration the national states will continue to be important agents within the framework of the capitalist reproduction process for the predictable future. And if today's strategic task is to recover the sovereignty of the peoples, then it must be not against each other but within mutual cooperation in the face of the financial markets. Thus, the democratic self-determination of the populations and their control of their states have to be defended. And this, of course, implies the right of every country to leave the EU and the Euro as well as the right of every progressive government to disobey those rules which impede the wellbeing of their states and societies.

However, despite the growth of disintegrative tendencies, a disorderly breakup of the EU, at least under conditions of peace, is a rather improbable scenario. What can be expected from a present-day perspective is a condition of lasting paralysis of the institutions, which have proven ever more incapable of solving urgent social and ecological problems, that is, a circumstance which, in turn, continually feeds right-wing populism and nationalism. In this scenario, most probably the old lines of conflict, which haunted Europe during the nineteenth and the first half of the twentieth century, between a Central European bloc under the aegis of Germany and a Western bloc led by France, will re-emerge, but this time in a world much more complex and dangerous than it was between the wars.

It is certain that neither prospect – either the abrupt falling apart of the EU or its slow waning away – would create favourable conditions for the left. It is stating the obvious to say that the left's essential power bases are located in the nation-states. However, this is a double-edged sword, since, as the defeat of the Syriza government proves, staying in the struggle confined to the national level turns out to be the Achilles heel of the radical left. Therefore, we need to refute the false dilemma of European versus nation-state strategy. Instead, the relevant focus should be, on the one hand, the efficient and transparent division of competences, with checks and balances between the national and the European level and, on the other hand, the democratisation of supranational institutions.

For any progressive reform agenda that encompasses the strengthening of the social infrastructures, the reconstruction and ecological transformation of Europe's industries, the elimination of regional disparities, the building of effective energy and transportation nets, with the mobilisation of the necessary financial capacity reaching beyond the scope of the current EU budget – for all this, long-term, resilient supranational cooperation is needed.

However, the European programme of the radical eco-socialist left must contain more than catalogues of the demands of trade unions, NGOs, and social movements; it must be a political programme, which competes with other programmes for political leadership.

On one point there seems to be agreement between the diverse tendencies of Europe's left: a change that addresses the roots of the crisis would be unfeasible within the framework of the European Treaties – and this is precisely expressed in the call for a necessary refounding of the EU.

Today in Europe, a claim to political leadership must strive for the expansion of democracy. The argument of the liberals – that the deficit of European democracy is due to the absence of European public opinion – is weak. It is more accurate to say that European civil society – the trade unions and social movements – only have limited capacities to influence European policy, for which the decisive factor still is, apart from the structural neoliberal and non-democratic characteristics of the EU itself, the hierarchy of its member countries as determined by their relative economic and political weight.

If Europe is to be refounded, then – also from the perspective of a post-capitalist vision – a crucial step in the long process of getting there is a fully fledged, sovereign parliament interacting with the trade unions and the social, ecological, and civic movements. In place of entrusting the steering of the integration process to the national executives and ministers and heads of states who meet in the European Council, and have failed in nearly every respect, the European Parliament must become the centre of decision-making in those affairs for which the EU has authority. In it, the key factor would be the intervention of political parties at the European institutional level. The Party of the European Left has the duty to try to boost its own role and that of the European Parliament by proposing that its member parties run candidates in European Parliament elections on a pan-European list, allowing citizens to vote for a multi-national European slate.

Today, the EU exists as a strange hybrid: It has created the world's most powerful free-trade zone with a common currency. Yet its constitution is characterised by the prevalence of the executive powers, that is, the European Commission and the national governments in the European Council. A Parliament exists, but it is deprived of full sovereignty since it can neither initiate legislation nor nominate the European Commission, nor does it have full budget authority. It is directly elected, but not through a unitary electoral law. This squeezing of parliamentary power less resembles what occurs in a two-chamber-system than it does the kind of power sharing between the executive and the representative body typifying enlightened absolutism.

It is true that the future of the EU is dependent on its capacity to lead the social and ecological transformation on the transnational level.

In order to make this possible, we ought to remember: From the English Chartists to Lassalle and to the enactment of women's suffrage in Europe, social progress has been inextricably linked to the struggle for dismantling the executive power of the monarchs and transferring it to parliaments elected by universal and equal suffrage. Although incomplete and deficient, this democracy was largely achieved at the national level; but on the European level it is has not yet been won.

Who if not the radical left should be called to fight for it?

NOTES

1   'OXFAM-Bericht: Die Reichsten werden noch reicher' [The richest become even richer], *Frankfurter Allgemeine Zeitung*, 25 January 2021, <https://www.faz.net/aktuell/wirtschaft/arm-und-reich/oxfam-bericht-die-reichsten-werden-noch-reicher-17162878.html>; *The Inequality Virus: Bringing together a world torn apart by*

coronavirus through a fair, just and sustainable economy, <https://www.oxfam.org/en/research/inequality-virus>.
2. 'Internationale Arbeitsorganisation: Langzeitfolgen für die "Lockdown-Generation"' [International Labour Organisation: Long-time consequences for the 'lockdown generation'], <https://www.finanzen.at/nachrichten/aktien/internationale-arbeitsorganisation-langzeitfolgen-fuer-lockdown-generation-1029237333> (27 May 2020); *ILO Monitor: COVID-19 and the world of work. Fourth edition, Updated estimates and analysis*, <https://www.ilo.org/wcmsp5/groups/public/---dgreports/---dcomm/documents/briefingnote/wcms_745963.pdf>.
3. Oxfam, *The Inequality Virus*.
4. Xe Hui Han, Paolo Medas, and Susan Yang, 'The Pre-Pandemic Debt Landscape – and Why it Matters', *IMF blog*, 1 February 2021, IMF blog, <https://blogs.imf.org/2021/02/01/the-pre-pandemic-debt-landscape-and-why-it-matters/?utm_medium=email&utm_source=govdelivery>.
5. Tribune – Collectif, 'L'annulation des dettes publiques que la BCE détient constituerait un premier signal fort de la reconquête par l'Europe de son destin,' *Le Monde*, 5 February 2021, <https://www.lemonde.fr/idees/article/2021/02/05/la-bce-peut-offrir-aux-etats-europeens-les-moyens-de-leur-reconstruction-ecologique-sociale-economique-et-culturelle_6068861_3232.html>.
6. European Commission, *A Clean Planet for All. A European strategic long-term vision for a prosperous, modern, competitive and climate neutral economy*, Brussels, 28 November 2018, <https://eur-lex.europa.eu/legal-content/EN/TXT/HTML/?uri=CELEX:52018DC0773&from=EN>.
7. Federal Constitutional Court, 'ECB-decisions on bond purchasing programme violate competences', Press release number 33/2020 of 5 May 2020, <https://www.bundesverfassungsgericht.de/SharedDocs/Pressemitteilungen/DE/2020/bvg20-032.html>; judgement in English: <https://www.bundesverfassungsgericht.de/SharedDocs/Entscheidungen/EN/2020/05/rs20200505_2bvr085915en.html>.
8. 2 BvR 1651/15 -, III. Dr. G […], <https://www.bundesverfassungsgericht.de/SharedDocs/Entscheidungen/EN/2020/05/rs20200505_2bvr085915en.html>.
9. In 1307, according to legend, the Habsburg bailiff, Albrecht Gessler, raised a pole in the market square of Altdorf, Switzerland, placed his hat atop it, and ordered all the townsfolk to bow before it, which Wilhelm Tell refused to do.
10. See 'Lagarde als Krisenmanagerin: So fällt die Bilanz ihres ersten Jahres aus' [Lagarde as a crisis manager: That is the balance sheet of her first year], *Handelsblatt*, 26 October 2020, <https://www.handelsblatt.com/finanzen/geldpolitik/ezb-praesidentin-lagarde-als-krisenmanagerin-so-faellt-die-bilanz-ihres-ersten-jahres-aus/26303040.html>.
11. See Tobias Kaiser, 'Halb Europa fordert Schuldenerlass – doch aus Deutschland kommt eine Warnung' []Half of Europe is Demanding Debt Cancellation – But From Germany There Is a Warning. *Die Welt*, 15 February 2021, <https://www.welt.de/wirtschaft/plus226346127/Staatsfinanzierung-durch-EZB-Gutachten-warnt-vor-EU-Schuldenschnitt.html?cid=onsite.onsitesearch>.
12. Wolfgang Münchau, 'Beware of smoke and mirrors in the EU's recovery fund', *Financial Times*, 20 September 2020, <https://www.ft.com/content/0ba23192-5f43-402d-8f26-6fce0ab669f3>.
13. <https://www.eca.europa.eu/lists/ecadocuments/inrw20_01/inrw_tracking_climate_spending_en.pdf>.

14 Münchau:,'Beware of smoke and mirrors'.
15 Gita Goinat, 'A Race between the Vaccines and the Virus as Recoveries diverge', IMF blog, 26 January 2021, <https://blogs.imf.org/2021/01/26/a-race-between-vaccines-and-the-virus-as-recoveries-diverge/>.
16 'Data show efforts by Trump to decouple economies has fallen short […] Instead of decoupling financially, the US and China now have one of the largest and fastest-growing investment relationships in the world', James Kynge, 'US-China inverstment flows belie international tensions', *Financial Times,* 4 February 2021, <https://www.ft.com/content/b3dcc262-a153-4624-bc1d-156179d6e914?desktop=true&segmentId=7c8f09b9-9b61-4fbb-9430-9208a9e233c8#myft:notification:daily-email:content>.
17 European Commission: Joint Communication to the European Council and the European Parliament, *Elements for a new strategy on China*, 22 June 2016, <https://eeas.europa.eu/archives/docs/china/docs/joint_communication_to_the_european_parliament_and_the_council_-_elements_for_a_new_eu_strategy_on_china.pdf>.
18 European Commission Press Release: 'Commission reviews relations with China, proposes 10 actions', <https://ec.europa.eu/commission/presscorner/detail/en/IP_19_1605>.
19 <https://trade.ec.europa.eu/doclib/docs/2021/january/tradoc_159342.pdf>.
20 The Belt and Road Initiative, known in Chinese and formerly in English as One Belt One Road (OBOR), is a global infrastructure development strategy adopted by the Chinese government in 2013 to invest in nearly 70 countries and international organisations.
21 Instex (Instrument in Support of Trade Exchanges) is a European special-purpose vehicle (SPV) established on 31 January 2019 to bypass the US sanctions without breaking them by allowing non-US dollar and non-SWIFT transactions with Iran.
22 Jim Brunsden, Sam Fleming, Philip Stafford. 'EU sets out plans to curb reliance on dollar in post-Trump era', *Financial Times*, 16 January 2021, <https://www.ft.com/content/20f39e33-e360-479e-82e2-5441d24f0e0b>.
23 European Union, External Action Service, European Neighbourhood Policy (ENP), 8 February 2021, <https://eeas.europa.eu/diplomatic-network/european-neighbourhood-policy-enp/330/european-neighbourhood-policy-enp_en>.
24 'EU neighbourhood "in flames", warns Borell, calling for "strong and united" response', Euronews, 19 September 2020, <https://www.euronews.com/2020/09/13/eu-neighbourhood-in-flames-warns-borell-calling-for-strong-and-united-response>.
25 'Digital transformation - Statistics & Facts', Statista.com, 4 August 2020, <https://www.statista.com/topics/6778/digital-transformation/?utm_source=browser&utm_medium=push-notification&utm_campaign=cleverpush-1599119161>.
26 The 'Frugal Four' is the nickname of an informal cooperation among like-minded fiscally conservative and ideologically neoliberal European countries: Austria, Denmark, the Netherlands, and Sweden.
27 It is by no means superfluous to point out that a military-political component was also integrated into this administrative structure in 2019; see 'Command and control structure of the European Union', <https://en.wikipedia.org/wiki/Command_and_control_structure_of_the_European_Union>.
28 'European Parliament resolution of 15 May 2020 on the new multiannual financial framework, own resources and the recovery plan', <https://www.europarl.europa.eu/doceo/document/TA-9-2020-0124_EN.html>.

29 European Commission, *White Paper on the Future of Europe*, 2017, <https://ec.europa.eu/info/future-europe/white-paper-future-europe-and-way-forward_en>.
30 Emmanuel Macron, full text of the Sorbonne speech, <http://international.blogs.ouest-france.fr/archive/2017/09/29/macron-sorbonne-verbatim-europe-18583.html>.

Capitalism's Ecological Crisis and Radical Left Alternatives

MONTHLY REVIEW
AN INDEPENDENT SOCIALIST MAGAZINE

MONTHLYREVIEW.ORG
134 W 29TH STREET, SUITE 706 NEW YORK, NY 10001

*group solidarity discounts available on our website

The Planetary Rift:

John Bellamy Foster Interviewed by Haris Golemis

Haris Golemis: With your path-breaking article 'Marx's Theory of Metabolic Rift', you challenged the then prevalent view, even among non-dogmatic Marxists, that the effects of capitalist growth on nature was not of interest to Karl Marx. Could you briefly explain your thesis?

John Bellamy Foster: In 'Marx's Theory of Metabolic Rift',[1] I argued that the widespread view on the left that Marx had adopted a Promethean (extreme productivist) view of the human domination of nature and hence had failed to perceive the natural limits to production and ecological contradictions in general – giving them at most only marginal attention – was contradicted by his theory of the metabolic rift, which played a key role in his overall analysis. Marx built on the German chemist Justus von Liebig's notion of the robbery of nature in which nutrients were systematically removed from the soil and shipped hundreds and even thousands of miles to the new urban centres, polluting the cities, rather than being returned to the soil. Based on this, he constructed an ecological critique of capitalism, rooted in the concept of social metabolism, standing for the human relation to nature as a whole through production. Capitalism's disruption of this metabolism generated an 'irreparable rift in the interdependent process of social metabolism, a metabolism prescribed by the natural laws of life itself'. For Marx, the labour and production process constituted nothing less than the social metabolism between humanity and the universal metabolism of nature, mediating between the two. But under capitalism this had become an alienated mediation, rupturing this metabolism, which needed then to be restored under socialism, as an eternal requirement of life itself. In these terms, Marx developed a notion of sustainability, arguing that no one, not even all the people in the world, owned the earth, but rather they needed to sustain it for 'the chain of human generations' as 'good heads of the household'. Socialism itself was defined in volume 3 of *Capital* as the rational regulation by the associated producers of the metabolism of nature and society, so as to conserve energy, and promote human development.

In short, Marx's critique of political economy ushered in the most profound ecological critique ever developed, since integrated with his overall analysis of capitalist production and constituting the basis of the creation of a higher society of the future. Later scientific ecology, including the concept of ecosystem, were to be developed on this same basis, with the concept of metabolism leading to systems ecology.

The power of Marx's analysis in this respect and the depth of his understanding of natural science surprised me and forced me to rethink Marx's entire body of work. How had he developed such a profound ecological critique? The answer had to lie in his materialism, which went much deeper than most Marxist theorists had perceived. This led me back to the very beginnings of Marx's thought, starting with his doctoral thesis on Epicurus, the greatest materialist thinker in antiquity, and analysing the development of Marx's materialist and ecological perspective from that point on, including his relation to thinkers such as Liebig and Darwin. That reinterpretation of Marx's thought, resulted in my book, *Marx's Ecology: Materialism and Nature*, published in 2000.[2]

HG: In a March 2020 interview you gave to Farooque Chowdhury (*Monthly Review online*, April 1, 2020),[3] you said that David Harvey was critical of the theoretical scheme presented in your book *The Vulnerable Planet* (Monthly Review Press, 1994).[4] Would you say that since then his and your analyses of contemporary capitalism have come closer?

JBF: David Harvey is a major Marxist theorist, and his wide-raging work is always illuminating, presented with an elegance all of its own. In the last decade or so, he has moved closer, particularly since his *The Enigma of Capital* (2011),[5] to the Marxian economic analysis pioneered by *Monthly Review*, focusing on the problem of surplus capital absorption under monopoly-finance. So there are a lot of places where our analysis overlaps.

However, Harvey and I have long had major differences in how we see the planetary ecological crisis and of the significance of Marxist theory in this respect. In the 1990s, he denied the severity of the overall environmental problem, arguing in response to my book, *The Vulnerable Planet* (1994), in his *Justice, Nature, the Geography of Difference* (1996),[6] that with respect to the human impact on the planet, 'The worst we can do is to engage in material transformations of our environment so as to make life less rather than more comfortable for own species, while recognizing that what we do also does have ramifications (both positive and negative) for other living species.' In these quiescent terms, he rejected the argument in my book that biogeochemical cycles of the Earth System were being disrupted by the increasing scale of capitalist production. Instead, he strongly criticised all notions that 'ecocide is imminent' due to capitalist development, claiming rather that such a view was vulnerable to right-wing criticisms that said that human conditions were constantly improving.

In a debate between Harvey and myself that followed in *Monthly Review* (April 1998)[7] he declared that the 1992 'Warning to Humanity' focusing on the dangers of climate change signed by over 1,500 of the world's scientists, including more than half of the recipients of the Nobel Prize among living scientists, was 'every bit as problematic as the literature [of climate change deniers and anti-environmentalists such as Julian Simon and Greg Easterbrook] they rebut'. He insisted that a Marxist perspective should prevent us from falling for the ecological rhetoric 'that we are reaching some limit, that environmental catastrophe is around the corner or that we are about to destroy planet earth'. His overall emphasis at the time was to downplay and to a considerable extent deny the planetary ecological emergency – on putatively Marxist grounds.

It took him several decades, but Harvey has now come to recognise the environmental problems and to admit to the shortcomings of his analysis in this regard. In his *Anti-Capitalist Chronicles* (2020)[8] he indicates that a graph from the National Oceanic and Atmospheric Administration (NOAA) – the kind of graph that has been around for decades based on the Mauna Loa Observatory, but this one showing the rise in carbon concentration in the atmosphere all the way to 400 ppm (reached in 2013) – finally convinced him that climate change was as serious as the scientific consensus had long contended. The question is why had he taken so long to realise the full environmental dangers, despite coming from a historical-materialist perspective? In answering this, Harvey goes into a long discussion on how he had been misled by focusing too much on weaknesses of some of the environmental rhetoric on the left. In 2020, he says it was the NOAA graph showing the speed with which the Earth System had gone from 300 ppm to 400 ppm of carbon concentration in the atmosphere that 'changed everything in my world view. The question of climate change went from something I thought to be manageable by normal techniques and sensible interventions to a recognition of the need for radical transformation of all our ways of thinking.'

Even with this revelation, however, his emphasis in *The Anti-Capitalist Chronicles* tends to favour ecomodernisation perspectives, whereby technology will save the day by carbon sequestration: taking the carbon out of the atmosphere and putting it in the ground. The fact that such technology does not exist at scale, and poses its own cataclysmic problems is not considered in his analysis. There is simply no attempt to pose this problem in ecological Marxist terms as one of ruin or revolution.

HG: In the same interview you say that 'it has suddenly become easier to imagine the end of capitalism than the end of the world, and indeed the former would likely preclude the latter'. What do you really mean by reversing Jameson's quote? It is true that the number of radical left intellectuals and activists who believe that capitalism is not the end of history has considerably grown. However, the ruling classes are using the pandemic to hide this truth, by presenting the virus as an external threat, and in view of the power of the mainstream media, I am afraid that the TINA narrative still prevails in the general public. I would be happy if you could convince me that I am wrong.

JBF: You will recall that Fredric Jameson's statement in *New Left Review* (March-April 2003) read: 'Someone once said that it is easier to imagine the end of the world than the end of capitalism.'[9] Well before I was conscious of his authorship of this statement, we commonly used that same exact phrase over and over in our discussions in the graduate programme in environmental sociology at the University of Oregon, discussions and debates that included some of those who are now among the world's leading environmental sociologists, who had come to study at Oregon, primarily in order to engage with Marxian ecology. In fact, I had used the exact same wording early in this century in talks I gave, though usually in the question-and-answer sessions after the talk, more as a kind of riposte to get the audience to think – just as we often raised it ironically in our seminar discussions in environmental sociology.

The reason why the notion that 'it is easier to imagine the end of the world than the end of capitalism' was approached in this circumspect way in our discussions at the time was that, although capturing part of the contemporary environmental predicament – and the dystopian consciousness that was so pervasive among youth – it tended to represent a negative, even defeatist outlook, when not put into a concrete historical context. The problem is closely related to what Derick Jensen and Aric McBay in *What We Leave Behind* (2009) were to call 'the inversion of the real and the not real' such that 'the end of the world is less to be feared than the end of industrial capitalism'.[10] If such a view were to be presented, however, it needed to be placed in a context of generating a revolutionary ecological consciousness, rather than signalling defeat. It was a question of countering the dominant ideology and received views in general.

This was such an important part of our overall discussions on the environment that when I became aware that the phrase had been introduced in print by Jameson who had prefaced it with 'someone said' I thought it had emerged somehow from our own discussions. Now, however, I think we must have picked it up from him indirectly, probably from Cade Jameson, Fredric Jameson's son, who is himself a great environmental sociologist, who now teaches in Hawaii, and who was part of our programme at the University of Oregon. It may be Cade, knowing his father's work, who inserted this phrase early on into our discussions. I am not sure.

The point, though, is not that the consciousness of capitalism's role in the destruction of the planet as a safe home for humanity is wanting, rather the point is to change this. In reversing the famous Jameson quote, and indicating that 'it has suddenly become easier to imagine the end of capitalism than the end of the world', I was pointing to the fact that the Covid-19 pandemic, coming on top of climate change, was threatening the ideological hegemony of the system, demonstrating that our ecological-epidemiological crises were products of capitalism itself. The illusion of the Emperor's clothes had vanished and suddenly the Emperor was revealed as naked. The United States, at the centre of capitalism, has now experienced over half a million deaths from Covid-19, which everyone knows have to do with the privatisation of public health, not to mention the circuits of capital, as historical-materialist epidemiologists like Rob Wallace explain. For many, this allows them to see that what is constantly projected as the end of the world is indeed properly seen as the question of ending capitalism. You are right, of course that in presenting the virus as an external threat to the system the ruling ideology was attempting to steer the population away from such critical conclusions.

You ask me about the views that prevail in the general public, given the constant outflow of propaganda on TINA (there is no alternative) under capitalism. I think that that is the wrong way to think about it. A snapshot of public opinion tells one very little given that the material conditions of humanity – the very conditions of life on earth – are changing more rapidly than at any time in human history. People are volcanoes and will erupt when the molten rock rises to the surface. If one starts simply with ideas, from an idealistic perspective, it looks like capitalism is supreme and will remain forever so. But the Catholic Church got Galileo to disavow his science, and yet, as legend has it, he touched the ground and said, 'it still moves'. TINA is correct, but in a different way than Margaret Thatcher believed. *There is no alternative* to a society of substantive equality and environmental sustainability, that is, socialism – if humanity is to survive.

HG: How do you evaluate the work of Murray Bookchin, a non-Marxist thinker, who has also tried to bring the ecological issue into the public debate? Indeed, we see radical leftists and anarchists fighting together in the streets of many cities in the world against the policies of governments that are destroying the environment and increasing class, race, and gender inequalities. In view of such an 'alliance', do you think that a theoretical and programmatic dialogue between different anti-capitalist traditions is desirable and possible?

JBF: I have always thought a great deal of Bookchin's work in ecology, though it was seldom directly influential on my own thinking. I was first introduced in the early 1970s to his *Post-Scarcity Anarchism*,[11] which, however, left little impression. But his 1962 *Our Synthetic Environment* (written under the pseudonym of Lewis Herber),[12] which came out in the same year as Rachel Carson's *Silent Spring*, was pathbreaking. One of my favourite books by him is his *The Limits of the City*.[13] Another is his *The Ecology of Freedom*.[14] He could be very polemical and was a strong critic of Marxism on ecology. But he was careful in doing so to criticise Marxism and not Marx himself, for whom he always retained great respect. I cite Bookchin at various points in my work, though not extensively. When I was on the editorial board of *Capitalism Nature Socialism* in the early years, there were a stream of harsh criticisms of Bookchin and one edited collection opposed to his analysis that came out of the journal. I declined to be part of it. Instead, not soon afterward, when I was coeditor of *Organization and Environment*, we published a very favourable assessment of Bookchin's ecology by Steven Best. *Monthly Review* has always been open to Bookchin's ecological analysis. Brian Tokar, who is perhaps the most important figure in Bookchin's social ecology tradition, has written for Monthly Review Press. In fact, *Monthly Review* as an independent socialist magazine has always been open to anarchist views, particularly where they overlap with Marxism, as part of the conversation. Our whole orientation from the beginning has been to unite various anticapitalist traditions. Of course, there are differences but there is plenty of room for commonality. The role of anarchists in fighting neofascism; in the racial solidarity protests in the United States; and in the ecological movement has been very great. Forging coalitions in this respect is necessary in the common cause.

HG: Ever since the 1960s, *Monthly Review* has been well known for its interest in developments in the Global South, or the 'Third World' in the language of the period. As editor of the periodical you maintain what I think is a very useful, internationalist tradition. In this framework, can you tell us the differences between the effects of catastrophe capitalism in the Global South as compared to the Global North?

JBF: *Monthly Review* has always focused on imperialism, especially in terms of the relations of the Global North to the Global South, as the key to the critique of the capitalist world system. In terms of 'catastrophe capitalism', I think our two most important contributions in the last couple of years have included the article on 'Imperialism in the Anthropocene', written by myself Hannah Holleman, and Brett Clark,[15] and the work that we have done on Covid-19 in relation to Rob Wallace, especially his books *Big Farms Make Big Flu* and *Dead Epidemiologists*[16] and his article with others on 'Covid-19 and the Circuits of Capital',[17] as well as the article that Intan Suwandi and I did on 'Covid-19 and Catastrophe Capitalism'.[18]

In 'Imperialism in the Anthropocene', we developed an argument that departs from most traditions on the left, in that it takes physical geography seriously, as the climate catastrophe demands. Thus, we explained how low latitude countries, essentially the Global South, are affected most, as a result of Earth System dynamics, by climate change, independently of the fact that they are already economically exploited by the nations of the Global North. Moreover, the effects of climate change on such factors as the elimination of glaciers (or water towers); desertification; the flooding of islands and other low-lying areas; the eradication of tropical forests and coral reefs; the extinction of species; and the creation of hundreds of millions, even as many as a billion, climate refugees expected this century – are all being factored into the global imperial strategy of the United States and other nations in the Global North. We, therefore, desperately need a theory of imperialism in the Anthropocene that would take all of this into account.

In the work of Rob Wallace and other theorists of what is known as Structural One Health (a historical-materialist approach to epidemiology), the emergence of Covid-19 and other zoonoses are seen as connected to the circuits of capital and the extension of agribusiness into ecosystems and wilderness areas. This work provides a rich understanding of the relation of global commodification to global contagions. Moreover, the same analysis points to the effects of the privatisation of public health under neoliberalism and the effects on the spread of disease, especially among the poor, pointing to the contemporary significance of Frederick Engels's notion of 'social murder'.

HG: As the US is one of the two world superpowers, its government's economic policies play a crucial role in the climate crisis. Would you say that the Trump administration has left its footprint on the development of catastrophe capitalism and if so how? And do you believe that Biden might follow a different path?

JBF: The Trump administration accelerated catastrophe capitalism in a number of ways. As detailed in our article 'Imperialism in the Anthropocene', it expedited the expenditure of trillions of dollars on the building of fossil fuel pipelines and fracking in North America in order not only to expand fossil fuel production but to entrench fossil fuel production so that it could not be displaced. It pulled out of the Paris Agreement on Climate Change, and removed environmental protections wherever it could, both nationally and internationally. Meanwhile, it started a New Cold War directed at China. This included putting a tariff on Chinese solar panels imported to the United States.

Politically, the Trump phenomenon had its basis in the development of a neofascist political movement/political formation based in the white lower middle class, with its nationalist, racist, misogynist ideologies and its hatred of both the greater part of the working-class majority (the most diverse section of the population) and of the upper middle-class professionals. In essence, monopoly capital has drawn on the rearguard of the capitalist system, as C. Wright Mills called it, to stabilise itself during a period of declining US hegemony, increasing class polarisation, and the rise of a significant socialist movement.

The Trump administration backed by the Federal Reserve poured trillions into the coffers of corporations and the rich in tax reductions followed by aid in response to the pandemic. The result is that US billionaires are running off with the store. While the economy has had negative growth, Jeff Bezos saw his wealth *increase* by $74 billion this year, and Elon Musk by some $76 billion in this year to date. All of this has been supported by expanding US federal deficits. The financial system has been expanding at a record pace during the pandemic. All of this means a bubblier economy, which will burst in the end.

Unfortunately, not much help in any of this can be expected in the Biden administration, which represents a neoliberal politics, which differs from that of Obama and Hillary Clinton only to the extent that the situation is now considerably more desperate. The current administration seems destined to attempt to expand its reach to elements of the non-Trumpist right, as the Democrats and Republicans continue to fight to gain the support of the lower-middle class section of the electorate. In terms of the forward movement of society we will see very little. In fact, Biden promised Wall Street that nothing would change if he were elected. This seems to be confirmed by the fact that 83 percent of the top thirty members of the Biden team have close connections to the billionaire-plutocratic class (see the article by Laurence Shoup in the May 2021 issue of *Monthly Review*). In short, the Biden administration has no interest in rocking the boat. Part of this has to do with the already destabilised state of the system, resulting from the overaccumulation and financial crisis of capital, for which the ruling class and its political representatives have no answers. The current 'solution' is in the direction of the greater repression of the population via an enhanced surveillance capitalism, the promotion of the carceral state, continuing privatisation of public schools, a New Cold War with China, etc. Biden is openly opposed to the Green New Deal (his proposed $2 trillion of spending in this area is only one-twentieth of that proposed by the Green Party's Green New Deal, and one-eighth of what was proposed by Bernie Sanders), Medicare for All, and to nearly every other needed progressive program. The result is likely to be a neoliberal disaster leading to a restoration of the neofascist wing. The left's only choice is to find a way to break the current undemocratic rules of the game.

HG: The new virus originated in China, the second world superpower and at the same time the world's biggest polluter. Can we expect that China's ruling Communist Party will have learned the lessons of the pandemic, and change its policies in the future?

JBF: To say China is the world's biggest polluter is true in one respect and misleading in others. China, it is true, is the biggest carbon emitter. But it is way below the United States and the other wealthy countries in its carbon emissions per capita. Moreover, in terms of the carbon that has accumulated in the environment as a result of historic emissions (the really important figure), the bulk have come from Europe and North America. Finally, a very large share of China's emissions is associated with production for multinational corporations in the core of the capitalist system, which import this production to their own countries. Essentially, production that would have occurred in the capitalist core is now happening in the periphery, for the capitalist core. It makes sense to see the bulk of such emissions as associated with the core countries. The United States has a trade deficit with China. China supplies produced goods and the United States asks them to hold dollars in return.

The fact that the Covid-19 virus originated in China has less to do with China itself than with the circuits of capital globally and the destruction of ecosystems and wilderness areas, with zoonotic spillovers. No doubt China will institute and is instituting new regulations, for example, in relation to wet markets. But this is not the core of the problem.

In terms of overall ecological responses, China, while an epicentre of ecological destruction, is also an epicentre of ecomodernism and environmental reform. It has made 'ecological civilisation' an official goal, unlike countries in the West. How we understand this is important. There are indications that China under its current leadership is taking decisive environmental steps (although hardly the ecological revolution that is needed). China is now the world leader in clean technology. I just read a very interesting book by Barbara Finamore, published by Polity, entitled *Will China Save the Planet?*.[19] We have plenty of reason to be sceptical. Yet, given all that China is actually doing in terms of seriously addressing its ecological crisis and that of the world, the question remains. As a post-revolutionary state, with a quite different social construction from that of the mature monopoly capitalist economies of the West, China, with all of its contradictions, may still have a hidden potential to move in the direction of its official goal of an 'ecological civilisation'. My view is that this depends ultimately, as elsewhere, on the spread of a genuine ecological revolution emerging from the ground up. That this is at least possible in China is suggested by its current rural reform movement.

HG: The pandemic has not only considerably reduced US-China trade, but it has also intensified the struggle between the two countries for global hegemony. Could this lead to broader geopolitical changes, and do you think that it could also signal the beginning of the end of globalisation?

JBF: This is an easy question to answer. A New Cold War is being launched by Washington against Beijing, explicitly aimed at bringing down the Chinese Communist Party, and then resubordinating China to the world imperial system, in a replay of the demolition of the Soviet Union. All of this is spelled out by the US State Department and in foreign policy circles, and is being supported by the US capitalist class and multinational corporations, which realise that a China Century, replacing the American Century, is not in their interests. The Trump-initiated trade war and military buildup directed at China (and indeed both China and Russia) is now entrenched and is continuing in the Biden administration. US allies, like Australia, are being asked to sacrifice their own trade interests to the New Cold War pact. This is meant to be a major geopolitical shift. China is responding in its own way by furthering its Belt and Road Initiative and creating with the 2020 Regional Comprehensive Economic Partnership the largest trade bloc in the world.

I don't think this will signal the end of globalisation, which has its basis in the global labour arbitrage, whereby multinational corporations mainly centred in the Global North locate industrial production as measured by employment primarily in the Global South. The object is to exploit low unit labour costs, providing large profit margins (or rates of surplus value) for these corporations. But we are seeing a geopolitical shift in the growth of global blocs within this. US multinational corporations are pulling out of China to some extent and relocating in other low unit labour cost countries such as India and Mexico.

HG: In February, at the beginning of the Covid-19 outbreak, the Italian radical philosopher Giorgio Agamben wrote that the lockdowns and other government measures against the virus are intended to permanently establish a 'state of exception' and make this appear to be normal. He was also worried by people accepting the restrictions of their freedoms almost with no complaint. However, we later saw people protesting violently in the streets against the lockdowns and refusing to comply with instructions even to wear facemasks and keep social distancing. Do you agree with Agamben, and how do you explain these reactions of a large part of the populations to their governments' measures? Is their reaction progressive or reactionary?

JBF: It is hard to answer this since international situations vary so much. In the United States, we saw with racial solidarity protests in the May and June Days the biggest mass protests in the country since the US Civil War, with working-class whites and youth on a scale never seen before crossing the colourline to join protest/revolt against the public police lynchings of Black men. But this was also a response to the pandemic, the lockdowns, and the laying off of millions of people. In many places, it took the form of a revolt against capital showing that there is a suppressed anger at the base of society. Of course, the neofascist, white supremacist movement based in the lower-middle class also was in evidence, but they lacked the numbers and power of those revolting against the system. For the neofascists, their main advantage is their ability to pull out their guns and even to fire them in some cases, with the support of the police. The Trump administration did everything it could to promote these 'militias' and back them up with its own paramilitary forces. This is the situation in the United States. It is lessening somewhat on the surface with the coming into office of the Biden administration. But the contradictions remain.

HG: To combat the virus, governments all over the world have resorted to, or are seriously contemplating unprecedented state-interventionist measures (supplementary direct payments to people who cannot go to work due to the lockdowns, nationalisation of private hospitals and healthcare providers in Spain, nationalisation of railways in Wales, etc.), which conflict with free-market ideology. Can this lead to a change of the capitalist paradigm in a way similar to what happened with the New Deal in the US following the 1929 crisis and the consensual implementation of Keynesian policies in Europe after the Second World War?

JBF: One would hope so, but I am sceptical. It is strange to me that Europeans are looking to the US New Deal, which was not nearly as radical as many historic changes that developed in Europe in the same period. The First New Deal, during Franklin Delano Roosevelt's first term of office, was to a considerable extent a form of conservative corporatism. The New Deal only radicalised, and we are only talking here of about four years, in the Second New Deal, beginning in 1935, due to the Great Revolt from Below with the formation of industrial unionism, which involved pitched battles all across the country. It was not a top-down development. Roosevelt merely saw a chance to get at the head of this movement and contain it, to save capitalism. The New Deal did not increase overall government spending on consumption and investment in the United States, since the federal increases in civilian government spending merely compensated for the drop in government spending at the state and local levels. In 1937-1938, there was a recession within the depression decade. All sorts of radical things were proposed in 1938 but nothing really happened. In 1939, the war orders from Europe began and the New Deal and the Great Depression ended with the Second World War. There were some important results, particularly Social Security. But overall, the New Deal did little in transforming the system. It merely stands out in relation to the period of entrenched ruling class power that followed. US civilian government spending on consumption and investment as a percentage of GDP has remained pretty much on the level of 1939. To change this in the United States would require a New Great Revolt from Below. Some of the nationalisations occurring in Europe could have a positive effect, but unless it is part of a movement toward socialism, it will be the usual nationalisations for capital, buying them out when they are losing money, and reprivatising once these markets are profitable again.

HG: It seems that even a section of mainstream politicians in the US and Europe support a 'Green New Deal', a name that directly refers to Roosevelt's 1933 New Deal. Do you see this as a victory of the eco-socialist movement or an initiative to promote 'green capitalism'?

JBF: It is difficult to say what the Green New Deal represents because there are so many versions of it, all of which are rejected of course by the Biden administration. (Obama, incidentally, officially included a corporatist 'Green New Deal' in his first presidential race and then dropped it as soon as he was elected.) The Green New Deal with a 'just transition' proposed by Alexandria Ocasio-Cortez and Bernie Sanders could be described as a Peoples' Green New Deal and would be important if it inspired a genuine ecological revolution, forcing ever greater efforts. But this is not in the cards now without a massive movement from below, which briefly looked possible when the climate movement was on fire, but now has abated in 2020, due largely to the pandemic. Some versions of the Green New Deal are so feeble from the start as to be meaningless. And with Biden now in office anything resembling an actual Green New Deal is off the agenda of the Democratic Party. In general, US politicians will sign up for things that sound good if the polls point to a lot of public support, and if it is so nebulous as to not constitute a recognisable threat to business. So the mainstream political support for real change in this sense is largely illusory, unless there is some push from below powerful enough to challenge capital. This, however, requires real organisation, and there is little to point to in that respect.

HG: The inability of capitalist states to fight the pandemic, largely due to the underfunded and understaffed health systems – together with the fact that vulnerability is closely tied to class, race, and gender – and the concomitant economic crisis have created hope among some radical leftists that an increasing number of people in the world might envision a non-capitalist alternative. Do you think that this hope is realistic?

JBF: The question of whether hope is realistic always sounds strange to me. The question is whether hope is necessary. We shouldn't be trying to predict the future so much as to engage in the necessary struggles, recognising that the world's population now has its back to the wall. I think this is what scares the ruling classes. They know a struggle is inevitable and they know they could lose. Marxists have long argued for freedom as necessity. At no time has this stance been more realistic today, since the reality of our world is one of catastrophe capitalism. If it is impossible to save the world, humanity, and most of the world's known species, then the struggle must become that much fiercer, the impossible has to be made possible.

HG: In a discussion you had with Michael Yates, published in the 19 April 2020 online edition of *Janata Weekly*,[20] you say that the way we can confront catastrophe capitalism is 'the building of a vast, unstoppable socialist (or ecosocialist) movement'. This is a normative general statement, which however does not specify in what way the various national movements can achieve their anti-capitalist goals: through revolution, or through the Poulantzasian 'democratic road to socialism'? What is your view?

JBF: I don't think that revolution and a democratic road to socialism are necessarily contradictory. Nicos Poulantzas wrote numerous important works on the state but they were a product of the Eurocommunist period, and quickly receded. I personally, prefer the analysis of Ralph Miliband, since he started with the harsher reality of the failure of the British Labour Party as a socialist party, as depicted in his *Parliamentary Socialism*.[21] Since he was responding to a major defeat, he saw the problem of the capitalist state as a greater challenge and therefore raised harder questions. We need a more critical theory of the state than Marxist theory provided in the 1960s and '70s, which was removed in many ways from the question of revolution – so much so that the Italian political theorist Norberto Bobbio once declared there was no real Marxist theory of the state. It is necessary to turn back to the classical tradition of the withering away of the state associated with Marx and Lenin, and powerfully revived by István Mészáros in his *Beyond Leviathan*, which will be published by Monthly Review Press at the end of 2021. The Bolivarian Revolution in Venezuela, despite the fact that it has been deeply scarred by the international siege warfare imposed on it by the United States, has things to tell us about how to promote a revolutionary strategy aimed at 21st-century socialism, based on Hugo Chávez's notion of the communal state. But, of course, the conditions in every country are different. There is no universal model.

HG: Thank you very much for the time you spent answering my questions. Before we end, I wonder if you could say a few words about your latest book *The Return of Nature: Socialism and Economy*.[22]

JBF: *The Return of Nature* was written to carry forward the story told in *Marx's Ecology*, covering the period from the death of Darwin and Marx in 1882 and 1883, respectively. *Marx's Ecology* ends with the death of Darwin and Marx. *The Return of Nature* begins with their funerals. It explores the interrelations between socialism and ecology in the century that followed, providing concrete research into ecology as it developed in relation to socialism and materialism. Of course, the developments went in all directions and the story becomes quite complex, especially if given historical depth so that we can comprehend the context in which the various figures emerged. Basically, the thesis is that socialists (some of them social democratic, some of them Marxist but deeply engaged with each other) generated ecology as a critical form of thought.

In arguing this, I follow an analysis that is not only historical but also genealogical. One genealogical line can be seen in terms of those influenced by Marx's ecological ideas directly, including figures like E. Ray Lankester and William Morris, and those who they in turn influenced, such as Arthur George Tansley, H.G. Wells, and Julian Huxley. The other genealogical line derives more from Engels's ecological thought and especially his dialectics of nature, which are the focus of Part Two of the book. This leads to the dialectical and ecological contributions of such important scientists as J.B.S. Haldane, Joseph Needham, J.D. Bernal, and Hyman Levy. Some thinkers, such as Christopher Caudwell, Lancelot Hogben, and Jack Lindsay can be said to be products of both lines of development. All of these thinkers were involved not only in the development of ecology, but also in the debates on race, gender, class and the making of socialism in their time. Nearly all of them contributed to materialist dialectics. The direct influence on the ecology movement in the 1960s and 1970s in the United States and Britain is quite evident, leading to discussions in the Epilogue of the work of figures such as Rachel Carson, Barry Commoner, Virginia Brodine, Richard Levins, Richard Lewontin, Stephen Jay Gould, Steven Rose, Hilary Rose, and E.P. Thompson. We thus get a much wider picture of why ecology is such a critical, and indeed revolutionary, doctrine.

The book also challenges the Western left to recognise that a materialist conception of history is meaningless without a materialist conception of nature – plus the role of dialectics as necessarily related to both. In this way, the long detour of Western Marxism away from the natural-material world is transcended, a necessary task in the deeper ecological and social revolution required in our times.

NOTES

1. John Bellamy Foster, 'Marx's theory of metabolic rift: classical foundations for environmental sociology', *American Journal of Sociology* 105,2 (1999):366-405; see also John Bellamy Foster, 'Marxism in the Anthropocene: dialectical rifts on the Left', *International Critical Thought* 6,3 (2016), 393-421
2. John Bellamy Foster, *Marx's Ecology : Materialism and Nature*. New York: Monthly Review Press, 2000.
3. <https://mronline.org/2020/04/01/catastrophe-capitalism-climate-change-covid-19-and-economic-crisis/>.
4. John Bellamy Foster, *The Vulnerable Planet: A Short Economic History of the Environment*, New York: Monthly Review Press, 1999.
5. David Harvey, *The Enigma of Capital: And the Crises of Capitalism,* Oxford England: Oxford University Press, 2011
6. David Harvey, *Justice, Nature, and the Geography of Difference,* Cambridge, Mass.: Blackwell, 1996.
7. John Bellamy Foster, 'The Scale of Our Ecological Crisis', and David Harvey, 'Marxism, Metaphors, and Ecological Politics', *Monthly Review* 49,11 (April 1998).
8. <https://anticapitalistchronicles.libsyn.com/>.

9   Fredric Jameson, 'Future City', New Left Review 21 (May-June 2003).
10 Aric McBay and Derrick Jensen, *What We Leave Behind*, New York: Seven Stories Press, 2009.
11 Murray Bookchin, *Post-Scarcity Anarchism*, 3rd ed., Working Classics Series, 3, Edinburgh: AK Press, 2004.
12 Lewis Herber (pseudonym of Murray Bookchin), *Our Synthetic Environment*, Barakaldo Books, 2020 (1962).
13 Lewis Herber (pseudonym of Murray Bookchin), *The Limits of the City*, New York: Harper and Row, 1974.
14 Murray Bookchin, *The Ecology of Freedom: The Emergence and Dissolution of Hierarchy*, Oakland, CA: AK Press, 2005.
15 <https://monthlyreview.org/2019/07/01/imperialism-in-the-anthropocene/>.
16 Rob Wallace, *Big Farms Make Big Flu: Dispatches on Infectious Disease, Agribusiness, and the Nature of Science*, New York: Monthly Review Press, 2019; Rob Wallace, *Dead Epidemiologists: On the Origins of Covid-19*, New York: 2020.
17 Rob Wallace, Alex Liebman, Luis Fernando Chaves, and Rodrick Wallace, 'Covid-19 and the Circuits of Capital: New York to China and Back', *Monthly Review* 72,1 (May 2020), 1-15.
18 John Bellamy Foster and Intan Suwandi, 'COVID-19 and Catastrophe Capitalism – Commodity Chains and Ecological-Epidemiological-Economic Crises', *Monthly Review* 72,2 (June 2020), 1-20.
19 Barbara Finamore, *Will China Save the Planet?*, Cambridge UK: Polity, 2018.
20 <https://janataweekly.org/trump-neo-fascism-and-the-covid-19-pandemic/>.
21 Ralph Miliband, *Parliamentary Socialism: A Study in the Politics of Labour*, 2nd ed., London: Merlin Press, 1973.
22 John Bellamy Foster, *The Return of Nature: Socialism and Ecology*, New York: Monthly Review Press, 2020.

On the Political Economy of the Ecological Crisis

Birgit Mahnkopf

In the first months of 2020 we frequently read and heard that the cosmopolitan Covid-19 pandemic and the massive spread of the ensuing fear was ushering in a 'new historical epoch'. The illness and its consequences were seen as constituting a 'caesura' that could make possible a 'turn to less' – especially in terms of mobility and consumption, and therefore also of production, with the positive result of reducing CO_2 emissions. The dangerous viral disease was seen as having thoroughly 'positive side effects': greater solidarity among people and greater appreciation for the people working in healing and care professions (and their potentially better remuneration). Because a more local scale in production, consumption, and leisure time suddenly became more important, there was speculation that the pandemic could lead to greater regionalisation, to a turn away from private transport and possibly also from consumption, but resulting in a better quality of life.

Just two months later there was no longer any talk of this. In the programmes launched so far to boost the economy only 3 to 5% of the total of 12 to 15 billion of Covid Stimulus Funding have been provided for 'green investments'.[1] In view of the increasingly threatening ecological crisis, the pandemic has certainly not proven to be a 'game changer'. It is not only in Europe that political discourse is completely concentrated on the economic and social consequences of the pandemic; if its ecological causes are ever mentioned it is only marginally. Nowhere has the health crisis been treated as an opportunity to change basic structures and the direction of economic and social development. Confronted with the worst recession since the world economic crisis of nearly a century ago and with labour markets that are becoming ever more clearly polarised – in which low-wage workers, youth, and women are those who suffer most during the crisis – the first opportunity after the post- 2008 financial crisis for a turnaround is being squandered.

In the EU too a quite large Pandemic Recovery Package Fund has been launched; it is to direct public and private investments towards 'green infrastructures', increase the number of jobs, and stimulate new growth as quickly as possible – and at the same time not only reduce CO_2 emissions but achieve zero emissions by 2050! These promises have been combined through a new buzzword, 'net carbon neutrality', which is to be reached by mid-century. This term is seldom mentioned without referring to another one: 'digitalisation'. Already before the outbreak of the Covid-19 pandemic digital automation was seen in Europe as a technological development that is as inevitable as it is beneficial, from which no one can nor should escape. With the epidemiologically compulsory lockdown of normal social life in the course of the pandemic, this perspective became the shared common sense.[2]

The following arguments attempt, first, to substantiate the thesis that with the announced political measures aimed at 'decarbonisation' and 'digitalisation' in Europe – and possibly in other industrialised countries as well (including China) – 'greening' of the economy is aimed at invigorating the stalled accumulation dynamic of industrial capitalism. The second main thesis is that 'green capitalism' cannot defuse the ecological crisis; for this crisis is so closely entwined with modern industrial capitalism that it can only be resolved in the process of transforming/transcending the latter.

2020: The 'new normal' of terrifying disasters

In an increasingly industrialised, urbanised, and in many respects networked world, people are encroaching on the last refuges of wildlife; through poaching, uncontrolled livestock trade, the destruction of rainforests, housing developments, and above all through the constant expansion and intensification of agriculture and livestock farming they are in increasing contact with virus-carrying birds and mammals. Thus, viral infections from Zika, AIDS-HIV, SARS, Ebola, and now SARS-Covid-2 are expectable and unavoidable. The Intergovernmental Platform on Biodiversity and Ecosystem Services, founded in 2012 as a sister organisation of the Intergovernmental Panel on Climate Change, estimates that among the possible 1.7 million as yet undiscovered viruses in host animals, from a half million to 850,000 have pandemic potential. But we also must expect increasing 'reverse zoonoses', that is, the retransmissions of viruses through animals that have been infected by people.

The political economy of the ecological crisis certainly explains why the spread of a mutation of the virus in Danish mink farms in fall 2020 only triggered fear, because the mink-specific mutation of the virus might call into question the efficacy of future vaccines. But the ensuing killing of up to 15 million minks is exclusively seen as the inherent consequence of a 'business that is dying out' anyway and not as a cause for outrage; for these animals were already being bred to be slaughtered somewhat later – their skins making possible an 'animal outfit' for rich people.

Understandably, pandemics are seen as serious crises with far-reaching health, economic, and social consequences. Most people want state power to be deployed on all policy levels to contain such crises and, whenever possible, tackle their causes. But the same cannot be said of other manifestations of the ecological crisis, even though we all know that it threatens not only the life of people, animals, and plants that now inhabit the beautiful blue planet but even the lives of many of their (potential) progeny.

The manmade ecological crisis is throwing the earth system's climate equilibrium out of balance, a balance which has developed over a long period of 1.2 million years, and it is ensuring that a 'well-tempered' geological epoch highly conducive to human development will come to an end. This was the Holocene phase in which homo sapiens was able to spread his dominion throughout the entire globe.

Everything is pointing towards the conditions of existence for living beings, of whatever species, not being nearly as pleasant in the near and far future as they were in the geological age now coming to an end. Just as threatening, but far less frequently seen as cause for worry, is another dimension of the ecological crisis: Man, the intelligent being, who has learned how to dominate the other animals with an 'ecology of fear',[3] destroys – sometimes by leaps, but mostly gradually – the 'network of life' that emerged in the course of billions of years and in so doing is narrowing the path of future evolution on the planet.

Quite clearly, we are dealing here with the phenomenon of the shifting bottom line: it seems to have already become the new normal that new records of destruction of life possibilities are being broken on an almost daily basis. Most people appear to be getting used to much of this destruction which derives from their doings; they are especially adaptive where they are unable to protect themselves from the sudden or creeping destruction of the essential bases of life – and ignorant where they, although aware of the consequences of their action, (still) hope to escape their disastrous effects.

The year 2020 may go down in history books as the year of the Covid-19 pandemic. As a global average, however, it is also one of the hottest since the beginning of recorded temperatures. The last time the earth's atmosphere reached a CO_2 concentration as high as that of November 2020 was 3 to 5 million years ago – at a time when there were not 7.7 billion people on the planet as there are now.

We are very well informed about the consequences of this development: The polar ice caps are melting faster than ever before, and what happens in the Arctic, as we know, does not stay there. In summer, the North Pole area now has half the ice cover measured in the 1970s and the ice's thickness is down by half. With this the reflection of sunlight has changed and the ice sheets in Greenland and even in the Antarctic are shrinking still more quickly. This not only makes sea levels rise; it also changes the circulation of warm and cold air masses, with a weakening of the so-called jet stream. This in turn has the consequence that heat waves in many places are becoming longer and deadlier and the number of tropical storms in the Atlantic is increasing. At the same time, other 'tipping points' of the earth system are constantly coming closer: permafrost soils have by now thawed out to the point that climate researchers were predicting for 70 years from now. Water in the oceans is rising; it is warming, becoming acidic, and losing oxygen – with dramatic consequences for sea life and for the global climate, for with rising sea temperatures continually less heat can be absorbed by the oceans.

It belongs to the 'new normal' of 2020 that what continues to be called 'extreme weather events' follow each other at a nearly monthly rate: devastating tropical storms with attendant flooding in Southeast Asia and the Caribbean; heavy rainfall in an atypical season in Africa, which favour breeding conditions for locusts, which then fall upon the fields of farmers in Eastern Africa, in the Arab Peninsula, and later in the eastern regions of Afghanistan and Pakistan, destroying crops; the increasing draught in the Sahel region that each year drives ever more people from the land into the overpopulated cities – and beyond them into cross-border migration, especially to Europe. In this part of the world the connection between developments in sub-Saharan countries and the advance of Islamist militias (especially in Mali) is seldom noted. Yet both phenomena need to be seen as expressions of a brutal struggle for survival in a region of the world increasingly inhospitable to life, a struggle that certainly cannot be contained by military intervention (for example, on the part of Europe through France).

In contrast to the catastrophic developments in many countries of the Global South, which always involve the same poor people to whose misery those in the rich North have become accustomed, the huge fires of the year 2020, which supplied the media with spectacular images, managed to stay in daily news reports for a long time. 2020 began with devastating bush fires in Australia. In the same year in Brazil more rainforest burned down than ever before. In California the forest fires could not be extinguished for months, and at the end of the year Australia was still ablaze. Every additional report of catastrophes makes the previous ones lose their newsworthiness, and a 'new normality' take hold.

And nothing indicates that a policy change will occur in reaction to such 'natural catastrophes. Australia provides a good example. There a rise in the average temperature of just 1° C over the pre-industrial level will be enough to destroy half of the Great Barrier Reef and forests of the size of the whole isle of Ireland, annihilating a billion animals and making the Tasmanian Tiger extinct. And yet there are no signs that the 'black summer' of 2019/2020 will call into question the 'business model' on which Australia's wealth is based. The world's biggest exporter of coal and liquid gas, with one of the highest rates of CO_2 emissions per capita, has up to now done nothing to stop its coal production, which is set to double by 2030, nor has it put a hold on its plans for 50 new coal mines. Therefore, the grandiose announcement of a gigantic Asian Renewable Energy Hub for the export of hydrogen to Southeast Asia in 2027 and other huge green future projects, in which components of the Australian state will be involved alongside private entities, probably must be seen as wishful thinking.

None of the ecological catastrophes of 2020 has turned into a wake-up call.[4] It seems that the final extinction of probably a million animal species is causing even less pressure for action than the reports of the catastrophic consequences of unchecked climate change. If the 'sixth greatest mass extinction'[5] in the long history of the planet can attract brief attention it is mostly only in connection with the water and food crisis coming to a head in the highly populated equatorial countries. Meanwhile in the everyday parlance of the rich industrialised countries, the dramatic loss of biodiversity and the related loss of humus-rich soils is not seen as a catastrophe whose consequences can both deepen and go beyond climate change. Biodiversity is mostly seen as the concern of apprehensive 'conservationists' who are out of touch with people's everyday lives. They, with their concern for bees and earthworms, tend to be derided and appear distant from the problems of making a living that occupy the majority of people.

Today everyone can know – not just the young people who are active with Fridays for Future or Extinction Rebellion – that we are leaving behind the realm where there is still room in the earth systems for manoeuvre, now producing important tipping points that, once reached, will unleash a cascade of massive and then irreversible changes – and change the face of the planet for hundreds of thousands of years.[6] If the geophysical dominos that provide the planet's precarious equilibrium fall one after the other, our beautiful blue planet will become an annealing oven in which people, many animals, and plants can only barely survive.

In the Covid-19 crisis, fear for one's own life and those of one's family and friends has in many places helped state power to gain new legitimation; this appears to be the case at least for the majority of Europe's populations.[7] In the pandemic we see how quickly many people can adjust to the new circumstances, even to severe restrictions of their individual freedom. But how is it that the same thing is obviously not happening in regard to the by now foreseeable consequences of global ecological crisis? Nowhere are politicians forced by growing fear in the population to take decisive measures that will possibly put limits on private property and individual freedom, but could stem the further destruction of the bases of life.

It is very clear that an unconditional orientation to the present moment prevents people from imagining their future as, or even wanting it to be, something other than a prolongation of the present. Therefore, as Günther Anders once wrote in terms of people's blindness to their possible extinction from an atomic bomb, their fear is mainly focused on the loss of their jobs, even if they are in danger of losing their lives tomorrow and the whole world the day after tomorrow.[8]

A majority of people especially favour those promises that hold out the prospect that essentially nothing has to change; that although here and there a couple of screws have to be readjusted, the socio-economic system can stay the way it is. For, as the popular formula goes, the last 100 years have shown that the historically unique symbiosis of capitalism, democracy, individual freedom, and unlimited economic growth is superior to any systemic alternative, especially a socialist one.

In the meantime, innumerable think tanks, international organisations, associations, and politicians from almost all parties claim that they are taking the voices of the international climate movement seriously, which they demonstrate by including 'Green Deals' in their agendas as all-purpose weapons to confront almost all economic, social, and ecological problems of our time – in ways that range of course from light to dark green as dictated by their position in the spectrum of competing parties. Especially in the EU, the 'Green Deal' – here always closely tied to a comprehensive 'digitalisation' of economy and society – is being propagated as the key to reaching 'climate neutrality' – in the spheres of electricity supply, mobility, construction and housing, and industry and agriculture.

The promise of 'green growth'

Starting in the 1970s the Club of Rome, and after it many other organisations and personalities, has drawn attention to the 'limits of growth'. And ever since that time the EU's environmental policy has professed the principles of 'precaution' and 'prevention'. The 'precautionary principle' was recognised by many countries around the globe with the 1992 Rio Declaration. However, this did not prevent the foreseeable aggravation of the ecological crisis. It is true that, above all in many areas of the richer European countries, 'dirty pollution' could be curbed, for this can be reduced through technology investments that promise lucrative profits. The 'clean pollution' released by greenhouse gases, which are not directly experienced as compromising human health, had in the meanwhile broken all records within a few decades. Added to this was the emissions trading in the framework of the Kyoto Protocol. This created an entirely new market. Through state-securitized rights to pollute the atmosphere and the creation of artificial scarcity (through 'caps' on emissions) economic assets were created that could be included in the capital value of companies. At the same time, during the first trading period until 2008, a market for innovative and profitable financial instruments for trading in certificates emerged, which made 'windfall profits' possible for companies that had not provided services to reduce pollution. Only true believers in the market could wonder why CO_2 emissions continued to rise.

Innumerable studies on the ecological crisis have been financed at the global level and in national contexts in the last decades. There are many multilateral agreements – mostly not binding, which is not surprising, considering that the UN is structurally defined as having a petitioning function in relation to its Member States.[9] In addition, multilateral agreements (for example, the UN Convention on Biological Diversity) are systematically undermined by organisations outside the UN system (especially by the WTO's regulations and the bilateral and regional trade agreements based on them). And even the 2015 Paris Agreement, celebrated as a breakthrough, relies on countries pledging themselves to a *voluntary* reduction of greenhouse gases.

The national, supranational, and global consequences of the environmental and climate policy that for decades now has been constantly said to be 'ambitious' are well known: there is only one direction in which increasing radiation levels in Mauna Loa in Hawaii, due not to the sun but to anthropogenic greenhouse gases, can go: up! And the destruction of animal and plant species is continuing at an accelerated pace.

But today public discourse has moved away from the noble goals of sustainable development – as if the comprehensive Sustainable Development Goals were to be shelved simply because by the time of the Great Financial and Economic Crisis of 2008/2009 and the following global economic and social crisis no one any longer believes they can be met in 2030. Instead everything is now to become 'green': industry and jobs, cities, automobile and air transportation, even heavy industry, and agriculture in any case.

This is not a new message; in the years after the financial crisis, in the ambit of the G20 countries, there had been talk of a 'Green New Deal' (GND). In the UN Environment Programme the term 'green economy' came into fashion, and in the EU 'bioeconomy' was discovered, while the OECD and the World Bank had already been talking unmistakeably of 'green growth'; only the ILO preferred to dream of 'sustainable development and green jobs'. But ultimately, all these protagonists and organisations of the then not yet ruined 'global governance' promised that the wasteful, non-sustainable use of scarce resources (including those that are not renewable) would be 'more efficiently used' with the help of technological innovations and on the basis of the wonderful mechanism of market prices (established through supply and demand). In this way, along with a change in individual consumption practices, capitalism was to become 'green'.[10]

Since that time the green narrative has held out the prospect that, *first*, there can be technological progress especially with new industrial processes and products and a great deal of digital services; *second*, that with the help of market mechanisms (first and foremost the pricing of CO_2 emissions) a 'sustainable', 'quality', that is, 'green' growth would be possible, through a combination of intelligent macroeconomic policy including wide-ranging and judicious state intervention, but above all with targeted subsidies. Whatever the adjectives chosen according to party preferences, this is said to involve a kind of growth that does not (any longer) destroy the environment and needs less raw materials. However, growth is still seen as essential – that enables an increase in private property for the real economy, rewards the protagonists of the financial economy with increased profits, heaps growing tax revenues on the states, and creates more jobs and wage income so that the necessarily growing mass of commodities can also be consumed.

These glad tidings are based on some underlying assumptions loaded with presuppositions. *First of all*, the unavoidable 'externalities' of economic activities must be given a monetary expression, that is, they have to have a price; only under this condition can the markets work their magic and through the pricing of the 'externalities' cause the latter to disappear – so that ultimately nothing would stand in the way of the infinite growth of these markets. *Second*, the state's continued functioning must be ensured so that it can create and expand ('brown' or 'green') markets and compensate for inevitable market failures. However, this is only allowed with an aim to open up new, and today 'green ecological', spheres for the private sector and not, for instance, for the purpose of making the state into an economic protagonist itself. And, *third*, with some propagandists of green capitalism there are the additional glad tidings – though admittedly hard to square with physical laws – that economic activity entailing lower CO_2 emissions could at the same time set in motion a 'dematerialisation' of production. As if bridges could be built with significantly less, or no, cement and steel, chairs with almost no plastic or wood, and as if computers worked just through freely accessible information without energy supply or material components.

European Green Deal and the goal of 'net-zero emissions' by 2050

With the media's rosy picture of a Green Deal, which is to save 'the climate' and sometimes even 'nature' as a whole, but above all 'our economy', it is well to recall that a green agenda for the EU is no novelty. Since the adoption of the 'Lisbon Strategy' in 2005, relaunched as the Europe 2020 agenda, the integration of energy and environmental policies and the expansion of capacities for production of renewable energy are supposed to give a powerful boost to 'growth and jobs'. Through a strict cost-benefit analysis the incorporation of environmental policy into the neoliberal agenda has the effect that competition was seen as the efficient method of promoting technological innovation related to environmental police - and not government control, strict regulation with requirements and prohibitions – and above all *not planning*. At the same time, the concept of 'technological neutrality' was pursued, which meant that all 'low-carbon technologies', including nuclear energy, were to be promoted in equal measure; any preferential treatment of technologies based on renewable energy was consciously excluded. At the same time energy-intensive industries, and not just in the eastern EU Member States, have continued to enjoy state support. This has always occurred with the reasoning that the competitiveness of European corporations in international markets should not be endangered by an 'ambitious environmental and energy policy' and high energy costs.[11]

In short, 'green investments', essentially understood as the expansion of renewable energy in the electricity sector, have for years now been seen as a promising strategy to increase economic growth; it served the goal of securing and developing competitive advantages for EU-based enterprises in the energy- and resource-intensive branches through more or less voluntary 'decarbonisation'. This policy is supported by market-based incentive schemes. However, only cynics could call the Europe 2020 strategy successful; that emissions in the three decades from 1990 to 2020 have been reduced by 24% is only partly due to those technological advances in wind and solar energy that have clearly cheapened electricity production. The more important cause has been the 'greatest deindustrialisation programme' ever undertaken in the 20th century: the so-called 'transformation' of

Central and Eastern Europe. If starting in 2020 emissions in the EU (and also in other industrialised countries) need to drop much more drastically – the specific recommendation of the European Parliament's Environmental Committee is at least 60% by 2030 – we will not be able to rely on another such quirk of history.

A further important goal of the Europe 2020 strategy has been increasing the share of renewable energy sources within the energy mix. This has been successful in some EU Member States, but it has changed comparatively little in terms of the composition of the primary energy consumption of all economic sectors. In the former 'pioneering country', Germany, the share of renewable energy in total primary energy consumption amounts today to just 17%, of which half is accounted for by biomass, a quarter by wind, and only a tenth by solar energy. Throughout Europe the addition of renewable energy was simply used up by overall increased energy consumption. Not to mention that in the same period emissions from the transport sector in the EU rose by 30%!

Against the backdrop of these 'successes' of the EU, which was once praised as the role model for a shrewd integration of energy and environmental policy, we can expect that the European Commission's European Green Deal (EGD) will – in so far as it comes into being – also prove to be a sham. This plan is supposed to achieve 'CO_2 neutrality by 2050', and at the same time set in motion a revival of Europe's pandemic-shaken economy. It provides for a lowering of emissions in the next three decades not only by ca. 24%, as happened in the last three decades, but by a phenomenal 75% – and this without the help of large-scale deindustrialisation in a part of Europe! Even if it were to be honest and admit that the use of many material resources (among them especially many kinds of metal) would have to decline by about the same rate in the same period this grandiose promise would be no more credible.

The necessity of setting such goals can hardly be doubted. However, it is one thing to formulate ambitious goals and make promises open to different interpretations in the haze of a smoke candle called 'climate neutrality', and another story to take the political measures through which such goals can actually be realised. At present we only know of 'recommendations' that are to be 'made more precise' during an at least two-year negotiating process between the European Parliament, the European Commission, and the European Council – all this under constant pressure from innumerable lobbying organisations, which, as is well known, have made their influence felt on all protagonists in both Brussels and the Member States throughout all phases of the negotiations.

The focus of the EGD is almost exclusively on a reduction of CO_2 emissions and on measures aimed at reducing greenhouse gas emissions, especially by substituting fossil fuels with electricity generated from other energy sources. But there are no possibilities for substituting plant and animal populations; and so the critical condition of ecosystems in the EU plays a rather marginal role in the announced package of EGD measures. That our economic and social system is dependent on exosomatic energy, as the junkie is on drugs, is accepted as an incontrovertible and necessary condition of existence for capitalist industrialised societies. Thus, the EGD remains focused on technological innovations; with their help energy sources are to be tapped that will guarantee to us all the possibilities that fossil resources have so far given us, not only at the same level but to a greater extent. This is to have less undesirable 'side effects' ('externalities') than those coming from the burning of fossil fuels.

By contrast, the disappearance of forms of life, whatever their genus and species, has less importance; no provisions are made for them to grow again into acceptably large populations and in adequate variety. Clearly, the underlying logic is that the consequences will become visible only indirectly, after much time, only in particular places, and above all not to the majority of the people who have contributed most to the destruction of biological diversity. As a result, this dimension of the ecological crisis only appears at the margins of the EGD.

But even the promise of net-zero emissions by 2050 seems to be more of a tranquilizer than a courageous policy project. And this is not just because several Eastern European member countries only want to undertake greater CO_2 cuts if they get more financial support than provided by the Corona Package. In reality, among the majority of EU member countries there is no readiness for a true policy change; the elimination of state subsidies for coal, oil, and gas is only planned to start in 2025; when subsidies for exports of extraction technology for fossil fuels will be abolished (which would particularly involve the German and French export companies) is written in the stars. The EGD framework does not even envisage a freeze on member countries' airport and highway projects; the announcement is only that starting in 2022 the European Investment Bank (EIB) will no longer facilitate investments in airports and airplanes with conventional drive systems but will continue to promote road projects; and starting in 2022 agricultural activities that demonstrably damage the climate are no longer to be facilitated by the EIB.

Contrary to all announcements made in recent years, it is equally unlikely that the next years will see a significant boost to the 'circular economy' in the EU, in which all physically finite and economically increasingly scarce raw materials will be reused several times. Already in 2020 a majority of member countries have not complied with the recycling rates fixed by a 2018 legislative package. It is thus improbable that things will be any different with the goals set for upcoming years – although we frequently hear about how many billions in funds would be freed up by a closed-loop economy and what positive effects this could have on the labour market and the reduction of social inequality. Of course, collecting household refuse is not especially lucrative. But it is a different story with construction, extractive mining, and manufacturing wastes, and from waste processing itself, for this recovery of materials through 'waste mining' really does promise considerable profits in times of 'Peak Everything' and geopolitically disputed resources.[12]

In the past the EU could achieve, by international standards, quite high recycling rates through the export of all second-class waste. But now that China and other Asian countries, and even some African countries, have since July 2018 begun to tighten their rules for the import of recyclable waste, recycling rates within the EU necessarily have to be increased. Thus, it is said, there is to be an end, finally, to the 'waste of money' – the value added from refuse is to be accelerated. Admittedly, this does not create an incentive for waste prevention in the absence of powerful public subsidies for it. For everywhere where refuse can (through comparatively large investments) be transformed into energy, private companies lobby push those politically responsible to guarantee a specific large quantity of refuse supply for a long period (up to 50 years) so that their investments in recycling technology actually pay off. This is equivalent to a lock-in effect that makes it impossible to reduce refuse in the case of valuable resources. This effect could only be avoided if waste disposal and recycling occurs in public enterprises and with public financing for all types of waste.[13] But such proposals – which the Club of Rome has recently called the 'North Star for a prosperous sustainable Europe' – are nowhere to be found in the EGD.

A further important component of the 'new star' in the political heaven is the 'Farm to Fork' strategy; this is closely entwined with the long overdue reform of the Common Agricultural Policy (CAP). There is no doubt that a reduction in CO_2 emissions requires more carbon sinks in Europe, that is, intact forests, meadows, and wetlands. But, as in many other regions of the world, these are largely in a catastrophic condition; according to the European Environment Agency (EEA)[14] only 15% of all habitats have been well conserved. Therefore, to counteract a further loss in biodiversity more land areas have to be removed from industrial, infrastructural, and housing construction and from intensive agriculture, and intensive logging has to be stopped and large surfaces reforested. This has been known for years now. According to an EEA estimate, at least 10% of European land and sea territory needs to be protected and another 15% re-naturalised; 15% of rivers must have their original courses restored. Consequently, the 'Farm to Fork' goals provided for a 25% expansion of organic farming in the EU by 2030, cutting pesticide and antibiotics use by 50%, the strong regulation of fertiliser use, and an increase in biodiversity in all ways possible. But in order to reach these goals, at least 70% of EU agricultural subsidies would have had to be directed towards them, for the previous CAP is a 'costly and expansive folly neither we nor nature can afford'.[15]

By now this point of view has even penetrated parts of the business world – certainly not the agricultural lobby and the closely connected food and fertiliser industry, but it has, for example, influenced the insurance sector. For to the degree that natural spaces are shrinking, their 'performance', that is, what nature provides, is systematically registered, evaluated and traded. Thus, insurance corporations like Swiss Re have broadened their business and now calculate on a dollar basis how much these 'services' contribute to each country's GDP; conversely, interference with this money/value-creating function of ecosystems is seen as 'lost assets'. Companies and environmentalists are therefore asked to cooperate in integrating the value of 'nature's contributions' (the 'benefits') into their operations and their culture.[16]

But in the case of the EU itself this does not seem to work, for in fall 2020 a large majority of EU parliamentarians and a parallel decision of the European Council under the presidency of the German minister of agriculture strictly rejected anchoring the Farm to Fork goals of the EEA in the CAP. With this nothing stands in the way of continuing the subsidisation of industrial agriculture in the EU – in the form of direct payments to agricultural businesses according to farmed area without any environmental restraints. This will also contribute to aggravating the ecological crisis in the next seven years.

Thus because other forms of use yield more profit we cannot expect agriculture in the EU to make an important contribution to the conservation of the remaining EU biodiversity. For lands have by now everywhere become objects of speculation; they have to serve as a 'parking place' for accumulated capital that cannot be profitably invested elsewhere. In expectation of short-term gains, profit-hungry domestic and foreign investors, whose primary concern is not the agricultural use to which the purchased land is put, are acquiring not only fertile agricultural lands in Romania but also far less profitable lands in Germany and elsewhere. This makes it continually more expensive for agricultural businesses to lease land, while the prices they get for their products from the food industry and from food trade no longer suffice to cover their production costs. In short, even European agriculture drops out as a bearer of hope for reaching the net-zero carbon goal by 2050!

Thus, the whole weight of the grandiose promise rests on technological solutions to the 'energy question' – or more precisely for the electrification of transportation, heating, and industrial production and on the 'digitalisation' of practically all social and economic activities.

The new scramble for metals and growing geopolitical conflicts

With the catchwords 'decarbonisation' and 'digitalisation' two tracks of a development trajectory have been named that only know one direction. Naturally, even the proclaimed 'green'-tinted economic model has the same basis as the 'brown fossil fuels' of the last 250 years – the fundamentally infinite accumulation of capital. This economic model has, from the second half of the twentieth century, spread to the entire world economy, at the same time creating a global ecology.[17] As is well known, the peculiarities of this system consist in its resting not only on the private ownership of the means of production and propertyless wage labour but also on the separation of economy from politics and governance by self-referential markets. There can be no such thing as 'enough' within this system, for boundlessness is its lifeblood – and this is in no way just to be thought of as an ethical maxim, although that is contained in it. For money in its form as credit *must* always generate a surplus; money is only capital if it generates a surplus and is valorised/expanded via constantly new investments. The expansion of production beyond any needs conditions a very specific relation of human and non-human nature: The 'gifts of nature' not produced by labour – which according to Marx belong to no one, no person, no state, and not even to humanity as a whole, to which these are only left to be carefully used – are processed, transformed in terms of their material and energy, economically valorised, and thereby dispersed and ultimately irreversibly destroyed.

The maintenance of this system that is so destructive of human and non-human nature thus also underlies the 'decarbonisation' and 'digitalisation' hype, for both slogans promise infinite (monetary) growth in a world that is materially finite. In this a central role is played by the fixation on scientific-technical progress as the motor of social development. For ever since the Enlightenment and, even more, since the Industrial Revolution in England, the nearly boundless trust in science and technology has suggested that rational human beings can liberate themselves from the constraints of a finite world through ever new technological solutions to all possible problems. Nowhere is this fiction more powerful than in the current debate on 'artificial intelligence'.

It is not only the political decision-makers in the EU who have proclaimed 'decarbonisation' and 'digitalisation' to be the royal road to lead out of the ecological crisis in the system of natural use values and at the same time solve the real valorisation problems that are consolidating into 'tipping points' in the system of (monetary) values.[18] We have also heard from important industrialised countries such as Japan and South Korea – which are now superior to the EU in the field of digital automisation around which the conflicts over future technological leadership and contested world market share will be fought – that they intend to reach 'net-zero carbon emissions' by 2050. Even China, the big player in 21st-century digital capitalism, is aiming at the same goal by 2060 in its new 5-year plan. There is good reason to suppose that this announcement by China, as the 'strategic competitor', involves keeping one step ahead with the manufacture of electric batteries for automobiles and of super-computers for the next stage of digitalisation. China could possibly outsource its carbon-intensive production spheres of heavy industry for a long period to those countries along the Belt and Road initiative in which it is now financing and developing a great many coal and nuclear power plants. The emissions this causes would then no more have to be taken into account than is currently done by the EU in its imports of industrial goods, whose production in China is associated with high emissions.

If such important players among the industrialised countries announce that they want to resolve the ecological crisis by a quick transition to 'clean energy', this means there must be strong signals to stop the speeding train of global industrial capitalism as it rages towards an ecological nightmare – to then no less quickly reroute the train in another direction via sustainable tracks. But nothing of this is being heard anywhere. The mantra of 'CO_2 neutrality', which in the best of cases is supplemented by some lip service to 'rescuing' dwindling biodiversity, is based on a central gospel: the 'electrification' and 'digitalisation' of as many industrial production processes and services as possible, above all of mobility in all its forms. In this, it is taken for granted that electrification and digitalisation are to become 'clean', alternatively 'green' or (to use an expression that has gone somewhat out of fashion) 'sustainable', that is, to be derived through energy produced from renewable sources.

We are dealing here with many inconsistencies, contradictions, and probably also with deliberately concealed impediments and 'trade-offs'. They all have a common core: In the interest of a new industrial cycle promoted through government industrial policy (in China as well as in Japan, South Korea, Germany, and France), the raw-material basis of the industrial-capitalist developmental path is to be 'renewed'. However, this occurs not instead of, but in addition to the exploitation and climate-damaging burning of fossil raw materials; for these are far from being left in the ground. Their share in primary energy consumption may go down in the long term, but this changes little if at the same time this consumption increases. If fossil energy sources prove to be more economical in comparison to the alternative energy sources that are technically expensive to develop, such as hydrogen, then fossil raw materials will continue to be burned.

At the same time the efforts to keep the industrial capitalist system of production alive at all costs but while burning less fossil raw materials go along with a geopolitically tense run on metal raw materials. Like oil, gas, and coal, these too are non-renewable, and due to their economically relevant presence in only a few countries they are just as fiercely fought over as the fossil raw materials oil and gas. Parallel to this, a ruinous 'competition for water' has been fomented, whose consequences can predictably lead to vast human misery; for the 'financialisation of water', including the speculative 'future-trading' well-known in the oil market, will first and foremost follow the lust for investment returns on the part of the owners of monetary assets – and make water, as the basis of all life, into an economically 'scarce resource'. Not to mention that in many areas of the world it could also become a 'scarce good' in the physical sense as well.

In contrast to the 'green brainwashing' that dominates the EU politics and media, the data-supported scenarios of the International Energy Agency (IEA) look almost soberly realistic: If there really were preparations made in all countries that have currently made declarations of intent or where there is proposed legislation to reach 'zero-emission' goals by 2050, and if investments in developing the necessary infrastructure were made, energy consumption would have to be cut by 50% from 2010 to 2030. This would be occurring starting in 2021 at a time when every country in the world will use any available means to stimulate a 'recovery' of its national economy.

The demand for coal would nevertheless have to drop by almost 60%, in other words, to the level of the 1970s; for those power plants which continue to be operated the ecologically highly risky and universally disputed Carbon Capture and Storage technology would have to be deployed. The IEA has calculated that the share of renewable energy in global electricity supply would have to increase from 27% in 2019 to 60% in 2030 (which does not take account of the problem of renewables' lower Energy Return on Energy Invested – ERoEI), while coal power plants would have to cover only 6%

and nuclear power plants 10% of demand. From this the IEA deduces a powerful increase in investment need just for the expansion of the electricity sector alone from $760 billion in 2019 to $2,200 billion in 2030.[19]

Its prognoses for the transportation and industrial sector in the net-zero carbon scenario also support the conclusion that this scenario is unrealistic: By 2030 already half of all, and in 2050 all, automobiles would have to be running on electrical propulsion. In this, neither the IEA or other 'e-mobility' enthusiasts wonder about the existence of millions of used vehicles with combustion engines. These, along with the rest of the growing mountains of second-hand electrical waste that are not able to be recycled very profitably in the industrialised countries, will surely be sent to the poor countries in still greater quantities than now – with the well-known ruinous effects on the health of people and the 'rest of nature'.[20]

By 2030, likewise, half of all industrial production would have to get its heating from electricity. Especially in the heavy industry branches of chemicals, steel, and cement this is quite simply unimaginable.[21] A doubling or even quadrupling of demand for the products of these branches is anticipated for the coming decades, not least due to the development of infrastructures and technologies for the production of renewable energy. At the same time, the processes of production in these key branches are extraordinarily energy-intensive; for many production procedures extremely high temperatures of 1000° to 1500° C are needed; on the basis of technologies available today, and with 'acceptable' costs, these temperatures can only be reached by having recourse to energy-dense fossil resources. What is more, industrial plants in these branches have been in production for 15 to 40 years now and reinvestments on a completely new, emission-poor or emission-free technological basis would have to be put into effect today (and not just in a couple of years) if they are to achieve the desired effects in 2030.[22]

Certainly, we can hope for a breakthrough in hydrogen technology. But when this can fuel industrial production processes is anyone's guess – and the same can be said of where the hydrogen can be obtained, at what costs, and under what geopolitical constellations. No wonder then that the confusion sown by the new 'colour theory' is causing fantastical flowers to blossom: Because it is predictable that energy from renewable sources will not be available for economic growth on the required scale, the public is already becoming attuned to the new play of colours, as there is not just fantasising about a quixotic 'green hydrogen' but already gestures towards producing hydrogen with 'grey' energy – meaning fossil gas – or 'violet' energy – behind which nuclear energy lurks.

The consequences are already foreseeable today that are tied to the promise of a far-reaching or even the complete conversion of cars and lorries to electric propulsion: the worldwide production of batteries, for whose production there is still no alternative to lithium. According to research provided by "Deutsche Rohstoffagentur" (German Raw Material Agency – DERA), the overall demand for lithium will double or even triple by 2025, due to the industry's very high expectations for the application of rechargeable batteries in e-mobility.[23] However, it is not just e-mobility that cannot do without lithium but also all the technologies and products that are to guarantee us zero-net carbon emissions and a digitalisation of all possible infrastructures, industries, administrations, services.

In addition, other metals such as rare earth, germanium and steel refiners such as niobium, vanadium, and tungsten also have high potential procurement risks. These metals are 'scarce', for one thing, in the *geopolitical sense* because they only exist in economically meaningful concentration and conveniently located in a handful of countries. China is not only the most important mining country in the world, the most important refinery producer and the most important net importer of intermediate products in metal production; it also intends to build up large parts of the higher added value in its own portfolio – and it already controls well over 70% of the market for gallium, indium, and magnesium.

However, most of these metals are also scarce in the narrower *economic sense*, for example because the soaring demand for batteries, fuel cells, wind turbines, robots, 3-D printers, GPS, and drones will lead to exorbitant price hikes. In the case of some metals around whose exploitation conflicts have already flared up today there is already a *physical shortage*, for they are found in constantly rarer concentrations and locations on the earth's crust that would make their mining useful.

Further, we should not forget that 'critical raw materials', which form the basis of almost all so-called future technologies, and thus ultimately also underlie the promise of 'climate neutrality', are 'dual-use', that is, suited to both military and civilian purposes. But this can be interpreted to mean that there will be as much 'critical materials' left over for civilian uses as are not claimed first by the security apparatuses and the military – and the demand for which only points, as in the case of the ecological crisis, in one direction: upward!

A European left prepared for the challenges ahead?

Let us be absolutely clear: In order to bring global energy demand back down to the level of 2006, although the extent of economic activities is twice as great today as it was then, the EU, as well as governments of other industrialised countries, favours instruments that all come under the label Business As Usual: *First*, markets will be newly created through government industrial policy, trade agreements, and – if these are not effective – through instruments of 'hard power' (sanctions and military intervention), reinforced, and extended beyond one's own territory into foreign states. This is particularly important today in terms of access to 'critical metals' but also in terms of access to land and all forms of so-called intellectual property rights. *Second*, the reduction of greenhouse gases is not to be achieved through requirements and bans for the large-scale emitters and through long-term planning that draws in as many citizens as possible but through market-driven trade in pollution rights for climate-damaging gases. *Third*, what is involved is stimulating efficiency increases in industry in order to cut costs and be able to produce and sell just as many or more products and services with less deployment of energy, raw materials, and labour power. *Fourth*, there will continue to be a campaign for voluntary changes in individual consumer behaviour.

Can we, however, even imagine other reactions to the ecological crisis – at least on the part of Europe's political left? In parliamentary democracies many structures, rules, and processes ensure that even where strong political movements push for a 'socio-ecological transformation' these are blocked – through policy's dependency on the lobbying power of 'brown' (and nuclear) industry at the national and European levels; through the legitimation of parties and governments in the face of voters who expect such improvements for themselves, or for society as a whole, that make an impact 'today' and not just tomorrow or the day after; through the thinking of politicians in legislative periods who also foster short-term thinking; and through the fact that voters like promises of 'more' of anything rather than calls, however well justified, for doing with 'less'. Majoritarian democracies are therefore fundamentally rooted in safeguarding the 'status quo' and less oriented to radical and quick transformation. The structural conservatism built into parliamentary democracy does make possible incremental change but through the systems of checks and balances between the executive, legislative, and judicial branches blocks precisely what is now needed – a profound and very quick transformation.

But if this does not take place, not only will nuclear energy, against all reason, be proclaimed the saviour as a CO_2-free energy source in a time of great need. All possible experiments in 'geo-engineering' will be inflicted on the planet. Global demand for gas will explode. In the meanwhile the poorer countries will continue to count on coal; and oil will continue to be burned for the production of more or less useful products. Climate-damaging emissions will thus continue to increase and the 'point of no return' will be reached by mid-century at the latest. The ongoing degradation of forests, wetlands, freshwater reservoirs, and oceans will be accepted as the 'price' that just has to be 'paid' for maintaining the 'prosperity' of the rich third of the world population including the poorer parts of the European population.

Those who by contrast demand quick and radical change quickly manoeuvre themselves into political marginality. The narrative of 'green capitalism' will probably continue to have its sedating effect for some time still to come – although the path of a fossil-nuclear capitalism has in fact never been abandoned. Especially in Europe a majority of citizens will be content that all kinds of 'turns' (in energy, mobility, and food) are being introduced in system-compatible doses, regardless of whether they have the promised effect.

The political left will insist that all answers to the ecological crisis first and foremost take account of social justice. It will thus demand a reinforcement of regional economic circuits, a clear-cut reduction of necessary week or lifetime working hours, a re-municipalisation of care services, and the establishment of solidary social security systems. It will be adamant that debt be cancelled and that therefore the financial claims of owners of money assets cannot be honoured because the accumulation of debt on the one side and of assets on the other have reached a level that far exceeds the capabilities of state borrowers to service the debt. They will be right in pointing out that the concentration of capital in very few hands will ultimately lead to the undermining of entire democracies and the tendency of state power to be narrowed down to its disciplinary, controlling, and violent aspect.

But under these conditions is it honest and prudent to hold out hope of 'a good life for all'? In light of capitalism's ecological crisis – which can, following Marx, be called a crisis in the system of nature's use values—and of its mirror-image crisis in the system of monetary values – can we really still plan on an incremental change in social and economic forms (that is, on a 'transformation')? Particularly since the second phase of globalisation is coming to an end and the antagonisms between the great powers are once again becoming so intense that not only are uprisings, revolts, and armed conflicts within states but also confrontations between them becoming more probable – but now with 'cyber weapons' whose destructive potential can reach that of nuclear bombs.

If the epidemic spread of economic and social inequality claims far more human lives than the spread of a zoonosis like Covid-19, intervention in the system of ownership is unavoidable – and harsh conflicts with the profiteers of the old system that has no future. If the climate catastrophe can be averted at all then 80% of fossil energy has to be left in the ground. But then destructive and useless branches of industry would also have to be radically downsized; alongside the armaments economy this would also surely involve parts of the chemical and building materials industry as well as large part of the advertising and marketing sectors. And there is no question that finance would have to be forced back into its function of serving the real economy.

If total raw-material consumption is going to really be cut back and 'critical metals' not swiftly scraped out of the earth, in conditions that are extremely harmful to the environment, for purposes of e-mobility and digital products and services and thus end up as toxic waste after being consumed – then there is probably no way forward without limits on mobility. Then probably more rather than less physical labour will be needed. And this not only in all sectors of personal care services but above all in the re-use, retooling, repair, and (for waste materials) recycling of the finite materials, which in the last decades have been dug out of the earth's crust, dismembered, burned, and converted. This presents our educational systems with completely different challenges than are suggested by the current digitalisation euphoria – and probably does not jibe with the dreams of many young people.

If social inequality is to be reduced through redistribution, then it is certainly not just the 'super rich' who will be affected but also the 40% of the world population that are seen as part of the middle strata – to which, for example in Germany or Austria, almost the entire population, when classified according to income, belongs. If biodiversity is not to be further destroyed, then this will drive up food prices in the cities – and in Europe too less money will definitely be available for non-essential consumer goods. If the countries of the Global South, which are rich in raw materials, want to free themselves from their dependency on demand from and competition among the industrialised countries, and, beyond this, if the finiteness of raw materials is to be recognised, then a policy of 'managed austerity' has to be envisaged that no longer prioritises the needs of the buyer countries.

The expected objection to such a perspective that suggests a revolution rather than a transformation is that no elections can be won by anyone who articulates it. Certainly, one can sooner win elections by announcing Business As Usual. But processing the ecological crisis today requires of social movements and political parties that want to be part of the solution that they attempt the 'impossible' – simply because the 'possible' leads to ecological catastrophe, to lethal conflicts, and to a chaos in comparison to which the present looks like paradise on earth.

NOTES

1. C40 Global Majors Covid-19 Recovery Task Force, *Technical report: The case for green and just recovery*, 2020, <http://c40.my.salesforce.com>.
2. Birgit Mahnkopf, 'Europas Weg in den digitalen Kapitalismus – planiert durch die Covid-19-Krise', in Hans Baumann, Joël Bühler, Roland Herzog, Ronja Jansen, Samira Marti, Simon Rutz, and Hans Schäppi (eds), *Jahrbuch Denknetz 2020: Europa zwischen Reform und Zerfall: Die große Zäsur: Europa, EU und die Schweiz*, Zurich: Edition 8, 2020, pp. 185-194.
3. Jens Soentgen, *Ökologie der Angst*, Berlin: Matthes & Seitz, 2018.
4. It may even be that one of the lessons learned from Covid-19 is simply: 'drive more!' This is suggested by the findings of a survey of 26,000 people in 25 countries conducted by the YouGov-Cambridge Globalism Project in cooperation with *The Guardian* during the summer of 2020. Although many more than three-quarters of those questioned admit that climate change is man-made, few of them plan to fly less in the future, and in almost all countries surveyed the great majority plan to use their cars even more frequently after the pandemic than previously. See Jonathan Watts, 'People plan to drive more post-Covid, climate poll shows', *The Guardian*, 11 November 2020.
5. Elisabeth Kolbert, *The Sixth Extinction: An Unnatural History*, New York: Henry Holt, 2014.
6. Will Steffen et al., 'Trajectories of the Earth System in the Anthropocene', *PNAS* 115/33 (15 August 2018), 8252-8259.
7. This is not the case for Latin America and certainly not for the USA. In many Latin American countries, where the armed forces have taken over tasks that state organs were unable or unwilling to fulfil, the power of the military has tended to expand during the course of the pandemic, which will surely remain in place long after the pandemic ends. In some countries (like Mexico and Colombia), on the other hand, the organised criminal cartels have provided financial and material support to poor people and so further consolidated their power in the country.
8. Günther Anders, 'Die Wurzeln der Apokalypse-Blindheit', in Günther Anders, *Endzeit und Zeitenende. Gedanken über die atomare Situation*, Munich: Beck, 1962, pp. 106-125.
9. Apart from its one body endowed with powers, the Security Council, whose composition is determined by an anachronistic mechanism.
10. Gareth Dale, Manu V. Mathai, José A. Puppim de Oliveira, *Green Growth. Ideology, Political Economy and the Alternatives*, London: Bloomsbury, 2016.
11. Birgit Mahnkopf, 'Lessons from the EU: why capitalism cannot be rescued from its own contradictions', in Dale, Mathai, and Puppim de Oliveira, *Green Growth*, pp. 131-149
12. Elmar Altvater and Birgit Mahnkopf, 'The Capitalocene: Permanent capitalist counter-revolution', in Leo Panitch and Greg Albo (eds), *Socialist Register* 2019, London: Merlin, pp. 79-99.
13. Vera Wegkmann, 'The "circular economy" - neither safe nor sustainable', *Social Europe*, 13 Oct 2020.
14. European Environment Agency, *State of nature in the EU. Results from reporting under the nature directives 2013-2018*, EEA Report No. 17/2020.
15. European Environment Agency, *State of Nature in the EU*.
16. Swiss Re Group, 'A fifth of countries worldwide at risk from ecosystem collapse as biodiversity declines, reveals pioneering Swiss Re index', Zurich 23 September 2020,

<https://www.swissre.com/media/news-releases/nr-20200923-biodiversity-and-ecosystems-services.html>.
17 Elmar Altvater, 'The Capitalocene, or: Geoengineering against Capitalism's Boundaries', in Jason M. Moore, *Anthropocene or Capitalocene? Nature, History, and the Crisis of Capitalism*, Oakland, CA: PM Press, 2016, pp. 138-152.
18 Birgit Mahnkopf, 'Der Kapitalismus an ökologischen, ökonomischen und sozialen Kipppunkten', *Kurswechsel* 1/2020, 11-19.
19 International Energy Agency, *World Energy Outlook* 2020, Paris: IEA.
20 According to the UNEP, between 2015 and 2018 ca. 80% of the 14 million light commercial vehicles from the US, Europe, and Japan were sent to Low-and Middle Income Countries, with 40% going to Africa alone. The EU is the biggest exporter and annually ships 7.5 million vehicles to northern and western Africa, <https://www.unep.org/resources/report/global-trade-used-vehicles-report>.
21 International Energy Agency, *The challenges of reaching net zero emissions in heavy industry*, Paris: IEA, 19 September 2020, <https://www.iea.org/articles/the-challenge-of-reaching-zero-emissions-in-heavy-industry>.
22 International Energy Agency, *The challenges of reaching net zero emissions in heavy industry*.
23 <https://www.deutsche-rohstoffagentur.de/DERA/DE/Downloads/Studie_lithium_2017.pdf;jsessionid=2109BF3AB47E7F244E3FE6D94A6CB9A0.2_cid284?__blob=publicationFile&v=3>.

Climate Change and Capitalist Development

Teppo Eskelinen

In contemporary politics, climate-change mitigation might appear to be everywhere. Almost every government reports on its advances in sustainable development, and even global firms have ever more environmental responsibility programmes and sustainability initiatives. Given these developments, and with a large number of responsible and conscious consumers, the acutely deteriorating state of the climate is striking. The question to be asked is: Is there something inherent in the existing economic system that pushes it towards climate disaster, or can the crisis be governed away with more environmental policies, without addressing the underlying system?

In what follows, I will briefly review climate change in the context of and in relation to capitalism. This requires taking into account the key aspects of the economic system which press towards environmental destruction. A further question that needs to be asked is: Are capitalism and climate change inextricably interwoven, or could there be a capitalist system without such an environmental impact? I will begin by discussing the currently dominant narrative on climate change and then turn to the particularities of capitalism's relation to nature. Finally, I will discuss the prospects of capitalism without climate change.

The dominant climate-change narrative

While there are several sides to the ongoing global environmental crisis and many 'planetary boundaries' have already been exceeded,[1] the currently most acute environmental problem is climate change. As humanity is in a crisis which it may not be able to overcome, it would be either misleading or completely cynical to say that climate change can be ignored. However, 'the mitigation of climate change' is not a question of a uniform set of policies based on a technical analysis of facts; rather, the chosen approaches in climate-change mitigation reflect political and explanatory hegemonies.

We can distinguish two typical explanations for environmental problems in general and climate change in particular in mainstream political discourse:

First, seeing the climate issue as a question of inadequate technology and thus of finding less polluting technology to replace it. From this point of view humanity has chosen fossil fuels as a source of energy instead of a more sustainable alternative such as solar or wind, and so humanity simply needs to switch to a new energy source to avert climate chaos. This will be assisted by technological developments in the renewable energy sector. Indeed much of climate policy focuses on technology, with the hope of fixing the problems with suitable innovations.

Second, arguing that environmental problems are simply caused by people's selfish motivations and urge to overconsume. According to this line of thought, climate change is brought about by the tendency of people to consume what they can, and the only ways to avoid ecological destruction are through a collective change of values or very strict coercion suppressing this spontaneous drive.

Both ideas are influential today – and both have serious problems. Believing in technology alone ignores the economic system. Technological change does not occur independently of economic power, and productive relations always have an impact on both the form of technological innovation and the utilisation of technology. Envisioning eternally greedy consumers leads easily to ecofascist-style calls to restrict democracy and blaming the consumers regardless of their social position.

It is noteworthy that such ideas lean heavily on liberal political philosophy and bourgeois economics. The underlying idea is that the economy can be modelled as 'the market' which people enter with pre-existing wants and an intention to meet these wants maximally. Technological innovation and consumer desire are seen as exogenous to the functioning of the market. The market is thus understood as a neutral medium for the communication of preferences and their translation into production decisions. Since the political nature of the economic system is ignored, changes in preferences or technological developments are viewed as natural pathways to prevent environmental damage, in addition to restricting the operation of the 'spontaneous' market.

The same perspective is visible in 'market-based solutions' to climate change, in which existing preferences and the urge to maximise consumption are taken as given but pricing is used to steer consumption in less polluting directions. The most prominent of such approaches has been the cap-and-trade system, in which climate is commodified into pollution rights so that polluting has a price, and the price mechanism is believed to manage pollution effectively. In other economistic approaches, the whole climate crisis is interpreted as a cost-benefit problem, that is, with the destruction wrought by climate change expressed in monetary values the argument can be made that it is economically rational to invest in climate-change mitigation.[2]

Capital and nature

It would be misguided to treat climate change as a contained problem – obviously because climate change is connected to other ecological problems such as biodiversity loss. But in addition to its diverse environmental consequences, climate change is also not an isolated phenomenon because of its many social drivers. These social drivers are not about the human greed for consumption but the system of production. Whether or not 'greed' is part of human nature, capitalism as a system largely determines humanity-nature relations. Therefore, the imperatives of this system should be properly taken into account when considering the essence of and remedies to climate change.

Crucially, capitalism organises not only human relations but also the humanity-nature relation: the term 'capitalocene' is sometimes used to refer to the existing system of organising nature.[3] While economic decisions concern the value dimension of capitalism, being ultimately based on the economic rationality of profit maximisation, these decisions have significant impacts on the material dimension (system of material and energy flows in production and consumption) and thus on nature.[4] The systemic economic and productive logic on which capitalism is based then translates as a systemic logic in human-nature relations.

Capitalism has also been analysed as a forcible reorganisation of the metabolic exchanges between humans and nonhuman nature, so that some people are disadvantaged and natural processes are disturbed.[5] This reorganisation is an aspect of the reorganisation of the relations of production. For example, Marx saw that capitalism caused a disturbance of humanity-nature relations chiefly through the capitalist organisation of agriculture. More obviously, capitalist industry is characterised by a specific logic in the way resources and pollution sinks are used.

In addition to being a form of production, capitalism also determines consumption. In its origins, capitalism required wage labour and created significant dependency on it. Historically, this was possible due to the enclosure of the commons and the creation and enforcement of debt relations. By debt-enforcement and dispossession strategies, workers are made dependent on the capitalist value form.[6] Today, the increase in money dependency continues through generating new social necessities, goods without which it is almost impossible to function in contemporary society. For instance, the environmental impact of much of communication electronics is not due to people's massive desire for electronics but to the fact that many aspects of communication and even living in contemporary society are hardly possible without them.[7] Because the system functions through the creation of social necessities and money dependency, blaming individual consumers for being greedy is hardly a feasible strategy.

Some characteristics of the system of production

Let me outline two necessary characteristics of capitalism and two further features of fossil capitalism. These do not take account of all of capitalism's essential features but indicate features that are significant from the perspective of climate change.

First, the priority of the profit motive as the dynamic force driving the system. The profit motive not only explains exploitation but also technological innovation. Thus it largely determines technological choices. In designing and making use of new technologies, the question is not whether a technology is 'smart', advanced, or rational but whether profit can be generated through the technology and associated mode of production. This has been documented by many Marxist historians. For example Andreas Malm has shown how steam replaced water as a source of power in early industry not because of its technological superiority or cheaper price but because it allowed locating factories where production would be most profitable – above all where there was a dense supply of labour-power .[8] William Lazonick has shown how capital-labour relations determined the choice of technology in the cotton spinning industry in the late nineteenth century.[9]

Second, growth as reproduction. While every productive system includes some system of reproduction of the society (its material and cultural basis, key social relations, etc.), capitalism is unique in this sense because its reproduction is based on expansion. Capitalism is not only dependent on the growth of output, but also on the expansion of commodification to new geographic areas or spheres of life. This was already theorised by Rosa Luxemburg.[10] Luxemburg saw the reproduction of capitalism as dependent on the capture and closure of 'natural economies' and forcing them to adopt the capitalist value form.

The priority of expansion also shows the very limited options that exist within a capitalist system: contrary to what the market theory says, an economy will not easily find an equilibrium at a lower level of output. Rather, despite growth contributing directly to climate change, in its absence capitalism enters into crisis.

As for the specificities of contemporary fossil capitalism, it first of all largely operates in an abstract market space. A capitalist market is indeed easier to sustain if it is detached from its material and natural basis. Fossil energy has been preferred because it is easy to transport and not dependent on immediate natural processes (for example whether there is enough wind to drive wind power), which has given rise to 'logistical networks which today cover the globe'.[11] Nor is the location of manufacturing dependent on the local availability of energy resources.

In addition, politics in the prevailing system is strongly influenced by corporate power. Firms have great impact on policy design and priorities – at least they do in the absence of a strong counterforce. This corporate capture, while a persisting feature of capitalism, has become particularly noteworthy in environmental policy in recent decades. At least since the Business Council for Sustainable Development document 'Changing course', released at the 1992 Earth Summit, the corporate environmental agenda has been quite uniform: no obstacles to growth, efficiency through pricing mechanisms, and voluntary regulation.[12] Consequently, environmental politics should not be understood as a matter of making rational choices but of power and clashes of interests.

Immaterial capitalism and energy transition

In the light of the above, capitalism as a system of production needs to be seen as the societal basis for the existing humanity-nature relations, climate change included. The big question for the future of the climate then is: Is a sustainable capitalism conceivable? If a given way to organise nature is so intimately linked to the development of capitalism, could capitalism organise nature differently? Perhaps turning polluting rights into commodities can be seen as a strategy in this direction. A further question is: What does renewable technology imply in the capitalist framework of profit maximisation, expansion, and abstract market space?

Perhaps the most common strategy proposed for impeding climate change within the capitalist system of production is 'decoupling'. This means a shift from material to immaterial production while maintaining the growth paradigm. It would mean that the generated economic value would still increase while emissions would increase less ('relative decoupling'), or decrease ('absolute decoupling'). The feasibility of this strategy is doubtful, not least because of the historically very strong linkage between climate change and capitalism – fossil fuel emissions have increased hand in hand with capitalist expansion and increased output. Nevertheless, some evidence points to the possibility of a decoupling of CO_2 output and growth in a geographically limited area (for example, at the national level), while evidence hardly exists for the possibility of decoupling on a larger scale, or for sufficiently rapid decoupling.'[13]

One difficulty with 'decoupling' is that immaterial goods tend to have connections to material goods. Currently, most of the value generated in the immaterial economy comes from finance, which if it is not based on a growing real economy becomes largely unstable. But it is not completely impossible for value generation to shift its focus to immaterial goods. Such a turn to the immaterial practically means that new accumulation regimes come into existence – indeed much of culture, communications, and care is commodified and reorganised so as to generate profit. It is another matter whether this is desirable for the mere purpose of rescuing growth.

An important aspect of the decoupling strategy is energy transition to renewable sources. While there are several ways to produce energy from renewable sources, solar stands out as technologically the most promising; it is also to some extent even symbolic in the sense of being available virtually without limits. Furthermore, solar power has developed in quantum leaps technically and in terms of its energy ratio.

Another alternative that has been prominent in the economic policy alternatives discourse is the so called Green Keynesian approach. As such, the fundamentals of Keynesianism as economic policy are quite straightforward: markets never reach full employment equilibrium because of the persistent uncertainty that prevails within a capitalist system. Therefore, governments need to make significant public investments to keep aggregate investment levels sufficiently high and the employment rate at effective full employment.

While the concept of Green Keynesianism is sometimes used merely to mean global taxes and regulation,[14] a truly Keynesian approach emphasises government financing. The argument amidst the ecological crisis then is that since public investment is needed in any case it could be used to facilitate ecological transformation. Especially in an economic downturn coinciding with an ecological crisis, it would be sensible to employ as much workforce as possible in green reconstruction jobs: transforming the energy production and supply system, housing infrastructure, and traffic and logistics infrastructure into green systems. The recurring financial crises and more recently the economic downturn caused by the Covid-19 pandemic, have offered humanity 'a unique opportunity to address financial and ecological sustainability together'.[15]

Climate change mitigation: within or against the system of power?

A Green Keynesian strategy and an energy transition will surely be needed. But like technology as such these strategies too do not tell us much about the underlying questions of power and capitalism's logic of expansion. As noted above, energy transition or 'decoupling' are not merely technical questions. If they were, then early capitalists would have preferred water power to steam power. In capitalist logic, the questions arise: How does a given system of energy supply relate to the control of the workforce? How does it enable profits? How does it facilitate expansion and protecting the abstract space of the market? And, ultimately, who controls energy? From the perspective of profit-making, solar energy might be too accessible – there is no way of making sunlight scarce as small solar panels can be used technically by anyone: this reduces the possibilities for invested capital to generate profit. Just as it is not coincidental that fossil power and capitalism as a system of production emerged together and have remained intimately connected, so solar capitalism will not emerge automatically or easily, for its emergence would require changes in the existing social relations.

The real question of Green Keynesianism then is: Can it be used for transformation? In other words, could government investment be used to reduce the capitalist sphere to the benefit of a non-capitalist sector, or champion another value conception altogether.[16] In capitalism it is relatively easy to add new investment or new regimes of accumulation but difficult to replace old ones, at least without political confrontation. Indeed the history of energy production is a history of new complementing forms of production, rather than replacement. Perhaps also today, wind power only complements coal, and more energy is produced and consumed. Perhaps trains only complement aeroplanes, and the aggregate of travelled distances increases. Indeed it is very difficult to undo the growth logic with increased investment. Practically, transformation to sustainability requires that much of the physical capital in the fossil infrastructure loses its value. As massive amounts of capital have been invested in the oil drilling and refinement infrastructure, it seems naïve to believe that the holders of this capital would agree to its destruction merely due to rationality or the attractiveness of other investments.

It is quite obvious that energy means power; this is all too easy to observe by looking at the existing fossil energy companies. By implication, energy transition means contesting power and remaking power relations. Elmar Altvater, for instance, has referred to solidarity economy, co-operatives, etc. as the social basis of a society based on renewable energies.[17] Optimistically, one could imagine the creation of a more sustainable and dispersed system of production, which would mean new social relations, productive relations included. In a Green Keynesian spirit, strategically directed government investment could be instrumental in the shift towards this system of production. Furthermore, as already noted by Michał Kalecki,[18] the boosting of aggregate demand by government investment is always also a form of class politics, and the bargaining power of the workers is increased as full employment is approached. Indeed, while there may be various reasons to count on, or be dubious about decoupling and Green Keynesian strategies, their success seems inseparable from a transformation of existing power relations.

Conclusions

As noted above, capitalism is not only a productive system but also a way of organising nature, so understanding environmental challenges such as climate change requires an analysis of the capitalist system of production. The intimate connection between capitalism and climate change is due to the usefulness of fossil fuels in profit generation, organisation of the labour force, and the creation of an abstract market space. Thus, the question of whether there can be capitalism without climate change is a complex one. We can imagine a 'solar capitalism', or a turn to immateriality but not a capitalism without profit maximisation. For capitalism to exist, it needs to be based on some sort of accumulation regime. Capitalism as we know it has long been defined by carbon – Lewis Mumford coined the term 'carboniferous capitalism' already in the 1930s,[19] and climate change has been linked to Fordist and post-Fordist accumulation regimes.[20] Yet this does not mean that a different kind of accumulation system would be completely inconceivable.

It may well be that climate change proves to be a symptom of a general crisis of capital[21] and that system change will occur because of the exhaustion of possibilities for increasing capital accumulation, not least because of the using up of available cheap resources and sinks.[22] But, while anticipating this, strategies are needed for mitigating climate change. It is true that technologies and policies cannot be detached from the prevailing system of power; at the same time, however, capitalism is not a monolithic system occupying all of social space; on the contrary, all social systems are hybrid forms, exhibiting capitalist and non-capitalist social relations. While climate-change mitigation requires anti-capitalist impulses – limits, commons, anti-capitalist governments and politics – they can be promoted within and despite capitalism.

Sustainable anti-capitalist spaces – common ownership of natural resources, democratic management of production, and so forth – can be expanded. Some theorists indeed consider the key task to be making visible the largely existing non-capitalist space of being, doing, and caring, currently made invisible by the dominant value form.[23] A climate-change mitigation strategy can then also be anti-capitalist within capitalism. Even solutions in which the market plays a crucial role seem to be effective to the extent that they deviate from market logic. For example in the cap-and-trade strategy, it is exactly the 'cap', in other words the limits, which produces the desired effect.

Others see that capitalism always comes in 'varieties', with some forms having a stronger government-sector presence and more co-ordination of labour through unions. These varieties can be analysed by looking at these balancing features.[24] Moreover, in climate-change mitigation a stronger government sector and related political power will be needed in setting limits. As noted, there is a strong expansionary dynamic within capitalism. If some commons, such as climate, are to be protected, there needs to be a very strong political push to create and maintain these necessary limits. Naturally, government activity is also required by the Green Keynesian strategy. Most importantly, while climate-change mitigation will require going against capitalist logic in many areas, waiting for the demise of capitalism would mean giving up on the most urgent ecological challenge of our time.

NOTES

1   Johan Rockström, Will Steffen, Kevin Noone, Åsa Persson et.al., 'Planetary boundaries: exploring the safe operating space for humanity', *Ecology and Society* 14,2 (2009), 32.
2   Nicholas Stern, *The Stern Review on the Economics of Climate Change*, Cambridge: Cambridge University Press, 2006.
3   Jason W. Moore (ed.), *Anthropocene or Capitalocene? Nature, History, and the Crisis of Capitalism*, Oakland: PM Press, 2016.
4   Elmar Altvater, 'The social and natural environment of fossil capitalism', The Socialist Register 2007: Coming to terms with nature, 37-59.
5   John Bellamy Foster, *Marx's Ecology: Materialism and Nature*, New York: Monthly Review Press, 2000.
6   Tero Toivanen amd Markus Kröger, 'The role of debt, death and dispossession in world-ecological transformations: swidden commons and tar capitalism in nineteenth-century Finland', *The Journal of Peasant Studies* 46,7 (2019), 1368-1388.
7   Teppo Eskelinen, 'Living with the extreme demand', *Etikk I Praksis - Nordic Journal of Applied Ethics*, 7,1 (2013), 73-87.
8   Andreas Malm, *Fossil Capital: The Rise of Steam-Power in the British Cotton Industry, c. 1825-1848, and the Roots of Global Warming*, Lund: Lund University, 2014.
9   William H. Lazonick, 'Production Relations, Labor Productivity, and Choice of Technique: British and U.S. Cotton Spinning, *The Journal of Economic History* 41,3 (1981), 491-516.

10 Rosa Luxemburg, *The Accumulation of Capital*, Oxon: Routledge, 2003 (1913).
11 Altvater, 'The Social and Natural Environment of Fossil Capitalism'.
12 Joshua Karliner, 'The Globalization of Corporate Culture and its Role in the Environmental Crisis', in Richard Hofrichter (ed.), Reclaiming the Environmental Debate: The Politics of Health in a Toxic Culture, Cambridge: MIT press, 2000.
13 Tere Vadén, Ville Lähde, Antti Majava, Paavo Järvensivu, Tero Toivanen, Emma Hakala, and Jussi Eronen, 'Decoupling for ecological sustainability: A categorisation and review of research literature', *Environmental Science and Policy* 112 (2020), 236–244.
14 Servaas Storm, 'Capitalism and Climate Change: Can the Invisible Hand Adjust the Natural Thermostat?', *Development and Change* 40 (2009), 1022-26.
15 Tim Jackson, *Prosperity without growth? The transition to sustainable economy*, Sustainable Development Commission, 30 March 2009, p. 6.
16 Teppo Eskelinen, 'The possibilities and limits of green Keynesianism', in Kaysa Borgnäs, Teppo Eskelinen, Johanna Perkiö, and Rikard Warlenius (eds), *The Politics of Ecosocialism. Transforming Welfare*, London: Routledge, 2015, pp. 101-115.
17 Altvater, 'The Social and Natural Environment of Fossil Capitalism'.
18 Michał Kalecki, 'Political Aspects of Full Employment', *Political Quarterly* 14,4 (1943), 322-330.
19 Lewis Mumford, *Technics and Civilization*, New York: Harcourt, 1934.
20 Max Koch, *Capitalism and Climate Change: Theoretical Discussion, Historical Development and Policy Responses*, London: Palgrave, 2012.
21 Larry Lohmann, *Should We Put a Price on Carbon? That Depends - Who Are the 'We'?*, London: The Corner house, 2018.
22 Immanuel Wallerstein, Randall Collins, Michael Mann, Georgi Derluguian, and Craig Calhoun, *Does Capitalism Have A Future?*, Oxford: Oxford University Press, 2013.
23 J. K. Gibson-Graham, *A Postcapitalist Politics*, Minneapolis: University of Minnesota Press, 2006.
24 Peter A Hall and David Soskice (eds), *Varieties of Capitalism: The Institutional Foundations of Comparative Advantage*, Oxford: Oxford University Press, 2001.

The UN Climate Summits: Not a Solution to the Climate Crisis – But it is Important to Be There

Nadja Charaby and Katja Voigt

There is a moment when you enter the registration pavilion of the next United Nations (UN) climate conference with a thrill of anticipation and enthusiasm. You are prepared, you already contacted your allies from all over the world to discuss the strategy. You are ready! Then two weeks later on the last day of negotiations, you are at the same spot and about to pull off your registration badge, out of desperate resignation. You walk through the empty hallways, look into the tired faces of hopeless negotiators and civil society activists. And you are tired and disappointed. What happened in these two weeks? Or should we ask what didn't happen?

Before we go into a more detailed analysis of the Conference of the Parties (COPs) to the United Nations Framework Convention on Climate Change (UNFCCC),we can summarise in one sentence what is happening with the climate crisis: it is not on pandemic break!

We will probably always remember 2019 as the year with millions of young people in the streets demanding governments take action on climate. The news was full of updates on the climate catastrophe and the climate strikers' growing movement. In 2020, the ongoing horrors of natural disasters, fuelled by human-made climate change, made it clear that the climate crisis is very much here and that governments' inaction along with 25 years of climate negotiations have so far not contributed to stopping it. Just to remind us, the disasters we faced this year included the Australian bushfires, devastating swarms of locusts in Eastern Africa, in the Middle East, and South Asia, the burning Siberian and Californian forests, the dramatically accelerated melting of the Arctic ice shield – many more could be added. It has become clear by now that political decision-making has not done enough to tackle the climate crisis. What we are experiencing is a climate emergency – and nobody is sending an ambulance.

The lockdowns caused by the pandemic in the first half of 2020, which included a partial shutdown in several economic sectors, created a window of opportunity for a more sustainable path after the pandemic. A growing demand appeared on the part of countries (and also the European Union), cities (for example, the C40 Global Mayors[1]), and NGOs (such as WWF[2]) for a just and green recovery – with less greenhouse gas (GHG) emissions, more investments in renewable energy sources, a commitment to a fossil fuel phase-out in the coming 20-30 years (net zero), and an expansion of sustainable transportation.[3] What is often missing in these discussions however, is a global perspective. The ideas and discussion mainly focus on inward-looking political solutions based on the national state or groups of countries, like the European Union.

When we look at the global context, we come across the slogan 'Build Back Better', a concept introduced during the third UN Conference on Disaster Risk Reduction in 2015. Secretary General António Guterres filled the three words 'Build Back Better' with the aim of 'a comprehensive welfare system that [is] accessible to all. […] creating a fair taxation system, promoting decent jobs, strengthening environmental sustainability, and reinforcing social protection mechanisms.'[4] But we have to ask whether the countries that are hit by the climate crises and the pandemic more severely than others are really able to build back better and accomplish a just and green recovery? They might be if they were to receive financial support from the large emitting countries to cope with the climate crises.

On a smaller scale we can also see discussions of this kind in public debates, for example in Germany where different sorts of ideas are addressed with an emphasis on how to integrate them into our lifestyles – consuming less, producing regionally, working less, and travelling locally, and so forth. These approaches, however, only work in a wealthy environment, in a state that is able to support its citizens, for example with Corona subsidies. It becomes increasingly clear that those who can afford good healthcare and a healthy lifestyle, who do have a place to stay during the lockdown and have regular income even during a pandemic, experienced the recent months differently from those with less wealth and resources who lost their income and their homes and are facing an insecure future. However, it rarely happens that the systemic imbalance is questioned, and this leads to a business-as-usual attitude that we have also experienced during the COPs.

In what follows we will focus on the UN and its international climate negotiations within the UNFCCC and explain why these negotiations and spaces are important, even though the results sometimes seem nowhere near what is needed. We start with a summary of what has happened in the 25 years of negotiations and why we are seeing downsized ambitions since COP 21 in Paris 2015. We will also look at the state of global climate diplomacy in 2020 as well as the impact of the COP26 postponement to 2021. And we will consider the meaningful alternatives, even under the recent special circumstances, opened up by the promising climate justice mobilisations.

Let us look back in order to understand how it is possible to negotiate for 25 years and come up with a multilateral climate agreement like Paris yet still be headed toward a 3° C global average temperature increase with a slightly greener business-as-usual.[5] It all started with the UN Earth Summit in Rio 1992 when state leaders of 193 countries and over 2,400 registered civil society observers came together to discuss global environmental questions – the first conference of its kind. The outcome was promising: a sustainable development concept was introduced, also known as Agenda 21, the UN Forest Declaration and UN Convention to Combat Desertification were adopted, and the milestone in international climate conferences reached with the endorsement of the UNFCCC.[6] The multilateral system seemed to be on a promising path toward dealing with environmental problems like loss of biodiversity and a changing climate.

From Berlin to Kyoto

The first COP under the UNFCCC took place in 1995 in Berlin and 24 more COPs followed. In 1997 at COP3, the parties agreed, after long discussion, on the first binding document – the Kyoto Protocol. The 192 parties committed to reducing GHG concentrations in the atmosphere to 'a level that would prevent dangerous anthropogenic interference with the climate system'.[7] This applies to six different GHGs, among others carbon dioxide (CO_2) and methane (CH_4). The Protocol distinguishes between emerging, developing, and industrialised countries. Because of their historical responsibility for the increase in GHG emissions, industrialised countries had to commit themselves to reducing their emissions by at least five percent compared to 1990.

This principle of common but differentiated responsibilities – meaning those emitting most must decrease their GHG emissions more than others and making clear the nexus of industrialisation and climate change – has since its introduction been a core issue in the climate negotiations and respective disagreements between industrialised countries and, principally, emerging economies. In the first stage of commitments from 2008 to 2012, 37 states and the European Union (EU) (now called Annex I countries, since these 37 designated industrialised countries and countries in transition were listed in the first annex to the Protocol) agreed to reduce their emissions by a certain percentage in relation to a base level, which in most cases refers to the 1990 emission level. The EU, for example, committed to reducing its emissions by 8 percent between 2008 and 2020 compared to 1990. In order to reach this target, the member countries agreed to set their own emission targets: Germany committed to reducing its own GHG emissions by 21 percent compared to 1990. Emerging economies such as China or India, whose economic growth has increased energy consumption and GHG emissions, as well as developing countries, did not have to take any binding measures to protect the climate. By signing the Protocol, they nevertheless had to recognise the need to take action against climate change.

Behind what sounds fair and ambitious there is also a deceitful component. On the one hand, the ambitions differ a great deal between the Annex 1 states. On the other hand, the Kyoto Protocol introduced some so-called flexibility mechanisms – which turned out to be one of the biggest mistakes. We know these mechanisms as the Clean Development Mechanism (CDM) and the International Emissions Trading or Joint Implementation. In brief, these mechanisms make sure that global emissions will not effectively decrease. They allow large polluting countries to implement emission reduction projects in other countries (often in the Global South), like reforestation projects, or to buy for a more or less symbolic price Certified Emission Reduction units from countries with low emissions. With these mechanisms in place, polluting countries can buy their way out without a guilty conscience. The emissions-trade market crashed in 2012 and the value of credits collapsed within days. Other programmes also developed under the CDM, such as REDD (reducing emissions from deforestation and forest degradation), exhibited their dark sides. They often lead to displacement of local communities and take away their livelihoods by preventing them from using the forest. They recreate power structures in the local regions at the expense of the marginalised.[8]

Moreover, we must not forget that the Kyoto Protocol only came into effect in 2005 after enough countries ratified the international treaty, which remained in force only until 2020. The biggest polluter at the time, the United States, signed the Protocol in 1998 but actually never ratified it, leaving the Protocol just three years later. All in all, the Kyoto Protocol – through the time it took to come into effect and the US' refusal to ratify it – not only clearly demonstrated how the world has gambled with climate, but through the insertion of false solutions into the global climate architecture's DNA also showed that climate diplomacy, with its dismissal of the issue of fossil capitalism, was, and until now is, very far from getting to the root cause of the climate crisis.

Copenhagen and Paris

In 2009, twelve years after Kyoto, the negotiation arena moved to Copenhagen (COP15). Starting as 'Hope-nhagen' accompanied by confident civil society mobilisation, it soon turned into 'No-penhagen'.⁹ The aim was to negotiate regulation for the post-Kyoto era, but parties left what is known as the worst COP of all time with an unbinding Copenhagen Accord. COP15's devastating outcome for people and the planet only brought to 2° C the vague idea of a limitation of average global warming along with a financial pledge of 100,000 billion US $ annually from 2020 on. Reactions from civil society representatives, climate justice movements, the scientific community, and ambitious politicians ranged from disappointment to frustration. Excessive police intervention and arrests of about 1,000 protesters during the Copenhagen climate march crowned COP15's failure and put a definite end to any sort of trust the climate justice movements had in the UNFCCC process.

But was this poor performance perhaps necessary to spark a commitment to more ambitious policies in reaction to it? At least this is how the relief expressed by the French president at the outcome of the Paris COP21 in 2015 could be interpreted. With the Paris Agreement in place and the promise to 'limit global warming to well below 2, preferably 1.5 degrees Celsius, compared to pre-industrial levels',¹⁰ a new agreement was created to succeed the Kyoto Protocol. What was celebrated at COP21 as a successful and historic negotiation, a global achievement, and a surprise even for critical civil society organisations, turns out to have kicked off a long and rocky road when it comes to implementation. It shows that mere diplomatic sensitivity and agreements full of idealistic rhetoric cannot save the climate, since there are no binding consequences. Moreover, a closer look at the new Paris rulebook – negotiated during the COPs after Paris - reveals all the gaps and false promises that come along with what was negotiated in Paris. The results of COP21 remain ambiguous up to the present day. On the one hand, we probably all remember the emotional moment with weeping negotiators as world leaders showed their willingness to approve a multilateral agreement needed so urgently for dealing with the climate emergency – an emergency or crisis that was by then, in 2015, still referred to with the softer phrase 'climate change'. On the other hand, the agreement's contents are far from what real solutions to climate change would be. The climate justice movement had unambiguously formulated its demands for coping with the climate chaos. Paris should have set a clear limit to global warming of 1.5 degrees. Even a 1.5-degree warming will bring catastrophic consequences for global justice, since the 2-degree target is really only a desperate attempt to deal with climate chaos. For the 1.5-degree goal, clear commitments to a fundamental transformation of the world economic system would have been necessary. A decarbonisation of the global economy, an end to the paradigm of unlimited growth and excessive free-trade agreements would have been necessary steps into this direction. Similarly, there were justified calls for an end to the Kyoto Protocol's market-based climate protection instruments, which were demonstrably inefficient and resembled an ecological trade in indulgences. Other demands warned of the dangers of so-called climate-smart agriculture and called for small-scale farming, food sovereignty, and agro-ecology as real solutions. Thus, the Rosa Luxemburg Stiftung declared after COP21:

> The agreement is dishonest because it claims to be able to stop climate change with flaccid paragraphs, while at the same time governments continue to push hard-core free trade agreements that drive the West's destructive production and consumption model ever more crassly and undermine national environmental and climate legislation. And the agreement is contradictory because it pretends to protect the climate, while the text does all it can to protect the interests of business. The only alternative we now have is for the social movements to force changes through pressure from below.[11]

The parties approved a dedicated Article 8, of the Paris Agreement, on climate-induced loss and damage. Previously this problem was negotiated within the discussions on adaptation, but Article 8 creates an independent space for negotiations specifically on loss and damage. This will hopefully bring substantial financing at some point. It has been a crucial demand put forward by countries most affected by climate change, such as the least-developed countries group (LDCs) and the small island states (AOSIS). The demand for loss and damage financing is closely linked to the debate on climate reparations and the ecological debt to be paid by industrialised countries. Article 8 of the Paris Agreement, however, does not include a liability clause for financing or climate debt settlement. The negotiators representing polluting countries managed to guarantee their countries' interests in preventing possibilities of being sued for the climate damage they have caused.

Five years after Paris

What happened to that spirit of ambitious and optimistic negotiations for a global solution to climate impacts? Or was it just a fairy tale? When we reflect on the last five years of climate negotiations we hearken back to the mood of setback in Copenhagen, an excluded civil society and a scientific community that produced an over 500-page long special report about the impact of 1.5°C global warming that nobody reads.[12] What we can observe after Paris is fear, the fear of compromise, the fear of telling the voters that their life has to change, . The Paris Agreement has had a hard time since its birth in 2015. US President Donald Trump stepped out of the Agreement in 2017. In 2018, the Polish COP24 presidency tried to sell coal as a green energy source. Moreover, negotiators were not able to agree on the Paris Rulebook, which was scheduled to be finalised in Katowice. In 2019, the Philippine government did not send a delegation to the negotiations, Brazil's President Jair Bolsonaro did not want to host COP25, and civil society was locked out in Madrid, where COP25 finally took place. Meanwhile, considering the rate of global warming it is clear that solving the climate crisis is a task that has to already begin now. Forests are burning with alarming frequency and in ever more places, the hurricane or typhoon seasons are longer and more intense, we are seeing a huge loss of biodiversity, and every year a new record is set in temperate latitudes as the hottest summer month to date.

Despite all criticism of the COPs, there has been no other global institution that brings together so many critical stakeholders. It is thus still important that ambitious politicians, civil society, and movement representatives make use of this contested space, raise their voices, and exert pressure on those who participate in them. We simply cannot allow the COPs to get too cosy. And we should not let seats to be occupied by representatives of the fossil-fuel industry.[13]

COPs are a long way from climate justice

Overall, there is perhaps the good news that the UN system is generally paying increasingly more attention to the climate crisis. The year 2019 was one of climate action. During the intermediate negotiations of the UNFCCC, which take place every early summer in the headquarters of the UNFCCC in Bonn, Germany, it became obvious how gridlocked the negotiations had become. Climate diplomacy in 2019 was not to lead to a successful outcome of the COP25 summit. Thus, UN Secretary General António Guterres organised a Climate Action Summit in late September 2019 in New York. His aim was to mobilise financial resources and urge states to expand their ambitions. In his concluding remarks Guterres listed all the different commitments: small islands states that will become carbon neutral by 2030; UN pension funds abandoning their investments in coal industries; 77 countries, including 'industrialised countries' committed to net-zero carbon emissions by 2050; and businesses that pledged to move to green energy. 'We can win this race!' he said.[14] However, the Secretary General's summit did not dare to deliver what the youth strikers, who were present, had asked him to do:

> 'Guterres' concluding speech presenting the 'ambitions' of the government representatives one after the other was quite uninspired and more of a technical summary. [...] Perhaps the UN Secretary General had not really listened to Greta Thunberg after all. Instead of naming the economic model based on permanent growth as the main cause of the climate crisis, he praised the belief in the 'green economy' as the solution.[15]

Then we met in Madrid for COP 25, a summit where states should have raised their national ambitions and pledged their climate targets – or, alternatively, at least decided on a uniform timeframe for them. But what we got was political inertia in which those countries which emitted the most were still not willing to pay for the losses they create. COP25 was dramatic in many senses and they showed a clear split between the need for emergency action and the unwillingness of parties to abandon the logic of self-interest and competition. Not much was left of the Paris spirit. Maybe it was good that governments did not agree on the new market mechanisms, but it was definitely disappointing to see the scarce (financial) commitment shown to deal with demands of the Global South such as a suitable architecture and funding for climate-induced loss and damage. The participants put Nationally Determined Contributions (NDCs) on the table in Madrid that were miles away from any global warming limitation agreed on in Paris. According to the Climate Action Tracker's Global Warming Projection, they still would lead to a temperature increase of approximately 2.7 degrees by 2100.[16] With ever more authoritarian governments in power globally, with the reluctance of all governments to put the solving of the climate crisis – as the largest global justice crisis - before national (economic) interests, the Madrid negotiations also showcased the crisis of multilateralism and the UN. In a protest action inside the COP location in Madrid, civil society constituencies raised their concerns over the protracted and unambitious negotiations. The failure of COP25 was symbolised by the ejection from the conference of 300 civil society representatives who had taken part in this protest.

> For climate movements worldwide, COP25 is yet another piece in the puzzle of an ominous reality. 2019 has been a significant year: never before have so many people demonstrated in the name of more climate action.

Political and economic decision-makers have deftly taken this up, but in a merely rhetorical manner. The Spanish government, for example, put up big posters around Madrid that read 'Don't call it climate change, call it a climate emergency'. Over and over at the UN climate conference people kept saying 'The world is watching us'. It would be dangerous to be lulled into a false sense of security by this and by the at times very consciously staged summit dramaturgy, both of which primarily attempt to do one thing: generate legitimacy for those involved. Real and substantial reductions of greenhouse gas emissions and real and comprehensive financial and technological transfer are the only adequate responses to the crisis. Climate movements are right to refuse to accept anything less in this regard.[17]

Climate diplomacy gridlock versus climate justice movements

Due to the Covid-19 pandemic, what otherwise would have been a significant year – 2020 – for the rollout of the Paris Agreement had to be postponed to 2021. It is now up to COP26 in Glasgow to solve open issues related to the Paris Rulebook, such as Article 6 on a new global carbon-market mechanism. In addition, from 2021 onwards countries have to implement their climate policies in line with the NDCs.[18] Traditionally, the COP host country's government is supposed to set a good example for climate action. If we look at the United Kingdom's COP presidency and how it is framing its ambitions, we see again that climate diplomacy is still very distant from real solutions to limit global warming below 1.5 degrees. Instead, we see the promotion of green capitalism. So-called green recovery from the Corona crisis includes renewable energy investments along with risky technology approaches such as carbon capture.[19] The UK's announcement of turning carbon emissions from its electricity system negative by 2033 is part of the myth that technologies like carbon capture or a widespread rollout of electric vehicles could solve the climate crisis.[20] Let us not forget that carbon capture technology is a dangerous intervention in the planet's geology. E-mobility in its production and operation will emit quite a lot of GHGs that are usually not counted for the consuming party. It also entails the problem of containing rare earth materials in its batteries that often are imported from countries with poor labour rights. Further, it perpetuates neocolonial trade schemes by importing raw materials from the Global South in order to maintain the lifestyle of private car transportation. Instead of transforming the whole mobility sector towards climate-friendly public mass transport, the promise of e-mobility simply replaces fossil-fuel cars with battery driven cars.

In the run-up to COP26 in Glasgow a broad coalition of NGOs and social movements has started to mobilise, combining different strains of the overall struggle for justice such as climate justice, racial justice, social justice, etc. As in many previous COPs, the political space that is generated locally will be used to create a counter narrative to the official climate action propaganda. The UK COP26 Coalition will bring together local and international activists and provide a space for debate and the development of alternatives. However, and this is perhaps something we can take away from the Covid-19 related lockdowns and travel restrictions, mobilisation does not have to wait for a major intergovernmental meeting; instead, a global gathering for climate justice will already have taken place online before November 2021.[21]

'By 2020 we rise' was the international call for action – and without the pandemic there would have been plenty of action. There are more and more people on the streets, in social media and in local politics that are raising their voices and demanding active policies. The Fridays for Future school strikes, and demos organised by other climate justice groups might have had their largest physical demonstrations before the pandemic, in 2019 – with millions of young people joined by older people, several global strikes, and the emergence many self-organised climate action groups, with direct action and diverse forms of civil disobedience putting additional pressure on political decision-makers. But these movements remain strong and are inventing new modes of protest to increase the pressure on the political and economic sectors, despite or even because of the pandemic.

However, there are yet other form of protest and resistance that have been ongoing for some time now: For instance, in the US and Canada, the indigenous First Nation protests against mega pipelines like Keystone XL with marches, blockades, camps and legal challenges to enforce indigenous rights. There are the anti-fracking movements in Chile and Argentina and anti-oil protests organised by the Ogoni people in Nigeria; they have used legal instruments to sue for the environmental destruction and dirty extractivism of Shell and other large fossil companies. The small island community in the Torres Straight Islands, for instance, is suing Australia for its lax climate policies. Education and empowerment also play a huge role in the struggles against climate change. Educating people about their rights and advocating environmental justice is one form of activism in Indonesia where indigenous women are organising people to stand up against palm oil companies.[22]

There are many forms of climate activism. One is to join the UN global climate summits and raise awareness about the injustice produced by the current economic system, with the power politics carried on by countries of the global north and their inability to accept their responsibility vis-à-vis countries and communities that already suffer from the climate emergency. We are aware that COPs will never deliver climate justice, but as spaces in which to fight for justice, we will not abandon them.

NOTES

1. <https://www.c40.org/other/agenda-for-a-green-and-just-recovery>.
2. <https://www.wwf.eu/what_we_do/eu_affairs/green_just_recovery/>.
3. <https://www.wri.org/blog/2020/09/coronavirus-green-economic-recovery>.
4. <https://www.un.org/en/coronavirus/building-back-better-requires-transforming-development-model-latin-america-and-caribbean>.
5. <https://climateactiontracker.org/global/temperatures/>.
6. <https://www.un.org/en/conferences/environment/rio1992>.
7. <http://unfccc.int/cop4/conv/conv_004.htm>.
8. <https://demandclimatejustice.org/2019/06/29/false-solutions/>.
9. Hans Joachim Schellenhuber, *Selbstverbrennung: Die fatale Dreiecksbeziehung zwischen Klima, Mensch und Kohlenstoff*. München: C. Bertelsmann Verlag, 2015.
10. <https://unfccc.int/process-and-meetings/the-paris-agreement/the-paris-agreement>.
11. <https://www.rosalux.de/en/news id/8583?cHash=2618b225a35678d76dc69bf83c034c2d>.
12. <https://www.ipcc.ch/sr15/>.
13. <https://www.corporateaccountability.org/wp-content/uploads/2018/04/PRIMERConflictofInterestUNFCCC_Final.pdf>.
14. <https://www.un.org/sg/en/content/sg/statement/2019-09-23/secretary-generals-remarks-closing-of-climate-action-summit-delivered>.
15. <https://www.rosalux.de/news/id/41037/und-sie-wagen-es-doch?cHash=6d91646641f66ecb5b1ae5f7da7ac458>.
16. <https://climateactiontracker.org/global/temperatures/>.
17. <https://www.rosalux.de/en/news/id/41383?cHash=3a21b7e1339170db068eade86786f6cc>.
18. <https://unfccc.int/process-and-meetings/the-paris-agreement/the-paris-agreement/nationally-determined-contributions-ndcs#eq-3>.
19. <https://www.theguardian.com/environment/2020/jul/27/uk-electricity-grids-carbon-emissions-could-turn-negative-by-2033-says-national-grid>.
20. <https://www.theguardian.com/environment/2020/jul/27/uk-electricity-grids-carbon-emissions-could-turn-negative-by-2033-says-national-grid>.
21. <https://cop26coalition.org/>.
22. <https://www.rosalux.de/en/publication/id/42979?cHash=b950ffc1b363aaa7207a089eac29331c>.

The EU's Green Deal and the Betrayal of a Generation: A Strategy to Fight Back

David Adler and Paweł Wargan

In December 2019, Ursula von der Leyen introduced the European Union's landmark plan to address the crises of climate and environment that are gripping the planet. 'The European Green Deal is about reconciling our economy with our planet', the incoming European Commission President said, 'reconciling the way we produce, the way we consume with our planet and respecting the environment we live in.' The EU Green Deal, according to von der Leyen, would make Europe the world's first carbon neutral continent – a promise to a new generation of young people striking for a sustainable future in town and city squares across Europe. 'Our European Green Deal is for them', von der Leyen said.

Announced in the wake of the largest climate protests in history, von der Leyen's plan was hailed as a momentous step forward in the movement for a global just transition – and a breakthrough in the politics of the Green New Deal everywhere. 'EU Beats US, Adopts Its Own Green New Deal', one headline proclaimed. Commission officials jumped at the opportunity to seize the mantle of the Green New Deal for themselves, claiming a leading role in the global push for decarbonisation. 'I bring back a message from Madrid', EU Commission Vice-President Frans Timmermans told the Parliament following his visit to the United Nations Climate Change conference in 2019. 'The message is this: we need European leadership. The message is also this: some of us are insecure what we should do, but if Europe leads we might go in the same direction.'[1]

Timmermans was right to stress the importance of Europe's climate commitments. The member countries of the European Union have been history's great leaders in the drive toward fossil fuel extraction and emission, both across the continent and throughout their respective empires. Indeed, the Union itself was forged in fossil fuel. Binding the signatories of the 1951

Treaty of Paris to a cartelised system of carbon emissions, the European Coal and Steel Community sought to overcome an age-old rivalry between Germany and France. The Common Agricultural Policy (CAP) – which absorbs over a third of the EU's annual budget and channels it predominantly to industrial agricultural holdings – was introduced soon afterwards to shore up the support of rural communities, ensuring internal cohesion against the allure of communism. As a result, beef farming now generates more emissions than all of Europe's cars and vans combined,[2] pesticides are decimating biodiversity,[3] and cheap European produce is undercutting farmers in the Global South, devastating sustainable farming practices the world over.

Europe's actual leadership in the global green transition, however, is dubious. A careful analysis of the Green Deal suggests that it is less a pathbreaking vision for an ecological future than a colossal effort to greenwash Europe's political and economic status quo. In all but name, Ursula von der Leyen's agenda bears no resemblance to the Green New Deal paradigm popularised by social movements like Sunrise and affiliated congressional representatives like Alexandria Ocasio-Cortez in the United States. The latter is rooted in a Keynesian model of the economy and a Rooseveltian theory of political change. Like the original New Deal, introduced in the wake of the Great Depression, the Green New Deal aims to respond to the particular economic conditions confronting developed economies today: high private savings, low public investment, and a gaping wealth gap that has only grown during the Covid-19 pandemic. The Green New Deal links two concepts – overaccumulation by the rich and underinvestment for the poor – with the crises of environment and climate – promising to push idle savings into green public investments. And, in its strategy, the Green New Deal hopes to channel the crises of unemployment and underemployment towards building worker support for a programme that would create millions of green jobs.

The European Green Deal contains no such provisions. In contrast to the Rooseveltian tradition, the Green Deal is a programme of upward rather than downward economic distribution, seeking explicitly to deepen the logic of private competition over the promise of public cooperation. Far from providing relief to Europe's ailing communities, the Green Deal strives to accommodate the concerns of capital by guaranteeing its profits in the green transition. Far from directing a democratic transformation of the economy, the Green Deal strengthens the EU's technocratic control in Brussels, Luxembourg, and Frankfurt. In this sense, the deficits of the Green Deal are both a reflection of the European Union's institutional architecture, and a lack of political will and courage to challenge them. In what follows we will go into the details of the Green Deal, making the case for a clear distinction between von der Leyen's programme and the proposals for a Green New Deal that have given hope to millions of people elsewhere in the world. There is no doubt that Europe needs a Green New Deal. But to get it, we must avoid the familiar traps of activism and civil society consultation into which Europe's protest movements continue to plunge. We conclude with considerations of a political strategy that can win a just transition, and resist the great betrayal of Europe's Green Deal.

Breaking down the Green Deal

Ursula von der Leyen has gone to great lengths to establish the Green Deal as a global benchmark for climate ambition. It is Europe's 'man on the moon moment', she has said, to dramatise her broader vision of a 'Union that strives for more'. But a close reading of the Green Deal and its component parts suggests the inverse: it does not strive for more as much as it strains to preserve the existing political economy of the European Union. Specifically, the Green Deal fails as a programme for political, economic, and ecological transformation across five key dimensions: speed, size, scope, strategy, and structure.

The clearest measure of any climate programme is its speed. When von der Leyen announced the Green Deal, she pledged to raise the EU's decarbonisation ambitions from 40% to 50-55% below 1990 levels by 2030, reaching "net-zero" by 2050. But that target is as misleading as it is insufficient. It is misleading because it is premised on the idea that the EU can continue emitting greenhouse gases while relying on largely unproven and potentially dangerous mitigation techniques – like carbon capture and storage – to offset emissions. And it is insufficient because it fails to take into account Europe's historical legacy of polluting around the world. The EU is today the world's third largest emitter of greenhouse gases, responsible for nearly 8% of all emissions globally.[4] By 2100, Germany on its own will account for 3.9% of the global temperature increase – taking into account its outsized historical legacy.[5]

The failure to redress the long history of colonial extraction is common across proposals for the green transition among developed economies. Critics of Green New Deal proposals in the United States have emphasised that the country's rapacious demand for resources and energy could accelerate social and environmental exploitation abroad. The same holds true for the EU, and the Green Deal makes little accommodation for the impacts its policies will have on other countries – let alone the reparations owed to the victims of its historical practices of excessive pollution. The EU's appetite for agricultural imports, for example, has already led to deforestation abroad –

even as EU officials celebrated the reforestation of large swathes of Europe.[6] The CAP, a policy of industrial protectionism at home, has severe impacts when combined with Europe's policies of advancing economic liberalisation abroad. In Ghana, for example, the percentage of poultry demand satisfied by domestic production dropped from 95% in 1992 to 11% in 2002 – at a cost of 200,000 jobs.[7]

In this regard, the Green Deal not only violates the Common But Differentiated Responsibility principle enshrined in the 2016 Paris Agreement, which holds that states with greater financial and technological capacities should shoulder more of the burden – a principle that EU negotiators vehemently opposed.[8] By failing to address its historical contributions to climate change and shifting the burden to other countries, the Green Deal is also aggravating the unequal distribution of climate change and the capacities of other states to respond to it. Such inequalities, as a paper in *Nature* argued, amount to 'a massive transfer of value from the hot parts of the world to the cooler parts of the world'.[9]

In its size, too, the Green Deal falls far short of what is necessary, and in what its public relations managers in Brussels have sold to the world. To fund her 'moonshot', von der Leyen introduced the Sustainable Europe Investment Plan,[10] a promise to turn the European Investment Bank (EIB) into a climate bank, mobilising €1 trillion over the next decade towards the green transition, or €100 billion each year. But that figure falls far short of all estimated costs of transition. The Commission itself put the cost at approximately €260 billion per year in additional funding to secure Europe's climate and energy targets by 2030.[11] The European Court of Auditors estimated that the EU needs to spend €1.115 trillion *each year* between 2021 and 2030 to meet its climate targets.[12] Even the latter figure is likely to be insufficient, based as it is on emissions reduction targets that predate the announcement of the Green Deal.

The inadequate funding of the Green Deal brings us to the narrowness of its scope. In the face of a real opportunity – and urgent need – to break with a status quo that continues to aggravate Europe's economic, social, and democratic crises, the Green Deal doubles down on the broken policies that have generated these crises in the first place. When introducing the Green Deal, von der Leyen took pains to reassure the EU's fiscal hawks by emphasising the programme's fidelity to the Stability and Growth Pact. Europe's 'fiscal straightjacket', as the SGP is sometimes called, is designed to maintain GDP growth while setting a ceiling on public expenditure, shifting ownership and opportunities for wealth creation into private hands. The EU's growth strategy is not only incompatible with planetary boundaries, as the European Environmental Agency made clear in its 2020 report;[13] it also maintains the fiscal logic that has seen public investment across the Eurozone collapse – with devastating consequences for public services, worker training, and public infrastructure.

The so-called NextGenerationEU programme threatens to aggravate that logic. Europe's flagship Covid-19 recovery package introduces, for the first time, a mutualised debt instrument that promises to flatten borrowing rates by consolidating the risk profiles of all Eurozone states into a single financial instrument. But the measure fails to break out of the straitjacket. Instead of abandoning the SGP and advancing an agenda that would benefit all those who live in Europe, the funds of the programme will be distributed unequally, with poorer nations receiving a greater share of the relief package. When budget talks resume next year, the imperative to balance the books will take centre stage – and, rather than draw the ire of their electorates, the EU's core members are likely to shift the burden of that balancing act onto net recipients of the recovery funds. NextGenerationEU, in other words, risks adding velocity to the hammer of austerity wielded against the Eurozone's poorer members in the years to come, deepening rather than healing the rifts that have repeatedly brought the European project to the brink of collapse.

If the Green Deal fails to redress Europe's structural imbalances its political strategy risks deepening its democratic deficit. Many advocates of the Green New Deal have advanced the policy under the banner of 'climate populism', suggesting that its sweeping ambition could unite a broad coalition of workers, communities, and concerned citizens. The Green Deal, by contrast, has no coalition. Von der Leyen claims to have been motivated by the youth movement that exploded around Europe in the year before the announcement. For all of its inspiration, however, the climate movement remained largely focused on the 'children'; workers, and the labour militancy that powered the demands underpinning the original New Deal in the 1930s, were absent. Indeed, the climate agenda is often portrayed as a threat to workers – and their concerns an insurmountable barrier to a truly ambitious programme. On the surface, through meetings with young activists, EU officials took pains to show that they were 'listening' to demands from the streets. But, behind the scenes, they met with over 11 business lobbyists each week, the effects of which are becoming clearer as money is poured into fossil fuel projects, and decarbonisation legislation is postponed.[14] By reducing the scope of democratic engagement to a series of minor 'consultations', the Green Deal seeks to co-opt democratic demands, and repurpose their rhetoric in order to inject fresh legitimacy into an existing, and unpopular, political economic paradigm.

This successful co-optation of the climate movement in the form of the Green Deal reflects an ugly truth about the politics of decarbonisation. The contemporary climate movement has emerged in large part from the left side of the political spectrum, with the result that its more ambitious proposals – like the Green New Deal – reflect principles of equity and democracy that are held close by climate activists themselves. In many cases, this has led advocates of the Green New Deal to suggest that decarbonisation is in itself a progressive or redistributive project. But the Green Deal suggests, instead, that decarbonisation can equally serve to entrench inequality and reduce the scope of democratic politics. The Green Deal therefore presents a novel case of what we have called '*decarbonisation without democracy*,' a political economic vision of the green transition that aims to reduce overall emissions while preserving the existing distribution of power between rich and poor, north and south, creditor nations and debtor ones.[15] In other words, Europe is indeed pioneering a new model of climate politics – it just happens to be a different model than the headline of the 'Green Deal' would suggest.

Finally, in its structure, the European Green Deal deepens the crisis of public investment that has plagued the Eurozone since the sovereign debt crisis. Instead of committing to a programme of public investment sufficient in size to address the looming crisis, it seeks to leverage public money toward private investments, socialising the costs and privatising the gains of the green transition. In this regard, the Green Deal resembles its immediate predecessor – the Investment Plan for Europe, also known as the 'Juncker Plan'. Like the Green Deal, the Juncker Plan sought to mobilise roughly €100 billion per year by using public funds to guarantee private loans – socialising the risk of investment while privatising the gains. This model allows the EU to mobilise significant amounts of funding without incurring the full balance-sheet costs of investment. Its logic is simple: 'to nudge private finance toward the public good', as EIB President Werner Hoyer said in 2019.[16]

This approach of public-private co-financing not only elevates short-term budgetary considerations over long-term sustainability – the products of these investments do not remain in public hands; it has also been shown to generate disproportionate gains for private investors. In a 2018 report, the European Court of Auditors said that the risk allocation between private and public partners in such arrangements 'was often inappropriate, incoherent and ineffective' with 'remuneration rates (up to 14%) on the private partner's risk capital' that did not reflect the risk borne.[17] In other words, the model has served to siphon public wealth into private hands.

Winning a Green New Deal for Europe

The concept of a 'just transition', at the very heart of the Green New Deal, requires a more thorough interrogation of its Rooseveltian namesake. The New Deal emerged at a time of great economic and social turmoil. The programmes that it enacted – which sought to bring relief to the poor, recovery to an ailing economy, and reform to a broken system – represented perhaps the greatest gains for workers in US history. Yet, bulwarked as he was by labour militancy, Roosevelt could not escape the ideological and coalitional constraints of his time. The product of those constraints delivered, as historian William Leuchtenburg wrote in 1963, 'a halfway revolution; it swelled the ranks of the bourgeoisie but left many Americans – sharecroppers, slum dwellers, most Negroes – outside of the new equilibrium'.[18] The New Deal that emerged was, in short, a life raft for capitalism, which condensed rather than eliminated the chasm between owner and worker, setting the stage of its undoing in the decades to follow.

The challenges facing a 'just transition' today are greater still. Climate and environmental breakdown are not neatly circumscribable by national frontiers – nor are their root causes. A hundred multinational corporations, overwhelmingly from the Global North, are responsible for 71% of all emissions.[19] The hyper-mobile 1% of the world's wealthiest individuals is responsible for more than double the emissions of the bottom 50% of the global population.[20] The Intergovernmental Panel on Climate Change has long maintained that a changing climate would be responsible for the unparalleled displacement of this population, which primarily resides in the Global South.[21] The International Organization for Migration warned that between 25 million and one billion people might be forced to move because of the climate by 2050.[22] Recent years have provided ample forewarning of these impacts: towns seared out of existence or swept away in biblical floods; entire regions forced to escape the accelerating creep of the desert sands.

A European just transition must therefore operate simultaneously at different levels of scale. It must lift up workers and communities within Europe – calming the centrifugal forces of reaction that are deepening the decades-long crisis of democracy on the continent. It must provide robust support to countries across the Global South that are already reeling from the effects of a collapsing climate. And it must challenge the systems of financial and trade multilateralism that – without accountability to national democracies – support the siphoning of wealth from the world's poor to the world's rich.

To bring that vision to life, our Blueprint for Europe's Just Transition[23] – developed alongside researchers, academics, and activists from across the continent and beyond – proposes three major initiatives. The first is the Green Public Works: a historic investment programme to kick-start Europe's equitable green transition: Among many proposals, the programme includes the rapid transition of industries towards worker ownership, a process for the elimination of the global war industry, and the wholesale shift towards public investment for all the infrastructural and social projects that undergird the transition. The second is an Environmental Union – a regulatory and legal framework to ensure that the European economy transitions quickly and fairly, without transferring carbon costs onto frontline communities. The third is an Environmental Justice Commission – an independent body to research and investigate new standards of 'environmental justice' across Europe and beyond its borders, while facilitating robust reparations for historical wrongs, and supporting nations in their green transitions. In our conception, the Green New Deal for Europe must be grounded in the practice of internationalist solidarity rather than the framework of neoliberal multilateralism on which the EU was built.

It would be naive to assume that a change of this magnitude – however ready-made the policy prescriptions – could be willed into existence. Unlike Roosevelt, von der Leyen operates in an ideological and institutional environment that is designed to lock in the status quo and rein in ambitions to undermine it. Meanwhile, her notional adversaries – the climate movements that began on Europe's streets and have since found homes in civil society organisations, themselves funded by the European Commission – sustain a vision of activism grounded in the belief that the sheer volumes of young people can alchemise political action. In this vein, many of the movement's demands are framed as pleas. 'The EU must lead the way', Greta Thunberg said in an impassioned address to the European Parliament in 2019. 'You have the moral obligation to do so and you have a unique economical and political opportunity to become a real climate leader.'[24] The tragedy of European politics lies in the broken mechanism of transmission from its organs of civil society to the control centre of its political decisions. As a set of governing institutions and political frameworks, the EU has proven unwilling and unable to deliver on policies that protect its own frontline communities, let alone redress its historical record.

Indeed, the evidence could not weigh more heavily against the dominant strategy of European activism. In 2019, activists organised the largest climate strike in history. In Germany alone, some 1.4 million people took to the streets to demand action.[25] Just a few months later, Germany opened a new coal plant[26] – to significant but fruitless opposition from activist groups – and the European Parliament voted through a €27 billion investment in fossil fuels for that year's budget, nearly twenty-seven times more than the annualised budget for the proposed Just Transition Fund. More successful projects of climate activism, like the months-long occupation of Dannenröder Forest in the German state of Hesse, are met with disproportionate state violence for simply trying to safeguard a stretch of woodland.[27] In short, the pipeline from protest to policy – even in places like Germany and France, far less hostile to such mobilisations than neo-authoritarian contexts like Hungary – does not work, and no amount of consultations at Berlaymont or the European Parliament will fix it.

To deliver a radical Green New Deal for Europe, then, it is insufficient to speak in the language of civil society as a category of European governance. Reciting scientific models to confounded officials might expand awareness of the urgency of the moment, but it does little to shape our strategic response. Much of this activism is phrased in negative terms. Fridays for Future defines its mission as the 'protest against the lack of action on the climate crisis'.[28] It is less clear what it demands, for whom, and how it hopes to win. We must stop dreaming of access to a decision-making process designed to exclude us, and start thinking about the levers of power that are actually at our disposal: this is how we will win a true just transition of our political economies.

Climate mitigation, as we have shown, is less a question of scientific urgency than of the gross imbalances of economic power in our societies. To build mass popular power, it is vital for movements to articulate *positive* demands for change: ones whose fulfilment can lift communities across Europe, overcoming the stranglehold that decades of neoliberal entrenchment has exerted on them. These demands must in the first instance be aimed at reclaiming power – economic, political, and cultural – within our communities. Counterintuitively, the climate crisis might not be the most appropriate vector through which to advance that mission, despite its existential stakes. On the contrary, a climate agenda that is abstracted from the material needs of communities promises only to alienate those communities from the project of ecological justice; the generational politics of the EU climate movement, pitting student activists against their working parents, is evidence enough. In a continent where one out of five live in poverty, which faces rising homelessness in each country, and where inept responses to the Covid-19 pandemic have left millions destitute, the most powerful demands may be those that are aimed at satisfying the basic material needs of communities: for food, healthcare, and shelter.

These demands have strategic force because they can shatter the primary obstacle to climate action in Europe today: the so-called *black zero*. Within the EU, member countries have had a morbid obsession with balanced state budgets, eroding their capacity to respond to crises and deepening inequalities across various geographic and social axes on the continent. Channelled in the right ways, a break with the economic orthodoxy sustaining inaction could unleash public funding for needed jobs and public services – the first steps in the construction of the Green New Deal for Europe. That in turn could disable the attempts to position labour as the enemy of the just transition. From Polish miners to the French *gilets jaunes*, workers have been wary of climate mitigation because, within the austerity realities of 21st-century Europe, decarbonisation can provide cover for regressive taxation and forced unemployment. In the raw arithmetic of democratic politics, then, the climate agenda can only be won in coordination with workers whose concerns are placed at the centre of its political demands.

But the activation and organisation of labour inside the climate movement is not only necessary for this reason in the electoral arena. Workers also possess the material power to challenge the paradigm of decarbonisation proposed in Brussels. By withholding working hours, unions can throw a spanner in the gears of the economy and create new sources of democratic leverage against the managers of the EU technocracy. It is a lesson that Europe has learned before, and it is a lesson that we are learning again from social movements further afield: in Bolivia, for example, the regime installed by the coup of November 2019 was not defeated by the ballot box; to restore democracy to their country, workers across Bolivia launched waves of mass strikes and highway blockades to force Jeanine Áñez to deliver an election date in the first place. Their fight for democracy, in other words, was won – not petitioned.

The success of labour struggles in the advance of democracy points to a new strategy for the European climate movement. In particular, it suggests the need to forge a strategic climate coalition that brings environmental activists into existing institutions of community organisation — unions, especially – in order to advance a shared agenda and plan common strategies. Using productivity gains to reduce the working week would, for example, have powerful environmental benefits, reducing material throughput and infrastructure use, and cutting per capita emissions and resource exploitation in the process. Together, unions and activists could demand ownership and control within the workplace, or exit the workforce and begin constructing new modes of democratic economic organisation outside the sphere of capital accumulation.

But even these simple demands represent tectonic shifts in the balance of power within our political economies – shifts to which key constituencies in EU policymaking (for example, bankers, the hedge fund managers, and the fossil fuel corporations themselves) will not readily yield. Recognising capital's institutional entrenchment, studying its instruments of power, building a new type of praxis designed to pierce through the armour of EU technocracy – in a word, *politicising* a climate movement that too often frames its demands in merely scientific terms – are the first steps in the construction of a robust front for eco-socialism.

Here again, history can serve as a compass of what may lie on the horizon. From Thomas Sankara planting 10 million trees in just a few years, helping to halt desertification of Burkina Faso;[29] to Evo Morales inaugurating the first 'people's summit' on the climate in response to the failures of the United Nations process,[30] lessons from the successes and failures of socialist construction ground our analysis and policy proscriptions in the material struggles for – and experiences of – what we now call 'systems change'. They also expose the often clandestine obstacles to our political aspirations, tearing away the convenient myth that radical change is just within reach, that one more protest or one more election might tilt the scales toward a new political economic paradigm. And, most importantly, these lessons from history reveal that the sources of power and wealth lie in the control of the ores, metals, foods, and fuels that we draw from the earth; the fish, water, kelp, and algae that we draw from the oceans; the energy that we draw from the sun; and the labour that creates use value from them. To take seriously the call for a just transition, we must set our sights on full popular sovereignty over these resources. And it is a striking feature of our political moment – a moment defined by mass recognition of the existential crises on the horizon, and the plague of economic inequality that is reaching new heights – that bears stressing today.

Conclusion

As the hallmark of Ursula von der Leyen's mandate at the Commission, the Green Deal was presented as a holistic overhaul of Europe's political economy. Both in breadth and ambition, the Green Deal promised to transform key pillars of the European economy. These included plans for a Farm to Fork Strategy that would 'cherish and preserve our rural areas and invest in their future', aiming to reduce agricultural emissions and align farming practices with the EU's new climate goals. They included a New Circular Economy Action Plan that would support Europe's construction and textile industries to pollute less and curb the production of plastics. And they included the plan to leverage €1 trillion in sustainable investments over the following decade, including a Just Transition Fund to ensure that 'we leave nobody behind'.

But on closer inspection, the Green Deal bears virtually no resemblance to the original New Deal – in style as in substance – and falls far short of the expansive vision of political and economic transformation so urgently needed today. While borrowing the rhetoric of the just transition, the authors of the Green Deal stripped the programme of its promise to confront the failures of speculative capitalism and drive an economic transformation to replace it. If Roosevelt 'welcomed the hatred' of high finance and the capitalist class at large, Ursula von der Leyen has sought to accommodate their interests, if not to serve them outright. If Roosevelt's New Deal aimed to instantiate a new set of rights for workers and their families, Ursula von der Leyen's Green Deal contains no social dimension, and virtually no provisions for the social dislocation associated with its decarbonisation project. In short, not only does the Green Deal not qualify as a Green New Deal, as Roosevelt would have understood it – it is also in direct and irresolvable conflict with the promise of a just transition. But in its historic betrayal, in its dilution and cooptation of our existential struggle, it also reveals something important about the nature of our political institutions: they are redundant. Are we prepared to build new ones in their place?

NOTES

1 <https://ec.europa.eu/commission/presscorner/detail/en/SPEECH_19_6753>.
2 <https://storage.googleapis.com/planet4-eu-unit-stateless/2020/09/20200922-Greenpeace-report-Farming-for-Failure.pdf>.
3 <https://apnews.com/article/46c52a31c79b0628d07d5d5fa44b5806>.
4 <https://www.wri.org/blog/2020/02/greenhouse-gas-emissions-by-country-sector>.
5 <https://climateanalytics.org/media/historical_responsibility_report_nov_2015.pdf>.
6 <https://www.nature.com/articles/d41586-020-02991-1>.
7 Sylvester Bagooro, 'Report of the national civil society forum on the EPA', Accra: Third World Network-Africa, 2011.
8 <https://www.carbonbrief.org/old-battlelines-resurface-as-countries-meet-for-last-time-ahead-of-paris-climate-summit>.
9 <http://web.stanford.edu/~mburke/climate/BurkeHsiangMiguel2015.pdf>.
10 <https://www.europarl.europa.eu/RegData/etudes/ATAG/2020/659314/EPRS_ATA(2020)659314_EN.pdf>.
11 <https://ec.europa.eu/energy/sites/ener/files/documents/recommondation_en.pdf>.
12 <https://op.europa.eu/webpub/eca/lr-energy-and-climate/en/>.
13 <https://www.eea.europa.eu/publications/soer-2020>.
14 <https://corporateeurope.org/en/2020/07/disclosed-intense-fossil-industry-lobby-undermines-eu-green-deal>.
15 <https://jacobinmag.com/2020/03/decarbonize-democracy-european-union-green-new-deal/>.
16 <https://www.eib.org/en/press/news/the-eu-climate-bank-channeling-private-capital-into-sustainable-finance>.

17 <https://www.eca.europa.eu/Lists/ECADocuments/SR18_09/SR_PPP_EN.pdf>.
18 William E. Leuchtenburg, *Franklin D. Roosevelt and the New Deal: 1932-1940*, New York: Harper & Row, 1963.
19 <https://www.cdp.net/en/articles/media/new-report-shows-just-100-companies-are-source-of-over-70-of-emissions>.
20 <https://www.oxfamamerica.org/press/carbon-emissions-richest-1-percent-more-double-emissions-poorest-half-humanity/>.
21 <https://www.ipcc.ch/report/climate-change-the-ipcc-1990-and-1992-assessments/>.
22 <https://www.iom.int/migration-and-climate-change>.
23 <https://report.gndforeurope.com/>.
24 <https://www.europarl.europa.eu/news/en/headlines/society/20200227STO73520/greta-thunberg-urges-meps-to-show-climate-leadership>.
25 <https://www.theguardian.com/environment/2019/sep/21/across-the-globe-millions-join-biggest-climate-protest-ever>.
26 <https://www.bloomberg.com/news/articles/2020-01-13/germany-s-farewell-to-coal-complicated-by-new-uniper-plant>.
27 <https://www.dw.com/en/germany-water-cannon-fired-at-dannenr%C3%B6der-forest-activists/a-55831581>.
28 <https://fridaysforfuture.org/what-we-do/contact-us/>.
29 <https://www.bbc.com/news/world-africa-41580874>.
30 <https://www.theguardian.com/environment/2010/apr/21/evo-morales-grassroots-climate-talks>.

Sleepwalking from One Crisis to the Next

Kateřina Konečná

Do you remember a time when you last felt the world and Europe was not in a crisis? The new millennium brought us new hope after the destructive and bloody twentieth century, but we did not have much time to enjoy it. Soon enough 9/11 came, and afterwards still more crimes against humanity were committed and international law violated during the so-called 'War on Terror', which continues to this day. How sure we were at the time that the US would never have a president worse than George W. Bush. How little we knew! Then, after a few years of disgusting images from the war brought to our TV sets by 'the coalition of the willing', the unleashed Wall Street bull brought the economic crisis to the rest of the world and most especially to those who did nothing to deserve it. Then everything accelerated with the Arab Spring, the Syrian Civil War, the Ebolavirus epidemic, the migration crisis, and the Black Lives Matter movement. And while the world's news-agency cameras were giving us the impression that the world was on fire, it actually was, not only because of wars and conflicts but mainly because of global warming and humanity's exploitation of nature.

In that sense, it is not hard to understand why many people feel as if the Covid-19 pandemic is essentially nature's way of getting even with humankind for its long-term destructive activity. It is true that capitalism managed to adapt when facing these challenges, but the absolute need for growth is still at its core; it is impossible to imagine it otherwise. The first victim to pay the price of this need for constant growth is nature, but since we are very much dependant on nature, we are basically all paying the price for this need for immediate profit, and this price is far greater than the gains obtained by the few.

The obsession with the highest GDP possible is one of the main factors in the race to the bottom. The consistent use of business optics through which those in charge look at all of the world's problems makes creating a sustainable and peaceful future absolutely impossible. We see this with global warming and with the current pandemic. And very sad to say, EU policies often not only do not help but can even make the situation still worse. Now more than ever we must decide what the foundation of our future is to be – greed or wellbeing.

This clash has characterised life on the planet for centuries, but never before has it been as visible as it is today on a daily basis. I believe the image that I will always associate with the year 2020 and possibly with the upcoming decade is the cartoon in which a group of scientists are looking at a wave labelled Covid-19, hoping it will soon be over, while behind them there is an even bigger wave called Economic Crisis, which is followed by a massive wave called Climate Change. Beyond this we will need to deal with additional 'waves', as for example the Fourth Industrial Revolution.

The big challenge now is to deal with all the issues without resorting to short-term solutions of the sort that will create additional problems in the near future. It is for example evident that austerity policies raised the mortality rate during the pandemic and must be ended. We need complex change that will not cause problems but will lay the basis for a sustainable future. The question now is: Who will push for this change, which will necessarily be directed mainly against big business? Since the UN does not have the power to do so many may pin their hopes on the EU, but, sadly, this will probably only be wishful thinking.

Profitable fires

Like many others on the left, I was already aware of the EU's unsatisfactory record when it comes to the environment. The EU, it is true, talks about climate and global warming a great deal and enjoys the reputation of an environmental champion on the international level, but in concrete reality the EU far too often fails to address the ecological challenge, instead favouring business's point of view. If there is a clash between international trade and the environment, the EU decides in favour of international trade. Many examples can be cited to illustrate this, but I would like to use just one, which I have been working on for many years – deforestation.

As a person coming from an inland country, the Czech Republic, I cannot sufficiently stress the importance of forests. 'Natural forests are the basis of life itself. They create the soil, maintain the water cycle, and are vast sources of nutrients. They shape the weather, cool down the climate, and protect us from hurricanes, droughts, and floods, which are intensifying as the planet warms up. They feed and shelter more creatures than we can count.'[1] The forest is a key factor boosting economies and underlying wellbeing since it is an object of recreation and tourism and provides everything from medicine to timber, fish, fruit, nuts, and vegetables. Even though the EU and the Member States do not do enough to protect European forests, the situation is even worse in Third World countries.

For quite some time now we have known that 'EU finance and imports of timber, palm oil, soy, beef, paper, cocoa and other commodities are causing vast deforestation and forest degradation. In many places, forests are being converted to tree plantations, losing their value for people, climate and nature.'[2] This raises a crucial question: How can an important international organisation, such as the EU, support the struggle against global warming and, at the same time, business activities that undermine this struggle?

I therefore believed it was necessary to open this subject in 2015 in the European Parliament, the immediate catalyst being the disastrous fires in Indonesia and Borneo which occurred that year. If you were paying attention to the news in 2019, you were continuously hearing about fires. They were breaking out in so many places that even mainstream media had to pay attention to them. But in 2015 not many heard about fires in Southeast Asia. Whether the lack of interest was due to a disinterest in the topic of the environment or the fate of the Third World its absence was shocking. I believe no one expressed the feeling of despair at this better than George Monbiot when he wrote: 'I have often wondered how the media would respond when eco-apocalypse struck. I pictured the news programmes producing brief, sensational reports, while failing to explain why it was happening or how it might be stopped. Then they would ask their financial correspondents how the disaster affected share prices, before turning to the sports […]. What I did not expect was that they would ignore it.'[3] But that is precisely what happened, and I was very afraid the EU would do the same, all the more so that, when it comes to deforestation, the EU is very much part of the problem.

The 2015 wildfires in Indonesia and Borneo were the worst observed for almost two decades and occurred as a result of global climate change, land-use changes, and deforestation, exposing 69 million people to dangerous air pollution and causing thousands of premature deaths. Fires in Indonesia are typically the result of the clearing of land for palm oil plantations and other agricultural uses, and 52% of the 2015 fires occurred in carbon-rich peatlands, turning the country into one of the largest contributors to global warming on earth. In only three weeks the fires released more CO_2 than Germany's annual emissions. It would, of course, be far too easy to blame the Indonesians for wanting to escape poverty and improve their socio-economical condition by taking advantage of the high demand. Isn't that what in theory capitalism is actually about? The problem here is that this is a demand for something that is directly linked to massive forest fires, the drying up of rivers, soil erosion, peatland drainage, polution of waterways, an overall loss of biodiversity, forced evictions, armed violence, child labour, debt bondage, and discrimination against indigenous communities. Moreover, the countries or organisations purportedly fighting for the environment and human rights are looking the other way.

One of these organisations, unfortunately, is the EU since at least 30% of global deforestation is linked to products traded and consumed there. That is why the EU often tries to make the issue more of a consumerism problem than an EU one, which ignores one significant factor – EU policy on biofuels. 'The EU is the second-largest importer of crude palm oil in the world, and the majority of those imports (53%) are currently subsidised to make "green fuel" for cars and trucks. This increases pressure on agricultural land which leads to deforestation.'[4] This is not only fascinating for its inherent contradiction but also because the Commission tried to hushed up the results of a study showing that biofuels from palm oil produce a volume of emissions three times greater than conventional fuels.

Therefore when it comes to deforestation the EU is certainly not the champion of the battle against it but is very clearly part of the problem, since 'The EU demands (imports and consumes) a range of commodities (and commodity-based products), while a range of EU-based actors plays a role in investments in forest risk sectors and supply chains. This translates into an EU land footprint that contributes to global land pressure'[5] and, of course, is contrary not only to the Paris Agreement on climate change but also the 2030 Agenda for Sustainable Development.

In 2017, for this reason, I presented a document in the European Parliament on 'Palm Oil and Deforestation' calling for the EU to introduce minimum sustainability criteria for palm oil and products containing palm oil that enter the EU market, making sure that they do not lead to ecosystem degradation, such as deforestation of primary and secondary forests and the destruction or degradation of peatlands or other ecologically valuable habitats, whether directly or indirectly; does not cause a loss in biodiversity, foremost of all endangered animal and plant species; does not give rise to changes in land management practices which have negative environmental impacts; does not give rise to economic, social, and environmental problems and conflicts, including the particular problems of child labour, forced labour, land grabbing, or the eviction of indigenous or local communities; fully respects fundamental human and social rights and is in full compliance with social and labour standards designed to guarantee the safety and wellbeing of workers; enables small-scale palm oil cultivators to be included in the certification system and ensures that they receive their fair share of profits; and ensures that palm oil is cultivated on plantations that are managed using modern agro-ecological techniques in order to drive the conversion to sustainable agricultural practices with the goal of minimising adverse environmental and social outcomes.[6]

Since my report, the EU has been taking the issue more seriously, and there is more political will to deal with it. But true to form the EU is sending a mixed message, since the EU-MERCOSUR trade deal is yet again threatening to fuel more deforestation in the Amazon rainforest. 'To meet the huge new demand for beef and soybeans that would be created by the agreement, it is expected that large areas of the Amazon rainforest in Brazil – the world's largest carbon sink – will be destroyed to create more space for intensive farming. [...] If this goes ahead, carbon emissions will rise by 1.3 gigatons a year, according to the country's scientists, as well as reducing biodiversity.'[7]

Yes, people need to become more enlightened consumers, but the EU policies are most to blame. The EU can criticise Brazil, Indonesia, and Malaysia for how they treat the environment, but since they are signing free-trade agreements with them, these are in the end just empty words .

Critics of current capitalism

Speaking of empty words for the sake of appearance, I always find it tragicomic when government leaders or corporations pretend to have awakened and they suddenly use the language and arguments of the left. When you read 'What we're facing right now – in terms of the rise of populism and divisive and fearful narratives around the world – it's based around the fact that globalisation doesn't seem to be working for the middle class, for ordinary people,'[8] you can agree with this criticism of globalisation only working for the privileged, but this was said not by Chomsky, Klein, or Žizek but by Canadian Prime Minister Justin Trudeau.

Ironically enough, Trudeau made this statement in 2016 to support CETA (the free trade deal between the EU and Canada), an agreement that could lead to more than 200,000 jobs being lost in the EU as a result of further market liberalisation. CETA is very problematic mainly because there is extraordinarily little basis for all its big promises of jobs and economic growth while it carries enormous risks for our labour rights, environmental protection, and consumer rights. The EU and Trudeau used good PR lines and talked a great deal about CETA's beneficial effects on the environment, but 'CETA's environmental provisions cannot be enforced through trade sanctions or financial penalties if they are violated. Victims of environmental abuse cannot bring a claim. Also, CETA does not include provisions that would allow urgently needed environmental and climate policies to overrule, or otherwise be exempt from, CETA rules that might endanger them'.[9] It is greenwashing all over again since trade is seen as far more important than the environment. The international trade advocated by the EU is bad for its populations and the planet.

While searching sources for this contribution, I came upon an article highlighting the need for a change in the current socio-economical system. The author points to the need for a more local approach and argues that 'We also need to change the economics of the system and move away from linear economies to more circular ones, which eliminate waste from the outset and maximise the continued use of resources rather than depleting them. Establishing regenerative and restorative economies which focus on ensuring that we live within environmental limits, where everyone can meet their basic needs, and which reduce inequality, must be our focus coming out of the current global crisis.'[10] Again, not much can be said against this argument, but since it was written by someone speaking on behalf of Nestle, I believe we can question the motivation behind it.

Big companies like to talk about the environment and a more ecological approach since it is always more comfortable to talk about these matters rather than really act on it. Nestlé, for example, said in 2010 that by 2020 they would only use those ingredients that do not contribute to deforestation in their products. That promise was not kept.[11] On the one hand, it is true that these companies generally try to be more ecological, but they do so mainly for PR reasons and because they are under much scrutiny from NGOs. Maintaining the current status quo is much more important for them than some minor 'green' changes.

Moreover, when Nestlé talks about the need to 'reduce inequality' it might start by its pledge of nearly two decades ago to stop using cocoa harvested by children. The company broke this promise too since it can track only 49% of its global cocoa supply to farms.[12]

Another critic of current capitalism is perhaps even more untrustworthy – French president Emmanuel Macron. 'Macron says he sees the crisis (meaning the pandemic) as an existential event for humanity that will change the nature of globalisation and the structure of international capitalism [...]. And he wants to use a cataclysm that has prompted governments to prioritise human lives over economic growth as an opening to tackle environmental disasters and social inequalities that he says were already threatening the stability of the world order.'[13] Those are undoubtedly smart words, but since they have been uttered by a person at the heart of the power establishment, they sound grotesque.

Did it really require a pandemic for the French president and French institutions to realise that human lives must be prioritised over economic growth? Did this pandemic have to occur for the political elites throughout the world to discover the fundamental facts about wellbeing and sustainable development? Environmental change has been a known threat to everything living on our planet for decades now, and yet the struggle against it is more a matter of promises than action. People in power do not think of the future as their problem; they care more about this year's GDP than what might happen in a few decades. As politicians on behalf of companies, they need 'profits' now and not in the future.

Luckily, real critics like Yanis Varoufakis did not hold back. 'COVID-19 found capitalism in this zombified state. With consumption and production hit massively and at once, governments were forced to step into the void to replace all incomes to a gargantuan extent at a time the real capitalist economy has the least capacity to generate real wealth.'[14] Once again, it was the state hated by neoliberals that had to help business. But the economic crisis of a decade ago taught us that this probably will not lead to a more stable and fairer economy, but more likely to 'socialism for the very, very few (courtesy of central banks and governments catering to a tiny oligarchy) and stringent austerity, coupled with cruel competition in an environment of industrial, and technologically advanced, feudalism for almost everyone else.'[15]

It is clear that Trudeau, Nestlé, and Macron want mere cosmetic changes. Their arguments may be correct but they are talking about resets and not about fundamental change. True, globalism is not working for everyone, but how can it since it is merely a stage of capitalism, which certainly does not work for everyone. How can governments prioritise human lives when they are dependent on economic growth? How can we deal with climate change in a system focused on profits today rather than on a sustainable future? Those are the questions that cannot be answered by the establishment and by beneficiaries of the current status quo, but sadly these are the people who will now deal with the question if or how the pandemic will change our lives.

Game-changing pandemic?

There are unfortunately many connections between the reactions of states and international organisations to climate change and the pandemic. Many criticise the response for being often fragmented and ineffective. That was the case with the EU when Member States first panicked and the EU did nothing. The EU does not have many powers when it comes to health issues, but 'in theory, it should have been European Council President Charles Michel's role to coordinate EU member states. But apparently, he did not, or did not manage to. His role in this crisis has been low-profile at best.'[16] In addition, Italy's call for urgent help was ignored by the Member States.[17]

Needless to say, not all EU institutions and agencies failed to rise to the occasion. The European Centre for Disease Prevention and Control (ECDC), for example, was very active im putting forward many crucial proposals. But Member States, having for decades ignored the experts on climate change, once again failed to heed them. Covid-19, however, is a particularly intense result of climate change. As climate economist Gernot Wagner wrote: 'It's amazing to see how Covid-19 is climate change on warp speed. It's *not* about levels, it's about growth rates. Yes, +1°C is bad. But it's nothing compared to +2, 3, or 4 expected by 2100. Well, a dozen Covid cases in NYC is bad. But it's nothing compared to 1,000.'[18] Once again, those in power ignored the issue until the roof was on fire. The danger must be imminent; otherwise, they are in denial or believe it is someone else's problem. When they are forced to face the facts, they turn to unprecedented desperate action. This did not happen with climate change since 'unlike coronavirus, it does not move at "warp speed", and governments have not yet been forced to confront the scale of the crisis. Nevertheless, this is the scenario we risk with continued inaction.'[19] The question then is: Did the EU learn from the pandemic? Sadly, I do not think so.

The first obstacle is the EU's relationship to big business; the EU's institutions are all too often connected to big companies, not only personally through the revolving door[20] but also because they speak with them more often than they do with anyone else. We need only look at who is shaping one of the most important documents of the current Commission's term – the European Green Deal (EGD). A hundred days after the official presentation 'key members of the Commission in charge of the EGD […] met 151 times with representatives of business interests. That amounts to 11 meetings a week! In comparison, it only met 29 times with public interest representatives, which means about 2 meetings a week.'[21] When the Commission negotiates trade agreements, the proportion is even more skewed towards business. We also know the Commission is willing to look the other way when corporations break European laws, as in the case of Dieselgate. However, in the case of vaccines against Covid-19 things are different.

The EU did a great deal to make sure there is a vaccine/cure for Covid-19 since it is afraid of another global lockdown. This is why it raised almost

€16 billion from 4 May through 14 August 2020 under the Coronavirus Global Response – the global action for universal access to tests, treatments, and vaccines against coronavirus and for the global recovery.[22] In terms of a vaccine developed in Europe the EU itself invested heavily in its development, but unfortunately without attempting to reach agreements with the pharmaceutical companies that would be more advantageous for European taxpayers who have paid for the development of the vaccine and will pay yet again for the actual vaccine. Through the end of summer 2020, the EU had already paid €336 million to secure AstraZeneca's potential Covid-19 vaccine and was also in advanced talks with Johnson & Johnson, Sanofi, Moderna, and CureVac for their vaccines.[23]

As to the advanced talks it is also interesting to look at who is negotiating these deals on the EU side. We know that there are seven people and that one of them is former pharma lobbyist and director of the European Federation of Pharmaceutical Industries, Richard Bergström. The identity of the other six is unknown.[24]

Thus, after investing a tremendous amount of money, the EU failed to make the anti-pandemic vaccines and treatments into a global public good freely accessible to everyone. This is in keeping with the European Commission's normal practice of writing checks to corporations with no questions asked. The Left (the the new name of the former GUE/NGL) therefore launched a petition:'#Right2Cure: No profit on pandemics. Vaccine and treatment for all'.[25]

The second obstacle is the Multiannual Financial Framework (MFF). The fact that the EU Member States agreed on the scaling back of recovery plan grants and curtailed proposals for the long-term budget – especially in agriculture, research, climate, transition-fund, and health policy – shows how little they learned from the extraordinary stupidity of austerity policies. It is easy for these politicians to cut funding necessary for the future since many of them will be long gone when the consequences have to be paid; but if we do not invest and plan for the future now we will continue to go from one crisis to the next without a safety net. It is doubtful that the pandemic would have been as bad as it is if, during the economic crisis, the EU had not carried out cuts in public spending.

Solidarity forever

One of the most fateful setbacks suffered by the left occurred when we tragically failed to use the opportunity presented by the economic crisis. If we do this once more, we risk falling into oblivion. Maybe it is because 'Neoliberalism and capitalism have deprived us from [sic] our imagination.

Thatcher's "There is no such thing as society" marked the transition from the social to the individual with detrimental effects on our language, our culture, our understanding of our communities. Living in our own silos, we struggle to infuse ourselves with solidarity.'[26] This dark vision has much that is compelling; neoliberalism and capitalism have indeed deprived us of our imagination. It is impossible to simultaneously tackle all the manifold problems this kind of society creates. Yet that often seems to be precisely what we try to do. Where I respectfully disagree with the above-quoted post on DiEM25's site is that it is less difficult to 'infuse ourselves with solidarity' than one might think – the pandemic showed us that the solidarity and empathy of our communities is very strong when facing a crisis.

I thought of ending this article by quoting John Holloway: 'How we come out of this pandemic will shape the future of humanity. Now, as never before, we have to break the deadly logic of capital.'[27] But I believe we all know this; we know there has to be change at this level. Instead of only focusing on the US and EU elites, capital, imperialism, the 1%, etc. I would like to draw attention to something else: the enormous amount of people during the pandemic who manifested solidarity and showed kindness to others.

During the lockdown, I was in the Czech Republic and witnessed the massive wave of solidarity when our government made facemasks mandatory, without actually providing them. Without waiting, Czechs began making them in their homes. Those without a sewing machine used other techniques or volunteered to help with distribution to old age homes, hospitals – anywhere they were needed. The government failed us, but we didn't fail each other; on the contrary, we bonded. Seeing videos from lockdowns all over Europe, I saw that the experience of other countries was very similar. Videos of people singing 'Bella Ciao' from their balconies give me goose bumps as have a great many videos and images of community strength and devotion.

Yes, we will have to face the second pandemic wave, the ensuing economic crisis, and climate change, but we should never forget that during all of this a massive solidarity wave continued. We can talk among each other every day about the need for change, but it will be useless without the direct participation of people constituting this solidarity wave. Let us restore our imagination by bringing these people onboard and asking them what world they want to see. I believe we can reach an understanding with them soon enough and that real change will be possible. While capitalism and the EU sleepwalks from one crisis to another, we should make sure 'that the corona crisis will help bring us into a new age of cooperation and solidarity and a realisation that we're in this together'.²⁸ Then we will no longer have to accept deforestation and other forms of degradation of nature, unfair trade agreements, inequality, and austerity, and we can rediscover our imagination together with those whose solidarity gives us hope.

NOTES

1. <https://www.fern.org/fileadmin/uploads/fern/Documents/Forest_Pledge_English.pdf>.
2. <https://www.fern.org/fileadmin/uploads/fern/Documents/Forest_Pledge_English.pdf>.
3. <https://www.theguardian.com/commentisfree/2015/oct/30/indonesia-fires-disaster-21st-century-world-media>.
4. <https://www.transportenvironment.org/news/biofuels-policies-massively-increase-deforestation-2030-study>.
5. https://ec.europa.eu/environment/forests/pdf/KH0418199ENN2.pdf, str 12.
6. <https://www.europarl.europa.eu/doceo/document/TA-8-2017-0098_EN.html#def_1_5>.
7. <https://www.guengl.eu/issues/explainers/eu-mercosur-free-trade-agreement-an-explainer/>.
8. <https://www.theguardian.com/world/2016/dec/15/justin-trudeau-interview-globalisation-climate-change-trump>.
9. <https://corporateeurope.org/sites/default/files/attachments/great-ceta-swindle.pdf>, str 5.
10. <https://www.nestle.co.uk/en-gb/media/news/climate-change-post-pandemic-world-capitalism-reset>.
11. <https://www.reuters.com/article/us-consumer-goods-deforestation/nestle-pg-say-they-will-miss-2020-deforestation-goals-idUSKBN1WC1WC>.
12. <https://www.washingtonpost.com/graphics/2019/business/hershey-nestle-mars-chocolate-child-labor-west-africa/>.
13. <https://www.ft.com/content/3ea8d790-7fd1-11ea-8fdb-7ec06edeef84>.
14. <https://diem25.org/something-remarkable-just-happened-this-august-how-the-pandemic-has-sped-the-passage-postcapitalism/>.
15. <https://diem25.org/something-remarkable-just-happened-this-august-how-the-pandemic-has-sped-the-passage-postcapitalism/>.
16. <https://www.euractiv.com/section/coronavirus/news/the-brief-was-the-no-panic-rhetoric-ultimately-effective/>.
17. <https://www.theguardian.com/world/2020/jul/15/revealed-the-inside-story-of-europes-divided-coronavirus-response>.
18. <https://twitter.com/GernotWagner/status/1237455830221496327>.
19. <https://www.aljazeera.com/indepth/opinion/coronavirus-failure-climate-failure-200318121417697.html>.
20. 'When European decision-makers – commissioners, MEPs, officials - leave office and go into lobby jobs, or when lobbyists join the EU institutions, the risk of conflicts of interest can be great, undermining democratic, public-interest decision-making' <https://corporateeurope.org/en/revolvingdoorwatch>.

21 <https://corporateeurope.org/en/a-grey-deal>.
22 <https://ec.europa.eu/commission/presscorner/detail/en/ip_20_1438>.
23 <https://www.euractiv.com/section/coronavirus/news/eu-pays-e336-mln-to-secure-astrazenecas-potential-covid-19-vaccine/>.
24 <https://m.hln.be/nieuws/binnenland/europa-laat-voormalige-topman-van-farmalobby-mee-beslissen-over-miljoenencontracten-covid-vaccins~a08ac32c/?referer=https%3A%2F%2Ft.co%2FlGxuLGJ3XK%3Famp%3D1>.
25 <https://www.right2cure.eu/>.
26 <https://diem25.org/the-much-needed-vision-of-a-post-capitalist-world/>.
27 <https://s3.amazonaws.com/supadu-imgix/plutopress-uk/pdfs/look-inside/LI-9780745343167.pdf>.
28 <https://www.dw.com/en/rutger-bregman-the-virus-is-contagious-and-so-is-our-behavior/a-52924554>.

Proposals for a Democratic Energy Programme in Turkey*

Oguz Turkyilmaz

The US and other traditionally imperialist powers, which consume the greatest part of the world's energy sources, are pursuing strategies and polices aimed at controlling all conventional sources in the world to protect their own interests and hinder other major powers' access to these limited resources. On the other hand, there are similar efforts by the Russian Federation (RF) and the People's Republic of China for similar purposes. World oil and gas reserves are concentrated in certain regions (RF, the Caucasus, the Middle East, North Africa, and Latin America) and conflicts are fanned and wars triggered to gain control over these regions. Countries such as the US, UK, and France do not bother to hide their imperial intentions; they overthrew the Libyan government, supported radical Islamic forces in the ²Syrian civil war, occupied Iraq, intervened in Latin American countries, and installed their own puppets in these areas.

Today the greatest danger faced by humanity is the global climate crisis. There is scientific consensus that rising global temperatures are caused by the widespread use of fossil fuels. The negative effects on people's lives of air and environmental pollution need to be counteracted and a limit set to the adverse effects of the climate crisis – such as droughts, rising ocean f temperatures, the shrinking of underground water resources, sudden heavy rains, floods, and drought – which endanger human beings and nature. For this two steps are of the utmost importance: First, the global temperature increase, which tends to be rapid, must be limited to a maximum level of 1.5-2 °C and, second, the share of fossil fuels in energy supply must be

* The author expresses his sincere thanks to his colleagues Mehmet Kayadelen, Orhan Aytac, Yusuf Bayrak, Olgun Sakarya, Nilgun Ercan, Prof. Aziz Konukman, Dr. Serdar Sahinkaya, and Dr. Ozan Zengin for their criticisms and contributions, and Can Ozgiresun, Dr. Yasemin Turkyilmaz van der Velden, and Prof. Gulay Toksoz for their reading of the English version.

reduced in a radical and decisive way.

Today, as resources are used up at a rate well beyond society's actual needs, WHO[1] and the World Bank[2] reports indicate how many billions of people still lack wash basins and decent kitchens. About one billion people have no access to electricity. Even in developed countries, many still lack the purchasing power to benefit from modern energy facilities.

Turkey's energy sector – an overview

According to the 2019 General Energy Balance Table of Turkey's Ministry of Energy and Natural Resources (MENR),[3] the primary energy supply has increased by half a percent and reached 144.39 Mtoe in 2019. Breaking down supply by resources, coal ranks first, oil second, and natural gas third. Fossil fuels total to 83.5%, while renewable sources makes up only a sixth – 16.5%. Import dependency is 69%, while domestic sources supply 31% of primary energy. The energy import bill was 41.6 billion USD in 2019; it will decline in 2020 due to a sharp slump in oil prices and decrease in gas prices, with energy demand remaining stable. Turkey is highly dependent on the Russian Federation, which ranks first in gas supply and leads in oil and hard coal supply, with a major share, about a quarter, of Turkey's total energy supply.

Due to the market-economy policies in force since 1980, the public presence in Turkey's energy sector has been all but eliminated. These policies were sustained by the Energy Market Regulatory Authority (EMRA), which was established in 2001. The greater part of the public-sector generation facilities have been privatised while. The public share in energy generation is now less than 20%, while the distribution and sales of electricity are completely in the hands of private companies. Due to a lack of planning, there is excess capacity of power generation and as a result, some facilities ceased operation while others were fully closed down. A couple of private sector groups together control the generation and distribution of energy. Oil is refined by two private groups, and import, distribution, sales, and marketing activities are done by a few private companies. Natural gas distribution and sales services are provided by private companies throughout the country, with the exception of Istanbul where these services are provided by the municipal gas company. Through tariff applications, EMRA aimed at maximising the revenues and profits of private companies and triggered an increase in energy prices.

The Word Bank ranks sectors, regions, countries, and private sponsors by number of project and investment commitments.[4] Astonishingly, the world leader in landing high-volume contracts is the Turkish company Limak, and four other Turkish companies, Cengiz, Kolin, Kalyon, and MNG are in the top ten. These companies, with the exception of MNG, have also been very 'successful' in tenders for privatisation of public power generation and distribution. Some private companies have been particularly favoured by the government, and they have been handed a number of major projects and contracts on a silver platter.

Energy policies in Turkey neglect public planning and control; instead they are aimed at maximising the profits of private interests. Through various mechanisms in the last three years, the government has transferred more than 110 billion Turkish Lira (TL) to private energy companies. The burden of these payments have been added to the electricity bills consumers have to pay.

Coal-based power plants constitute another case of special privileges granted to private power companies. Private companies which bought up power plants using local coal in the context of the 2013-2015 privatisation programme had committed to complete all necessary investments within two years to minimise adverse effects to environment. On the basis of a change in legislation on very dubious legal foundations, they were then granted an extension of the conversion period to the end of 2019. Some companies did not even bother with conversion at all and used the extra period as an opportunity to pollute the environment. Just before this extension expired, it was extended for another two and half years (until 30 June 2022). The extension met with strong public criticism and was vetoed by Turkey's President. The Ministry of Environment and Urbanisation (MEU) and the Ministry of Energy and Natural Resources (MENR) issued a joint decree and closed down a few power plants, vowing to ensure that necessary investments would be made to decrease negative environmental impact. But although it was very well known that the lignite-based power plants which were permitted to operate had very serious defects, the authorities neglected this and allowed them to continue to pollute the environment. Moreover, in June 2020, the closed power plants were also allowed to reopen, as if the required investments had been fully completed, which was not the case.

Rising energy prices and energy poverty

Energy bills have been steadily increasing in Turkey while energy poverty is becoming ever more serious. About a quarter of all the country's employees are not covered by the social security system, and about 57% of salaried workers survive on the minimum wage. The high electricity and gas bills represent a heavy burden for them and their families. Between January 2019 and January 2021, electricity and gas prices rose well more than the increase in the minimum wage. As of January 2021, the monthly average electricity, gas, water, and internet and phone bills of a household with 4 persons amounted to 23.70% of the minimum wage in Istanbul and 24.79% in Ankara.

On the other hand, due to the corona virus pandemic, millions of people have lost their jobs, with the official unemployed figure surpassing 10 million. Moreover, thousands of small businesses were shut down, with owners unable to pay their electricity, gas, water, phone, and internet bills. The Minister of Energy and Natural Resources said that in the first nine months of 2020, 2.6 million electricity and 600,000 gas invoices were not paid, with private electricity and gas companies cutting off supply to these consumers. More people are going to face energy poverty problems. Turkey's government, traditionally very generous to private corporations, is now consciously refusing to focus on the suffering of millions of people due to energy poverty. Those in worsening conditions due to the pandemic and economic crisis require public support. Clearly, the government should halt the cutoff of service to those unable to pay their overdue utility bills; these must be paid by the state until the resumption of normal conditions.

Power generation

Power generation has reached 94,801 MW and increased by 3.87% compared to 2019. In the breakdown of generation capacity by source in 2019, hydraulic took first place with a share of 31.84% and other renewable sources 18.93% totalling to 50.72%; fossil fuels made up 49.23%. Power consumption in 2020 has been 304.6 GWh with only a marginal 0.3% increase from 2019.[5] In the same period, the share of the different sources in power generation has shifted, with fossil fuels now making up 57 % and renewables 43% of power generated. Exaggerated demand forecasts and investment undertaken without any proper planning resulted in excess both of installed capacity and generation. However, the system needs to plan for a reserve margin between peak demand and installed capacity as well as preventing the waste of resources.

According to Turkey's 2019 Presidential Programme,[6] an installed capacity of 94,767 MW is able to generate 467 GWh of electricity, much higher than the annual demand for electricity since 2018 (300 GWh). The Programme's figure is quite close to Turkey's 2020 installed capacity, 94,801 MW. We should also note that the MENR forecasts electricity demand to be 452-515 GWh in 2030, 511-608 GWh in 2035, and 556-680 GWh in 2039, and that there are licensed power plant projects currently being constructed that will exceed 23,000 MW. Therefore, we can assume that existing capacity combined with the capacity provided by the projects now at investment stage will meet demand in the near future and in the medium term. Today there is no shortage of electricity supply in Turkey. However, the problems include, but are not limited to:

- steep increases in electricity and gas prices,
- the existence of millions of consumers who cannot pay electricity and gas bills, and billions of TL transferred from public budget to private electricity generation and distribution companies,
- private energy companies that are not repaying their loans,
- nuclear power plant projects that will increase external dependency and which may create environmental catastrophes, and
- an energy management which is pursuing policies to protect the interests of private companies, ignoring the rights and wellbeing of the majority and the most vulnerable citizens.

In a country like Turkey with a fragile economy and facing serious economic crises every seven or eight years, the blame for the squandering of resources and accumulation of idle installed capacity has to be laid squarely at the feet of:

- investors who do not bother with calculations and believe electricity prices will always be high, exchange rates stable, and the value of the TL in relation to foreign currency will not drop;
- banks and financial corporations that do not question the knowledge, experience, and management capacities of investors and do not even review the feasibility of projects they finance, assuming they are safe as long as the debtor provides secure guarantees;
- EMRA, which refuses to look at planning concepts and applications and issues licenses to every power plant project without questioning its need or whether it would increase external dependency, and
- the MENR, which assumes that demand for electricity will increase steadily by 5-6% per year and prefers the role of a silent onlooker rather than an intervening authority.

It is clearly impossible to overcome the current deepening and ever more destructive worldwide crises, by applying the existing capitalist and neoliberal policies. Solving the problem requires social programmes and policies that have a planning and social development perspective based on public ownership, public service, and social welfare aimed at meeting the essential needs of citizens and society. This is an urgent task and responsibility for all people and organisations which are on the side of the working classes. If similar movements and demands from all areas of social life come together and unite, it would be possible to overcome the forces that constantly repeat the mantra: 'There is no alternative'.

What would a democratic energy programme look like?

Left debates and efforts around building a democratic energy programme are open-ended and incomplete. New ideas, evaluations, proposals, contributions, and criticism are welcome not only from friends in the larger cities but also from people living in regions where there are problematic energy facilities and ongoing investments.

What steps would be necessary to shift the energy sector from the hegemony of private profit-making monopolies to the public sphere, to move to a low-carbon economy based on public planning and renewable energy sources, aiming at social welfare and the most efficient energy consumption along with democratic control?

First of all, we should be free to imagine the democratic energy policies and programmes we really want. And then we have to turn them into reality by establishing how their design, construction, and development would work.

A democratic energy programme would aim at undoing the neoliberal policies that have abolished labour's historic achievements, organisational capacities, and dismantled the social state for the benefit of capital, converting all public services, including education and healthcare, into commodities. Such a programme would be an inseparable component of the social, economic, and political struggle of the working classes against the capitalist forces, and would be centred on labour as the most important value in the struggle for building an equal, free, and just society and an independent and democratic country that might ultimately be able to transition towards socialism. This will require a process of widespread public debate and participatory decision-making.

We believe that the programme's cornerstones should be the following:

Public energy enterprises should play a key role in the public sector as a whole. These enterprises need to uninterruptedly supply citizens' energy needs at low cost – even when not profitable. This public perspective would result in policies that minimise losses in distribution and transmission, with savings that could be as high as 50% in some sectors through an increase in energy efficiency.

This public perspective would concentrate on projects that encourage the use of locally produced energy equipment, based on renewable resources, and would consequently increase employment, decrease dependency on imported resources, generate electricity at low cost, and support local industry by using locally made energy equipment. It would invest in the manufacturing of energy equipment, locating these plants in underdeveloped regions of the country, and thus create new jobs, directly and indirectly.

As a result of the splitting up, closure, and privatisation of enterprises occurring in Turkey since 1980, the public efficacy of all public enterprises, but especially in the fields of oil, gas, and electricity has diminished. The publicly owned oil distribution company, Petrol Ofisi, as well as Turkey Oil Refineries TÜPRAS were completely privatised; Turkish Electricity Authority (TEK) was split up, public investment for new generation facilities were limited, and most of the other public power plants were privatised. To confront this, the goals of a democratic energy strategy must be connected to industrial policies prioritising low-energy consumption, based on high-tech industries such as electronics, computer hardware and software, robotics, avionics, laser, telecommunications, genetics, nanotechnologies, and the abandonment of old, energy-intensive, polluting industries such as cement, ceramics, steel mills with arc furnaces, etc.

At the same time, there must be a major decrease in the number of superfluous shopping malls, over-illuminated buildings, and private cars instead of public transportation.

Let us imagine what government agencies would have to be established and what their roles ought to be:

In such a planned system the Energy Market Regulatory Authority would be irrelevant and needs to be abolished. The MENR, on the other hand, would be responsible for carrying out planning in cooperation with a Turkish Planning Corporation (TPC) to be created. MENR should be reorganised to carry out the required regulation, control, and auditing in all segments of energy, and would guide investments of public energy corporations.

The TPC would acknowledge that the specific needs and demands of local communities can be defined and determined at the local level more accurately than they can centrally, but at the same time it would aim to eliminate the inequality between regions as well as the unequal opportunities between citizens.

At the provincial level, Provincial Planning Departments and Provincial Planning Boards, in which municipalities and local divisions of state corporations and ministries are represented, also need to be established. In them, labour and professional organisations, universities, and consumer organisations would be represented.

In the Akkuyu Nuclear Power Plant, the Trans-Anatolian Gas Pipeline, Turkish Stream, as well as other projects, all decision-making authority has been transferred to foreign firms, with commercial contracts between two companies legitimised by ratification in parliaments. By this means commercial contracts are converted into international agreements between countries involved and are thus brought outside the control of national judiciary systems. In a democratic and rational planning system, such contracts would have to be reconsidered and all legislation and agreements detrimental to Turkey's interests annulled. We need energy projects that are not created through secret discussions behind closed doors. All procedures, meetings, discussions, and decision-making would have to be transparent, public, and accessible.

Moreover, the legal forced expulsion of people from their homes and lands for energy investments would have to reversed. All procedures and legislation which obstruct people's ability to seek redress in courts of law need to be abolished and access to the legal system simplified and made inexpensive.

Unfair support mechanisms, such as the state purchasing power from local lignite-based power plants with preferential prices over market price, which constitute a major transfer of funds to private fossil-fuel-based power plants, need to be terminated. There would also have to be an end to large subsidies to big power plants based on renewable resources – another way in which public resources have been channelled to big private companies. Supports and subsidies should be limited to small plants that really need support.

Power plants having serious adverse effects on the environment and social life would need to be closed immediately. The environmental impact analysis of projects would focus on the immediate and cumulative effects of particular projects or related projects nearby and in the same region. And the controls and audits would have to be continuous. No coal power plant should be permitted unless there is a clear social necessity for it.

Installing energy facilities on productive agricultural lands and otherwise harming agricultural areas must be prohibited. The authorities need to talk with people and understand why they oppose certain projects instead of threatening and trying to silence them.

The social rights of miners and workers in coal power plants and mines must be protected and guaranteed, while the operation of those plants which continue to pollute must be terminated. The owners/operators of coal-fired plants must install and operate $DeSO_x$, $DeNO_x$, waste water treatment systems, and solid waste/ash landfill facilities that are managed properly and in a timely manner.

★ ★ ★

Experience shows that to achieve the possible it is necessary to ask for what may not be immediately realisable. In history, change has only occurred through projection, through vision. We need to take to heart the slogan of the French May '68 quoted by Che Guevara: 'Be realistic: demand the impossible!'

NOTES

1. UNICEF, *Progress on household drinking water, sanitation and hygiene, 2000-2017*, 2019, <https://data.unicef.org/resources/progress-drinking-water-sanitation-hygiene-2019/>.
2. ESMAP, *The State of Access to Modern Energy Cooking Services*, 2020, <https://documents.worldbank.org/curated/en/937141600195758792/The-State-of-Access-to-Modern-Energy-Cooking-Services>.
3. MENR, '2019 General Energy Balance Table', 2020, <https://enerjiapi.etkb.gov.tr/Media/Dizin/EIGM/Raporlar/Ulusal_Enerji_Denge_Tablolari/2019%20Y%C4%B1l%C4%B1%20Genel%20Enerji%20Denge%20Tablosu.xlsx>.
4. World Bank, *Infrastructure Finance, PPPs & Guarantees, Featured Rankings*, 2020, <https://ppi.worldbank.org/en/snapshots/rankings>.
5. TEİAŞ – Turkish Electricity Transmission Corporation, *Electricity Transmission in Turkey*, 2020, <https://www.teias.gov.tr/en-US/electricity-transmission-in-turkey>.
6. *Official Gazette*, 27 October 2018, retrieved from Turkey Residency 2019 Programme, <https://www.resmigazete.gov.tr/eskiler/2018/10/20181027M1-1.pdf>.

Politics and Everyday Life Under the Pandemic

The Covid-19 Crisis and Socio-Economic Disruption in Europe: Threats and Challenges for Labour

Maria Karamessini

The corona crisis has shaken the world population and the global economy with its unprecedented character and intensity; a global public health crisis combined with a state-induced recession due to the mandatory shutdown of large parts of the economies throughout the world. In addition, the deep recession and disruptions caused by the pandemic have coalesced with the lingering structural problems of the global financial crisis, public and private over-indebtedness, and the continuing tendency to financial speculation and bubbles, as well as the ongoing climate crisis. This fateful conjuncture along with the new lockdowns caused by the second wave of the pandemic and the fears of a third wave are steadily transforming the Covid-19 crisis from a temporary shock into a major global socio-economic crisis of financialised neoliberal capitalism, the second in less than fifteen years.

Up to now, the labour market disruptions and their effects on workers across the globe have been unlike those of any crisis since the Great Depression. According to the International Labour Organization's (ILO) *Covid-19 Monitor*,[1] in the second quarter of 2020 the working hours[2] of all employed worldwide, wage earners and self-employed, dropped by 17.3% in relation to the last quarter of 2019, with the greatest losses recorded in Latin America, the Caribbean, and Southern Europe, while global labour income,[3] before income support measures, is estimated to have declined by 10.7% during the first three quarters of 2020 compared with the corresponding period in 2019, mostly in Latin America, the Caribbean, and Southern Asia. Last but not least, the huge employment crisis which stemmed from the economic recession generated by the lockdown has fuelled inactivity much more than unemployment in all countries across the globe, an entirely novel labour market phenomenon of the corona crisis.

This unprecedented crisis has led to an equally unprecedented policy response by governments to save the capitalist economies from collapse, much more so in the advanced economies and in countries with low public debt and great borrowing capacity from the international financial markets. To mitigate the anticipated severe socio-economic effects of lockdown and confinement measures, national governments have designed and implemented a large array of emergency economic, labour-market and social-policy measures, supported by important fiscal packages. Fiscal stimulus has been unevenly distributed worldwide between high- and low-income countries, but also across the advanced capitalist economies, including EU Member States. Unequal means with which to respond to the crisis translate into unequal capacities of state intervention and an exacerbation of economic and social inequalities between (groups of) countries and regional and geopolitical entities across the world.

As for the EU, this is the deepest economic recession in its history. Moreover, the pandemic struck the European economies before they had managed to overcome the major shortcomings inherited from the 2008 crisis, that is, the heavy indebtedness of states, firms, households, and banks and the low rates of productive investments. According to the latest Eurostat data, EU GDP contracted by 6.4% and employment by 1.6% in 2020[4] while the estimated overall loss of labour income by employees in the EU in 2020 is equal to 4.8% before and about 2% after the wage compensation provided by the various job retention schemes.[5] What is even more important is that we are unable to predict the full socio-economic effects of a pandemic which has recently entered its second wave and may well evolve into a third in the coming months. In a situation of fear of contamination, frustration created by social isolation, and uncertainty about the future, insecurity and anxiety have become pervasive in the population, further destabilising economic decisions and life.

In what follows we will consider the socio-economic effects of the Covid-19 crisis in the EU, with a particular focus on the upheaval of European labour markets and the effects of the crisis on workers and the working-age population, during the first two or three quarters of 2020, given the lack of available data for the more recent period. The paper also outlines and critically examines the policy measures that have been deployed so far at the national and European levels to curb the intensity and destructive potential of the recession. Contrary to what happened in the 2008 global financial crisis, this time all EU institutions have swiftly reacted to allow EU member countries to support businesses, jobs, and vulnerable groups and their banking systems to stay afloat and continue to provide credit to the economies. The European Central Bank (ECB) moved first, by enacting monetary and credit measures in mid-March while EU fiscal and state-aid rules were relaxed and new financial initiatives and instruments were made available to EU member countries, including the new Recovery Fund and the 'Next Generation EU' recovery plan. The risk of a second Eurozone crisis in case of inaction by the European institutions, triggered this time by Italy, after the first one provoked by Greece during the Great Recession, alongside the fear of a reinforcement of alt far and populist right forces in Europe and their accession to power in Italy, has changed the alliances of state interests and precipitated decisions at the EU level. Ironically, the remarkable and unprecedented compromise to finance the promised investments of the Recovery Fund through common European bonds issued by the European Commission would have been impossible without Brexit.[6]

In this article we attempt to gauge the danger that the corona crisis has created and is still creating for labour. We will explore the opportunities contained in the new EU policy context marked by the suspension of competition and fiscal rules and the search for a recovery compatible with the creation of a sustainable socio-economic development model aided by ample funding through the recently established EU financial instruments (Recovery Fund, new EU budget, etc.).

We first present the initial economic and employment effects of the Covid-19 crisis in Europe and the role played by the emergency measures taken at the EU level to mitigate their impact; then we critically examine the employment and social policy measures taken at the national level and the impact of the crisis on vulnerable groups and industrial relations; and, finally, we turn to the community level to discuss the implications of EU initiatives during the Covid-19 crisis for the future of 'Social Europe' i.e., the social dimension of European integration. In the conclusions we combine all these elements to explore the threats and challenges ahead for the working people and dominated social groups in European countries.

The economic and labour market effects of the Covid-19 crisis in Europe and the role of emergency measures enacted by EU institutions

The Covid-19 pandemic recession we are experiencing is a unique type of crisis, very different from the Great Recession, with asymmetric impact both between and within countries.[7] To begin with, the pandemic and the containment measures to limit its spread have caused a sharp slump in the global economy followed by a temporary rebound of the economic activity that was interrupted by a resurgence of infections and the re-introduction of containment measures in Europe and in other parts of the world.

The EU economy has been affected more than all the other regions of the world, with the exception of Latin America. In 2020, the world GDP excluding the EU is expected to contract by 3.8%[8] while the EU GDP has contracted by 6.4%. This represents the deepest output contraction of the European economy since the Second World War and is certainly much greater than the contraction that occurred during the 2008 global financial crisis when the EU GDP dropped by 4.3% in 2009 (the first dip) and by 0.8% between 2011 and 2013 (the second dip). The actual toll on the European economy taken by the corona crisis is already huge. Compared with the same quarter of the previous year, seasonally adjusted EU GDP decreased by 2.6% in the first, 13.9% in the second, and 4.2% in the third quarter of 2020, despite the rebound of economic activity in the third quarter. It also decrased by 4.8% in the fourth quarter of the year due to the second wave of the pandemic and the new series of lockdown measures taken by governments.

Fiscal stimuli and asymmetric output losses

The toll would have been much greater if more or less important fiscal packages had not been put in place in all EU countries to limit job losses and bankruptcies from the lockdown measures which halted economic activity in certain sectors and harshly disrupted the activity of others. To accommodate national policy responses by EU countries, EU institutions enacted emergency measures to suspend fiscal and state aid rules and relax monetary and credit policy in the euro area. The European Council activated the general escape clause of the Stability and Growth Pact to allow euro area countries to depart from the agreed budgetary requirements and provided them with the full flexibility under state aid rules to assist particularly affected sectors and companies. At the same time, the ECB and European Investment Bank (EIB) geared up to avoid liquidity shortages and credit contraction in the public and private sectors. The ECB expanded its asset purchase programmes of private and public sector securities and launched a new series of pandemic emergency longer-term refinancing operations; and the EIB mobilised a large amount of funds to support European firms early in the outbreak of the pandemic and then created a guarantee fund to scale up its financing, targeting small and medium enterprises in particular. Finally, to enhance EU Member States' policy responses to the social and employment crisis, the European Commission has accelerated the deployment of cohesion funds while the European Council has decided to create *SURE* (*'Support to Mitigate Unemployment Risks in an Emergency'*), a temporary loan instrument to help finance temporary lay-offs, short-term work schemes, and support measures for the self-employed across the EU. A few months later, in response to the disproportionate effect of lockdown measures on youth labour markets, the European Commission adopted a *Youth Employment Support Package,* promising at least 22 bn spending on youth employment measures to reinvigorate the Youth Guarantee adopted in 2013 at the end of the previous crisis.

Table 1: Discretionary 2020 fiscal measures adopted in response to coronavirus as % of 2019 GDP

	Immediate fiscal impulse	Deferral	Other liquidity / guarantee	Last update
Belgium	1.4%	4.8%	21.9%	3/6/2020
Denmark	5.5%	7.2%	4.1%	1/7/2020
France	4.7%	8.7%	14.2%	24/9/2020
Germany	8.3%	7.3%	24.3%	4/8/2020
Greece	3.1%	1.2%	2.1%	5/6/2020
Hungary	0.4%	8.3%	0.0%	25/3/2020
Italy	3.4%	13.2%	32.1%	22/6/2020
Netherlands	3.7%	7.9%	3.4%	27/5/2020
Portugal	2.5%	11.1%	5.5%	4/5/2020
Spain	3.7%	0.8%	9.2%	23/6/2020
UK	8.0%	2.3%	15.4%	16/7/2020
United States	9.1%	2.6%	2.6%	27/4/2020

Note: We calculate the ratio of the 2020 measures to 2019 GDP because the 2020 GDP outlook is very uncertain. The category 'Other liquidity/guarantee' includes only government-initiated measures (not central-bank measures) and shows the total volume of private sector loans/activities covered, not the amount the government put aside for the liquidity support or guarantee (the amount of which is multiplied to cover a much larger portion of private-sector activity).
Source: Anderson et al. <https://www.bruegel.org/publications/datasets/Covid-national-dataset/>.

According to Table 1,[9] the size of discretionary fiscal measures varies widely among the countries included in it. Germany, the UK, and France gave a much larger fiscal impulse to their economies than Italy, Spain, Greece, and Portugal, in addition to the measures enhancing the liquidity and facilitating the borrowing of firms. The North-South divide in fiscal policy is to some extent accounted for by the policy stance of governments but most crucially by the weight of public debt on economies.

To compare the magnitude of national responses to the Covid-19 economic shock with the size of those during the 2008 global financial crisis, we have calculated the fiscal policy stance in selected countries in 2009 and 2020 (Graph 1). The percentage point (ppt) change in the general government fiscal balance reflects both the discretionary measures of governments and the effects on public expenditure and revenues of automatic stabilisers. Most of the countries of the table have adopted a much more expansionary fiscal stance during the current crisis relative to the previous one, while Italy, Spain, Austria, Poland, and Germany were the EU countries with the most expansionary fiscal stance in 2020.

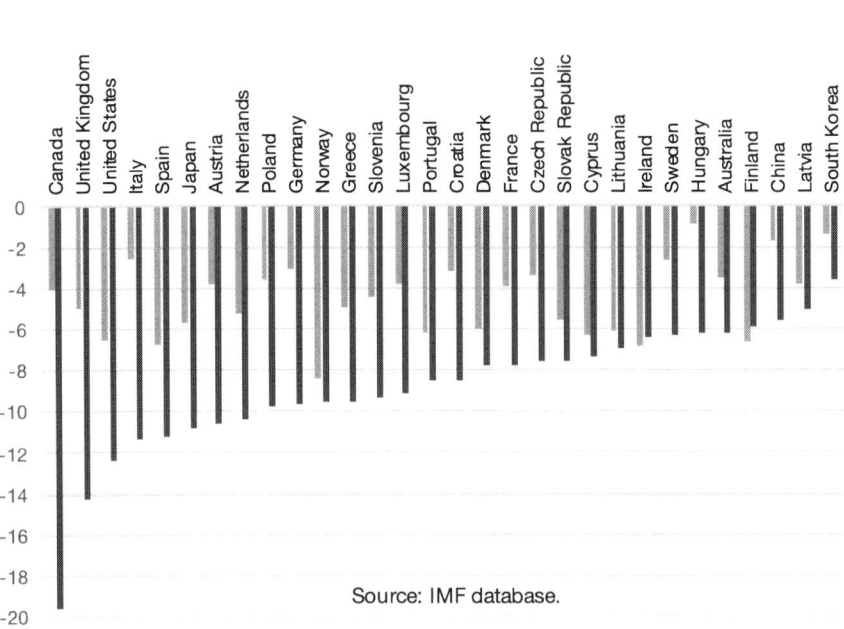

Graph 1: Change in general government overall balance (in ppt)

Source: IMF database.

Fiscal stimuli and expansionary fiscal policies have mitigated the deleterious effects of the Covid-19 crisis on the economy but have been unable to stem them. Graph 2 illustrates the latest forecasts on GDP decline in 2020 for EU Member States. Together with a few newcomers (France, Belgium, and Slovakia), the countries hardest hit by the 2008 global financial crisis

(Greece, Spain, Portugal, Italy, Ireland, Cyprus, and Croatia) will also incur the greatest output losses in the current crisis; which will foster economic divergence in the euro area and the EU once more.

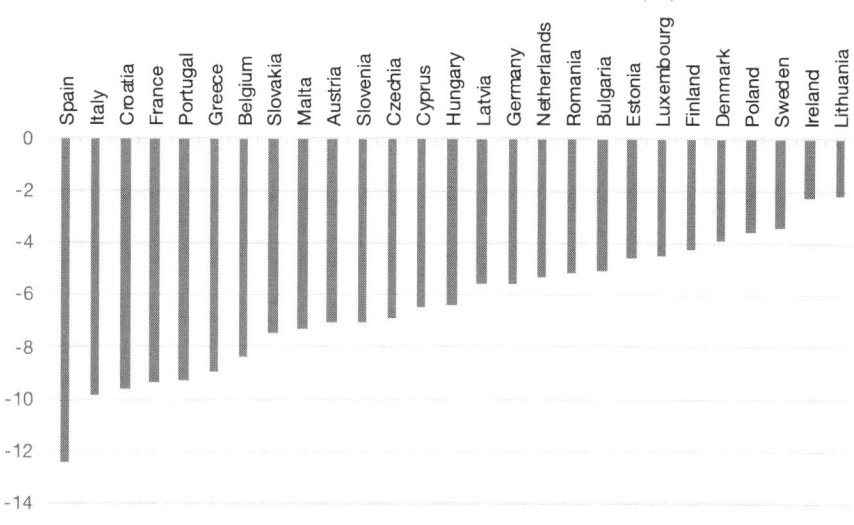

Graph 2: Forecast GDP decline in 2020 (%)

Source: European Commission, *European Economic Forecast – Autumn 2020* (Table 1, p. 1).

The magnitude of output losses by EU economies as a result of the Covid-19 crisis has not only depended on the size of fiscal stimuli and the expansionary fiscal policy of governments but also on factors such as the strictness of lockdown measures, the importance of tourism in the production system, and the quality of governance, i.e., the existing institutional arrangement whose role is to 'absorb adverse shocks'.[10] However, a longer-term divergence between euro area countries is by definition unsustainable for the survival of the European Monetary Union.

Labour market consequences

The Covid-19 crisis has provoked a labour-market upheaval around the world, with huge working-hour, job, and labour-income losses that are spreading insecurity and discouragement among the workforce and working-age populations worldwide. Total actual hours worked contracted more during the few lockdown months than during the years of the global financial crisis. They dropped by 15.5% in the EU on average between the last quarter of 2019 and the second quarter of 2020, against a 7.1% reduction between the second quarter of 2008 and the same quarter of 2013, the period of the 2008 crisis when total actual hours of work were constantly falling.

The very large reduction in actual hours worked in the EU between the last quarter of 2019 and the second of 2020 was not followed by a similar decline in employment, which contracted by 2.9% over this period. Job loss caused by the Covid-19 crisis would have been much greater if EU countries had not adopted wide-ranging policy measures to maintain activity, avoid business closures, and protect employment. Nevertheless, net job destruction was considerable and its intensity varied extensively among EU countries (Graph 3). The emphasis on job retention schemes, mainly temporary layoffs and short-time working schemes, largely explains why some of the EU countries with the highest drops in GDP do not belong to the group of countries with the greatest declines in employment, and vice versa.

Graph 3: Employment change (%) in the second quarter of 2020 (relative to the same quarter of previous year)

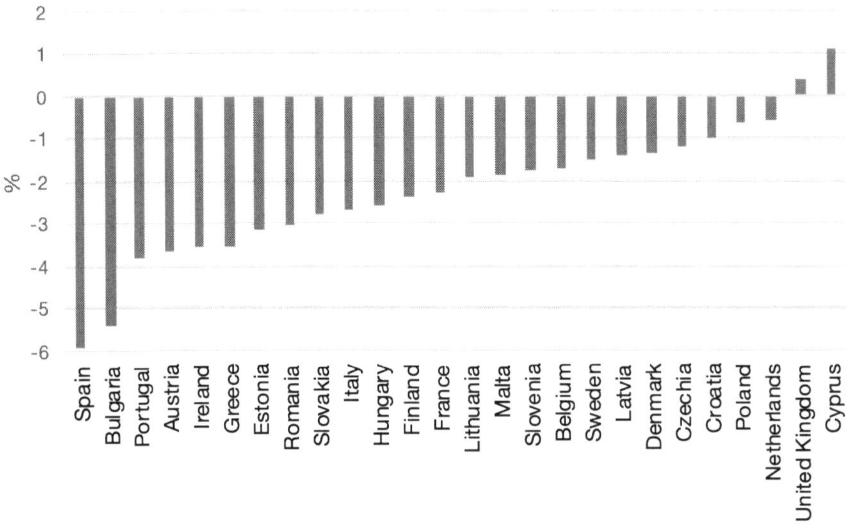

Source: ELFS, Eurostat database online.

The rebound of the economy in the third quarter of 2020 that witnessed a 11.5% rise in the EU GDP relative to the second quarter was followed by a similar increase (11.9%) in actual hours worked but also by a very timid job recovery equal to 0.9%. As a result, in the third quarter of 2020 employment was 2% less than the levels recorded one year earlier, that is, in the third quarter of 2019. The latest European Commission forecast for the annual decline in EU employment in 2020 is -2.4%.[11]

The unemployment rate in Europe almost remained stable during the first lockdowns in contrast with the US and Canada, the only OECD countries in which unemployment rose sharply. Between February and June 2020, the unemployment rate increased by only 0.3 percentage points in the EU on average. It increased slightly more during the rebound of the economy between July and October (Table 2). This remarkable resilience of the unemployment rate was determined by the relatively low rate of job destruction and the spectacular rise in inactivity rates.

Table 2: Unemployment rates (%)

	Feb 2020	April 2020	June 2020	Oct 2020
EU-27 (from 2020)	6.9	6.6	7.2	7.6
Canada	5.6	13.0	12.3	8.9
USA	3.5	14.8	11.1	6.9

Source: OECD Statistics Online <https://stats.oecd.org/>

Table 3: Inactivity rates (%)

	2019q4	2020q2	2020q3
EU-27 (from 2020)	26.5	28.2	26.8
Canada	21.0	25.4	21.7
USA	25.7	28.0	28.2

Source: OECD Statistics Online <https://stats.oecd.org/>

A remarkable and novel phenomenon of the Covid-19 crisis has been the universal increase in inactivity rates due to the decreased prospects of job searching perceived by the unemployed and those outside the labour force, in a context of employment contraction. In fact, the pandemic has reversed the long-term fall in inactivity and pulled the inactivity rate upward everywhere. The latter increased by 1.7 percentage points in the EU during the first two quarters of 2020 and returned to its previous level during the third. Canada and the USA saw even greater increases (Table 3).

From the labour market consequences described above, we conclude that the unemployment rate, as officially measured, has become a misleading indicator of the job crisis produced by Covid-19 recession. The underemployment and inactivity rates are better suited to capture the job crisis under the conditions of this unique recession.

Employment and social policy responses at the national level

There were three main 'policy innovations' in employment and social policy during the initial phase of the Covid-19 crisis meant to improve the social protection of workers:

(a) expansion of teleworking in order to minimise worker's exposure to the virus;
(b) generalisation of job retention schemes to protect employment;
(c) extension of income support to the self-employed and other non-standard workers to prevent impoverishment.

The aim of these 'innovations' was to provide health, employment, and income protection to workers and close gaps in the social protection system. However, the concrete measures also had shortcomings with regard to workers' rights, depending on the institutional context and the way they have been implemented at the national level, the involvement or otherwise of trade unions and other civil society organisations in their shaping, and the accompanying labour flexibility measures. For instance, in Greece, the new job retention schemes and working-time flexibility measures have been imposed on workers by the government without previous social dialogue. They were meant to increase employers' discretion in the use of labour power and have further undermined workers' rights in an already deregulated labour market by a host of Troika-led 'structural reforms' since 2020.

At the same time, the suspension of various workers' rights in essential activities during the lockdown phase in almost all EU countries, which has been justified by the need to cover social needs in an emergency situation, represents a real danger of backtracking on rights if these are not re-established after the end of the emergency and if the pandemic is used as an opportunity for a new cycle of neoliberal labour market reforms once the Covid-19 crisis is over.

Essential activities and labour rights

It is common knowledge that, since its initial lockdown phase, the Covid-19 crisis has been associated with differentiated economic, employment, and social effects on different sectors of the economy and groups of workers; the main divide being between activities requiring or not requiring physical proximity and mobility and the second between tasks that can or cannot be performed at home. Among the sectors whose operation requires physical proximity and mobility some were considered 'essential activities' (health and social care, agriculture, production and distribution of food and drugs, utilities, transport and logistics, public administration, and defence), which had to continue to operate smoothly in order to ensure social reproduction, while the rest were considered either 'teleworkable' (for example, education) or 'non-essential activities' and were shut down (non-food and drug retail, live arts and entertainment, hotels and restaurants, sports and leisure, etc.). In the sectors and firms that remained open, governments, in order to protect the health of employees, established special paid care or sick leaves for the workers.

To ensure business continuity and smooth functioning and enhance the delivery of essential services many EU countries enacted exceptional measures that suspended the labour-law entitlements of workers, especially regarding working time.[12] To overcome longstanding bottlenecks in labour supply, especially healthcare, and to cope with increased demand for services during the emergency, many governments introduced temporary derogations in maximum working hours and overtime work, minimum daily rest periods, work on Sundays or public holidays, and the right to take leave. The Slovak government went so far as to suspend the right to strike of healthcare workers while Hungary imposed a ban on medical staff leaving the country. All these developments increased workloads in essential activities and put a great strain on workers, especially in the health sector.

Although suspensions of and derogations from working-time provisions in essential activities were introduced everywhere except Hungary as exceptional and temporary measures to cope with the emergency of the pandemic, there is '*a need for worker representative organisations to stay alert to the threat of the emergency situations being used to roll back labour standards.*'[13]

Last but not least, the pandemic created greater visibility and elicited increased appreciation for workers in health and care services. However, apart from the provision of exceptional bonuses or other temporary benefits by governments in eleven EU countries, only France and Hungary have permanently improved the wages and relative pay of health and care workers in these strongly feminised sectors.[14]

Teleworking and labour rights

A major change in the world of work during the Covid-19 health crisis is the unleashing of the potential for teleworking, leading to more people working from their homes than at any time since the Industrial Revolution.[15] Pre-crisis teleworking accounted for a relatively marginal share of paid labour. Just 5.4% of the EU's working population regularly worked from home in 2019 – 3.2% of employees and 19.4% of the self-employed.[16] In April 2020, a Eurofound e-survey found that 39% of all employed people in the EU – 41% of employed women as against 37% of employed men – had begun to work from home because of the pandemic.[17] Teleworkers as a percentage of all employed workers in advanced non-EU economies during the pandemic was even higher: around 50% in Australia, the United Kingdom, and the United States, and 60% in New Zealand.[18] The next round of the Eurofound e-survey, published in July 2020, provided additional information only for employees: 34% of the respondents reported working exclusively from home during the pandemic while 48% having worked at home at least some of the time, with larger shares found among women, those with tertiary qualifications, and those working in education, financial services, public administration, and other services. The survey also showed a great variation in the share of teleworkers among EU countries.[19]

Teleworking was actively promoted for public health reasons by all governments in all EU countries. However, the countries endorsed different methods and tools, from suspending labour rights to financial incentives. Greece and Hungary amended pre-existing legislation giving employers the right to introduce teleworking without their employees' consent, a clear attack on individual labour rights, while Italy allowed companies and employees to arrange teleworking without a written agreement and without a prior agreement with unions. In contrast, Belgium enabled employers to grant their teleworking employees a tax- and social-security-free monthly allowance to cover telework-related costs, while Spain expedited existing programmes to support the digitisation of small and medium enterprises.[20]

Undoubtedly, telework has saved many people's jobs during the pandemic by ensuring the continuity of economic activity and the survival of businesses and has enabled working parents to continue to work while caring for their children full-time in the wake of school closures, prohibitions on children being under the care of grandparents, and interruption of services provided by paid domestic carers. However, for many workers, telework has also been accompanied by a greater work intensity, a heavier workload, and more overtime spilling into family and personal time due to blurred work-life boundaries.[21] In fact, in the April Eurofound e-survey, 27% of respondents working from home reported that they had worked in their free time to meet work demands while 22% of those with children under 12 reported that they were struggling to concentrate on work, compared to 7% of those with older children and 5% of those with no children.[22] Moreover, in the second round of the e-survey in July, 24% of the teleworkers declared they were working during their free time, compared to 6% of those who worked only at the employer's premises or locations outside the home.[23]

Stress and fatigue have been greater for teleworking mothers than fathers because of the unequal sharing of caring duties between women and men.

In this respect, we should also bear in mind that most new measures adopted by EU countries during the lockdowns to assist working parents and carers to cope with their increased caring duties were explicitly targeted at parents whose work had not been suspended and who were not working from home (see below).

Most probably, teleworking will become more widespread post-crisis than pre-crisis, if not a dominant form of flexible working. Employers and their organisations already maintain that teleworking has increased labour productivity and can help reduce the firms' workplace investment costs, but workers also seem to have formed a positive attitude towards teleworking during the pandemic. Over three-quarters of employees in the July 2020 (second) round of the above-cited Eurofound survey indicated a preference for working from home at least occasionally if there were no Covid-19 restrictions. Their preferred way of working is a mix of teleworking some days in the week and presence at the workplace for the remaining days. At the same time, the responses of workers to the same survey warn against the dangers of teleworking for labour rights and workers' well-being if left unregulated.[24]

If teleworking is to become widespread and a dominant form of flexible working across the EU, *it is even more critical for the labour movement to insist on legal and collective-agreement provisions guaranteeing the voluntary nature of telework, the suitability of specific tasks to teleworking, the contribution of employers to the expenses involved in working from home, the control of overtime as well as equal pay, and access to training for those working remotely.* Given the blurred work-life boundaries associated with any form of work at and from home, in addition to the regulation of teleworking it is of crucial importance for unions to establish by law or collective agreement 'the right to disconnect' to protect the family and personal life and health of workers, especially female, and their right to a work/life balance.

A neglected shortcoming of teleworking in international literature and not addressed by the above guidelines for action (regulation and the right to disconnect) is the social isolation of workers. This has negative repercussions not only on the emotional health of workers but also on their ability to join unions and engage in collective action. Teleworking thus brings more individualisation to industrial relations, further eroding the collective power of unions and labour that is already decreasing.

Special parental leaves and other support for working parents

Containment measures during the lockdowns have greatly increased demands for unpaid care work everywhere for a host of reasons. Schools and nurseries were closed and facilities for elderly and disabled people often suspended, limited hospitalisation opportunities obliged non-Covid patients to remain at home, grandparents stopped being available for childcare, while the shutdown of personal care networks affected both those needing care and their close relatives, especially female family members, asked to take over caring duties from previously employed domestic care workers.

Heightened demands for unpaid care work have exacerbated the work-life balance problems of workers with care obligations and still working outside home, female workers in particular. From the very beginning of lockdowns, in most – but not all – EU countries governments have intervened with ad hoc measures to tackle the childcare problem of families where both parents needed to work outside home (extra days or greater compensation for existing parental leave, special childcare leaves, vouchers for babysitters or nursing benefits, the right to reduce working hours, etc.). Workers who started teleworking because of the pandemic were excluded from work/life balance measures although most of them continued working the same or even more daily hours at the same or greater work intensity.

The most common parental support measure across Europe was special parental leaves[25] with 20 out of the 27 EU Member States having adopted such arrangements, though with considerable variation in how the leave was paid, whether it required employer consent, and whether the jobs of those taking leave were protected. Furthermore, 20 out of 27 EU Member States opted for ensuring the availability of childcare services either only for workers in healthcare and other essential services or for all families with both parents working outside the home. Sweden is the only EU country in which schools and nurseries never closed down and the service remained available through the whole duration of the Covid-19 crisis.

Employment protection and job retention schemes

To mitigate the employment effects of the Covid-19 crisis, EU countries adopted emergency measures since its outbreak. Very few imposed restrictions on dismissals[26] but all of them subsidised job-retention schemes whose distinctive feature is that employees keep their labour contracts even if their work is suspended. Such schemes have taken three forms[27]:

- temporary lay-offs, where workers do not work at all for a period, but their employment contract is maintained and they receive a certain level of income;[28]
- short-time work (STW), where working time and wages are reduced, but the employees continue to work in the company and receive a state allowance for the reduced hours;

- *ad hoc* temporary wage subsidies, which can be used by firms for hours worked (like standard wage subsidies) as well as for hours not worked (like short-term work schemes) while wages are kept at their previous level.

All three forms were enacted during the initial phase of lockdowns. As a result, the average share of laid-off workers in all employed in the EU-27 passed from 1.5% in the first quarter of 2020 to 7.4% in the second; in the third quarter it had fallen back to 1.1%. As for STW, most EU countries either introduced new schemes or amended and expanded pre-existing ones, many of which had been initially put in place during the global financial crisis.[29] At the peak of the first wave of the pandemic, the jobs on short-time work and temporary lay-offs covered 18.4% of all employees in the EU. The coverage rate in April/May 2020 ranged from 2.3% to 39.1% among EU countries, with all Southern European countries (except Malta) and Croatia, Austria, France, Belgium, the Netherlands, and Luxembourg being the most intensive users of such measures (Graph 4). Among all EU countries, only four preferred to use ad hoc temporary wage subsidies. Estonia and Poland introduced new schemes while Ireland and the Netherlands replaced existing STW with a temporary wage subsidy scheme. Such schemes may be

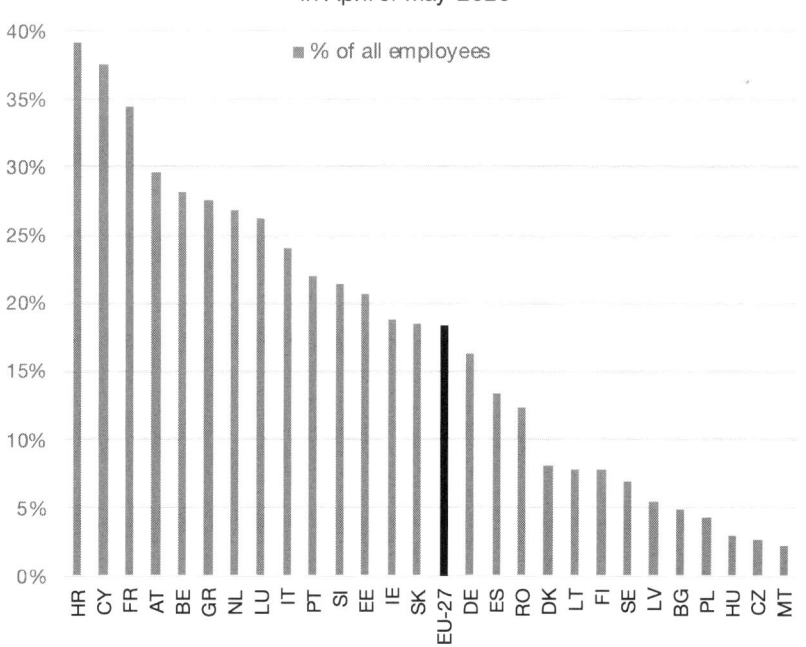

Graph 4: Employees temporary laid-off or in short-time work in April or May 2020

Source: EC, Labour Market and Wage Developments in Europe. Annual Review 2020. Table 3.1 p. 82

more flexible than STW schemes, but tend to be less well targeted (OECD 2020a).[30]

The European Commission has recently estimated the anticipated effectiveness of all job retention schemes implemented in the EU to mitigate the impact of the Covid-19 crisis on employment, claiming that 53% of the decline of this year's GDP in the EU will be absorbed by the reduction in working hours and another 15% by the decrease in labour productivity, that is, without reducing employment, while the respective shares in the 2009 recession were 30% and 28%.[31] In a similar vein, the OECD has argued that by May 2020 all job retention schemes supported about ten times as many jobs across the OECD as during the global financial crisis of 2008-9.

No one can contest the positive impact of job retention schemes in curbing the job crisis and in supporting the income of workers and households and aggregate demand in the economy. However, it should be understood that such schemes are not panaceas for stemming the job crisis. Employment was forecasted to decline by 4.5% in the EU on average in 2020 and even more in countries dependent on sectors with seasonal activity severely hit by the crisis, such as tourism. Moreover, in many countries job retention schemes may entail discrimination against non-eligible groups of workers, for example part-timers or temporary employees, and deepen inequalities between standard and non-standard workers.

Finally, although wage subsidy schemes provide full wage compensation for employees, this is not the case with temporary lay-offs and STW schemes in most countries, involving employment income loss by employees, which varies between EU countries. For instance, the replacement rate of previous wages for hours not worked in STW schemes ranges from 60 to 100%, the level in each country depending both on the generosity of state allowances and the top-ups negotiated by unions.[32] As a result, although job retention schemes are universally applied in all EU countries, the employment income of employees in 2020 is projected to shrink by 2.1% in the EU. The countries whose employees will incur the greatest losses are Croatia, Cyprus, Greece, and Ireland, while those where employees will incur negligible losses are the Netherlands, Denmark, Latvia, and Hungary.[33]

Income support to the self-employed and non-standard employees

Job retention schemes were not the only way to provide income protection along with employment protection to employees. Nearly half of EU countries improved protection by unemployment benefits, by extending the eligibility and the generosity or duration of unemployment benefits while some countries reinforced minimum-income benefit schemes and Spain, for the first time, introduced a minimum guaranteed income.

Despite these improvements, the Covid-19 crisis has revealed and accentuated the problem of social-protection gaps for workers in non-standard employment. The most innovative policy response to such revealed gaps concerns the self-employed who had more limited access than employees to social protection systems before the crisis and were severely hit by the lockdown measures and the contraction of economic activity during the reopening phase in sectors such as retail, culture, and entertainment or hospitality.

Until the end of April 2020, 19 EU countries as well as Norway and the UK had introduced measures covering the solo self-employed, freelancers, and the self-employed. Countries like Austria, Bulgaria, Croatia, Denmark, Estonia, and Italy had specifically included artists and individuals working in the creative industries who have been particularly affected by the closure of venues and cancellation of events and creative productions.[34] Spain had introduced a specific scheme to protect registered domestic workers who had stopped working because of the pandemic, while Croatia adopted an income support scheme for 'permanent' seasonal workers.[35] However, most of the schemes for the self-employed and other groups not previously protected offered a relatively low level of income protection, at or below the minimum wage rate.

It is thus no surprise that social protection offered by existing and new employment and income-protection institutions and schemes has insufficiently protected households from a fall in their disposable income, which has been all the sharper the greater the job crisis, the inadequacies of automatic stabilisers, and the holes in the social safety nets in the different EU countries. It is noteworthy that household consumption dropped by more than 10% in the first half of 2020 relative to the same half of the previous year in 19 EU countries and the UK, which indicates the difficulties their economies will face in their attempt to recover, due to the huge demand deficit thus created. Among the big EU economies, the Spanish, Italian, and French incurred the sharpest household consumption declines.

The Covid-19 crisis as an amplifier of labour market inequalities and an underminer of labour's power

Although the Covid-19 crisis is still evolving and the second wave of the pandemic has confirmed the 'double-hit scenario' that is expected to have further economic and employment implications, existing data on the first two quarters of 2020 illustrate that one of the most important labour-market consequences of the lockdown measures is their disproportional impact on vulnerable groups. This has amplified pre-existing labour-market inequalities. At the same time, the scaling back of social dialogue in most of EU countries and labour-market upheaval in a context of job crisis represent a threat and a further erosion of labour's collective power. The latter has been undermined in the past decades by falling union density and the absence of militant trade unions even in countries where unionism is still powerful.

Vulnerable workers: the greatest victims of the Covid-19 crisis

The more vulnerable workers, especially temporary, part-time and low paid workers, platform workers, the solo self-employed, and informal workers, are those who have borne the immediate brunt of the Covid-19 crisis, either by being more exposed to the virus while working in open workplaces or by losing jobs and income as a result of the lockdowns. Immigrants, young people, women, and the under-educated are overrepresented among vulnerable groups of workers, which may represent 40% of total employment in sectors most affected by containment measures across European OECD countries.[36] The heavy job or income losses by non-standard employees whose contracts were terminated and not renewed were compounded by their non-eligibility for job retention schemes and unemployment benefits in many countries. Moreover, during the lockdowns job postings and hirings were frozen; consequently, the unemployed, the young first labour-market entrants from all levels of education, and the labour-market reentrants, mainly prime-age women, were deprived of job opportunities and discouraged from looking for a job.

Despite the emphasis put on the deleterious impact of the Covid-19 crisis on the job opportunities of young people, it should be remembered that middle-aged or older people who experienced unemployment during the global financial crisis when they were younger and are now experiencing the second heavy economic crisis, may be permanently excluded from the labour market if unemployed.

The crisis has also exacerbated pre-existing gender inequalities on all fronts. It has increased women's unpaid work burden and the work/life balance problems of those working from home despite the emergency measures taken to support working parents after the closure of schools and childcare facilities and the prohibitions on letting children be cared for by grandparents. Moreover, social isolation, overcrowding in confined spaces and socio-economic insecurity increased domestic violence everywhere.[37] And, contrary to what happened in previous crises, female employment in the EU decreased more than male employment through the first three quarters of 2020 (-2% against -1.6%), since the sectors hardest hit by the

Covid-19 crisis have a higher share of women workers. Finally, female domestic workers, predominantly immigrants and working informally, stopped working during the lockdown, lost their income, and had no access to income support.

On a more positive note, the pandemic also gave visibility to women's huge contribution to social reproduction through both their paid and unpaid work. Namely, it became evident that women play a key role as workers in the health and care sectors which were so important for people during the pandemic (two-thirds of the health workforce worldwide and 90% of long-term care workers are women). They also represent the majority of teachers, cleaners, and frontline supermarket and pharmacy employees and perform the largest portion of unpaid domestic work. The greater visibility of women's contribution to the provision of services essential for social reproduction is an important side-effect of the current crisis, which provides an opportunity for the reevaluation of care work and pushing forward the feminist agenda for a recovery based on extensive social investment in a caring economy for all those in need of care and on the equal sharing of unpaid care between men and women.[38]

Marginalisation of collective bargaining and social dialogue during the pandemic – the erosion of labour's power

Big crises represent major challenges for collective bargaining, which suffered greatly during the Great Recession in Europe. In the aftermath of the 2008 global financial crisis, declining coverage accelerated in many countries – dramatically in those that introduced structural reforms undermining collective bargaining – while it remained stable in others. Bargaining coverage continued to fall steadily in the EU as a whole in the years after 2015.[39] At the outbreak of the pandemic, more than one third of EU Member States displayed extremely low rates (Graph 5).

The Covid-19 crisis brought new difficulties, problems, and challenges to the fore. It is still difficult to assess the importance of collective bargaining and tripartite and bipartite dialogue in addressing the impact of the Covid-19 crisis, since information is incomplete and restricted to the initial phase. The trade unions in the EU have generally been very active in voicing the demands of workers, negotiating for their protection at the workplace, and monitoring compliance with safety rules, while in a few EU countries (Denmark, Sweden, Germany, and Austria) they have also signed new collective agreements at the national, sectoral, or company level to implement and improve STW schemes.[40] However, according to a Eurofound study[41] even in these two areas (protection at the workplace and job retention) only 17% of all measures adopted during the initial phase of the crisis in the EU were an agreed outcome with the involvement of 'social partners'. The authors of the same study also argue that it is striking that over 50% of legislative measures taken by EU member-country governments and contained in the above-mentioned Eurofound database are *'reported to have been passed with no agreement or involvement from the social partners (other than being informed) and that social partners in a number of countries have reported a decline in their involvement as measures were rushed through the legislative processes'*.[42]

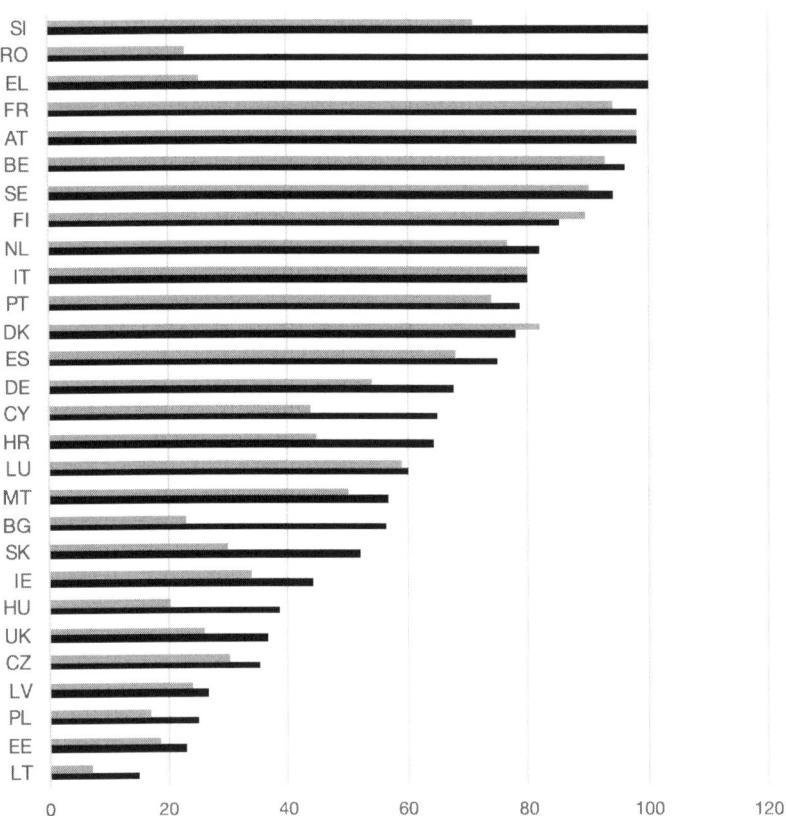

Graph 5: Bargaining coverage rate (%)

In the emergency context created by the lockdowns, the marginalisation of collective bargaining and social dialogue, the suspension of labour rights for workers who continued to work in open workplaces, rising employment and financial insecurity of workers and households, and the impoverishment of vulnerable workers have diminished the power of workers and unions to prevent the erosion of labour rights and industrial relations. This occurred mostly in countries with low union density and coverage by collective agreements. Given that the full socio-economic consequences of the Covid-19 crisis are yet to be seen, the future of collective industrial relations appears bleak, even in countries where unions seem to be still quite strong.

EU recovery, solidarity, and social policy in a post-pandemic world

The emergency measures taken at the EU level in March and April 2020 to assist member countries in their efforts to limit the economic and social consequences of the Covid-19 pandemic did not prevent the much larger effects of the pandemic on the heavily indebted Southern European economies, especially Italy and Spain, which had incurred the greatest economic and social costs during the Great Recession. The discrepancy did not only entail the risk of an unsustainable permanent economic divergence in the euro area but – primarily – the peril of a second Eurozone crisis due to the already explosive and ever-growing indebtedness of Italy, hard hit as it was by the pandemic.

To prevent a dangerous blow to the EU integration project caused by an Italian economic and political crisis and a further economic divergence of Southern Europe, the decision on the 'Next Generation EU' (NGEU) recovery plan by the extraordinary European Council meeting of 17-21 July 2020 included the establishment of a new Recovery Fund of €750bn in addition to the 2021-2027 EU budget of €1.1 tn. The funding of the NGEU would come from long-term borrowing from financial markets through the issuance of bonds by the European Commission, and funds would be allocated according to the needs of EU countries to a large extent as non-repayable grants and the rest as loans. Although the breach is stated as temporary, the above decision breaks two historic taboos of European integration: the steadfast opposition to large-scale common debt issuance and to explicit fiscal transfers between countries.[43]

There is serious criticism of the NGEU regarding its adequacy in both counteracting the economic and social consequences in the countries hardest hit by the pandemic and financing the ecological transition of EU economies. Based on barely 300 billion euros of subsidies over three years, it is far from the 2 trillion requested by the European Parliament. There is also criticism of the finally agreed balance between grants and loans, the size of redistribution between EU countries with low and high income, and the neglect of the social dimension. However, we must acknowledge that the political agreement on the NGEU signifies a qualitative turn towards more solidarity in the way of dealing with economic crises at the EU level and, more precisely, in overcoming them by investing in the future. Moreover, since the above-mentioned taboos have been breached once, the repetition, scope, and normalisation of this breach will depend on the balance of forces at the EU level.

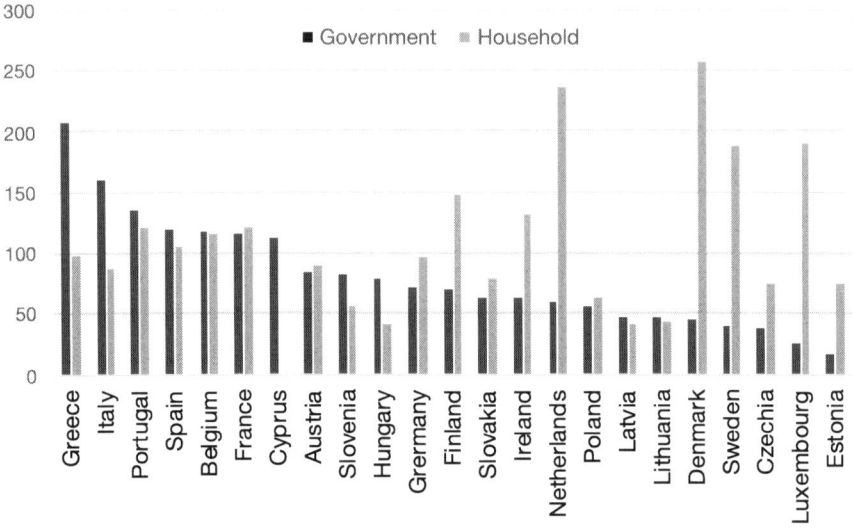

Graph 6: General government gross debt (% GDP) Household debt (% net disposable income) – 2019 or latest data

Source: EC, European Economic Forecast 2020; OECD (2021), Household debt indicator, https://doi.org/10.1787/f03b6469-en

The degree of solidarity between EU member countries expressed through their decision on the NGEU should, however, not be exaggerated for a number of reasons other than the slashing of the euro figure of grants in favour of loans in the final agreement. First, solidarity can be undermined by other measures. For instance, higher-income countries, especially those with lower public-debt burdens, can take greater advantage of the EU decision, relaxing state aid rules in order to reinforce their competitive advantage over lower-income and over-indebted countries, simply because they have more spending power.[44] Second, the funds from the Recovery and Resilience Facility (RRF) do not cover the immediate financial needs of EU member countries to provide assistance to workers and firms hit by the crisis while those from SURE add to the national sovereign debts. In fact, member countries are left alone to avert the labour-market and social crisis awaiting them in 2021. Third, sovereign debts are mounting fast. Debt ratios for Greece, Italy, and Portugal are expected to reach 207%, 160%, and 135% of GDP respectively in 2020 (Graph 6) and are also expected to rise in 2021 because the governments of these countries have decided to maintain large public deficits in order to offset the socio-economic effects of the ongoing crisis. Nobody knows whether, after the end of the pandemic, sovereign debts will be repaid through a return to austerity or they will be restructured, nor how and to what extent. *The great class confrontation over the distribution of the cost of state relief measures during the pandemic as well as the big battle for or against solidarity between EU member countries will thus both take place after the pandemic is over and are postponed for the time being.* The same holds for over-indebted households that will struggle to keep their homes/real estate from bank seizure. Household debt ratios in the EU are the highest in Scandinavia, the Netherlands, and Luxembourg (Graph 6).

What were the social policy initiatives at the EU level during the pandemic and what is the future of the social dimension of European integration after the corona crisis? To respond, we have to remember that the new European Commission which took office in December 2019 replaced the previous Europe 2020 Strategy by six headline strategies, prioritising among them the European Green Deal (EGD) and the Digital Strategy (DS) meant to ensure the transition to a 'fair, climate neutral and digital Europe'. The pursuit of social fairness was integrated both into the EGD through the aim of a just transition to a carbon-neutral economy and the establishment of the Just Transition Mechanism, as well as into the DS with the proposal for the establishment of social security benefits for platform workers, the review of the EU occupational safety and health strategy, and other initiatives for closing the digital skills gaps among workers and other social groups.[45]

Despite sharp criticisms of the EGD from a radical socio-ecological transformation perspective,[46] the EU's two strategic priorities have opened up new fields for mainstreaming employment and social-policy goals in environmental and digital strategies and policies at the national and EU levels, given that the recent RRF guidelines are under construction and the EU Member States are still finalising their national Recovery and Resilience Plans with the requirement of respecting a minimum allocation of 37% of expenditures to climate and 20% to the digital transition, and contributing to seven EU 'flagship initiatives', each of which sets targets for 2025 or 2030.

In the EU headline strategy 'An Economy That Works for People' announced by von der Leyen in December 2019, a strategy that incorporates all EU employment and social policy goals, the European Commission has included the following main components: an Action Plan to implement the European Pillar of Social Rights, a new Gender Equality Strategy, the full implementation of the 2019 Work-Life Balance Directive, a European Child Guarantee, a European Unemployment Benefit Reinsurance Scheme, and a legal instrument on Fair Minimum Wages.

The Covid-19 outbreak has ushered in the emergency measures at the EU-level described above, including SURE and the Youth Employment Package in the fields of employment policy and social protection. At the same time, it has provided the basis and arguments in favour of a further extension of EU healthcare competences and of an EU initiative on long-term care, given that the pandemic has revealed 'the dark side of long-term care provision i.e., the situation of institutional long-term care and of informal carers'.[47] Last but not least, the Commission's recent (October 2020) proposal for a Directive on adequate minimum wages has met the strong opposition of the European employers' association and Scandinavian trade unions. Notwithstanding its lack of a clear 'decency' threshold below which legal minimum wages cannot fall, strongly criticised by the European Trade Union Confederation, and the obvious inadequacy of a European minimum wage framework to combat in-work poverty in the EU,[48] the watering down or the removal of all the binding elements of the proposed Directive would be a clear defeat for left and progressive forces in Europe.

For all the death, hardships, and insecurity it has caused everywhere in Europe, the Covid-19 crisis has also produced new threats to the project of European integration and political alliances and compromises at the EU level, which have led to previously unimaginable political decisions and policy innovations. It is difficult to know how the impact of the pandemic will play out in the medium and long run as regards both EU and national social policy.[49] On the one hand, the social agenda may be strengthened by linking it to the climate and digital agendas and by an insistence on the implementation of the European Pillar of Social Rights. On the other hand, after the corona crisis is over, the distributional struggles over who will pay for the sovereign debts accumulated before and during the pandemic will determine whether or not social policy aims will be subordinated to fiscal consolidation goals. A new cycle of austerity, after the one following the global financial crisis, is very likely. It would entail a new series of attacks on the welfare state and labour rights in the EU, especially in the overindebted Southern periphery, as well as in France and Belgium, and – this time – might prove fatal for the continuity of the European integration project. This is why the debate on the partial cancellation of sovereign debts has already begun and is going to escalate in coming years.[50]

Epilogue

Our analysis has shown that the deepest recession in the EU's economic history has so far not led to a significant rise in unemployment due to an unprecedented policy response at the national levels. To curtail redundancies, national governments have forcefully promoted temporary layoffs, short-time work, wage subsidy schemes, and teleworking to cushion the impact of the economic shock on employment primarily by reducing working hours and secondarily by incentivising labour hoarding. At the same time, many more individuals than those forced into redundancies have, at least temporarily, withdrawn from the labour market because of the lack of job opportunities, pushing unemployment rates downward and inactivity rates, that is, hidden unemployment, upward. This cannot continue forever, but international organisations have repeatedly warned national governments worldwide not to withdraw job retention schemes and other income support measures before recovery is re-established after the end of the pandemic.

Policy interventions to cushion the effects of the crisis have been wide-ranging in all EU countries. However, in most of them they have also entailed a greater or lesser curtailment of labour rights, including wage cuts, for the workers involved, while collective bargaining and social dialogue have clearly receded and industrial relations deteriorated in many countries during the lockdown phase and beyond. Moreover, the measures put in place to protect incomes and jobs have provided less coverage and protection for the most vulnerable groups of workers, despite efforts to upgrade income support for non-standard workers, especially the self-employed. In similar fashion, the Covid-19 economic crisis has exacerbated gender inequalities in paid and unpaid work, has taken the greatest toll on women, youth, and migrants, and has widened inequalities between EU countries due to its asymmetrical effects on their economies and the economies' differing fiscal capacities to respond to the crisis. Southern economies were harder hit, just as in the global financial crisis.

The Covid-19 crisis has threatened the labour movement as well as opened the possibility of it meeting new challenges. The biggest threat comes from the further destabilising effects the second wave of the virus might have on European labour markets, due to shutdowns of entire sectors and local economies. This time it will be more difficult to hold back redundancies, avoid deterioration in labour rights and further erosion of union power, and keep collective bargaining and social dialogue alive. Preventing the negative consequences of the second wave on the economies and societies as well as preparing the recovery require a timely European contribution, that is, financial support for protective national policy measures, especially to EU countries with the greatest problems and heaviest public debt. Although the emergency measures of March and April 2020 and the political agreement on the NGEU constitute a turning point in the way EU institutions deal with economic crises, the NGEU funds will not begin to become available before mid-2021 while the available funds from SURE are loans that add to sovereign debts.

The second threat comes from the risk of policy reversal at the EU-level in the name of re-establishing fiscal credibility, repeating in 2022 the 2010 turn to austerity, after two years of expansionary fiscal policies that had been implemented in the wake of the 2008 global financial crisis. Although the EU economic governance framework is currently under review to allow for more flexibility in EU fiscal rules while, since the beginning of the pandemic, a host of emergency measures have been taken at the EU level and various financial instruments have been made available by European institutions to ease the fiscal pressure on member countries, there is a very great danger of a policy reversal toward austerity in the coming years.

In terms of the challenges the labour movement can hopefully meet, the biggest are: pushing for measures preventing a rise in unemployment and reducing hidden unemployment without curtailing labour rights; regulating teleworking so that it has no harmful effects on workers, unions, and collective action; increasing workers' participation in unions and strengthening collective bargaining, especially in Eastern Europe, Greece, and Ireland; increasing the relative wages of workers in essential activities; ensuring that the national recovery plans not only include public investments for 'greening the economy' but also social investments in the health and care sectors to ensure citizenship rights and promote gender equality.

The pandemic has caused hardships and spread insecurity now and for the future well-being of all European societies, but at the same time it has opened a window of opportunity for the social movements in Europe to push demands for new social rights. The national contexts are favourable because the majority of the populations have recognised the value of the welfare state, in particular the value of public healthcare and social care systems for the survival of the population and social reproduction. The EU policy context is also favourable, for the first time allowing an alignment of EU social policy with EU environmental and technology policies, which are key for achieving the green and digital transition of EU economies. It is time for the European left and progressive forces to push for a radical socio-ecological transformation of Europe. It would be tragic to miss this historical opportunity.

There is a prerequisite to seizing this opportunity. The European left and progressive forces must take the lead in advancing concrete proposals on sovereign debt cancellation across Europe, in addition to radical reforms of EU institutions and treaties, while, at the national levels, their main concern should be to assist vulnerable households in their struggle to protect their homes from bank seizures and to develop and propose socially just solutions to tackle the issue of private debt.

BIBLIOGRAPHY

Anderson, Julia, Enrico Bergamini, Sybrand Brekelmans, Aliénor Cameron, Zsolt Darvas, Marta Domínguez Jíménez, Klaas Lenaerts, and Catarina Midões, *The Fiscal Response to the Economic Fallout from the Coronavirus*, Bruegel Think Tank, 2020, <https://www.bruegel.org/publications/datasets/Covid-national-dataset/>.

Anderson, Karen M. and Elke Heins, 'After the European elections and the first wave of Covid-19: prospects for EU social policymaking', in Bart Vanhercke, Slavina Spasova and Boris Fronteddu (eds.), *Social Policy in the European Union: state of play 2020, Facing the pandemic*, Brussels: European Trade Union Institute (ETUI) and European Social Observatory (OSE), 2021, <https://www.etui.org/publications/social-policy-european-union-state-play-2020>, pp. 13-32.

Cahuc, Pierre, 'Short-time work compensation schemes and employment', *IZA World of Labor 2019: 11v2* 2019, <https://wol.iza.org/articles/short-time-work-compensations-and-employment>.

Eurofound, *Living, working and Covid-19*, Covid-19 series, Luxembourg: Publications Office of the European Union, 2020, <https://www.eurofound.europa.eu/sites/default/files/ef_publication/field_ef_document/ef20059en.pdf>.

Eurofound, *Covid-19: Policy responses across Europe*, Luxembourg: Publications Office of the European Union, 2020, <https://www.eurofound.europa.eu/publications/report/2020/Covid-19-policy-responses-across-europe>.

Eurofound, *Industrial relations: Developments 2015-2019*, Challenges and prospects in the EU series, Publications Office of the European Union, Luxembourg, 2020, <https://www.eurofound.europa.eu/sites/default/files/ef_publication/field_ef_document/ef20023en.pdf>.

EuroMemo, *EuroMemorandum 2021. A post-Covid 19 global-local agenda for a socio-ecological transformation in Europe*, forthcoming at <http://www.euromemo.eu/euromemorandum/index.html>.

European Commission, *European Economic Forecast. Autumn 2020*, Luxembourg: Publications Office of the European Union, <https://ec.europa.eu/info/sites/info/files/economy-finance/ip136_en_2.pdf>.

European Commission, *Employment and Social Developments in Europe 2020. Leaving no one behind and striving for more*, Luxembourg: Publications Office of the European Union, <https://ec.europa.eu/social/main.jsp?catId=738&langId=en&pubId=8342&furtherPubs=yes>.

European Commission, *Employment and Social Developments in Europe Quarterly Review - December 2020*, Luxembourg: Publications Office of the European Union, <https://ec.europa.eu/social/main.jsp?catId=738&langId=en&pubId=8364>.

European Commission, *Labour Market and Wage Developments in Europe. Annual Review 2020*, Luxembourg: Publications Office of the European Union, <https://ec.europa.eu/social/main.jsp?langId=en&catId=89&furtherNews=yes&newsId=9873>

European Women's Lobby, *Purple Pact. A Feminist Approach to the Economy*, 2019, <https://www.womenlobby.org/IMG/pdf/purplepact_publication_web.pdf>.

Eurostat, *Impact of COVID-19 on employment income – advanced estimates*, <https://ec.europa.eu/eurostat/statistics-explained/index.php?title=Impact_of_COVID-19_on_employment_income_-_advanced_estimates&stable=1#cite_note-4>.

Habermas, Jürgen, *Year 30. Germany's Second Chance,* Berlin/Brussels: Social Europe Publishing and the Foundation for European Progressive Studies (FEPS), 2020, <https://www.socialeurope.eu/book/year-30-germanys-second-chance>.

International Labour Organization, *ILO Monitor: Covid-19 and the world of work. Sixth edition. Updated estimates and analysis,* 23 September 2020, <https://www.ilo.org/wcmsp5/groups/public/---dgreports/---dcomm/documents/briefingnote/wcms_755910.pdf>.

International Labour Organization (2020), *Global Wages Report 2020-21. Wages and minimum wages in the time of Covid-19,* International Labour Office, Geneva. ≤https://www.ilo.org/wcmsp5/groups/public/---dgreports/---dcomm/---publ/documents/publication/wcms_762534.pdf>.

Kambouri, Nelli, *Towards a Gendered Recovery in the EU: Women and Equality in the Aftermath of the Covid-19 Pandemic,* Gender five plus (G5+) think tank, 2020, <https://f3a391c2-4245-4e49-aa95-5dc4452adce4.filesusr.com/ugd/530efa_fbea5a87a11643e6949b734c05c81e72.pdf>.

Laurent, Eloi, 'The European Green Deal: from growth strategy to socio-ecological transformation', in Bart Vanhercke, Slavina Spasova and Boris Fronteddu (eds.), *Social Policy in the European Union: state of play 2020, Facing the pandemic,* Brussels, European Trade Union Institute (ETUI) and European Social Observatory (OSE), 2021, <https://www.etui.org/publications/social-policy-european-union-state-play-2020>), pp. 97-111.

Merler Sylvia, *Next Generation EU: how does it work and what does it mean for Europe?*, London: Algebris, 2020, <https://www.algebris.com/policy-research-forum/next-generation-eu-how-does-itwork-and-what-does-it-mean-for-europe/>.

Müller, Torsten and Thorsten Schulten, 'Ensuring fair short-time work – a European overview', *ETUI Policy Brief. European Economic, Employment and Social Policy,* No7/2020, <https://www.etui.org/publications/policy-briefs/european-economic-employment-and-social-policy/ensuring-fair-short-time-work-a-european-overview>.

Moreira, Amílcar and Rod Hick, 'Covid-19, the Great Recession and social policy: Is this time different?', *Social Policy Administration,* 2021: 1-19.

Myant, Martin, 'The economic and social consquences of Covid-19', in Bart Vanhercke, Slavina Spasova and Boris Fronteddu (eds), *Social Policy in the European Union: state of play 2020, Facing the pandemic,* Brussels, European Trade Union Institute (ETUI) and European Social Observatory (OSE), 2021, pp. 53-69. <https://www.etui.org/publications/social-policy-european-union-state-play-2020>.

OECD, *OECD Economic Outlook, Volume 2020 Issue 1*, Paris: OECD Publishing, <https://dx.doi.org/10.1787/0d1d1e2e-en>.

OECD, *OECD Employment Outlook 2020. Worker Security and the Covid-19 crisis,* Paris: OECD Publishing, <https://doi.org/10.1787/1686c758-en>.

OECD, *Job retention schemes during the Covid-19 lockdown and beyond*, Paris: OECD Publishing, <https://www.oecd.org/coronavirus/policy-responses/job-retention-schemes-during-the-Covid-19-lockdown-and-beyond-0853ba1d/>.

Peña-Casas, Ramón and Dalila Ghailani, 'A European minimum wage framework: the solution to the ongoing increase in in-work poverty in Europe?', in Bart Vanhercke, Slavina Spasova and Boris Fronteddu (eds), *Social Policy in the European Union: state of play*

2020, *Facing the pandemic*, Brussels: European Trade Union Institute (ETUI) and European Social Observatory (OSE), 2021, pp. 133-153. <https://www.etui.org/publications/social-policy-european-union-state-play-2020>.

Rasnača, Zania, 'Essential but unprotected: highly mobile workers in the EU during the Covid-19 pandemic', *ETUI Policy Brief. European Economic, Employment and Social Policy*, No9/2020, <https://www.etui.org/publications/essential-unprotected-highly-mobile-workers-eu-during-COVID-19-pandemic>.

Rubery, Jill and Isabel Tavora, 'The Covid crisis and gender equality: risks and opportunities', in Bart Vanhercke, Slavina Spasova and Boris Fronteddu (eds), *Social Policy in the European Union: state of play 2020, Facing the pandemic,* Brussels, European Trade Union Institute (ETUI) and European Social Observatory (OSE), 2021, <https://www.etui.org/publications/social-policy-european-union-state-play-2020>, pp. 71-96.

Sapir, André, 'Why has Covid-19 hit different European Economies so differently?', *Policy Contribution* 2020/18, Bruegel, 2020, <https://www.bruegel.org/wp-content/uploads/2020/09/PC-18-2020-22092020-final.pdf>.

Vanhercke, Bart, Slavina Spasova and Boris Fronteddu, 'Conclusions. Facing the economic and social consequences of the pandemic: domestic and EU responses', in Bart Vanhercke, Slavina Spasova and Boris Fronteddu (eds), *Social Policy in the European Union: state of play 2020, Facing the pandemic,* Brussels: European Trade Union Institute (ETUI) and European Social Observatory (OSE), 2021, <https://www.etui.org/publications/social-policy-european-union-state-play-2020>, pp. 155-184.

Vargas Llave, Oscar, *Covid-19 unleashed the potential for telework – How are workers coping?*, 2020, <https://www.eurofound.europa.eu/publications/blog/covid-19-unleashed-the-potential-for-telework-how-are-workers-coping>.

NOTES

1. International Labour Organization (2020), *ILO Monitor: Covid-19 and the world of work. Sixth edition. Updated estimates and analysis*, 23 September 2020, <https://www.ilo.org/wcmsp5/groups/public/---dgreports/---dcomm/documents/briefingnote/wcms_755910.pdf>.
2. That is, the hours actually worked in the main job.
3. Which includes the wages of employees and a part of the income of the self-employed.
4. Eurostat, news release: Euroindicators, 23/21 – 16 February 2021, <https://ec.europa.eu/eurostat/documents/portlet_file_entry/2995521/2-16022021-AP-EN.pdf/eb164095-6de4-a6a1-cd87-60c4a645e5e1>.
5. European Commission, *Employment and Social Developments in Europe 2020. Leaving no one behind and striving for more*, Luxembourg: Publications Office of the European Union, <https://ec.europa.eu/social/main.jsp?catId=738&langId=en&pubId=8342&furtherPubs=yes>.
6. Jürgen Habermas, *Year 30. Germany's Second Chance,* Berlin/Brussels: Social Europe Publishing and the Foundation for European Progressive Studies (FEPS), 2020, <https://www.socialeurope.eu/book/year-30-germanys-second-chance>, p. 4.
7. Amilcar Moreira and Rod Hick, 'Covid-19, the Great Recession and social policy: Is this time different?', *Social Policy Administration* 2021: 1-19.

8   European Commission, *European Economic Forecast. Autumn 2020*, Luxembourg: Publications Office of the European Union, <https://ec.europa.eu/info/sites/info/files/economy-finance/ip136_en_2.pdf>.

9   Julia Anderson, Enrico Bergamini, Sybrand Brekelmans, Aliénor Cameron, Zsolt Darvas, Marta Domínguez Jíménez, Klaas Lenaerts, Catarina Midões (2020), *The Fiscal Response to the Economic Fallout from the Coronavirus*, Bruegel Think Tank, 2020, <https://www.bruegel.org/publications/datasets/Covid-national-dataset/>.

10 André Sapir (2020), 'Why has Covid-19 hit different European Economies so differently?' *Policy Contribution* 2020/18, Bruegel, <https://www.bruegel.org/wp-content/uploads/2020/09/PC-18-2020-22092020-final.pdf>.

11 By comparison with the 2008 global financial crisis, employment in the EU retreated by 1.8% in 2009 and 0.9% in 2010.

12 Eurofound, *Living, working and Covid-19*, Covid-19 series, Luxembourg: Publications Office of the European Union, 2020, <https://www.eurofound.europa.eu/sites/default/files/ef_publication/field_ef_document/ef20059en.pdf>.

13 Eurofound, *Living, working and Covid-19.*.

14 Jill Rubery and Isabel Tavora (2021), 'The Covid crisis and gender equality: risks and opportunities', in Bart Vanhercke, Slavina Spasova and Boris Fronteddu (eds), *Social Policy in the European Union: state of play 2020, Facing the pandemic*, Brussels: European Trade Union Institute (ETUI) and European Social Observatory (OSE), 2021, pp. 71-96, <https://www.etui.org/publications/social-policy-european-union-state-play-2020>.

15 Oscar Vargas Llave, *Covid-19 unleashed the potential for telework – How are workers coping?* 2020, <https://www.eurofound.europa.eu/publications/blog/covid-19-unleashed-the-potential-for-telework-how-are-workers-coping>.

16 Eurostat, ELFS, <https://appsso.eurostat.ec.europa.eu/nui/submitViewTableAction.do>

17 Eurofound, *Living, working and Covid-19*.

18 OECD, *OECD Employment Outlook 2020. Worker Security and the Covid-19 crisis*, Paris: OECD Publishing, <https://doi.org/10.1787/1686c758-en>.

19 Eurofound, *Covid-19: Policy responses across Europe*, Luxembourg: Publications Office of the European Union, 2020, <https://www.eurofound.europa.eu/publications/report/2020/Covid-19-policy-responses-across-europe>.

20 OECD, *OECD Employment Outlook 2020*.

21 Vargas Llave, *Covid-19 unleashed the potential for telework*.

22 Eurofound, *Living, working and Covid-19*.

23 Eurofound, *Covid-19: Policy responses across Europe*.

24 Eurofound, *Covid-19: Policy responses across Europe*.

25 Rubery and Tavora, 'The Covid crisis and gender equality'.

26 Italy imposed an explicit ban on all economic dismissals until mid-August, while France and Spain mandated increased oversight, France prohibiting collective dismissals in companies with more than 50 employees and Spain banning unfair Covid-19-related dismissals (OECD, *OECD Employment Outlook 2020*).

27 Eurofound, *Covid-19: Policy responses across Europe*; OECD; *OECD Employment Outlook*.

28 In official statistics, layoffs are classified as the temporary absence of employed persons from work, if they have an assurance of returning within a period of three months or receive 50% of their wage or salary from their employer (Eurostat definition).

29. Pierre Cahuc, 'Short-time work compensation schemes and employment', *IZA World of Labor 2019: 11v2* 2019, <https://wol.iza.org/articles/short-time-work-compensations-and-employment>.
30. OECD (2020a), *OECD Economic Outlook, Volume 2020 Issue 1*, Paris: OECD Publishing, <https://dx.doi.org/10.1787/0d1d1e2e-en>.
31. European Commission, *Employment and Social Developments in Europe 2020*, <https://ec.europa.eu/social/main.jsp?catId=738&langId=en&pubId=8364>, Table 3.3, p. 110.
32. Torsten Müller and Thorsten Schulten, 'Ensuring fair short-time work – a European overview', *ETUI Policy Brief. European Economic, Employment and Social Policy,* No7/2020, <https://www.etui.org/publications/policy-briefs/european-economic-employment-and-social-policy/ensuring-fair-short-time-work-a-european-overview>; Eurofound, *Covid-19: Policy responses across Europe*.
33. Eurostat, *Impact of COVID-19 on employment income – advanced estimates*, 2020, <https://ec.europa.eu/eurostat/statistics-explained/index.php?title=Impact_of_COVID-19_on_employment_income_-_advanced_estimates&stable=1#cite_note-4>.
34. Eurofound, *Covid-19: Policy responses across Europe*.
35. Eurofound, *Covid-19: Policy responses across Europe*.
36. OECD, *OECD Economic Outlook, Volume 2020 Issue 1*, Paris: OECD Publishing, <https://dx.doi.org/10.1787/0d1d1e2e-en>.
37. Nelli Kambouri, *Towards a Gendered Recovery in the EU: Women and Equality in the Aftermath of the Covid-19 Pandemic*, Gender five plus (G5+) think tank, 2020, <https://www.genderfiveplus.com/covid19-gender-equality-eu>; and see, in this volume, Joanna Bourke, 'Pandemics and Domestic Violence'.
38. European Women's Lobby, *Purple Pact. A Feminist Approach to the Economy*, 2019, <https://www.womenlobby.org/IMG/pdf/purplepact_publication_web.pdf>.
39. Eurofound, *Industrial relations: Developments 2015-2019,* Challenges and prospects in the EU series, Publications Office of the European Union, Luxembourg, 2020, <https://www.eurofound.europa.eu/sites/default/files/ef_publication/field_ef_document/ef20023en.pdf>.
40. OECD, *OECD Employment Outlook 2020*; Müller and Schulten, 'Ensuring fair short-time work'.
41. Eurofound, *Covid-19: Policy responses across Europe*.
42. Eurofound, *Covid-19: Policy responses across Europe*, p. 13.
43. Sylvia Merler, *Next Generation EU: how does it work and what does it mean for Europe?* London: Algebris, 2020, <https://www.algebris.com/policy-research-forum/next-generation-eu-how-does-itwork-and-what-does-it-mean-for-europe/>.
44. Martin Myant, 'The economic and social consquences of Covid-19', in Bart Vanhercke, Slavina Spasova, and Boris Fronteddu (eds), *Social policy in the European Union: State of play 2020 – Facing the pandemic,* Brussels: European Trade Union Institute (ETUI) and European Social Observatory (OSE), 2021, <https://www.etui.org/publications/social-policy-european-union-state-play-2020>, pp. 53-69.
45. Bart Vanhercke, Slavina Spasova, and Boris Fronteddu (2021), Conclusions. Facing the economic and social consequences of the pandemic: domestic and EU responses', in Vanhercke, Spasova, and Fronteddu (eds), *Social Policy in the European Union*, pp. 155-184.

46 See for instance Eloi Laurent, 'The European Green Deal: from growth strategy to socio-ecological transformation', in Vanhercke, Spasova, and Fronteddu (eds), *Social Policy in the European Union*, pp. 97-111: and EuroMemo, *EuroMemorandum 2021. A post-Covid 19 global-local agenda for a socio-ecological transformation in Europe,* forthcoming at <http://www.euromemo.eu/euromemorandum/index.html>.

47 Vanhercke et al. 'Conclusions', p. 177.

48 Ramón Peña-Casas and Dalila Ghailani, 'A European minimum wage framework: the solution to the ongoing increase in in-work poverty in Europe? in Vanhercke, Spasova, and Fronteddu (eds), *Social Policy in the European Union*, pp. 133-153.

49 Julia Anderson, Enrico Bergamini, Sybrand Brekelmans, Aliénor Cameron, Zsolt Darvas, Marta Domínguez Jíménez, Klaas Lenaerts, and Catarina Midões, *The Fiscal Response to the Economic Fallout from the Coronavirus*, Bruegel Think Tank, 2020, <https://www.bruegel.org/publications/datasets/Covid-national-dataset/>.

50 See for instance the letter signed by a group of more than 100 economists, including Thomas Piketty, published by several European newspapers, calling on the ECB to cancel the almost €2.5tn of government debt that it owns or to convert it into perpetual bonds in return for higher state investment. <https://annulation-dette-publique-bce.com/>.

The Coronavirus, Working People, and Precarity: Challenges for an Exit Based on Labour

Adoración Guamán Hernández, Guillermo Murcia López, and José Miguel Sánchez Ocaña

Work, precariousness, and globalisation: the pre-corona reality

The International Labour Organization (ILO) celebrated its first century of life in 2019, commemorating it with the approval of the *Declaration on the Future of Work*.[1] The text highlighted the 'radical transformation' of the labour market caused by 'technological innovations, demographic shifts, environmental and climate change, and globalization'. There was no shortage of criticism of this diagnosis that, while still being true for a part of the planet's workers, was unable to grasp the main problems that the other part of the world workforce faces every day, engulfed by precariousness and poverty.[2]

In fact, the ILO recognised almost simultaneously, in its 2020 report on social and employment prospects in the world, that poverty and inequality are continually expanding, with employment and labour regulation unable to solve them. Beyond the challenges posed by artificial intelligence and other future scenarios, the ILO admitted that for a good part of the 3.3 billion people who work in the world, having a job does not mean the end of poverty.[3] That labour markets do not adequately distribute the benefits of economic growth is confirmed by these studies, raising the question of the dignity of the populations studied. Thus, the work-poverty link, which was broken for the social majorities of the core economies in the golden decades of the social state, has returned under the guise of the word 'precariousness'.

The now ubiquitous term 'job insecurity' is often difficult to define, even for researchers and theorists specialising in the field.[4] For example, it has been identified with uncertainty about the continuity or stability of a job;[5]

a means for employers to transfer their entrepreneurial risks to workers;[6] or with a phenomenon in which workers accept risks but receive limited benefits.[7] It is a term that Izabela Florczak has defined as 'both known and unidentified',[8] and Alberti, Bessa, Hardy, Trappmann, and Umney have described as 'nebulous'.[9]

However one understands it, we cannot forget that the Great Recession of 2008 served as a way to sharpen policies based on internal devaluation, deepening accumulation by dispossession, rapidly transferring income from labour to capital , squandering decades of conquest of social rights and expansion of public services, and breaking the old capital – labour pact. The former 'standard' worker, with a permanent full-time contract, with full social security coverage and wages protecting him/her from poverty, became a rarity in the labour market, causing some to question whether at some point it was really a 'standard' fiction'.[10]

The extension of precariousness, which has become a contemporary hallmark of labour markets, has had a multi-causal origin, which can be traced both at the supranational and state levels and from the point of view of institutional action and the relationship of forces between the subjects representing the interests of capital and labour. On the one hand, in essence, the different labour models set out in national standards have been greatly influenced by trade and investment policies, for it is still undeniable that the 'labour policy' of the International Monetary Fund and other international financial institutions have penetrated the labour laws of many countries, subverting the labour regulatory sphere starting in the 1950s, with greater momentum since the 1980s through the different Washington and Brussels 'Consensuses' .[11] In addition, the trend is towards increased infringement of labour rights in trade and investment treaties and the ongoing introduction of new mechanisms such as regulatory cooperation, which opens a huge floodgate for *Lex mercatoria* ('law merchant') in the field of social rights.[12]

On the other hand, the increase in the economic power of transnational corporations (TNCs) and the development of their large global value chains[13] have also contributed to this labour scenario. Practices of decentralisation and territorialisation have affected the international division of labour, forcing regulatory competition between states and triggering a race to the bottom, functional social dumping, opacity and impunity of the activities of TNCs, and negatively affecting the creation of decent employment by limiting the ability to monitor and control adherence to labour regulations, thus effecting a drop in labour standards.[14] The pre-Covid scenario of Lex mercatoria's offensive against labour is still more complex when we additionally consider the findings of Oxfam's analysis of inequality,[15] modern slavery rates,[16] or the unpunished crimes of various transnational companies against human and natural rights.[17]

At the national level, the endless reforms were presented as solutions to a global economic crisis 'caused' by the rights won by workers in the post-war social pact. The reality of impoverished workers in 'atypical' jobs established itself, and work stopped being synonymous with emancipation and dignity, becoming a condition devoid of rights. The already eroded reality of the working class was worsened by the permanent offensive against labour – a hallmark of neoliberal policies since their model implementation in Chile. Factors such as the ongoing discrediting of the labour movement in the media, the reforms of collective bargaining, the criminalisation of the right to strike or the reconfiguration of the international division of labour and the spread of global value chains has entailed an accelerated loss of the power of unions and therefore of their ability to negotiate and act as a counter-power, at a national and international level.

The 'overcoming of the crisis' of 2008 in the workplace was nothing more than a mirage, at least in qualitative terms and from a global perspective. It is true, as the ILO report *World employment and social outlook: trends 2020* pointed out, that before the appearance of Covid-19 the recovery in quantitative terms of employment at a global level post-Great Recession occurred in some developed countries, particularly in the British and American economies, which have experienced notable increases in their employment rates. However, this quantitative recovery did not result in a qualitative recovery, and, as noted above, the ILO itself pointed to the fact that having a job most often no longer guaranteed decent work conditions or an adequate income.

One of the paradigmatic examples of this weak and tremendously unequal recovery from the effects of the Great Recession is the case of Spain, eternally suffering from structural deficiencies in its labour model, with the higher occurrence, in new jobs from 2006 to 2015, of temporary employment, night work, low wages and especially involuntary part-time work.[18]

In the so called 'recovery', those who had traditionally benefited during previous recoveries from economic crises, that is, young people, workers with low incomes or a lower educational level, saw no improvement, as they were transformed into hyper-vulnerable subjects during the Covid-19 pandemic.[19]

Before going into the specific impacts of the coronavirus syndemic, we should point out that the labour landscape was taking a particularly interesting turn in some countries, such as Spain, precisely in the months before the virus began to spread. The formation of a coalition government in 2019, for the first time in Spain's post-dictatorship history, consisting of a traditional social democratic and a left-wing party (Unidas Podemos), signalled a gradual shift towards welfare policies and a manifest desire to rebuild the social pact with its guarantees of decent work. In fact, on labour issues, the government's objectives were clear: the repeal of the labour reform of 2012 – an icon of neoliberalism – something that began with the elimination of layoffs due to numerous sick leaves, and most importantly, the drafting of a Labour Statute that would respond to the needs of a new labour social model for the 21st century.

As we will show, the presence of Unidas Podemos in the government has been decisive for the adoption of the key neo-Keynesian measures approaching the social effects of this crisis, in ways diametrically opposed to those carried out during the Great Recession.

The impact of the syndemic on the world of work: when it rains it pours

Covid-19 appeared in a reality already marked by precariousness in certain sectors and with economies highly dependent on trade, foreign investment, and labour performed under miserable conditions.

Covid-19 also exposed how superficial the presumption had been of an ever decreasing need for human labour, with the consequent transformation of the workplace. One of the main measures used by the media to depict the severity of the health crisis during both the first and second wave of Covid-19 has been the number of hospital beds occupied. But what this metonymy conveys is not only a calculation of infrastructure use, including the physical beds themselves, but a concern about the limited number of health workers and auxiliary workers in hospitals, who are absolutely necessary in facing the pandemic and whose efforts and exposure were recognised with daily applause from people's balconies during the lockdowns. Far from being obsolete or destined to disappear, given the unstoppable rise of robotisation or an absolute transformation of the workforce, workers – and the reality of human labour – have been reaffirmed during this health crisis as an absolutely essential centrepiece of social functioning.

It is not surprising that the coronavirus syndemic, which has cast its shadow over 2020 and is continuing this year, will leave behind a patently brutal balance sheet in the sphere of health but also in the economic / labour sphere, seriously affecting income and thus the capacities of citizens to live dignified lives. Current data on the tremendously affected workforce indicates a global and unprecedented impact on employment. According to the ILO's January 2021 analysis,[20] in the second quarter of 2020 there was a reduction in working hours of around 18.2 per cent (equivalent to 525 million full-time jobs). These estimates are greater for lower and middle-income countries, where the percentage of hours lost reached 29.0 percent for the same quarter. The estimates for the end of 2020 were expected to be worse as the spread of the virus and its management have evolved.

By sectors, the most affected are food and accommodation services, manufacturing industries, wholesale and retail trade, real-estate activities, and administrative and commercial activities. These sectors employ 1.25 billion people worldwide, or almost 38% of the world's workforce. These are labour-intensive sectors with high rates of precarious employment, very low wages, and informality. In other words, these are workers who cannot cope with a drastic drop in income without falling into existential hardship. In particular, people with informal labour relations, around 2 billion according to the ILO, and most of them in emerging and developing countries, are in serious danger of having to choose between becoming infected or not getting sustenance for their families.

Thus, the pre-corona scenario was already particularly serious for the world's most vulnerable workers and the coronavirus crisis has especially impacted on them. This is due to several factors that are traditionally combined in peripheral economies but which have also begun to spread to central economies: the existence of a larger informal sector and a smaller public sector, the difficulties in teleworking, and scant provisions that governments allocate for revenue compensation measures.

The data for the central economies is equally alarming. Published studies point to a foreseeable increase in unemployment in the United States and the United Kingdom, which has already affected the most vulnerable groups such as young workers, workers with less education, and ethnic minorities.[21] In particular, the United Kingdom experienced a relatively low increase in the unemployment rate during the first wave, perhaps thanks to the launch of the Job Retention Scheme, a programme through which the British Government provided up to 80% of wages to workers unable to continue work activity due to the pandemic, as well as improved social benefits for the unemployed.[22] The lack of active workers was also noticeable, among other sectors, in health, supermarkets, and delivery services.[23]

Something similar could be observed in Australia, where the number of hours worked fell by 9.5% from April to May, with a 'rebound' effect from May to June of 3.6 percentage points, unlike previous recessions in which the decrease in hours had been more progressive; the rebound could be attributed to the Australian government's crisis response, and in particular to its JobKeeper subsidy programme for particularly affected companies in order to avoid layoffs.[24] In Canada, Covid-19 resulted in a 32% decline in weekly hours worked for workers between 20 and 64 years of age and a 15% decrease in the employment rate.[25]

In the case of Spain, Covid-19 has had a serious impact on labour, even despite instruments such as the Ruling on Temporary Employment Regulation (ERTEs[26]), which we will address below. As Raquel Llorente argues,[27] the syndemic is having especially negative effects on vulnerable groups such as young people or new entrants in the unemployment rolls, unemployed workers without the right to these benefits, or those who have them to a limited degree, and workers over 45 years of age. Other forecasts of the pandemic's economic impact have emphasised the unequal weight of industry in various autonomous communities,[28] anticipating a greater effect in sectors more dependent on the hotel and restaurant industry but also where vehicle manufacturing had significant weight due to the closure of production plants and the carry-over effect from other sectors.[29] A report by the General Workers' Confederation (UGT) based on data collected up to March 2020 confirmed that it was the recreational activities sectors as well as construction, hospitality, and administrative activities and auxiliary services that experienced the most outflows in social security due to increased layoffs and thus increased payouts of social security benefits. But there was a notable rebound effect from April to May in the construction sector and, to a significantly lower degree, in the hospitality sector.[30]

Also of special interest is a study by Salas Nicás, Llorens Serrano, Navarro i Giné, and Moncada i Lluís.[31] It is based on a survey carried out between April and May 2020 examining in greater detail the effects of the pandemic on working people in Spain depending on their jobs and other parameters. According to the study, 37.8% of the people surveyed continued to go to work during the state of emergency, and 13.1% can be calculated to have done so with symptoms, with this last percentage increasing to 18,2% in the case of workers whose salary did not cover their basic needs Alongside the health sectors, most of the people affected worked at grocery stores or supermarkets, construction, sanitation, or home delivery companies.

In addition, the people who went to work without the necessary protective measures exceeded 70% of those working and were located in the same sectors. Teleworking was only possible for 30.1% of the workers. Job loss among respondents reached 5.7%, mainly due to lay-offs but also due to non-renewal of contracts. Men were slightly more affected than women, as were manual workers compared to non-manual workers, but the difference could be seen especially in how this catastrophe was felt among young workers, with 17% of people under the age of 25 having lost their jobs. The ERTE mechanism was applied to more than one in four workers surveyed, either because they were in suspension mode or because their working hours were reduced.

From the beginning of the syndemic, the ILO, with the analysis of the impact we have highlighted, and other international organisations warned that the severity of the social impact data would largely depend on policy decisions adopted by the different governments. The crisis approach adopted by the Spanish government, and especially the Ministry of Labour, the Ministry of Social Security, and the Second Vice Presidency of the Government,[32] is an example of a socially sensitive public response.

Institutional reactions: from neoliberal adjustment to a socially oriented public response

At the beginning of 2020, Spain declared a state of emergency with the 463/2020 Royal Decree of 14 March.[33] The first of the workplace measures were put into practice two days before the formal declaration of the state of emergency. RD Law 7/2020, of 12 March,[34] guaranteed temporary disability benefits due to work accidents for people subjected to periods of isolation, either due to infection or quarantine. Following the declaration of the state of emergency, the government adopted various measures to cushion the economic effects of the health crisis on salaried and self-employed people, companies, etc.

An avalanche of government regulations has enacted measures dealing with the suspension of employment contracts and the reduction of working hours due to the ceasing of activity but also with many other areas, implemented beginning with the pioneering Royal Decree- Law 8/2020, of 17 March[35] promulgating extraordinary and urgent measures to deal with the economic and social impact of Covid-19.

While these do not involve direct intervention by the state and public entities in the economy, there are some exceptions such as the regulation of protective equipment prices. And rather than direct economic intervention, the measures arbitrate mechanisms of business flexibility and their counterparts in the form of social protection at work. Significantly, practically all of them have been negotiated and agreed upon within the framework of the social agreement between the Ministry of Labour and the most representative trade unions and employer organisations.

Below we will briefly analyse the flexibility and social protection measures that have become more important for safeguarding jobs and employment levels, while articulating social benefits and protecting people's health.

The most important measures are those related to teleworking and the increased flexibility of working time: The 17 March Law contained a series of measures aimed at maintaining work activity combined with health and sanitary measures. Given the need to prevent the movement of the population, it was adopted as the first option in terms of emergency measures, establishing the possibility of teleworking and the obligation to make working time more flexible along with the need to maintain co-responsibility in care.

The second set of measures is the Ruling on Temporary Employment Regulation,[36] which allows temporary suspension of the employment contract or reduction of the working day. The 17 March law adapted an existing mechanism in the legal system, the ERTE, in order to 'guarantee that business activity and work relationships are resumed normally after exceptional health situations'.

Along with telework, this type of mechanism, which allows the suspension of work contracts and reductions in working hours, has become the main bulwark of job retention in a good number of countries of the European Union. After two months of lockdown, one in four salaried workers in the European Union was affected by an ERTE or a similar suspension measure. Both in absolute and in relative terms this type of mechanism has been extended to the greatest number of people in France and in Italy. If the need for it was indisputable, the public indebtedness that this type of measures is entailing and the difficulties in effectively paying benefits had also to be taken into account, as was done in Spain and Italy. In fact, the debate over extending ERTEs has continued, given the second wave of the pandemic and anticipation of further waves. These mechanisms were necessary, but what also seemed clear was that they were neither sufficient nor the only solution to keep the business world afloat, which needs the implementation of other support, stimulus, and regeneration measures.

The adoption and coverage by mechanisms similar to ERTE in other countries vary considerably, and so we will briefly explain the Spanish reality so that it can be used as an example. One of the most characteristic features of this mechanism that allows the suspension of contracts or the temporary reduction of the working day is the 'express' decision procedure that involves the labour authority, unions or worker representatives, and companies. This collective representation in the adoption of measures has been particularly characteristic in France and Italy.[37]

The ruling establishes the possibility of suspending or reducing working hours due to force majeure or for economic, technical, organisational, or production reasons related to the coronavirus. Although at first the distinction between ERTEs due to force majeure and ERTEs due to economic, technical, organisational, and productive causes – both owing to the health crisis – seemed important, the truth is that the legal difference affected protection measures for companies, but not for workers. In addition, it must be kept in mind that around 90% of the rulings promulgated during the first state of emergency decreed on 14 March had a proven force majeure cause.

ERTEs due to 'force majeure' affect the company and its employees. In terms of the former, three characteristics are worth mentioning: In the first place, they allow the suspension or reduction of working hours while exempting companies from paying the corporate Social Security contributions to the Treasury Department.. Second, and precisely because of the economic advantage it brings, these ERTEs include a corporate commitment to maintain employment for six months.[38] Lastly, the formalisation procedures of the ruling are made more flexible and streamlined, both by shortening the deadlines and by generally dispensing with control reports by the Labour Inspectorate.

On the side of workers, a mechanism was activated that will ensure they receive unemployment benefits, whether or not they meet the usual requirements for accessing them (for example, how long they have contributed to the fund) and without 'consuming' their already contributed right.[39] It is important to focus on the part of the wage that salaried people lose in this situation caused by Covid-19, since the unemployment benefits only cover 70% of the regulatory base to which the workers in question were contributing. The truth is that this loss of income is a common feature in legal mechanisms present in comparative law, and that while countries like the Netherlands and Denmark provide benefits amounting to 100% of salary, countries like France, Spain, or Italy contemplate a reduction – in the best case, the provision sets the benefits at 80% of the base, as in Italy.

With the return to the workplace of workers with a suspended contract, governments such as Italy's found it convenient to permit reductions in social security contributions, which resulted in a reduction of up to 30% in contributions between 1 October and 31 December 2020 for companies in southern Italy. This measure was intended to encourage job creation in the regions of the country with the highest levels of unemployment and lowest levels of industrialisation.

Apart from ERTEs due to force majeure, those having economic, technical, organisational, or productive causes (ETOP), known as causes of an objective nature, appeared on the scene. These have constituted 10% of all ERTEs declared.

The third group of measures is a guarantee against layoffs and termination of contracts. The Spanish government has tried to articulate mechanisms to halt the termination of contracts. Among the most important are the employment safeguard clause,[40] the prohibition on firing,[41] the interruption of temporary contracts, or the extension of some fixed-term contracts such as research contracts. The measures were introduced after two weeks of the state of emergency and, although their validity was intended to go until 30 June 2020, they in effect remained in force until 31 January 2021 and subsequently were extended until 31 May 2021.

Fourth, and extremely important, the government has approved a series of measures for the specific protection of people in situations of economic and social hardship.[42] These include the following: suspension of eviction procedures, extension of rental leases, moratoriums on rents, supply guarantees, support for self-employed workers and small and medium-sized companies. The regulation contains two particularly important labour measures in the form of two extraordinary allowances for family household workers and for situations of temporary-contract terminations.

Undoubtedly, the star provision within this fourth category was the Minimum Necessary Income measure approved by the government on 29 May, with the direct aim of ensuring a level of income for people in a situation of hardship for lack of sufficient economic resources to cover their basic needs. This minimum necessary income is 5,538 euros per year, which is equivalent to 416.5 euros per month and is only guaranteed for as long as resources remain insufficient. It is thus not a Universal Basic Income, as many social groups demanded but was never the government's intention. And this new benefit has limited scope, as it is not sufficient to satisfy human needs, being far lower than the minimum wage established at a monthly amount of 950 euros by Royal Decree 231/2020, of 4 February.

Conclusions

The uncertainty generated by the unexpected appearance and evolution of Covid-19 makes it impossible to predict with certainty its social and economic effects in the near future. Nevertheless, the data examined so far shows how its worst effects have been borne by people who had already been in more unprotected situations and thus particularly vulnerable to the effects of the pandemic: young workers, those with less education and income, those with manual occupations and in the cleaning, retail and food, health, and home-delivery sectors. It is important to prioritise the groups of workers who have been more exposed to the pandemic due to poor and unprotected work conditions. Public measures ought to focus on these groups even though their cases are not publicised in the media; they are the ones most affected by the situation and who will probably continue to be so.

Since they are so exposed, taking care of their health is tantamount to taking care of the rest of the population's health.

The urgent socioeconomic measures enacted by numerous EU governments, including Spain's, to deal with the pandemic-induced crisis have been of a clear social character. We will highlight three fundamental characteristics of these social policies. First, they consist of labour policies giving flexibility to companies, while creating mechanisms that legally ensure their proper use in order to prevent fraud and abuse and massive layoffs, etc. All of this has helped contain job destruction, to a greater or lesser extent, although the very haste of government responses has been partly to the detriment of progress in labour-law protection for workers. Second, social benefits have been ambitiously applied, providing a good degree of coverage but not enough to protect the people in certain specific situations of vulnerability. And third, the governments have opted, in general, for classic legal processes based on negotiating and establishing pacts between the government, the employers, and the union, which has meant that they have slighted more interventionist tools.

Future forecasts at this time are difficult, considering the variety of locally conditioned regulatory and labour policies carried out by governments and institutions. This will certainly have its effect on future social majorities in the short and medium term, but the consequences of this pandemic for labour must also be assessed in relation to the social imagination and shifts in the 'common sense' in the perception of labour. In fact, it is already possible to say that in these months the concept of work broadly recuperated some of its former core value.

Thus, different realities have become particularly visible and palpable. For decades, attention had been called to them by social movements and unions alike: the importance of healthcare and of healthcare personnel, the importance of care and caregivers; the precariousness of salaried jobs in the care sector and the invisibility of unpaid care work; the lack of workers in sectors fundamental to life, such as agriculture when the entry of immigrants is blocked; the scant supply of basic consumer goods (such as medical supplies) as the links in global production chains are cut; the need for strong government intervention in the economy to sustain work and production structures, which has not meant a blank check to cancel business losses but, in general, has required companies to act responsibly; the awareness of the terrible situation of people whose lives are tied to the global production chains of transnational companies; the evidence of the climate crisis and the ecological emergency we face, generating more awareness of the direct link between these and daily production activities; and so on.

Regardless of the political orientation of the governments and their containment and management policies, the above-mentioned realities have made it possible to start emphasising labour reforms based on dignity, to reconstruct work as a right that is respectful of life, human dignity, and the rights of nature. In addition, earlier critiques of the shortcomings of the post-war social state must now be taken up again in proposing an alternative that does not repeat those shortcomings and is at the same time a viable option for the well-being of the social majority and our future generations. In this sense, it is essential to put certain principles on the table such as: the defence of recognition, dignity, and co-responsibility in care work, eliminating the sexual division of labour; the respect for the rights of nature and the fight against extractivism, especially in the countries of the Global South; the importance of social dialogue as a tool to forge consensus and the need to extend it to all links in global value chains; the urgent need to hold the TNCs directly responsible for the working conditions existing in all the links of their production and distribution chains; the eradication of modern slavery, including the over-exploitation of temporary immigrant agricultural labour in the central economies; and much more.

Due to the pandemic, the right to employment, decently remunerated, which was never revolutionary but essential, has regained the centrality that it lost during the years of the Brussels Consensus.

NOTES

1   International Labour Conference, *ILO Centenary Declaration for the Future of Work, Adopted by the Conference at its One Hundred and Eighth Session, Geneva, 21 June 2019*, <https://www.ilo.org/wcmsp5/groups/public/@ed_norm/@relconf/documents/meetingdocument/wcms_711674.pdf>, p. 3.

2   The *Declaration* was preceded by the report of the Global Commission on the Future of Work, Geneva: 2019, <https://www.ilo.org/wcmsp5/groups/public/---dgreports/---cabinet/documents/publication/wcms_662410.pdf>..

3   The report highlights that more than 470 million people worldwide lack adequate access to paid work or are denied the opportunity to work their desired number of hours. ILO, *World Employment and Social Outlook – Trends* 2020, Geneva: 2020, <https://www.ilo.org/wcmsp5/groups/public/---dgreports/---dcomm/---publ/documents/publication/wcms_734455.pdf>, p. 12.

4   Martin Olsthoorn, 'Measuring Precarious Employment: A Proposal for Two Indicators of Precarious Employment Based on Set-Theory and Tested with Dutch Labor Market-Data', *Social Indicators Research* 119,1 (2014), 421–441.

5   Joseph Choonara, *Insecurity, Precarious Work and Labour Markets*, Cham: Springer International Publishing, 2019, <https://doi.org/10.1007/978-3-030-13330-6>.

6   ILO, *From Precarious Work to Decent Work: Outcome Document to the Worker's Symposium on Policies and Regulations to Combat Precarious Employment*, Geneva: 2012, https://www.ilo.org/wcmsp5/groups/public/---ed_dialogue/---actrav/documents/

meetingdocument/wcms_179787.pdf; Fernando Rocha Sánchez, 'Atrapados en el tiempo: notas introductorias sobre temporalidad y precariedad del empleo en España', in Adoración Guamán Hernández and Vanessa Cordero Gordillo (eds), *Temporalidad y precariedad del trabajo asalariado: ¿el fin de la estabilidad laboral?*, Albacete: Bomarzo, 2013, pp. 21-34).

7   Kevin Hewison, 'Precarious Work', in Stephen Edgell, Heidi Gottfried, and Edward Granter (eds), *Sage Handbook of the Sociology of Work and Employment*, London: Sage, 2016, 1-72; Arne L. Kalleberg and Kevin Hewison, 'Precarious work and the challenge for Asia', *American Behavioral Scientist*, 57,3 (2013), 271-288; Christine Monnier, 'Precarious Labor', in Vicki Smith (ed.), *Sociology of Work: An Encyclopedia*, London: Sage, 2013, pp. 704-705.

8   Izabela Florczak, 'Precarious Employment V. Atypical Employment in the EU', in Jerzy Wratny and Agata Ludera-Ruszel (eds), *New Forms of Employment: Current Problems and Future Challenges*, Wiesbaden: Springer, 2020, pp. 203-14, <https://doi.org/10.1007/978-3-658-28511-1_12>.

9   Gabriella Alberti, Ioulia Bessa, Kate Hardy, Vera Trappmann, and Charles Umney, 'Foreward', *Against and Beyond Precarity: Work in Insecure Times*, special issue of *Work, Employment and Society*, 32,3 (2018), 447-457, <https://doi.org/10.1177/0950017018762088>.

10 Marcel van der Linden, *Transnational Labour History: Explorations*, London: Taylor & Francis, 2017, pp. 197-200.

11 Adoración Guamán, 'The Corporate Architecture of Impunity: Lex Mercatoria, market authoritarianism and popular resistance', *State of Power 2020*, TNI, <https://www.tni.org/en/stateofpower2020>, p. 38.

12 Adoración Guamán, 'Cláusulas laborales en los acuerdos de libre comercio de nueva generación: una especial referencia al contenido laboral del TPP, CETA y TTIP', *Estudios financieros. Revista de trabajo y seguridad social: Comentarios, casos prácticos: recursos humanos* 398 (2016).

13 According to UNCTAD data, the world's top 100 multinational companies have, on average, more than 500 subsidiaries in more than 50 countries. Ownership structure has 7 hierarchical levels (ownership links with subsidiaries can cross up to 6 borders), 20 portfolio companies with subsidiaries in multiple jurisdictions, and almost 70 entities in offshore investment centres. UNCTAD, *World Investment Report 2016: Invester Nationality – Policy Challenges*, <https://unctad.org/system/files/official-document/wir2016_en.pdf>.

14 Guamán, 'The Corporate Architecture of Impunity'; *Report of the Committee on Decent Work in Global Supply Chains: Resolution and conclusions submitted for adoption by the Conference*, Geneva, 2016, <https://www.ilo.org/ilc/ILCSessions/previous-sessions/105/reports/provisional-records/WCMS_489115/lang--en/index.htm>.

15 Oxfam, *Time to care: Unpaid and underpaid care work and the global inequality crisis*, 2020, https://oxfamilibrary.openrepository.com/bitstream/handle/10546/620928/bp-time-to-care-inequality-200120-en.pdf

16 An estimated 40.3 million people were victims of modern slavery in 2016. This figure includes 24.9 million in forced labour and 15.4 million in forced marriage. Of the 24.9 million people trapped in forced labour, 16 million are exploited in the private sector, such as domestic work, the construction industry or agriculture, 4.8 million people are victims of forced sexual exploitation, and 4 million people are in a situation of forced

labour imposed by the state. ILO, *Global estimates of modern slavery: Forced labour and forced marriage,* Geneva: 2017, <http://www.ilo.org/wcmsp5/groups/public/---dgreports/---dcomm/documents/publication/wcms_575479.pdf>.

17 Adoración Guamán and Gabriel González, *Empresas Transnacionales y Derechos Humanos*, Albacete: Bomarzo, 2018.

18 Carmelo García Pérez, Mercedes Prieto Alaiz, and Hipolito J. Simón Pérez, 'Multidimensional measurement of precarious employment using hedonic weights: Evidence from Spain', *Journal of Business Research* 113 (2020), 348-359, here 354-55.

19 David N. F. Bell and David G. Blanchflower, 'US and UK Labour Markets Before and During the Covid-19 Crash', *National Institute Economic Review* 252 (2020), R52--R69.

20 *ILO Monitor: COVID-19 and the world of work,* seventh edition, 25 January 2021 – updated estimates and analysis, <https://www.ilo.org/wcmsp5/groups/public/---dgreports/---dcomm/documents/briefingnote/wcms_767028.pdf; see also sixth edition, <https://www.ilo.org/wcmsp5/groups/public/---dgreports/---dcomm/documents/briefingnote/wcms_755910.pdf>.

21 Bell and Blanchflower, 'US and UK Labour Markets'.

22 Ken Mayhew and Paul Anand, 'COVID-19 and the UK Labour Market', *Oxford Review of Economic Policy* 36 (2020), Supplement 1, 215-224.

23 Monica Costa Dias, Robert Joyce, Fabien Postel-Vinay, and Xiaowei Xu, 'The Challenges for Labour Market Policy During the Covid-19 Pandemic', *Fiscal Studies* 41,2 (2020), 371-382.

24 Jeff Borland and Andrew Charlton, 'The Australian Labour Market and the Early Impact of COVID-19: An Assessment', *Australian Economic Review* 53,3 (2020), 297-324.

25 Thomas Lemieux, Kevin Milligan, Tammy Schirle, and Mikal Skuterud, 'Initial Impacts of the COVID-19 Pandemic on the Canadian Labour Market', *Canadian Public Policy*, 46,S1 (2020), 55-65.

26 ERTE – expediente de regulación temporal de empleo – temporary layoff scheme)

27 Raquel Llorente Heras, 'Impacto del COVID-19 en el mercado de trabajo: un análisis de los colectivos vulnerables', *Documentos de Trabajo* (IAES, Instituto Universitario de Análisis Económico y Social) 2 (2020), 1-29.

28 Francisco Pérez and Joaquín Maudos, *Impacto económico del coronavirus en el PIB y el empleo de la economía española y valenciana,* Valencia: Instituto Valenciano de Investigaciones Económicas, 2020.

29 Elvira Prades Illanes and Patrocinio Tello Casas, 'Heterogeneidad en el impacto económico del Covid-19 entre regiones y países del área del euro', *Boletín económico/Banco de España* [Artículos] 2 (2020)..

30 UGT, *Impacto del coronavirus sobre el empleo en España,* 2020, <https://servicioestudiosugt.com/impacto-del-coronavirus-sobre-el-empleo-en-espana/>.

31 Sergio Salas-Nicás, Clara Llorens Serrano, Albert Navarro Giné, and Salvador Moncada i Lluís, *Condiciones de trabajo, inseguridad y salud en el contexto del COVID-19: estudio de la población asalariada de la encuesta COTS,* Barcelona: POWAH-Universitat Autònoma de Barcelona; Instituto Sindical de Trabajo, Ambiente y Salud (ISTAS-CCOO), 2020.

32 Both the head of the Ministry of Labour (Yolanda Díaz) and the Second Vice President (Pablo Iglesias) are members of Unidas Podemos.

33 <https://www.boe.es/boe/dias/2020/03/14/pdfs/BOE-A-2020-3692.pdf>.

34 <https://www.boe.es/boe/dias/2020/03/13/pdfs/BOE-A-2020-3580.pdf>.

35 <https://www.boe.es/buscar/pdf/2020/BOE-A-2020-3824-consolidado.pdf>.
36 *Disposición transitoria primera. Limitación a la aplicación a los expedientes de regulación de empleo,* <https://www.boe.es/buscar/pdf/2020/BOE-A-2020-3824-consolidado.pdf>..
37 Tatiana Sachs, Adalberto Perulli, Adoración Guamán, Hosé Miguel Sánchez, Judith Borckmann, Lukasz Pisarczyk, and Roberto Fragale Filho, 'Regards comparés sur le droit social à l'épreuve du covid-19', *Revue de droit du travail* 4 (2020), 273-274.
38 This exemption only covered 75% of the employer contribution when the company had less than 50 workers, according to art. 24 of RD ley 8/2020.
39 This is not something new. Zapatero attempted this when he still believed, in 2009, in an alternative management of the crisis with Royal Decree Law 2/2009. Its role was to maintain and create employment. The measure involved the replacement of the unemployment benefits (having 120- and 90-day limits) already consumed for those workers who had their employment contract suspended or working hours reduced with a subsequent termination of the employment contract; or if there were two suspensions of a work contract and / or reduction of working hours; all this was processed under the appropriate EREs (mass layoff), ERTEs, judicial adjudication of the dispute, or individual termination of the employment contract for objective reasons. But the measure was temporally limited to the immediate crisis, extending to 31 December 2011 in the case of administratively or judicially authorised terminations, and to 31 October 2009 in the case of approved suspension measures (with the same terms).
40 The RD Law 8/2020, in its sixth paragraph, known as the employment safeguard clause, provided for extraordinary workplace measures tied to the company's commitment to maintain employment for a period of six months from the date of resumption of activity.
41 Despite the establishment of the ERTEs, the unions began to denounce the adoption of layoffs from the beginning of the mobility restrictions and suspension of activities. To prevent companies from resorting to terminations they allowed the ERTEs as a mechanism for contractual suspension or reduction of working hours, as Art. 2 of RD Law 9/2020 approved on 27 March, which prohibited the use of these causes to justify a contractual termination; however, the effects of this prohibition were visible from the coming into force of the RD Law and thus those who had been dismissed up to that date were outside its protection. This is a measure that the Italian government already adopted in mid-March, by prohibiting dismissals for objective reasons for 60 days, regardless of the number of workers in the company or those affected, now extending the measure until March 2021. Thus far, it has also been extended in Spain.
42 Royal Decree-Law 11/2020, of 31 March. This rule provides that in order to establish the existence of economic vulnerability as a result of the emergency created by Covid-19, the rental tenant has to be simultaneously unemployed, or receiving ERTE, or have reduced working hours due to care-giving, and, if the person is an employer when he or she is in circumstances that similarly involve a substantial loss of income. And there is a second requirement – that the rental income, plus basic expenses and supplies (cost of heating, electricity, telephone, and house ownership fees) must be greater than or equal to 35% of the net income received by all members of the family unit. These are conditionalities also applied, adapted to each circumstance, to mortgage moratoria and non-mortgage financing credit (Art.16 RDL 11/2020).

A Left Perspective on the Economics of the Corona Crisis

Roland Kulke

We surely will remember 2020 as the first year of the pandemic, which will go down in history as a turning point in the relations of humanity to nature. This does not mean that things will be any better from now on but that this year will leave traces or even scars in our self-image in terms of the environment. Since autumn 2018, Fridays for Future (FfF) reminded the elite of the old colonial and industrial powers in Western Europe that the mode in which we have been structuring the metabolism of human beings with nature is a thing of the past. FfF was indeed a turning point in how to struggle for a more sustainable way of life, but it was essentially the result of an already ongoing shift of perception vis-à-vis nature in many of the post-Fordist societies of the 'old West'. Today, many more understand that CO_2 emissions must be drastically reduced if we want to bequeath a good life to our grandchildren's generation. Uttered cautiously, it has become a kind of consensus within the broader society. This has been a good thing, but then, out of the blue, the virus came. Very few people,[1] or even institutions, were prepared.

There are two discourses about the pandemic. That of the powers that be is that we are dealing here with a 'black swan'. This is the notion that from time to time highly improbable events occur, which since they are impossible to anticipate and only occur once in a lifetime do not require common learning processes. In 2007, ironically, a broker published a book by this title discussing stock market crashes. In the media, the term was used to shield financialised capitalism from demands for structural transformation. As for the pandemic, we saw the same argument when Trump deployed a national narrative, calling the virus the 'Chinese Virus', in an attempt to shield the American Way of Life from criticism. Alternatively, there is the argument of the Bill Gates of the world who advocate pharmaceutical innovations (and not so clandestine support for this industrial sector) and thus quick technological fixes. The 'Macronista' argument in favour of shortening the value chains to 'bring back our production' uses a combination of these two narratives.

A left perspective sees the virus very differently – for us the virus and its effect are embedded in the totality of our social formation. We know that capitalism draws on two resources: labour and nature. In the central economies, the TINA principle of the 1980s focused especially on the exploitation of human capital; in the (semi) peripheries instead it focused on both but with less restrictions on the exploitation of nature, as polluting industries were increasingly 'exported' to the poorer states, while first world countries enjoyed the cheap and supposedly clean products. The last decades have seen an institutionalised crisis of the super-exploitation of these two resources: human labour and nature – both to the benefit of private capital accumulation.

We can understand the current Covid19 pandemic only if we see the wider picture of this humanity/nature metabolism.[2] It is not humans per se, but humans under the pressure of capitalism who are coming closer and closer to nature, invading nature's last free spaces and thus increasing the risk of viruses 'jumping' from animals to humans.[3] The important point here is that Covid-19 is anything but a 'black swan'. The fact that hundreds of thousands of women and men have already died from a virus that derived from bats is the logical result of capitalism structurally crossing the 'planetary boundaries'. Dramatically lowering CO_2 emissions is only one of many tasks we now face.

In discussing the many-headed-hydra of the corona crisis in Europe we must always bear in mind that this is not primarily an economic or even a health crisis per se; it goes much deeper – it is part of the crisis of this civilisation.[4] Thus, any solution that would enable our societies to avoid such pandemics in the future must be a systemic solution. In what follows, after an overview of the human costs of the pandemic in Europe up to October 2020, we will discuss the economic impact and institutional reactions to this challenge and then attempt to lay out some initial reflections on what a left answer would have to entail: a democratically planned economy for the 21st century.

The virus and the people

The virus and the gender question

No, in the pandemic we are not all in the same boat. Comparisons with historical pandemics like that of cholera offer a clue as to the circumstances under which the elite is willing to invest resources in developing pandemic counter-measures . Cholera was confronted as a social problem only because the elite depended on the services of the commoners in their homes. Therefore, cholera became a public issue. The opposite is happening today with malaria or the plague – they are categorised as Third World problems , and pharmaceutical oligopolies do not care about the fate of these 'others'.

Although the virus can spread through the air (aerosols), not everybody is equally exposed to it. The most affected are those who have to work in close proximity to others, workers in what might be called the care economy. It is therefore obvious that women are among the most affected by Covid-19. We all remember the scenes of Europeans clapping their hands at 8 p.m. every evening. In so doing we were essentially thanking women.

But women are not only taking care of others in this sector who are most exposed to the virus. They also represent the majority of cashiers in stores. In 2018, 82% of cashiers were women, and in the crisis 'they were greatly exposed since supermarkets and essential shops never stopped operating'.[5] It comes as no surprise that on 20 October 2020 Ireland announced a six-week lockdown with the exception of the health and education systems and the supermarkets – all sectors where women are over represented.

If we talk about the social results of the crisis we also must mention the steep rise in domestic violence (plus 32% in France) and of course the rise in the workload for women. Furthermore, the European Committee of the Regions interestingly points out in its annual report that women are especially dependent on public transport and provides significant data in response to the question: 'In which areas do LRAs [local and regional authorities] expect the COVID-19 crisis to put pressure on expenditure?' 71% of the official respondents note 'high pressure' or 'moderate pressure' to cut public transport in municipalities.[6]

The new geography of pain

When the last crisis hit Europe starting in 2008, the left quickly adopted the terminology of critical social scientists to describe the geography of Europe, dividing it into centre (the old D-Mark bloc, and the Île-de-France) and periphery (southern and CEE) including, when necessary, a 'semi-periphery' (for example, Northern Italy, southern and eastern France).[7] This power-related geography has given way to an unexpected new geography of pain. It is no longer GDP and industrial export orientation that indicate the location of victims. The new distribution of pain and loss is far more multi-faceted.

On 24 January 2020, France announced its first two Covid-19 cases; it was also France that recorded the first Covid-related death on 15 February.[8]

By the end of February the virus had spread to, or appeared in, various regions: Lombardy, Veneto, Emilia-Romagna, Hauts-de-France, North Rhine-Westphalia, Madrid, and Navarre. It was only on 11 March that the WHO declared a worldwide pandemic. By mid-March Europe had become the world's worst affected area with Italy the first European country to impose lockdowns. By mid-May Europeans had already lost more than 100,000 people to the virus. Even mainstream media had to acknowledge that there was a connection between capitalism and the virus as business associations often successfully, as in Northern Italy, blocked the early closing of non-essential production.[9] In Germany, meat-processing plants and farms became the hot spots. Both production systems are based on the exploitation of workers from Southern and Eastern Europe.[10] Specific travel ban exemptions were established in Germany to guarantee the availability of workers from these regions. German farmer organisations even organised air transport to bring 80,000 (!) East European workers in April and May to Germany.[11] By mid-September Europe already had a Covid-related death toll of 142,000. In October, the new geography unfortunately shifted again and suddenly the Czech Republic became one of the most affected regions. By autumn 2020 we knew that no region is safe and that the virus does not distinguish between specific varieties of capitalism. Research shows some regional patterns – some related to capitalist structures, and some not.

The logic of difference between the regions

Whether a nation has the lowest per capita availability of critical care beds (CCB), like Portugal with 4.2 per 100,000 persons, or Germany, with the highest rate, at 29.2, obviously makes a difference.[12] The interesting fact is that the availability of CCBs is not determined by the old geography of centre vs. periphery since Romania has 21.4 and Sweden only 5.8 CCBs, or Croatia 14.7 against only 6.4 CCBs per 100,000 inhabitants in the 'mother of all frugal states', the Netherlands. Lombardy is Italy's number one region for CCBs with a total of 1,000 critical care beds as against the national total of 5,100 critical care beds.

Clearly, a machine cannot alone save people. While Germany's number of beds might look fantastic, the reality is that in Germany there are not enough workers to run the respirators – the availability of healthcare personnel comes into play here. The debate on care personnel obviously brings us to the international 'care drain' geography, with healthcare workers leaving the poorer countries (in the European periphery) to earn their living in the richer nations.[13] In terms of availability of healthcare personnel, Northern Europe is clearly in much better shape. Western Europe contrasts sharply with the CEE countries (including Greece), although with weak spots in Catalonia, Madrid, as well as some of the most affected Northern Italian regions and areas in Western France.[14]

Another factor is the elderly as a share of the population, as 'in Italy, Spain, France, Ireland, Belgium, between 42% and 57% of deaths from the virus took place in care homes'.[15] But perhaps the most relevant question is not numerical age itself but the question of how we deal with it as a society, as we can see from the horrifying mass deaths in Swedish care homes. Another arch-capitalist issue is poverty, with for example Seine-Saint-Denis with the highest death rate in the Île-de-France, which is also the French region with the highest poverty rate. An OECD report showed the same for the whole of the UK.

The Economy

In terms of the economy, this crisis differs fundamentally from the last crisis that befell the world economy after the collapse of Lehman Brothers. That crisis emerged in the financial sector and was largely fought out there until the neoliberal hegemony used real-economy surplus to save the banks. Only this led to the explosion of national debts and fundamentally affected the real economy. This time things are different – the financial system had been largely unaffected at the beginning, with the evening news full of reports of new bullish stock markets.

This crisis is foremost a crisis of the service sector. Obviously, this industry is very affected by the catastrophe, but what makes this crisis special is that the service sector is its focus. The virus forces social distancing on us, and services are by definition often based on close inter-personal activity. The service sector is particularly important in our post-Fordist, more or less post-industrial societies. We find well-paid jobs in the service sector, but more often David Graeber's *bull-shit jobs*.[16] We recognise many aspects of capitalist paradise in this sector: irregular contracts or none at all, often opened to low skills (hence workers can be exchanged easily), low degree of regulation, and, most importantly, low trade-union density. Therefore what we find in the service sector is quite the opposite of a workers aristocracy.

Another factor which will have a long-term impact is that the post-2008 crisis followed a period of strength in production and commerce.[17] But the 2020 crisis was preceded by slowing production and world trade. Already in 2019 in Germany there was 'Kurzarbeit' (short-time work) started in the important electronics and machinery sector. The German car industry was already in recession in 2019 with an 11% reduction of production to the 2018 level The loss of thousands of jobs in the metal and electro industry in Germany thus began already by September 2019. An IG-Metall briefing from July 2020 states that from September 2019 to July 2020 100,000 jobs were lost in this sector alone. Jürgen Kerner, the chief treasurer of IG Metall, worried that up to 300,000 jobs in this sector might be endangered.[18]

The peculiar structure of this crisis led to the problem of countries lacking the data to take appropriate measures. Researchers used alternative data like electricity consumption in buildings or truck toll data to understand what happened. The issue of the structure of data and public knowledge will be touched on below. Researchers had been complaining about the 'privatisation of data gathering' long before google and others entered the stage.[19]

Another way in which this crisis differs from the last is that the 2008+ crisis was systemic. It was a 'textbook' capitalist crisis, based on long years of de-regulation (as Jörg Huffschmid demonstrated) and pressure on wages, forcing people to be engaged in 'privatised Keynesianism' (Colin Crouch). The current crisis came from outside the core of the economic system. As mentioned above, this crisis is rooted in the wider humanity/nature metabolism, but not strictly speaking in the system of supply and demand.

The answer to the 2008+ crisis was, in this sense, simpler because in economic terms regulation and redistribution of wealth to the working class would have been the correct response to that crisis.[20] This time the crisis cannot be solved by shoring up demand through supporting social systems and higher wages alone. No, this time the supply side is a genuine frontier of problems.

It is in fact not a neoliberal slogan that this time enterprises need direct support. The reason is that supply chains were cut and goods and services cannot be sold. The crude oil type WTI made headlines in April 2020 when 'Oil prices crashed through zero, closing out the day at -$37 per barrel, an unprecedented meltdown. […] The second quarter is "likely to be the most uncertain and disruptive quarter that the industry has ever seen", Schlumberger CEO Olivier Le Peuch, said on the company's earnings call.'[21] But throwing money at otherwise viable firms surely is not left strategy. In what follows we will put forward first tentative proposals for a left answer to these real world supply-side shocks.

Democratically planned economies as an answer to the crisis

The corona virus has proven that the capitalist, profit-driven regime has already reached its limits, both in terms of the environment and human beings. We must therefore strengthen the deliberative-planning aspects of our economies. The violation of some of the 'planetary boundaries' show that we are on the path to self-destruction. We thus urgently need a very different production and consumption model, and to achieve it we can only use democratic means. Democratic debate and planning regarding what we want to consume, produce, how we distribute the goods and services, and also where we produce them need to occur at different levels within our society.

It is not only the general environmental catastrophe that forces us to democratise our economies, but more specifically the structure of the current corona crisis. We have shown that this crisis has strong supply-side effects. It is indeed necessary for the state to support the corporate sector and therefore end up acquiring shares in companies. Following liberal ideology, especially in Germany, the state invests billions of euros in enterprises but acts only as a silent partner, without sitting on the board and influencing the firms' policies. Taxpayer revenue is used to support private firms, thus bolstering highly concentrated private property.[22] The EU member countries invest tens of billions of euros in private firms – people need to decide what to do with this sudden public ownership. This, in a nutshell, is why we need immediate debate on how we can have a publically planned economy.

This is in part a theoretical endeavour, but it is also a practical journey. In hundreds of lived experiences left, green, and progressive protagonists are active in non-profit-oriented economic entities. We call them cooperatives, social economy actors, (re-)municipalised energy producers, just to name a few. However, in most cases these actors are situated in the most local scale of societies – in villages and cities. Only rarely do they cross municipal boundaries.

Real existing alternatives to capitalist production and distribution thus exist mostly in economic niches. The municipality movement in Europe has proven to be very inspirational and effective. On the other hand it does not seem strong enough to challenge the fundamental power of capital in our societies.

For ideological reasons, many leftists even advocate concentrating only on these decentralised and small-scale solutions. The implicit slogan behind this is that *small-is-beautiful*, and that real democracy can only exist in face-to-face social structures – a kind of left-wing communitarianism.[23]

This situation poses two challenges for the radical left. On the one side, we are leaving behind an ideological vacuum. People know that long-term planning takes place – but so far only within big multinational firms and not in the public sphere. The problem is that as long as we cannot demonstrate to the public that we as citizens can actually have a democratically structured planned society, people will not believe the left's claim that truly viable macro alternatives exist.

We must ask ourselves how these macro alternatives can be realised if only decentralised lower-scale solutions are adopted. Our societies are based on materially centralised structures like the car industries, power grids, ports, or basic research facilities. These structures cannot be decentralised. We therefore must search for democratic answers to the questions of how to manage and plan these *macro* social infrastructures.

Three models of planning within the left

Fully Automated Digital Planning

The first model could be called 'fully automated digital planning'.[24] It is based on an updated version of Salvador Allende's Cybersyn project (1970-73).[25] The great attractiveness of this approach is that it uses the means of production we all have in our pockets: the mobile phones, and also the 'oil of the future', that is, data. The new technologies in data processing invalidate the strong anti-socialist argument of Mises and Hayek in the socialist calculation debate.[26] For instance, Mises and Hayek based their argument, among other things, on the lack of processing power of mid-20th-century computers. But today a mobile phone 'in your pocket has more than 100,000 times the processing power of the computer that landed man on the moon 50 years ago'.[27]

The negative side of this model is its technocratic mechanistic approach. Technical solutions can only be the starting point for collective debates and decisions. Nevertheless, the reasoning behind this position is of the utmost importance in establishing the technological feasibility of public planning.

Decentralised cooperative federalism

The second approach exists particularly in the area of energy democracy. Here especially, we find strong green/left aversion to central planning. Instead of an allegedly de-legitimised state, they want the backbone of our economies to be decentralised self-controlled entities. The idea is that we need small social circles to achieve real accountability and keep management under control. Sociologically speaking, the belief is that a real democracy can only exist in a 'Gemeinschaft' (community), not in a 'Gesellschaft' (society), using Ferdinand Tönnies's distinction. One should note that this thinking has a romantic tradition.[28] In terms of administrative science, this model attempts to overcome the principal-agent problem.

The undisputable positive effect of this approach is people's self-empowerment. This has never been more important than in late modern post-democratic times. Besides its socio-psychological effects, it has the material impact of supporting people's direct income.

The idea's more problematic side effects are that it hinders democratic development at higher scales of production and does not take on the problem of mediation through the market, that is, that goods and services are distributed via the price mechanism. The result would be that while capitalism continues to function on the regional and world levels, people's counter-power would be limited to the local level.

Old-School Technocratic Planning

In Europe from the 1960s on, we saw a debate on the democratisation of industrial societies. Industrialisation with a focus on the production of consumer and producer goods underpinned societies in Eastern and Western Europe, irrespective of capitalist or communist orientation. In the West, overall economic and investment control, further nationalisation, and democratic workers' and citizens' control were discussed. In the East, decentralisation and democratisation of the production system were discussed, along with the introduction of market mechanisms (with Ota Šik as probably the best known economist in this regard). Both debates were short-circuited by Europe's flanking powers, the USA and USSR, in their respective spheres of influence, either by indirect of direct imperial rule.[29]

We can assume that these discussions, had they had real impact, might have prolonged the *trente glorieuses* in Western Europe, while enhancing, in the East, the attractiveness of the real existing socialist model. On the negative side, for the Western European debate, we have to realise that these debates had inbuilt elitist technocratic biases, of which we still see echoes in post-Keynesian circles in the EU.

The Covid-19 crisis and the quest for a popular economy of the 21st century

By October 2020 the economic and ecological data were breathtaking. The year was the hottest year ever recorded in Europe:[30] 'CO_2, methane and nitrous oxide [in 2020 are at [...] their highest levels in at least a few million years – if not longer'[31], 'new WFP [World Food Programme] figures indicate additional 130 million lives and livelihoods will be at risk'[32], and millions of jobs will be lost in the course of the Covid crisis in the EU.

The left must move forward in developing credible real-world alternatives to an economy that has run amok. Based on the three broad discourses on planned (and more or less non-market-based) economies we must wrestle with the following questions, to cite just a few, and find answers. It would be to the credit of Europe's left if we could learn also from the experiences of Africa, Latin America, and Asia:

What macro-economic planning examples for real industry do we have in today's heterodox economics? What have been good and bad experiences with social and regional councils (prominent in West Germany in the 1970s and 80s in transforming the coal and steel industries)? How can we scale up the positive examples of cooperatives, experiences in municipalism, and networks such as 'fearless cities'? What macro-economic planning tools have been developed and implemented in recent years? An example is the Bolivarian Alliance for the Americas with the Sucre as a currency.[33] A useful entry into the debate could be the discussion on the Green New Deal within DSA/USA, or how anti-car-industry activists envision a just transition of this sector.

In many countries in the EU we already see lively political and intellectual debates on these issues.[34] To paraphrase a famous appeal: 'Camarades, un effort de plus si vous voulez être économistes!'

NOTES

1. Mike Davis, *The Monster at Our Door: The Global Threat of Avian Flu*, New York: New Press, 2005.
2. On the genesis of ecosocialism see John Bellamy Foster, *The Return of Nature: Socialism and Ecology*, New York: Monthly Review Press, 2019.
3. Roland Kulke, 'The Pandemic as Part of a Much Broader Crisis of Civilisation', transform! Europe, <https://www.transform-network.net/blog/article/the-pandemic-as-part-of-a-much-broader-crisis-of-civilisation/>, June 2020.
4. Birgit Daiber and François Houtart (eds), *A Postcapitalist Paradigm: The Common Good of Humanity*, Brussels: Rosa Luxemburg Stiftung, 2012.
5. European Committee of the Regions: *2020 Barometer of Regions and Cities*, Brussels, October 2020, p. 85.
6. *2020 Barometer of Regions and Cities*, p. 45.
7. For a good introduction see Joachim Becker, Johannes Jäger, Bernhard Leubolt, and Rudy Weissenbacher, 'Peripheral Financialization and Vulnerability to Crisis: A Regulationist Perspective', *Competition and Change*, 14,3-4 (2010), 225–247.
8. See European Committee of the Regions, *2020 Barometer of Regions and Cities*, Brussels, October 2020, pp. 6 ff.
9. For background on the profit-driven interest of capital, see Matteo Gaddi, 'Confindustria - tutto a noi, niente agli altri', 11 September 2020, *Erbacce.org*; see also the document of Italy's entrpreneur association, Confindustria: *Agenda per la riapertura delle imprese e la difesa dei luoghi di lavoro contro il Covid-19* (Agenda for the reopening of businesses and the defence of workplaces against Covid-19), 8 April 2020; and 'Lettera del Presidente di Confindustria Vincenzo Boccia al Presidente del Consiglio dei Ministri Giuseppe Conte', Rome, 22 March 2020.
10. Florin Poenaru and Costi Rogozanu, 'Why Social Distancing "Doesn't Apply" to Germany's Migrant Farmworkers', *Jacobin*, 23 May 2020.
11. 'Germany to lift border controls imposed amid virus for harvests', *Aljazeera*, 3 April 2020.

12 On this see *2020 Barometer of Regions and Cities*, p. 17 ff.
13 Alejandro Rada, 'Migration of health-care workers from the new EU Member States to Germany', eObservatory for Sociopolitical Developments in Europe, *Working Paper* 14, October 2016.
14 Eurostat, *Majority of health jobs held by women*, 9 April 2020.
15 *2020 Barometer of Regions and Cities*, pp. 21 f.
16 David Graeber, 'On the Phenomenon of Bullshit Jobs - A Work Rant', *Strike Magazine*, August 2013.
17 See on this Wilfried Kurtzke and Beate Scheidt, *Wirtschaftspolitische Informationen*, IG-Metall, July 2020.
18 Kurtzke and Scheidt: Wirtschaftspolitische Informationen, p. 9
19 Stephan Hessler et al.: Die Neue Weltwirtschaft - Entstofflichung und Entgrenzung der Ökonomie, Fr/M. 1999, p. 278
20 See especially the EuroMemoranda 2008 "Democratic transformation of European finance, a full employment regime, and ecological restructuring - Alternatives to finance-driven capitalism" and 2009 "Europe in Crisis: A Critique of the EU's Failure to Respond"
21 Nick Cunningham, 'What's Next For Oil As Prices Go Negative?', *oilprice.com*, 20 April 2020.
22 In the year 2000 6.21 million Germans were direct shareholders, in 2019 only 4.16 million were, see: 'Zahl der direkten Aktionäre in Deutschland bis 2019', *Statista*, 4 March 2020.
23 E.F. Schumacher published his book *Small is Beautiful: A Study of Economics As If People Mattered* in 1973. It is interesting to note that this book was for many years one of the key inspirations for Hindu Nationalists, as they could use its arguments against left-wing centralised planning and in favour of private ownership. We also might remember that one of the first policies of the left in the French Revolution was the centralisation of power in the new French republic aimed at breaking the power of local 'big men'.
24 See especially Leigh Phillips, Michal Rozworski, People's Republic of Wal-Mart-How the World's Biggest Corporations are Laying the Foundation for Socialism, London: Verso, 2019, and also Aaron Bastani, Fully Automated Luxury Communism, London: Verso, 2019.
25 <https://uberty.org/wp-content/uploads/2015/10/Eden_Medina_Cybernetic_Revolutionaries.pdf>.
26 Hilary Wainwright, *Arguments for a New Left: Answering the Free-Market Right*, Oxford: Blackwell, 1994, in particular the chapter 'Frederick Hayek and the Social-Engineering State', pp. 43 ff.
27 Graham Kendall, 'Apollo 11 anniversary: Could an iPhone fly me to the moon?', *The Independent*, 9 July 2019.
28 Robert Sayre and Michael Löwy, *Romantic Anti-capitalism and Nature: The Enchanted Garden*, London: Routledge, 2020.
29 On the devastating effects of the CIA's covert war against Italy's democracy after 1945 see for example the chapter on Italy in Daniele Ganser, *NATO's Secret Armies: Operation GLADIO and Terrorism in Western Europe*, London: Frank Cass, 2005.
30 Kira Taylor, '2020 was hottest year ever in Europe', *Euractiv*, 8 January 2021.
31 CarbonBrief, *State of the climate-2020 on course to be warmest year on record*, 23 October 2020.

32 Food and Agricultural Organisation of the United Nations, *Risk of hunger pandemic as coronavirus set to almost double acute hunger by end of 2020*, 16 April 2020.
33 Dario Azzellini and Julia Eder, 'ALBA – an alternative regional alliance?', RLS Brussels, 27 March 2017.
34 See, in France: *Les Possibles* 23, Printemps 2020 'Dossier: la planification pour la transition sociale et écologique'; 'La planification aujourd'hui', *Actuel Marx* 2019/1, n° 65, dossier coordonné par Cédric Durand et Razmig Keucheyan; Durand and Keucheyan, 'Ecological Planning for Post-Capitalism – The future starts right here', Le *Monde Diplomatique*, May 2020; in Germany: Franziska Wiethold, 'Wirtschaftsdemokratie gegen den Strich gebürstet', *SWP (Zeitschrift für sozialistische Politik und Wirtschaft)* 5, 2019; Bernd Riexinger, *System Change: Plädoyer für einen linken Green New Deal – Wie wir den Kampf für eine sozial- und klimagerechte Zukunft gewinnen können*, Hamburg: VSA Verlag, 2020; in the USA: Leigh Phillips and Michal Rozworski, *The People's Republic of Walmart – How the World's Biggest Corporations are Laying the Foundation for Socialism*, London: Verso, 2019; Phillips and Rozworski, 'Where market forces don't work – Walmart's planned economy', *Le Monde Diplomatique*, March 2020.

Reaping The Whirlwind: Digitalisation, Restructuring, and Mobilisation in the Covid Crisis

Ursula Huws

This essay addresses the changes sweeping through global labour markets during the coronavirus pandemic, looking in particular at the concentration of capital and expansion of market share by global corporations, bringing with it the digital management of supply chains and an exponential growth in algorithmic control and surveillance of workers. Pandemic lockdown conditions have exposed very clearly the polarisations in the workforce between 'fixed' workers, physically isolated in their homes but closely monitored via their computers, working virtually, and the precariously employed mobile ('footloose') workers, disproportionately made up of black and migrant workers, equally closely monitored, who deliver the physical goods and services the home-bound need to survive and care for their bodily needs when they become sick, at great personal risk. This represents a sharp acceleration of existing trends but also brings new contradictions. The near-universal access to digital technologies that is a prerequisite for the management of workers also provides them with new ways to communicate and organise. In the vacuum left by government incompetence, communities have come together locally to develop their own solutions to support the vulnerable, discuss ideas about what reforms to campaign for, mobilise against employers and organise demonstrations to express their outrage against racism and state violence in an upsurge of initiatives many of which rely crucially on digital, online forms of organisation. In the process new social models are being developed that prefigure what a more inclusive post-Covid society might look like.

2008-2019: A decade of radical restructuring

The world economy in which the coronavirus arrived in 2019 was one that was already in upheaval. In the preceding decade, the restructuring of capital after the 2008 crisis sent convulsions throughout the global economy and its labour markets. The desperate search for new sources of profit led to increasingly cut-throat competition among manufacturing companies, intensifying the need to get their goods to market as quickly as possible. This drove investment in infrastructure, including China's Belt and Road Initiative, and exerted extreme pressure on production and logistics workers all along the value chain, from mine to assembly plant to port to ship to road to warehouse and, in the 'last mile', to the home of the consumer, without whose purchase no profit could be realised. Helped by ever more sophisticated digital technologies and the willing connivance of neoliberal governments, other companies found new sources of profit in the artificially created markets for outsourced government services, in the process rendering much public sector work precarious, casualised and low paid. Yet other companies transformed themselves into twenty-first century *rentiers*, collecting tithes from the public for their (increasingly essential) use of such virtual products as software licenses, maintenance contracts, insurance policies, phone contracts, or wi-fi networks. In other cases, labour itself became a commodity from which rent was levied, with a company taking a cut each time its online platform was used for ordering a taxi or a domestic task in a system that externalises all risk to the workers.

In the course of these upheavals, vast areas of life that were previously outside the direct scope of capitalism were brought within its orbit, generating new kinds of commodities ranging from bio products to ready meals, from cosmetic surgery to streamed entertainment.[1] And working conditions were transformed for tens of thousands of workers, now subjugated to the depersonalised, algorithmically managed discipline of global capitalism.

The scale of these changes is hard to overestimate. Here are just a few facts. In 2018 seven of the ten most valuable companies in the world (Apple, Google, Microsoft, Amazon, Facebook, Tencent, and Alibaba) were using platform business models, and it was estimated by McKinsey that 30 per cent of global economic activity would soon be mediated by digital platforms.[2] The global value of online retail sales (the main driver of growth in parcel delivery volumes) tripled from $1,196 billion in 2013 to $3,306 billion in 2019.[3] In the UK, by 2017 more than a third of all public spending was spent on procuring goods, works, and services from external suppliers.[4]

My own research,[5] carried out between 2016 and 2019 in thirteen European countries, revealed large numbers of people using online platforms to find work. Platform work is usually carried out as a top-up to other earnings, representing less than 10 per cent of their income for most, with only a small minority saying that it constitutes all their income. It forms part of a spectrum of casual, on-call work providing a subsistence income for the working poor. Some of this work is carried out in real time and space, often in public spaces. Those doing driving or delivery work range from 1.4 per cent (in the Netherlands and Sweden) to 12.3 per cent (in Czechia) of the adult population, but in the UK (the only country for which we have trend data) this proportion increased from 1.5 per cent to 5.1 per cent between 2016 and 2019, showing how rapidly it is growing. In every country the proportion doing this type of highly visible platform work in public spaces is exceeded by those doing more hidden types of work providing household services in other people's homes, ranging from 2.4 per cent in Sweden to 11.8 per cent in Czechia. But this too is exceeded by an even more common type of platform work – work that is carried out virtually, using online means. Independent of spatial location, as it is, online platform labour is carried out in direct competition with workers in other parts of the world – so, unsurprisingly, the highest levels are found where average earnings are lowest compared with international competitors.

It seems clear that at a time when earnings were falling in real terms or at best stagnating, and austerity policies had been biting hard, people were looking for any source of income they could find to make ends meet. One of the most important mechanisms for doing this before the financial crisis – credit – was much less readily available after the crisis, making the online economy an increasingly important resource to tap into.

In the UK (where we did surveys in 2016 and 2019) we can see the exponential growth of platform work. Over this three year period, the number of working age adults who said they did work obtained via an online platform at least once a week doubled from an estimated 2.8 million people to an estimated 5.8 million (from 4.7 per cent to 9.6 per cent of the adult population). People were turning to the internet to make money in other ways too: over the same period the proportion of people renting out rooms via online platforms such as Airbnb soared from 8.2 per cent to 18.7 per cent, while those selling self-made products via platforms like Etsy rose from 10 per cent to 20.2 per cent. A high proportion of the UK population (60.7 per cent) were users of platform services by 2019. Although wealthier households were more likely to do so, more than half (50.9 per cent) of those earning less than £20,000 per year were platform customers, including many who were themselves platform workers. Three quarters (76 per cent) of people who said that they provided driving or delivery services via platforms at least weekly were also users of such platforms at least monthly (rising to 92.8 per cent who did so at least yearly), while two thirds (67.2 per cent) of those who provided services in other people's homes at least weekly were also customers for such services at least monthly (89.6 per cent at least yearly).[6] There was thus effectively a doubling of both supply and demand for platform-based service labour during this short three-year period.

In the labour market, work for formally designated online platforms represented the visible tip of a much larger iceberg. Even more important than the growth of platform work was the phenomenally fast spread of digital management practices across the general workforce. In the UK in 2016 one person in ten reported using an app or website to be informed of new tasks but by 2019 this had more than doubled to 21 per cent of the adult working age population. Barely half of these workers were platform workers. The use of apps or websites to record what work had been done rose over the same period from 14.2 per cent to 24.6 per cent. Again, most people reporting these practices were *not* platform workers. Nearly a quarter (24 per cent) of UK adults surveyed in 2019 – of whom nearly half (11.7 per cent) were *not* platform workers – also reported having their work rated by customers. By 2019, therefore, the upheavals caused by the restructuring of capital over the previous decade were already reflected in titanic labour market turbulence, with an erosion of standard employment contracts and dramatic growth in the digital management and surveillance of the workforce.

2020: Economic and social impacts of the Covid-19 pandemic

The great lockdown imposed on most populations in early 2020 thus arrived in highly dynamic circumstances, as in a rapidly moving vehicle. In some sectors its impact was like the slamming of brakes, with activity coming to an abrupt, screeching halt. In others, it was more like an equally abrupt stamp on the accelerator sending existing trends careening forward at breakneck speed.

Stop and go in the labour market

Transport industries came to a standstill, with airline workers laid off and hundreds of thousands of seafarers marooned on their ships for months.[7] Companies in the travel and tourism sector, as well as Airbnb hosts, faced financial ruin.[8] Many production industries, as well as brick-and-mortar retail and other service industries, were shut down. As images of stranded oil tankers, boarded up high streets, and closed factories filled our screens, the environmental impacts became evident in clear skies and suddenly visible views of distant horizons, and audible in the sound of birds whose songs were no longer drowned out by traffic noise.

The braking effects on the labour market are likely to leave lasting traces as temporary layoffs are transformed into permanent job losses. Not only are many employees of small and medium-sized enterprises made redundant when their employers go out of business but it also seems likely that larger organisations will seize on the pandemic as an excuse to casualise or downsize.

Though the braking effects are dramatic, the acceleratory effects of these activities are likely to be even more far-reaching in their implications. These include huge increases in the numbers of people working from home, in the use of online ordering of goods and services, and in labour linked to their delivery. The coronavirus crisis has made visible and accentuated an increasing polarisation across the labour market between 'fixed' and 'footloose' work and workers,[9] whereby the needs of those who are immobilised, whether through job constraints, incapacity, old age or the risk of contamination, are increasingly met through the hyper-mobility of other travelling workers who must deliver them the goods and services they cannot fetch for themselves, provide them with physical care, or transport them to and from the locations where they need to be treated in person. This has swelled the ranks of the precariously employed workers, disproportionately made up of migrants and people from black and ethnic minorities (BAME), whose lives have been put physically at risk and, for this and other reasons, make up a shockingly high proportion of deaths from the Covid virus.[10] Though their personal safety is sacrificed, they are among the least likely to be protected by employment rights such as sick pay, job protection, or minimum wages.

The growth in this mobile workforce, expanded by the addition of many made redundant from other industries, obliged to work in 'real' time and space, has been mirrored by an enormous growth in 'virtual' working among white-collar workers (who are also more likely to be white-skinned[11]) obliged by office closures and demands for social distancing to work from their homes and connected digitally to their employers, clients or customers. A third of Europeans reported taking up teleworking as a result of the pandemic.[12] While working under very different conditions from the mobile workers who serve their needs, and better protected physically, these homebased workers do have one feature in common with them: they are ever more likely to be working under the digital gaze of a global corporation, something to which I will return later in this essay.

Concentration and expansion of capital

Meanwhile, these new conditions enabled an astonishing expansion of some sectors of capital and concentration of wealth. Research by the US Institute for Policy Studies and Americans for Tax Fairness reported in June 2020 that the wealth of the top five billionaires (Jeff Bezos, Bill Gates, Mark Zuckerberg, Warren Buffett, and Larry Ellison) had seen their combined net worth grow by $584 billion during the first three months of 2020, in a period when $56.5 trillion was wiped off the value of household wealth. That Bezos, CEO of Amazon, was the greatest winner in absolute terms, with a growth of $43.8 billion over the three-month period, comes as little surprise given the enormous growth in online shopping. In percentage terms, his 38.7 per cent increase was exceeded by a phenomenal 58.6 per cent expansion in the fortune of Zuckerberg (CEO of Facebook) over the same period, benefitting from the turn to online communication among a locked-down, isolated population. Two others of the big five, Gates and Ellison, also make their money from the digital economy (Microsoft and Oracle).13[13] The fifth, Buffet is a more classic capitalist with fingers in many pies, including a significant shareholding in Apple as well as banks and food companies. Berkshire Hathaway, the company of which he is CEO, cannily sold off all its airline holdings early in 2020.

These billionaires are emblematic of a much larger trend whereby large corporations are expanding their grip. Sometimes this is achieved by extracting various forms of rent, for example from software licenses, which rises in proportion to the growing use of digital technologies. Under lockdown conditions, needless to say, the demand for such technologies has grown exponentially. For example the videoconferencing service Zoom reported that by April 2020 its usage had grown to 300 million meeting participants a day, up from just 10 million in December 2019 (bringing in $328 million in revenue during its February–April quarter).[14] In other cases, global corporations (such as supermarkets, fast food chains and online platforms providing household services) are colonizing huge areas of the economy formerly dominated by small firms and individual traders, helped by their ability to organise just-in-time delivery to isolated consumers using a dispersed, digitally controlled workforce.

Further beneficiaries from the crisis include the companies whose profits are based on the outsourcing of public services. After an early dip in demand when the pandemic first emerged, before government policies had been formulated to address it, it became clear that the outsourcing companies saw the Covid crisis as a promising new source of contracts. In June, 2020 there was a 40 per cent increase in invitations to tender for public contracts, with the publication of £4.3 billion worth of Covid-19 contracts in the UK, including a £326 million contract relating to the creation of temporary hospitals for the treatment of Covid-19, and a £750 million contract for an infection survey, as well as several contracts to supply videoconferencing for remote consultations with patients. Demonstrating graphically how the poverty of the general population becomes an opportunity for further corporate aggrandisement, two large contracts were awarded by the Department for Education to support students from disadvantaged backgrounds, one for the provision of free school meals and one for laptops and educational devices.[15] The size of this sector can be illustrated by the fact that since 2012, the UK government has awarded private contracts to the tune of £3.5 trillion.[16]

The growth of 'logged' labour

We thus have a situation in 2020 where there is, on the one hand, a growing dominance of the labour market by very large global corporations relying heavily on digital technologies to organise workflow and manage their workforce and, on the other, a growing reliance by the general population on digital technologies not just to acquire the goods and services they need for survival but also to access paid work and carry it out – whether this is from the physical isolation of their homes, travelling to deliver goods or provide services, or in the risky settings of hospitals, care homes, schools, warehouses, fields, food processing plants, and other spaces deemed sufficiently essential for workers to be obliged to work there in face-to-face contact with others, despite the risk of infection.

This is expanding the amount of labour that falls into the category I have elsewhere described as 'logged'[17]– a form of work characterised by three features, each of which can be described as 'logged' using a different meaning of the term. First, the component labour processes are broken down into separate tasks, much as a felled tree is broken down into separate logs, which (although these tasks may in practice require considerable tacit skills to deliver) are treated as standardised and interchangeable from the point of view of execution and reward. Second, the management and control processes are mediated by online platforms, with the worker or service user required to be online (or 'logged on') in order to be notified of what work is available and report the progress of its delivery. Third, the very fact that every aspect of the work is managed online means that each interaction leaves a digital trace, generating data that can be used not only to record and track current activities but also to build ever more sophisticated algorithms to enhance the efficiency of future ones. Both workers and users are therefore subjected to close surveillance, meaning that their activities are also 'logged' in the sense that was historically used to describe the tracking of movements in ships' logs.

The surveillance of workers is achieved by a variety of means including GPS, facial recognition, audio recording of customer service calls and shopping and social media browsing history and covers the minutiae of labour processes in extraordinary detail. For example, the system used by

UPS to monitor its 450,000 drivers uses over 200 sensors in each delivery van to collect information that is combined in a continuous stream with GPS data and information from customers and hand-held scanners. This is analysed to prescribe precise protocols for driver behaviour right down to details such as how to start the truck with one hand while buckling with the other and where to put your pen.[18] Cogito, a system used in call centres to analyse recordings of calls, claims to 'measure and interpret data about speakers' energy, empathy, participation, tone, and pace in real time'. Another, CallMiner, 'sends three to five notifications a minute to an agent on a typical call, ranging from ... "messages of congratulation and cute animal photos when software suggests a customer is satisfied" to "a suggestion to 'calm down' and a list of soothing talking points" when caller frustration is detected'.[19] Another AI-based system, Isaak, already in use in the UK in several law firms, a training company and an estate agent, gathers data on a range of actions which it then uses to gain 'real-time insights into each employee and their position within the organisational network', showing managers 'how collaborative workers are and whether they are "influencers" or "change-makers"'.[20]

Such examples could be multiplied many times over. Suffice it to say that there has been a mounting use of such surveillance tools since the arrival of the pandemic. One example, Sneek, which 'stays on throughout the workday and features constantly-updating photos of workers taken through their laptop camera every one to five minutes', reported a tenfold increase in signups in March 2020, and boasted over 10,000 users.[21]

The logging of labour does not just contribute to its standardisation and intensification, putting workers under continuous pressure while increasing their inter-changeability. It also removes – or renders very difficult – the possibility of direct dialogue between workers and their managers. When the only means of communication is an anonymous digital interface, there is no possibility of identifying the source of power or negotiating with it. Even if the system malfunctions and there is a valid cause for complaint, the best that can normally be achieved by a determined worker is to get through, via an automated contact centre or chatbot, to another equally alienated worker with little or no power to over-rule the system, in a Kafkaesque world in which responsibility is endlessly deflected and there is no answering back to authority. The normative model of industrial relations laid down in developed economies in the twentieth century is thereby bypassed as conclusively as the normative standard employment contracts that were negotiated within this model.

The counter-movements

History tells us that to every movement there is a counter-movement and, moreover, the greater and faster the change, the larger and more vehement the backlash is likely to be. The unprecedented scope and scale of the pandemic crisis seems capable of provoking a veritable tsunami of reaction among the victims of this latest capitalist upheaval.

The end of 'there is no alternative'

One of the most striking impacts of the crisis has been the unmasking of the neoliberal notion that 'there is no alternative' that was part of the political common sense for so long that there can be few workers under the age of 55 who even remember a time when other views prevailed. Its dominance spanned the mass unemployment resulting from the deindustrialisation of the 1980s and the austerity policies introduced after the financial crisis of 2008, insisting that the sufferings of millions were inevitable and unchallengeable. In the long run, it claimed, only the market can win. Allowing the state to intervene is a distortion of that market and will ultimately only prolong the pain. But if we let that market rip, look what goodies it can bring us: cheap products, new technologies to support a lazy lifestyle, an endless stream of entertainment, personal fulfilment, freedom of choice, and flexibility!

The arrival of the pandemic exposed this myth for all to see, making it abundantly clear that the market cannot cope in a real crisis and the state has an important role to play and is, indeed, essential for many other purposes than the maintenance of law and order. Governments that claimed for decades that there was no cash to provide basic health and social services suddenly found the resources to spend billions on subsidies to employers to furlough workers and bail out ailing institutions. The sense of having been hoodwinked is accompanied by a dawning realisation that political choices were possible in the past – and still are. As this realisation has sunk in, a great wave of anger has been released that all that sacrifice was for nothing – an anger that has meshed with other forms of rage against the neoliberal state, for example the way that its policing and incarceration policies (always curiously exempt from the cuts that affected other public spending) are used murderously against BAME people.

This critique has not come from nowhere, of course. It was already evident, for example, in the growing support for the alternative visions promoted by Jeremy Corbyn and Bernie Sanders in the late 2010s, in particular among the generation that entered the labour market (or tried to) in the period following the 2008 crisis, whose life experiences had taught them that however 'self-reliant' or 'creative' they might be, the market did not offer them the opportunities it promised. Those who did not fall into depression or anomie were already actively campaigning for change before the virus struck, including exploring new political and social options. It was also fed by responses to the climate change crisis, which also peaked in 2019, as fires blazed across Australia and global icecaps melted. By mid-2020, it appeared that some kind of tipping point had been passed during the pandemic in which belief in 'there is no alternative' had been suspended among a critical mass of the population, suggesting a new openness to alternative ideas.

Mobilisation

The late 2010s did not just see a change in attitudes among the young, it also witnessed a growth in new forms of social mobilisation, of which the Black Lives Matter movement is perhaps the most celebrated example. There was also a mushrooming of new forms of organisation among precarious workers, such as the National Domestic Workers Alliance in the USA and the App Drivers and Couriers Union (ADCU) in the UK, both of which have expanded their membership and activities during the pandemic period. Both organisations have developed an analysis that lays particular emphasis on the fact that the majority of their members are BAME, and are building on this politically. Along with many other such bottom-up mobilisations, they have developed a shrewd analysis of labour market trends, illustrated recently in the observation by James Farrar, General Secretary of the ADCU, that after the Pandemic 'the apps are going to come roaring back. We're going to see a world dominated by apps'.[22] These organisations have also fostered international solidarity, for instance in the setting up of the International Domestic Workers Federation (IDWF) in 2014 and the International Alliance of App-Based Transport Workers (IAATW) in 2019.

As well as the development of new organisations to represent precarious workers, further evidence of this new mobilisation comes from a rise in the membership of traditional trade unions. In 2019, for example, the UK Trades Union Congress (TUC) reported a 100,000 increase in membership in a single year.[23] A year later, after the pandemic had hit, traffic on the TUC's Join a Union website page in May 2020 was six times higher than in May 2019 and most new members are from non-union backgrounds. Female union membership in the UK is at a record high, at 3.69 million. The influx of care workers into the public sector union Unison is up 202 per cent.[24] The late 2010s also experienced a wave of strikes and other forms of industrial action among low-paid workers in companies ranging from Amazon to McDonalds, a wave which swelled further during the pandemic crisis. For example, over 800 strikes, walkouts, sickouts and other disruptions were recorded in the US between March and June 2020, many of them in hitherto non-union workplaces.[25]

While most of these actions took a very physical form, their organisation could scarcely have been possible without the widespread use of electronic communications. And the success of these actions, in terms of engendering publicity and, very often, drawing attention to the outrageously hostile responses to them on the part of employers and police, can also be attributed to the distribution of live evidence captured on smartphones and broadcast via social media. Social media, too, have provide forums for serious discussion of alternative social models to be campaigned for when the world emerges from lock-down, ranging from worker co-operatives to universal basic income schemes, from alternatives to prison to the creation of green jobs.

Indeed, during the coronavirus crisis there has been an unprecedented flowering of collaborative, local, bottom-up community-based initiatives, often organised by digital means, for example to distribute food to the hungry, supply social support to the isolated elderly, arrange housing for the homeless, or provide refuges for victims of domestic abuse or alternative schooling for locked-down children.[26] Shocked by the failure of the state to provide them with the means of survival and personal protection, appalled by the irresponsibility and selfishness of employers, and enraged by the behaviour of the police, many people, equipped with their new technologies and the ability to use them creatively and, in some cases, with more time on their hands than usual, are emerging from the torpor of the neoliberal years with fresh energy and motivation. In doing so, they are developing prefigurative models of what an alternative post-Covid society might look like, and, by giving them concrete form, stimulating an awareness that such alternatives are possible and thus helping to bring such a society into being.

Conclusion

The history of capitalism is a double one in which each development contains within itself the seeds of its own destruction. Once the technical division of labour reached a point where it was necessary to have a workforce that was literate and numerate, that literate, numerate workforce used these new skills to organise itself and demand democratic representation. Once the spatial division of labour reached a point where it required fast international communications to coordinate it, workers were able to use the telegram and the telephone, and later the email, fax, and text message, to connect with each other and share their experiences. Now that we have a digitally managed global workforce that requires a smartphone or laptop with an app on it to be summoned to work, then these new tools too can be used for organising resistance. And while the further development of capitalism requires innovation, then the workers who experiment with new ways of doing things, generate new ideas, and imagine new applications and organisational solutions can turn their skill, intelligence, and creativity to inventing alternative ways of living and organising the economy and society. Sow the wind and reap the whirlwind.

NOTES

1. I have written at greater length about these developments in *Labour in Contemporary Capitalism: What Next?* London: Palgrave Macmillan, 2019.
2. Jennifer L. Schenker, 'The Platform Economy', *The Innovator,* January 2019, available at <innovator.news>.
3. Apex Insight, *Global Parcel Delivery Market Insight Report,* 2020, available at: <apex-insight.com>.
4. Tom Sasse, Benoit Guerin, Sarah Nickson, Mark O'Brien, Thomas Pope, and Nick Davies, *Government Outsourcing: What has worked and what needs reform?*, London: Institute for Government, 2019, available at <www.instituteforgovernment.org.uk>.
5. Ursula Huws, Neil H. Spencer, Matt Coates, and Kaire Holts, 'The Platformisation of Work in Europe: results from research in 13 European countries', Brussels: Foundation for European Progressive Studies, 2019.
6. Ursula Huws, Neil H. Spencer, and Matt Coates, *Platform Work in the UK 2016-2019*, Brussels and London: Foundation for European Progressive studies and the Trades Union Congress, 2019.
7. Tim Bowler, 'Seafarers in limbo as coronavirus hits shipping', *BBC News,* 16 April 2020.
8. Joan Faus, 'This is how coronavirus could affect the travel and tourism industry', *World Economic Forum with Reuters,* 17 March 2020, available at <www.weforum.org>; Tripp Mickle and Preetika Rana, '"A Bargain With the Devil" – Bill Comes Due for Overextended Airbnb Hosts,' *Wall Street Journal,* 29 April 2020.
9. I made this distinction in Ursula Huws, 'Fixed, footloose, or fractured: Work, identity, and the spatial division of labor in the twenty-first century city', *Monthly Review* 57,10 (2006), 34-44.
10. Haroon Siddique, 'Key findings from Public Health England's report on Covid-19 deaths' *The Guardian,* 2 June 2020.
11. Office of National Statistics, *Coronavirus and homeworking in the UK labour market: 2019,* available at <www.ons.gov.uk>.
12. Oscar Vargas Llave, 'COVID-19 unleashed the potential for telework – How are workers coping?' *Eurofound,* 9 June 2020, available at <www.eurofound.europa.eu>.
13. Chuck Collins, Institute for Policy Studies, 18 June 2020, available at <ips-dc.org>.
14. Jacob Kastrenakes, 'Zoom saw a huge increase in subscribers – and revenue – thanks to the pandemic', *The Verge,* 2 June 2020.
15. Tussell, *Factsheet #2: Covid-19 & UK Public Procurement,* May 2020; Tussell *Factsheet #4: Covid-19 & UK Public Procurement,* July 2020, available at <www.tussell.com>.
16. Tussell, *2019 Update on Strategic Suppliers*, March 2020, available at <www.tussell.com>.

17 Ursula Huws, 'Logged labour: a new paradigm of work organisation?', *Work Organisation, Labour and Globalisation* 10,1 (2016), 7-26.
18 Moritz Altenried, 'On the Last Mile: Logistical Urbanism and the Transformation of Labour', *Work Organisation, Labour & Globalisation* 13(1), 2019, 114-29.
19 Camilla Cannon, 'Recorded for Quality Assurance: The datafication of affect in the call-center industry', *Real Life,* 19 September 2019.
20 Robert Booth, 'UK businesses using artificial intelligence to monitor staff activity', *The Guardian,* 7 April 2019.
21 Aaron Holmes, 'Employees at home are being photographed every 5 minutes by an always-on video service to ensure they're actually working – and the service is seeing a rapid expansion since the coronavirus outbreak', *Business Insider,* 23 March 2020.
22 Accessed on 29 June 2020 from <www.facebook.com/ADCUnion>.
23 Carl Roper, 'Trade union membership rises by 100,000 in a single year – but challenges remain', TUC, 30 May 2019, available at <www.tuc.org.uk>.
24 Lesley Riddoch, 'Unions thriving amid national crisis', *The Scotsman,* 22 June 2020.
25 Jason Koslowski, 'A Historic Wave of Workers' Struggle is Sweeping the U.S. – and It's Speeding Up' *Left Voice,* 22 June 2020. On the actual number of strikes, see Chris Brooks, 'Fact Check: Have there been 500 wildcat strikes in June?', *organizing work,* 23 June 2020, available at <www.organizing.work>.
26 There is no space to detail here the many examples. Those who are interested can find some listed in the Facebook group 'Prefiguring a positive post-COVID society'.

The Pandemic Crisis and Its Impact on Women's Lives

Amelia Martínez-Lobo and Andrea Peniche

The impact of crises is never neutral, and the Covid crisis is no exception. Despite the lack of official data on its impact, the experience of inequality in daily life is increasing as never before. Women are disproportionately affected, with inequality already a deep stigma on their/our lives. The crisis aggravated it, and so that we must consider the pre-pandemic situation together with the visible difficulties we are going through now.

In terms of the pandemic crisis, a distinction should be drawn between being infected and being affected. If the virus itself has no gender bias, the gender difference in its effects of the crisis are quite clear. The pandemic reinforces pre-existing inequalities and exposes the vulnerabilities of the social, political, and economic systems, which are too fragile to enable the requisite solutions.

It is known that throughout the world women, in comparison to men, are paid less, have less capacity to save, and have more precarious work. They fill the majority of jobs in large areas considered non-essential (hairdressers, restaurants, aesthetic centres, clothing stores), but they also make up the majority of workers in areas that are essential during the pandemic: caregiving, hospitals (nurses, cleaners), supermarkets, etc., and represent the majority of the informal economic sector in which labour typically lacks the rights and protection afforded by contracts. This makes them particularly vulnerable, at risk of losing their income and social protection, with concrete implications in their ability to resist the economic, social, and mental impact of the pandemic crisis.

The official discourse, which is also responsible for the construction of public opinion, described lockdown as a factor in the stopping of the economy. But, we have to ask, what is the economy that has stopped? A part of the economy never did stop and, what is more, never does: the economy of the home and of care work. However, because this involves women's work, it remains invisible and unskilled, as if it were not part of the economy. During the crisis women care workers, and the unprotected and precarious labour sectors did not stop, and the large majority of these workers are women.

This crisis revealed the fragility of social protection systems, which year after year have been eaten away by neoliberal policies. But however that may be, the current crisis requires a strong response from the social protection systems, one that needs to look at the specificities of all the impacts. We were never all together in one boat and, consequently, if the solutions are not to fail they should not be planned as if we were.

The front line is feminine

Throughout the European Union, women make up the majority of healthcare workers. However, in the front line of workers most exposed to infection are not only healthcare professionals but also supermarket workers, hospital cleaning staff, public transportation workers, those preparing and delivering food, etc., as well as all the workers in community services such as those taking care of the elderly, the poor, the homeless, and the disabled, etc., and most of them are women.

The global formal care sector is very important in the economy and society: it corresponds to about 12% of global jobs and includes some 381 million workers. In the EU, 83% of these jobs are held by women. For them, social distancing and remote work were never an option. If we add informal and non-paid work in care to that of the formal sector, the world figure reaches 2 billion people, and in Europe the estimate of the number of people involved in some sort of informal care is 125 million. The non-paid reproductive work, performed essentially by women, has been calculated at about 9% of world GDP. In Portugal, its corresponding value has been estimated at four billion euros each year, and the number of people performing some type of non-paid care work at between 800 thousand and one million. Four out of five of these workers are women, or 80%. Nevertheless, with the temporary shutdown or bankruptcy of social institutions during the pandemic crisis, this figure has gone up. According to a survey by ANCI (Associação Nacional de Cuidadores Informais, Portugal's national association of informal health care), about 90% of those doing unpaid reproductive work in Portugal are now women.

Crisis in the sector of social reproduction

The period of lockdown and distance learning highlighted the inequalities in house and care work; separated from their paid workplace and imprisoned in remote work, many women performed a disproportionate part of family chores. Taking care of the kids and following their school homework, preparing all the meals, cleaning house and clothes, helping sick relatives, and simultaneously fulfilling the duties of their own work schedule demonstrated how exploitation occurs 24 hours a day: serving the family, the company, and the country.

According to a survey carried out by Sussex University, inequality in the sharing of parental responsibilities increased during lockdown, and British society regressed to a 1950s way of life: the proportion of mothers who were totally or almost totally responsible for childcare increased from 27% to 45%, and 70% of all women declared they were the sole person responsible for all tasks related to school activities. This superimposition of labour and care tasks implies a greater lack of free time and an enormous physical and mental overburden that limits women's autonomy and economic opportunities. Moreover, most mono-parental families are feminine (85% in Portugal), meaning that for many women there was never any possibility of sharing these tasks.

Several firms declined to hire women during the pandemic, fearing they might need to spend time at home with their children during what would have been school hours.

Therefore, the long-term effects of the pandemic crisis need to be considered – namely that, in terms of women's economic independence,, we are at risk of regressing to the epoch of our grandmothers.

Crisis of reproductive health and rights

By March, UNESCO estimated that the pandemic had prevented 1.52 billion children from attending school. In many parts of the world, schools are the safest place for vulnerable girls. As a result, setbacks may occur, specifically in terms of genital mutilation and forced marriage. Away from school, many girls have ceased having access to hygienic supplies such as menstrual products, which in turn, has a significant impact on their sexual and reproductive health.

Confinement and fear of contracting the disease has prevented many women from using health services. Marie Stopes International, an NGO that provides safe contraception and abortion services in several countries, estimates that the crisis may be preventing some 9.5 million women and girls from accessing their services. Maternal health is vulnerable and thus the prediction is that the rate of worldwide maternal mortality will increase. Difficult access to contraception, family planning support, or to abortion services and pre- and post-delivery aid are the direct results of the reduction of rights and of reproductive health.

The right to life at risk

The United Nations estimates that 249 million women and girls have suffered some form of sexual and physical abuse from a partner in the last 12 months, and the number increased during lockdown. The state of emergency isolated many women with their aggressors, which aggravated pre-existing violent relationships. In France, one week after mandatory lockdown, reports of domestic violence increased by 30%; in Argentina, requests for help went up by 25%; in Brazil from 40% to 50%; in Cyprus and Singapore, the phone lines helping women registered a 30% and 33% increase of calls respectively; in the United Kingdom, in only one day the NGO Refuge received 700% more calls to its victim support line than the previous average; in Spain, complaints increased by 18% and in the US by 35%. The same increase of divorce and violence was noticed in Wuhan, China, where the pandemic was first recorded. In Portugal, of the ca. 16,000 calls to the national network helping victims, 1,167 came from persons older than 66. Violence against elderly women is frequently committed by close relatives, which makes complaint very difficult.

As NGOs were responsible for most victim response and the pandemic exacerbated their activities, victims remained particularly unprotected and vulnerable. In addition, with Covid's overburdening of health professionals, the police weighed down by enforcing the safety rules, the judiciary under pressure, and with female unemployment, the stage has been set for this additional pandemic of violence against women.

Crisis of the invisible

With their work coming to a halt, sex workers were financially unprotected. And, as their activity is not recognised as work in most of the legal systems in Europe and the rest of the world, they are not accorded the same labour-law protections given to other workers. Their situations, and that of their families, became impossible. Without the benefit of social protection policies, they depend on solidarity to survive.

The urgent need to address the social and political conditions of sex work became patent. In the face of their complete invisibility and lack of social protection, the prohibitionist solution has clearly failed; it is based on a divisive moral discourse and ignores the needs of concrete people who are asking for social justice. Reducing these persons to sub-humans in the name of a moral dystopia leads to predictable results, and the pandemic crisis, with concrete immediacy, revealed this: a social sector with neither protection nor rights, depending exclusively on solidarity to survive the crisis, but whose workers, given their stigmatisation, have no social space in which to communicate their difficulties and demand help.

The crisis of democracy and instrumentalisation of the pandemic and of women's rights

The Covid-19 crisis has been and continues to be used as a new weapon by the extreme right. On the one hand, far-right governments have implemented necropolitics,[1] using people's lives, and using power, to decide who can live and who should die. In other territories, where neo-fascisms are not in positions of governmental and institutional power, the extreme right has been able to mobilise its followers in social networks and in the streets; they have flirted with denialism; and they have managed to get their messages onto the public agenda. In other words, this global health crisis has served as a pretext and impetus for an ideological rearmament by the extreme right. At the centre of their war of ideas, one sees the deployment of communication strategies structured by fake news and fuelled by hatred. They have various common features, but racism and misogynistic ideology stand out – and the attempt to curb the conquest of women's rights. This far-right consensus is clearly homophobic, Islamophobic, ultra-conservative, and anti-immigrant. It is well to remember the central role that anti-feminism has occupied in the agenda of the extreme right. 'The gender war is the main space for the coordination of the worldwide right–wing', Nuria Alabao,[2] journalist and anthropologist, has stated on numerous occasions.

The Covid-19 crisis has shown, still more clearly, that the 'internationalisation of this gender war is the main forum for coordinating worldwide rights'. This battle against 'gender ideology' adopts different expressions, depending on location, in order to adapt and be acceptable to particular idiosyncrasies, as Alabao explains.

The goal of the extreme right, she points out, is 'to stir the ranks with radical rhetoric'. And, she adds, 'they are playing to create their political and cultural base, but they don't necessarily want to win; they just want to agitate through the war on values'. In fact, some of their mantras, hatred of the LGTBIQ population and anti-abortion, are in decline throughout the world: 'They do not aim at the bulk of voters, they only agitate, they seek to shake the established consensus.'

There is no doubt that there is a misogynistic reactionary international tendency and that gender wars occupy a central place in this crusade against women's rights, with the extreme right renewing its discourses, proposals, and strategies along these lines. But in turn, we also see that the extreme right's rhetoric is not uniform. Moreover, we find a reactionary, ultra-Catholic, and conservative position, whose ideology is to relegate women to their traditional role, making them responsible for providing care and looking after the family.

The great replacement and rise of femonationalism

According to the Austrian researcher Judith Goetz, the theory of the 'great replacement' is based on a so-called 'demographic problem' involving the lower birth rate of the 'native population'. 'In their narrative of demographic change they use a racist discourse to affirm that the indigenous population will be replaced by the Muslim population, which wants to Islamise Europe', explains Goetz, referring to the extreme right. To counter this, the role of women is to have more children, that is, there needs to be a return to traditional values and a subordinate role for women, destined to carry out the work of social reproduction invisibly and gratis, a crucial condition of the capitalist system. The idea of the 'great replacement' refers, in a purportedly apolitical way, to 'nature' and to 'normal families' or to 'demography' and 'openly invokes nature to legitimise racist, colonial, or class structures'.

Alongside this idea of women's insecurity is the second great approach of the extreme right to a supposed defence of women's rights. They single out and stigmatise foreign men as rapists and set themselves up as defenders of the safety and rights of women. Under that mantra, they do nothing but hide their Islamophobic agenda and instrumentalise women's rights to the benefit of their racist propaganda. As Alabao points out, the main novelty of the extreme right parties, 'which began to resurface in response to May '68, is to present immigrants as sex offenders'. There are many examples of these unfounded accusations, but perhaps the most significant was the one deployed on New Year's Eve 2015 in Cologne. The objective of this discourse is to connect economic hardships to the idea of insecurity. 'They say that the material problems of society are due to a crisis of values, not to neoliberalism. And they link their idea of insecurity to the return to traditionalism, to the traditional hetero-normative family that cares for people'. She observes that labour precarity has benefited the extreme right and that although racist policies have been operating for a long time, 'racist rhetoric used to have no place, which it does today'.

While all these ideas appear to involve only what we know as a culture war or a battle for ideas, all gender issues are first and foremost material. The fight for the right to have an abortion is a fight for the material: it is a matter of control over the bodies of women and who decides it. The idea that women should occupy their traditional position is not just an idea; it is the material and economic foundation of the capitalist system, based on a system of care and gratis social reproduction of life. Denying sexist violence results in the dismantling of public policies, and the budgets to carry them out, designed to combat the scourge of the purely misogynistically motivated murders of women perpetrated by men.

What feminism do we need?

A collective feminist conscience is more necessary now than ever, one that is capable of creating and setting its own agenda. Feminism cannot settle for lobbying or for the game of institutions.

Feminism has given concrete and material answers to common problems: the right to abortion, with the recent example of Polish women;[3] recently in Mexico,[4] feminism has attempted to make visible and fight against sexual assault and femicides, as well as for rights such as equal pay, for which there is still a long road to travel;[5] and the list continues.

Feminism is, moreover, a bastion against the extreme right. Wherever the ultra-right governs, it is feminist organisations that lead the mobilisations against the racist, misogynistic policies of the ultra-right, such as the EleNão movement in Brazil.[6] Feminism is counter-power and as such it has to be shaped and built. It is thus urgent to continue giving collective, peaceful, anti-conservative, and anti-puritan feminist responses, for the rights of sex workers and the LGTBIQ and non-binary community, with a feminism that puts life at the centre, demanding rights and demanding a conception of work that includes the life of women in all its dimensions: those who take care of people and perform domestic tasks who are paid by the hour, those who provide care and are not paid, those who carry out their activity in the informal sector of the economy, without contract rights – the migrants, the invisible ones.

Therefore, a plural, anti-fascist, anti-capitalist feminism capable of mainstreaming both anti-fascism and anti-capitalism as pre-conditions for building a truly democratic society, like the one proposed by Rosa Luxemburg: a society where we are socially equal, humanly different, and totally free.

NOTES

1 Necropolitics is a concept that refers to the use of social and political power to dictate how some people can live and how some must die. It is also related to so-called 'thanatopolitics', which has been used as its synonym. Achille Mbembe, author of *On the Postcolony*, was the first scholar to explore the term in depth, in the article of the same name. Necropolitics is often discussed in connection with biopolitics, Foucault's term for the use of social and political power to control people's lives. Mbembe clearly saw that necropolitics goes beyond the right to kill (Foucault's droit de glaive), also including the right to expose other people (including the citizens of one's own country) to death. His vision of necropolitics also includes the right to impose social or civil death, the right to enslave others, and other forms of political violence. Necropolitics is a theory of the living dead, that is, a way of analysing how 'contemporary forms of subjugation of life to the power of death' force some bodies to remain in different states of being

situated between life and death'. Mbembe uses the examples of slavery, apartheid, the colonisation of Palestine, and the figure of the suicide bomber to show how different forms of necro-power over the body (statist, racialised, states of exception, urgency, martyrdom) force people to turn to precarious living conditions.

2   <https://nurialabao.blog/2020/04/12/contra-la-ultraderecha-luchar-en-tiempos-de-las-identidades-oscuras/>.

3   <https://www.amnesty.org/en/latest/news/2020/11/poland-crackdown-on-womens-strike-protests-continues-unabated/>.

4   <https://elpais.com/mexico/2020-11-21/la-onu-pide-al-gobierno-de-mexico-que-proteja-a-las-mujeres-y-no-ataque-a-las-que-se-manifiestan-contra-la-violencia.html>.

5   <https://ec.europa.eu/info/policies/justice-and-fundamental-rights/gender-equality/equal-pay/gender-pay-gap-situation-eu_en>.

6   <https://ctxt.es/es/20181024/Politica/22535/elecciones-brasil-jair-bolsonaro-dilma-rousseff-corrupcion.htm>.

Pandemics and Domestic Violence

Joanna Bourke

Pandemics are a stark reminder of human vulnerability. Of course, at the most fundamental level, we are all vulnerable: sentience involves suffering; death is a certainty in life. However, pandemics, armed conflicts, and other calamities force us to acknowledge our fleshy finitude. To be vulnerable (from the Latin 'vulnus', meaning 'wound') is to be open to injury. In this chapter, I will be focusing on vulnerability to domestic violence in the midst of a pandemic. This form of vulnerability is always interpersonal. The possession of specific traits, characteristics, or identities do not automatically make people more or less vulnerable; people are *made* vulnerable by a complex mix of ideological, economic, political, and spatial systems which construct and maintain hierarchies of power. Vulnerable people are rendered 'wound-able' *by* someone; they are denied the humanity and personhood upon which that recognition is based.

The 1918-20 pandemic

Let me begin by briefly turning to the domestic abuse experienced by four women and their children in the midst of a global pandemic.

When Jessie Webster Cooper was desperately ill with the virus, her husband (an unemployed builder from south London) told her and their feverish son to 'go to hell, and the sooner they went the better'. He would return home late at night and drunk, slam doors, swear at them, and scatter onion skins all over the floor. When she threatened to leave him, he shouted, 'I will kill you if you do' and 'the best place for you is to go to hell'. Jessie was 'suffering from general nervous exhaustion, sleeplessness, and fright'.[1]

John Cook, a tent maker in Forfar (Scotland) had a 'violent and uncontrollable temper' and, according to his wife Mary Ann Allardice, 'was in the habit of seizing hold of her and pushing her about roughly', once 'knocking her against the mantlepiece, and upsetting a pot of boiling tea over her'. When both of them were in bed with the virus, he 'struck her a blow on the breast', so hard that she 'landed on a chair at the side of the bed'. She and her children lived 'in fear of their lives'.[2]

Stephen Stubbings and Florence Kate Stubbings lived in of Loughton, Essex. They had an 'unhappy marriage' and did not live in a 'proper home' but squatted in the bedroom and sitting room of a woman who had borne two illegitimate children with Stephen's brother. Stephen refused to work, was habitually drunk, and was 'always in a temper'. He had syphilis, which he transmitted to Florence. A witness claimed that the two could be heard 'jangling [quarreling] all night long'. When he was in a 'weakened state' due to the virus, Florence complained that he 'smacked my face' because she attempted to prevent him from drinking copious amounts of beer.[3]

While suffering from the after-effects of the virus, Robert Williams, a gardener from Porthmadog in Wales, attacked his wife with a razor and his children with a hatchet. He then slit his own throat.[4]

These stories of domestic violence in the midst of a pandemic sound familiar to us today. Throughout the world, levels of domestic violence have skyrocketed, especially after self-quarantining, physical distancing, and 'safer-at-home' mandates were imposed. However, the violence suffered by Jessie, Mary Ann, Florence, and a woman known only as the wife of Robert Williams occurred during a pandemic that swept throughout the world one hundred years ago. The 1918-1920 pandemic – which infected 500 million people (that is, one-third of the world's population at the time) and killed around 50 million – also saw rising levels of domestic violence. The exact number of women and children affected by domestic violence in those years is unknown. Familial violence was hushed up, divorce was considered scandalous, and only the most extreme cases of domestic cruelty were aired in court. However, newspaper reports of women seeking separation orders from their husbands regularly mention the influenza virus as exacerbating already aggressive male behaviour due to its effect on familial finances, increased alcohol consumption, and general irritability.

The current pandemic

By contrast, during the current pandemic, statistical evidence documenting rising levels of intra-family violence world-wide has proliferated. Jingzhou, a city in China's Hubei Province, witnessed a tripling of domestic violence cases between February 2019 and February 2020, 90% of which were attributed to Covid-19.[5] Domestic violence helplines in Singapore, Cyprus, Argentina, and France are receiving 30% more calls compared to the period prior to the pandemic.[6] In Brazil, reports of domestic violence have jumped by between 40 and 50%.[7] According to the World Health Organization, there has been a 60% rise in emergency calls about domestic violence in the EU since the pandemic.[8] Similar increases in domestic violence are reported in US cities.[9] In the UK, the national domestic violence charity Respect was almost overwhelmed by desperate women: the number of calls to their helplines increased by 97%; they received 185% more emails; and 581% more people visited their website.[10] Femicide rates have also risen. The UK-based organisation Counting Dead Women reported that deaths from domestic abuse between 23 March and 12 April more than doubled compared with the average rate in the past decade.[11] The United Nations Population Fund has issued alarming statistics suggesting that continuing lockdowns for six months could result in an extra 31 million cases of gender based violence globally.[12] It would also significantly impede programmes focusing on ending female genital mutilation (FGM) and child marriage, resulting in two million more cases of FGM and 13 million more child marriages over the next decade.[13]

Similarities and differences

What can exploring domestic violence during these two pandemics, 100 years apart, tell us about diverse historical responses to crisis? The broad cultural contexts within which the virus emerged are very different. In 1918-1920, people were unaware of what caused the disease. Influenza was not identified as being caused by a virus until 1930. Although the barriers to leaving an abusive husband remain extremely high today, women during the earlier pandemic faced more formidable legal and social barriers as a result of extremely limited employment opportunities for females, discriminatory property laws, unsympathetic juridical responses, and the stigma of divorce. In every country throughout the world, charging a husband with marital rape was not even possible until the 1970s (and it is still not possible in 48 countries today). Most notably, during the earlier pandemic, people were still at war when the virus began infecting and killing millions. They all would have experienced war-related disruptions; most would be mourning the killing of a friend or member of their family. In other words, fear of contracting influenza coexisted with other imminent threats of death. And abusers were adept at exploiting such terrors. As Jessie Webster Cooper recounted, during air raids over London, her sadistic husband took great delight in banging on her bedroom door, shouting 'There's another bomb, and another one will drop soon'. She recalled that it 'used to frighten her' and her 16-year-old son 'very badly', which is why they slept in the same room.[14]

But certain contextual similarities also existed, including the lack of a vaccine which meant that preventive measures focused on repeated hand-washing, social distancing, and the closure of schools, places of worship, theatres, movie houses, dance halls, shops, and courtrooms.[15] In 1918-1920, wearing face masks was mandatory in all public spaces in much of the US: even the President wore one.[16] During both pandemics, social gatherings were suspended, public funerals were curtailed, and city centres emptied as people retreated into their homes and other supposedly 'safe' spaces.[17] Hospitals and clinics quickly reached breaking point and public health professionals became overwhelmed by their heavy workloads.[18] Then, as now, quackery flourished. During the earlier pandemic, charlatans advised anxious Americans and Britons to ward off influenza by eating large quantities of brown sugar, drinking copious amounts of whiskey, rubbing raw onions into their chests, and prolonged soaking in creosote baths.[19]

During both pandemics, vulnerability to domestic violence has been unevenly distributed. Girls and women, residents in care homes or orphanages, refugees, undocumented migrants, people with physical or learning difficulties, and members of ethnic, racial, social, religious, or sexual minorities are more vulnerable to domestic abuse than others. It is no coincidence that the women who reported being subjected to domestic cruelty during the 1918-1920 influenza pandemic also complained of their husbands' lack of employment, of not living in a 'proper home, but in a bedroom and sitting room', and of poverty. In both epidemics, fear, frustration, and financial anxieties led to confusion, irritability, low mood, depression, insomnia, and anger.

Seeking help was also difficult for victimised women during both pandemics. For many, leaving the family home was not an option because of financial dependency on the male breadwinner, lack of access to divorce, and feelings of shame. The curtailment of social activities meant that vulnerable women lost the support of friends and family members; instead, they were required to share often-limited domestic space with aggressors.[20] Scarce health resources meant that medical attention was diverted from familial violence into tackling the deadly infection. Many places where abused women could seek refuge were over-stretched and under-resourced *before* the pandemics: the disease catapulted them to breaking point, forcing many to close.[21] During the 2020 lockdown, formal support services such as hotlines, shelters, and counselling services were cut and personnel was severely reduced.[22] Many victims refrained from reporting their abuse to the police or visiting health facilities due to fears of exposing themselves to a deadly disease or due to an attempt not to strain already overstretched health systems.[23] The extent of this avoidance in 1918-1920 is unknown but, in the UK today, there has been a 25% decline in the number of people attending emergency departments.²⁴

Accessing help is difficult. In 1919-1920 as well as 2020, courts were closed or started severely restricting their proceedings because of fears of infection. This has also meant that the forensic and other health professionals who would be called to give testimony stay away as well.²⁵ In the UK, sexual assault referral centres (SARCs) saw a 50% reduction in the number of referrals for forensic examinations in the first six weeks of the 2020 lockdown.²⁶ In those cases where a face-to-face interview is held (something that is only allowed in the most serious cases of domestic violence), doctors complain that wearing a mask or visor 'notably shifts the patient-doctor relationship, making building trust and rapport and expressing empathy – crucial when working with sexual assault patients – challenging'.²⁷

Lockdowns, alcohol, and quackery

Both pandemics generated passionate debate about the relationship between alcohol abuse and domestic violence. Nearly all cases of domestic cruelty reported in the press during the 1918-1920 pandemic mentioned excessive alcohol consumption. Similar concerns have been noted in 2020. People were consuming *more* alcohol in *greater quantities* at home, since bars and other drinking establishments were closed.²⁸ In the UK in the week to 21 March, sales in alcohol stores increased by 67%, compared to a 43% increase in overall supermarket sales.²⁹ Well-known statistics published by the Institute of Alcohol Studies did not bode well. In one of their surveys in 2014, they found that between one-quarter and one-half of perpetrators of domestic abuse had been drinking at the time of the assault; some surveys put this percentage as high as three-quarters.³⁰ In those instances where the violence was classed as 'severe', the perpetrators were twice as likely as others to be abusing alcohol at the time.³¹

Aggressive men typically used the fear of the virus as a weapon in their arsenal of abuse.³² They ramped up controlling mechanisms. The exact *form* this took was culturally specific. As mentioned at the beginning of this chapter, Jessie Webster Cooper's husband 'kept his room in a filthy condition. There were onion peelings lying all over the floor'. The mention of onion skins is important because of the belief that onions could prevent influenza infection. It was widely reported in the press that 'eating of raw onions is a complete protection against influenza and indeed all sorts of evil'.³³ Even more relevant in understanding the behaviour of Cooper's husband was the conviction of one 'distinguished London physician' that 'a raw onion in a fever-stricken room soon decays, because it attracts the germs'.³⁴ In other words, Cooper and her 16-year-old son had contracted influenza; by scattering onion skins throughout the home, her husband was not merely undermining her attempts at keeping the house clean, he was also attempting to 'soak up' the germs that she and her son had brought into the house.

In 2020, widespread 'lockdowns' introduced specific forms of abuse aimed at further isolating victims. Perpetrators tell their family that they are infected with the virus and therefore cannot leave the home; others invite people home, telling their wives that the visitor has Covid-19 and is 'going to infect them' unless they submit to certain conditions.[35] Crystal Justice, the chief development officer for the National Domestic Violence Hotline, reported that victims in essential jobs (such as health care) complained that their abusers accused them of 'purposely trying to infect them with COVID-19 by going to work'; other abusers forbid victims 'from taking preventative measures [...] using such tactics like restricting hand sanitizer, soap or access to the shower'.[36] They may ban or limit handwashing.[37] Perpetrators routinely impose restrictions on social media or the internet.[38]

Children in danger

In households with abusive men, children are in especially vulnerable positions, especially when schools, summer camps, youth and sports clubs, and faith-based societies are closed.[39] In the US today, around one-fifth of all reports of abuse and neglect of children are made by educational personnel: this makes teachers the primary reporters of abuse.[40] Combined with restricted access to members of the extended family (particularly grandparents), the closures of schools greatly reduces opportunities for children making their mistreatment known. This increased risk has been exacerbated by reduced numbers of staff working in child-protection charities; an understandable reluctance of health professionals to visit homes which potentially harbour the virus (especially in the context of limited protective equipment) further reduces physical visits to high-risk homes. In 2020, this has been starkly revealed in places like Connecticut, California, Michigan, Kentucky, New Hampshire, and Louisiana, which have seen a *reduction* in reports of child mistreatment to hotlines due to what health experts have identified as a 'precipitous decrease in contact between children, educational personnel, and other community youth programmes'.[41]

It is also important to note that many children do not have homes, let alone 'safe' ones: the millions of children living in immigrant or displaced persons camps, detention facilities, and orphanages are frequently targeted by abusers precisely because of their vulnerability.[42] Other high-risk children are those identifying as LGBTQ, that is, approximately 16% of all youth.[43] As two researchers explained, providers should be aware that it is sometimes difficult to ensure privacy with telemedicine practices. For instance, using correct pronouns or names or making reference to patients' LGBTQ identities may put them at risk for additional harm.[44]

The double-edged sword of digital communications technologies

These broad similarities in levels and risk to domestic violence during pandemics mask more important differences. Radical differences in communicative technologies are an obvious one. Telephones were not commonly available in deprived homes in 1918-1920; in contrast, medical personnel in 2020 quickly began conducting consultations via telephone or video link. However, such compromises turned out to be technically difficult, especially for the elderly and those without sophisticated mobile phones, as well as creating problems of privacy (such as when assessing wounds to genitalia).[45]

The 2020 pandemic has also seen dramatic upswings in the use of the internet and social media more generally – it has become crucial for work, schooling, and sociability. As a result, cyber-violence has thrived, especially online sexual harassment, zoombombing, and sexualised trolling. An Australian-based study revealed that such forms of abuse have increased by 50%.[46] There have also been increases in online attempts to access content relating to child sexual exploitation, a serious issue since the number of officers tasked with policing cyberviolence is falling.[47] This has affected young people in particular due to their increased reliance on texts, social media, and mobile apps to communicate with friends. As bored children turn to online platforms, the opportunities for offenders to abuse them increases.[48]

Getting help can be difficult if reliant on digital technologies: internet connectivity problems occur especially in rural areas or where there is low coverage.[49] Many low-income people cannot afford the computing technologies and elderly people may not be conversant with them. In poorer regions, there are 'profound gender digital divides', disadvantaging abused women.[50] The technologies are also harnessed by abusers who use Global Positioning Systems (GPS), digital trackers, and spyware to 'covertly and overtly monitor their victim's online presence to maintain coercive, even deadly control'.[51]

Landlord blackmail and firearms

Specific dangers to women and other vulnerable people can be expected to rise, especially since, in some countries, there are plans to give early release to certain categories of prisoners, which include those convicted of domestic abuse.[52] Some landlords have been accused of pressuring women for sex in exchange for the rent.[53] According to the International Labor Organization, 61% of women in the world (that is, two billion women) are engaged in the informal sector, so are especially vulnerable to economic uncertainty and the risks that go with that.[54] Many girls and women in the global South find themselves increasingly precarious since it is their responsibility to collect water necessary for adequate washing of hands and utensils. There is evidence that they are exposed to sexual harassment and rape in the course of carrying out this chore.[55]

More specifically, in the US, a large proportion of homes contain unsecured firearms, increasing the likelihood of intimate partner homicides. Research in 2003 found that abused women are five times more likely to be killed by their abuser if he owns a firearm.[56] In other words, the risk is increasing given that domestic firearms have risen as a result of anxieties and societal unrest during the pandemic.[57] According to the FBI, in March 2020, there were over one million *more* pre-sale background checks for firearms compared to March 2019: this amounts to a total of more than 3.7 million checks.[58] Small Arms Analytics and Forecasting (SAAF), the independent research consultancy firm focusing on small arms and ammunition markets, noted that retailers sold more than 2.5 million firearms in March alone, an 85% increase in a year.[59] Long-gun sales also rose by 74%.[60] This will have a longer-term impact, as Jurgen Brauer, the SAAF's chief economist explains, because 'It's now possible that at least a proportion of first-time buyers will be converted into repeat buyers, so that there may be a higher base of firearms owners in the years to come'.[61] In the short term, however, the risk posed by the proliferation of small arms is widely acknowledged. As the authors of an article in the *Annals of Surgery* warned, the 'stay-at-home ruling in many states does not recognize shooting ranges as essential businesses'. As a result, first time gun owners might not be receiving adequate training in firearm use and storage, leading to 'more deadly' domestic violence incidents. Unsafe storage might also make firearms 'easily accessible to bored and curious children that are currently stuck at home, which increases opportunities for tragic, unintentional shootings'.[62]

Conclusion

We have considered various vectors of vulnerability for girls, women, and other minoritised groups during two pandemics. Importantly, domestic violence does not exist outside broader societal practices, ideologies, and power struggles. After all, in 'normal' times, one in three women experience sexual or other violence by an intimate partner in her lifetime[63] and, worldwide, 37% of murders of women are committed by intimate partners.[64] Indeed, it might be inaccurate to call the rise of domestic violence during the pandemics as 'crises' since for many vulnerable people, violence is an everyday norm, not exceptional. This is crucial because the stress of domestic abuse has a cumulative effect on the immune system (known as 'weathering'), meaning that populations at high risk of domestic abuse prior to the pandemic are *particularly* susceptible to the harmful impacts of the virus. It is also important to interrogate the language used to discuss vulnerability in order to avoid labelling some groups (girls and women, minoritised people, and so on) as inherently vulnerable rather than *constituted* as vulnerable by structural relations of domination. Finally, the stories of intimate partner violence as told in this chapter risk reducing victims to spectres of vulnerability. However, the girls and women mentioned here are more than 'victims'. Domestic violence exposes a person's dependency to *known* Others, with whom the woman might also have experienced affection, even love, in the past. By focusing attention on domestic violence, we must not elude all other aspects of a subject's identity, including the ongoing ways she expresses agency and contests injustices.

NOTES

1. 'A Gipsy Hill Wife's Claim', *Norwood News* (21 February 1919), 6.
2. 'Unhappy Home', *Forfar Herald* (4 April 1919), 3.
3. 'Bury Woman's Marriage', *Bury Free Press* (2 August 1919), 8.
4. 'Madman's Terrible Crime', *The People* (15 December 1918), 3. For other examples of influenza-affected men killing their families, see 'Father's Awful Crime', *Belfast Tragedy* (26 November 1918), 3; 'Influenza Tragedy', *Aberdeen Evening Express* (26 November 1918), 3; 'Shocking Tragedy at Stowmarket', *Bury Free Press* (9 November 1918), 8; 'Strange Effects of Influenza', *Cambridge Independent Press* (8 November 1918), 5; 'Strange Effects of Influenza', *Cambridge Daily News* (2 November 1918), 4; 'Suicide Following Influenza at Milverton', *Western Times* (28 February 1919), 7.
5. Bethany Allen-Ebrahimian, 'China's Domestic Violence Epidemic', *Axios* (7 March 2020), at <https://www.axios.com/china-domestic-violence-coronavirus-quarantine-7b00c3ba-35bc-4d16-afdd-b76ecfb28882.html>, viewed 1 August 2020.
6. UN, 'UN Supporting "Trapped" Domestic Violence Victims During COVID-19 Pandemic' (2020), at <https://www.un.org/en/coronavirus/un-supporting-'trapped'-domestic-violence-victims-during-covid-19-pandemic>, viewed 1 August 2020 and UN, 'Women, COVID-19 and Ending Violence Against Women and Girls' (2020), at <https://www.unwomen.org/-/media/headquarters/attachments/sections/library/publications/2020/issue-brief-covid-19-and-ending-violence-against-women-and-girls-en.pdf?la=en&vs=5006>, viewed 1 August 2020.

7   Andrew M. Campbell, 'An Increasing Risk of Family Violence during the Covid-19 Pandemic: Strengthening Community Collaborations to Save Lives', *Forensic Science International: Reports* (2 December 2020), 2. Also see Emanuele Souza Marques, Claudia Leite de Moraes, Maria Helena Hasselmann, Suely Ferreira Deslandes, and Michael Eduardo Reichenheim, 'Violence Against Women, Children, and Adolescents During the Covid-19 Pandemic: Overview, Contributing Factors, and Mitigating Measures', *CSP. Cadernos de Saúde Pública. Reports in Public Health*, 36.4 (2020), 1-2, at <https://www.scielo.br/scielo.php?pid=S0102-311X2020000400505&script=sci_arttext&tlng=en>, viewed 1 August 2020.

8   Elisabeth Mahase, 'Covid-19: EU States Report 60% Rise in Emergency Calls about Domestic Violence', *British Medical Journal* (2020), 369.

9   For summaries, see Brad Boserup, Mark McKenney, and Adel Elkbuli, 'Alarming Trends in US Domestic Violence During the COVID-19 Pandemic', *American Journal of Emergency Medicine*, (20 April 2020), 1 and Yasmin B. Kofman and Dana Rose Garfin, 'Home is Not Always a Haven: The Domestic Violence Crisis Amid the COVID-19 Pandemic', *Psychological Trauma: Theory, Research, Practice, and Policy* (2020), 1-3.

10   UN, 'UN Supporting 'Trapped' Domestic Violence Victims During COVID-19 Pandemic' (2020), at <https://www.un.org/en/coronavirus/un-supporting-'trapped'-domestic-violence-victims-during-covid-19-pandemic>, viewed 1 August 2020.

11   Jamie Grierson, 'Domestic Abuse Killings "More Than Double" Amid Covid-19 Lockdown', *The Guardian* (15 April 2020), at <https://www.theguardian.com/society/2020/apr/15/domestic-abuse-killings-more-than-double-amid-covid-19-lockdown>, viewed 1 August 2020.

12   United Nations Population Fund, 'Millions More Cases of Violence, Child Marriage, Female Genital Mutilation, Unintended Pregnancy Expected Due to the COVID-19 Pandemic' (28 April 2020), at <https://www.unfpa.org/news/millions-more-cases-violence-child-marriage-female-genital-mutilation-unintended-pregnancies>, viewed 1 August 2020.

13   United Nations Population Fund, 'Millions More Cases of Violence'.

14   'A Gipsy Hill Wife's Claim', *Norwood News* (21 February 1919), 6.

15   Julian A. Navarro, 'Influenza in 1918: An Epidemic in Images', *Public Health Reports*, 125, supplement 3 (April 2010), 12.

16   Kate Marshall, *Corridor: Media Architecture in American Fiction* (Minneapolis: University of Minnesota Press, 2013), 117 and 133; and Navarro, 'Influenza in 1918', 11.

17   Stuart Galishoff, 'Newark and the Great Influenza Pandemic of 1918', *Bulletin of the History of Medicine*, 43.3 (May-June 1969), 250-51.

18   Monica Schoch-Spana, '"Hospital's Full-Up": The 1918 Influenza Pandemic', *Public Health Reports*, 116, supplement 2 (2001), 32-3.

19   See 'Plenty of Sugar as Influenza Cure', *Leeds Mercury* (12 March 1919), 4; 'More Sugar as Cure for Infleunza?', *Daily Mirror* (12 March 1919), 3; 'Science and Alcohol', *Orkney Herald and Weekly Adviser and Gazette for the Orkney and Zetland Island* (5 March 1919), 2; 'Sugar and Influenza', *Leicester Daily Post* (12 March 1919), 4; 'Sugar for Influenza', *Banffshire Reporter* (19 March 1919), 3; 'Whiskey for Influenza', *Evening Despatch* (16 December 1918), 3. See also Navarro, 'Influenza in 1918', 12.

20   Samantha K. Brooks, Rebecca K. Webster, Louise E. Smith, Lisa Woodland, Simon Wessley, Neil Greenberg, and Gideon James Rubin, 'The Psychological Impact of Quarantine and How to Reduce It: Rapid Review of the Evidence', *The Lancet*, 395.10227 (14 March 2020), 912-20.

21. Casey Tolan, 'Some Cities See Jumps in Domestic Violence During the Pandemic', CNN (4 April 2020), at <https://www.cnn.com/2020/04/04/us/domestic-violence-coronavirus-calls-cases-increase-invs/index.html>, viewed 1 August 2020.
22. Elisabeth Roesch, Avni Amin, Jhumka Gupta, and Claudia García-Moreno, 'Violence Against Women During Covid-19 Pandemic Restrictions', *The British Medical Journal* (7 May 2020), 369; Katy Johnson, Lindsey Green, Muriel Volpellier, Suzanne Kidenda, Thomas McHale, Karen Naimer, and Ranit Mishori, 'The Impact of COVID-19 on Services for People Affected by Sexual and Gender-Based Violence', *International Journal of Gynaecology and Obstetrics* (2020) 1-3, at <https://obgyn.onlinelibrary.wiley.com/doi/full/10.1002/ijgo.13285>, viewed 1 August 2020.
23. Adriene O'Neill, Stephen J. Nicholls, Julie Redfern, Alex Brown, and David L. Hare, 'Mental Health and Psychosocial Challenges in the COVID-19 Pandemic: Food for Thought for Cardiovascular Health Care Professionals', *Heart, Lung and Circulation*, (16 June 2020), 4.
24. Peter Green, 'Risks to Children and Young People During Covid-19 Pandemic', *British Medical Journal*, 2020), 1.
25. Katy Johnson et al., 'The Impact of COVID-19'.
26. Katy Johnson et al., 'The Impact of COVID-19'.
27. Katy Johnson et al., 'The Impact of COVID-19'.
28. [Editorial], 'Drinking Alone: COVID-19, Lockdown, and Alcohol-Related Harm', *The Lancet*, 5 (July 2020), 625. Also see UK Office for National Statistics, at <https://www.ons.gov.uk/businessindustryandtrade/retailinbusiness/bulletins/retailsales/march2020>, viewed 1 August 2020; Alcohol Change UK, at <https://alcoholchange.org.uk/blog/2020/covid19-drinking-during-lockdown-headline-findings>, viewed 1 August 2020.
29. Ilora Finlay and Ian Gilmore, 'Covid-19 and Alcohol – A Dangerous Cocktail', *British Medical Journal* (2020), 369.
30. Institute of Alcohol Studies, 'Alcohol, Domestic Abuse, and Sexual Assault' (2014), at <http://www.ias.org.uk/uploads/IAS%20report%20Alcohol%20domestic%20abuse%20and%20sexual%20assault.pdf>, viewed 1 August 2020.
31. Institute of Alcohol Studies, 'Alcohol, Domestic Abuse, and Sexual Assault'.
32. Mélissa Godin, 'How Coronavirus is Affecting Victims of Domestic Violence', *Time* (18 March 2020), at <https://time.com/5803887/coronavirus-domestic-violence-victims>, viewed 1 August 2020.
33. For just a few examples, see 'Allotment Notes', *Hull Daily Mail* (11 July 1918), 3; 'Harvesting the Onion Crop', *Blyth News* (16 September 1918), 1; 'Onions for Nerves', *Diss Express* (16 July 1920), 3; 'The Ever-Useful Onion', *The Hampshire Independent* (16 November 1918), 1; H. J. Swann, 'Correspondence', *Coventry Evening Telegraph* (31 October 1918), 2; 'Influenza', *Western Morning News* (26 February 1919), 6; 'Onions and Influenza', *Wigton Advertiser* (13 July 1918), 3.
34. 'Onions and Influenza', *Whitby Gazette* (19 July 1918), 2. For identical reports, also see 'The Onion Cure', *Halifax Evening Courier* (12 July 1918), 7; 'When Cholera was in Leeds', *Yorkshire Evening Post* (12 July 1918), 4.
35. Mary Gearin and Ben Knight, 'Family Violence Perpetrators using COVID-19 as a "Form of Abuse We Have Not Experienced Before"', in ABC News (28 March 2920), at <https://www.abc.net.au/news/2020-03-29/coronavirus-family-violence-surge-in-victoria/12098546>, viewed 1 August 2020.

36 Rachel Sandler, 'Domestic Violence Hotline Reports Surge in Coronavirus-Related Calls As Shelter-in-Place Leads to Isolation, Abuse', *Forbes* (7 April 2020), at <https://www.forbes.com/sites/rachelsandler/2020/04/06/domestic-violence-hotline-reports-surge-in-coronavirus-related-calls-as-shelter-in-place-leads-to-isolation-abuse/>, viewed 1 August 2020

37 Campbell, 'An Increased Risk', 2.

38 Campbell, 'An Increased Risk', 1-3.

39 Maya I. Ragavan, Alison J. Culyba, Fatimah L. Muhammad, and Elizabeth Miller, 'Supporting Adolescents and Young Adult Exposed to or Experiencing Violence during the COVID-19 Pandemic', *Journal of Adolescent Health*, 67 (2020), 18.

40 Elizabeth York Thomas, Ashri Anurudran, Kathryn Robb, and Thomas F. Burke, 'Spotlight on Child Abuse and Neglect Response in the time of COVID-19', *The Lancet*, 5 (July 2020), e371; Campbell, 'An Increased Risk', 2.

41 Elizabeth York Thomas et al., 'Spotlight on Child Abuse'.

42 Ritwik Ghosh, Mahua J. Dubey, Subhankar Chatterjee, and Souvik Dubey, 'Impact of COVID-19 on Children: Special Focus on the Psychosocial Aspect', *Minerva Pediatrica*, 72.3 (June 2020), 229.

43 Rachel I. Silliman Cohen and Emily AdlinBosk, 'Vulnerable Youth and the COVID-19 Pandemic', *Pediatrics*, 146,1 (July 2020), at <https://www.researchgate.net/publication/340985147_Vulnerable_Youth_and_the_COVID-19_Pandemic>, viewed 1 August 2020.

44 Cohen and Bosk, 'Vulnerable Youth and the COVID-19 Pandemic'.

45 Katy Johnson et al., 'The Impact of COVID-19'.

46 'Cyber Abuse Up by 50 Percent Amid Covid-19 Restrictions', at <https://www.skynews.com.au/details/_6148739344001>, viewed 1 August 2020.

47 Europol, 'Catching the Virus: Cybercrime, Disinformation, and the COVID-19 Pandemic' (3 April 2020), 7, at <https://www.europol.europa.eu/publications-documents/catching-virus-cybercrime-disinformation-and-covid-19-pandemic>, viewed 1 August 2020; Ghosh et al., 'Impact of COVID-19 on Children', 229; UN Entity for Gender Equality and the Empowerment of Women, 'Online and ICT Facilitated Violence Against Women and Girls During COVID-19' (2020), at <https://www2.unwomen.org/-/media/headquarters/attachments/sections/library/publications/2020/brief-online-and-ict-facilitated-violence-against-women-and-girls-during-covid-19-en.pdf?la=en&vs=2519>, viewed 1 August 2020.

48 Ghosh et al., Mahua J. Dubey, Subhankar Chatterjee, and Souvik Dubey, 'Impact of COVID-19 on Children', 229.

49 Chuka Emezue, 'Digital or Digitally Delivered Responses to Domestic and Intimate Partner Violence during COVID-19', *JMIR Publications* (11 May 2020), 10, at <https://publichealth.jmir.org/2020/3/e19831/>, viewed 1 August 2020.

50 Emezue, 'Digital or Digitally Delivered Responses'.

51 Emezue, 'Digital or Digitally Delivered Responses'. See also Diana Freed, Jackeline Palmer, Diana Minchala, Karen Levy, Thomas Ristenpart, and Nicola Dell, ''A Stalker's Paradise': How Intimate Partner Abusers Exploit Technology', in *Proceedings of the 2018 CHI Conference on Human Factors in Computing Systems* (April 2018), 1-13.

52 Campbell, 'An Increased Risk', 1-3; Lisieux E. de Borba Telles, Alexandre M. Valença, Alcina J. S. Barros, and Antônio Geraldo da Silva, 'Domestic Violence in the COVID-19 Pandemic: A Forensic Psychiatric Perspective', *Brazilian Journal of Psychiatry* (2020),

53. at <https://www.scielo.br/scielo.php?pid=S1516-44462020005015211&script=sci_arttext>, viewed 1 August 2020.
53. Sharon Goiuveia Feist and Monica S. Herrera, 'How to Improve Security Outcomes During a Pandemic? Start with a Gender Lens', *Daniel K. Inouye Asia-Pacific Center for Security Studies* (2020), at <https://apcss.org/wp-content/uploads/2020/04/Security-nexus-pandemic-gender-lens.pdf>, viewed 1 August 2020.
54. Max de Haldevang, 'Coronavirus is Imperiling Billions of Informal Workers – especially Women', (2020), at <https://qz.com/1831326/coronavirus-imperils-billions-of-informal-workers-especially-women/>, viewed 1 August 2020.
55. Imran Saqib Khalid, 'Managing Risks to Water and Sanitation amid Covid-19: Policy Options for Pakistan', *Sustainable Development Policy Institute* (2020), at <https://www.jstor.org/stable/resrep24356?seq=1#metadata_info_tab_contents>, viewed 1 August 2020.
56. Jacquelyn C. Campbell, Daniel Webster, Jane Koziol-McLain, Carolyn Block, Doris Campbell, Mary Ann Curry, Faye Gary, Nancy Glass, Judith McFarlane, Carolyn Sachs, Phyllis Sharps, Yvonne Ulrich, Susan A. Wilt, Jennifer Manganello, Xiao Xu, Janet Schollenberger, Victoria Frye, and Kathryn Laughon, 'Risk Factors for Femicide in Abusive Relationships: Results from a Multisite Case Control Study', *American Journal of Public Health*, 93,7 (July 2003), 1092.
57. Heath Druzin, 'Gun Sales Skyrocket in March on Pandemic Fears. Guns and America' (1 April 2020), at <https://gunsandamerica.org/story/20/04/01/gun-sales-skyrocket-in-march-on-pandemic-fears>, viewed 1 August 2020.
58. Druzin. Also see Justin S. Hatchimonji, Robert A. Swendiman, Mark J. Seamon, and Michael L. Nance, 'Trauma Does Not Quarantine: Violence During the Covid-19 Pandemic', *Annals of Surgery* (2020), 3.
59. Druzin, 'Gun Sales'.
60. Druzin, 'Gun Sales'.
61. Druzin, 'Gun Sales'.
62. Thomas K. Duncan, Jessica L. Weaver, Tanya L. Zakrison, Bellal Joseph, Brenda T. Campbell, A. Britton Christmas, Ronald M. Stewart, Deborah A. Kuhls, and Eileen M. Bulger, 'Domestic Violence and Safe Storage of Firearms in the COVID-19 Era', *Annals of Surgery* (2020). Also see Hatchimonji et al., 'Trauma Does Not Quarantine'.
63. WHO, *Global and Regional Estimates of Violence Against Women: Prevalence and Health Effects of Intimate Partner Violence and Non-Partner Sexual Violence* (Geneva: WHO, 2013), at <https://www.who.int/reproductivehealth/publications/violence/9789241564625/en/>, viewed 1 August 2020.
64. WHO, *Global and Regional Estimates of Violence Against Women*.

Testing Borders: Covid-19 and the Management of (Im)mobility

Sandro Mezzadra

The question of borders has been occupying my attention for the last two decades. In particular, working with Brett Neilson, I have emphasised the deep heterogeneity of 'border' as a semantic field, arguing that the conflicts and struggles surrounding geopolitical borders need to be framed within a wider consideration of a panoply of boundaries and lines of demarcations – from urban to linguistic boundaries, to mention just two important instances.[1] Nevertheless, I had never taken into serious consideration the existence of 'regional borders' in Italy – of those borders we were not allowed to cross for a month after the end of the lockdown in early May 2020. This is significant in pointing up how the Covid-19 pandemic and its management produced new borders while reinforcing and reorganising the functions of old ones. This is of course no surprise, since the virus circulated across the transborder conduits and channels that make up the material skeleton of globalisation and the governing of the pandemic was first of all a governing of mobility.

The experience of borders and bordering devices was and continues to be particularly harsh for migrants and refugees in many parts of the world, including the Mediterranean, the U.S./Mexico border, and the Bay of Bengal. Many migrants and refugees remained stuck during the pandemic, experiencing forced immobility. This is true for instance for many migrants working in the 'informal economy' who literally lost the material basis for the reproduction of their lives without usually having any access to public benefits. But it is also true for dozens of thousands of transmigrants from Central America to Mexico, who continue to be caught in the double pincer of the army and criminal cartels. Others lived through the pandemic in detention centres in Libya, on the Greek islands (with the infamous hotspot of Moria, a source of shame for Europe), or within European or North American territory, where living conditions were often hotbeds for viral spread.² Border crossing, in general, has become even more difficult and risky in the last months, as the increase in the number of shipwrecks in the Mediterranean demonstrates.

Mobility/Immobility – social and racialised containment

But the predicament of migrants is not limited to such conditions of forced immobility; it can also coincide with forced *mobility*, as the massive and painful exodus of internal migrants from metropolitan spaces to the countryside in India amply demonstrates.³ Internal boundaries played key roles in framing such forced mobility. This is an important point, since it demonstrates that a defining feature of the pandemic and its management is a reorganisation of the whole economy of mobility and immobility, with far-reaching consequences for the structures and subjective experience of domination and exploitation. Xiang Biao, a Chinese anthropologist based in Oxford, proposes the term 'shock mobility' to describe the unusual traffic patterns that involved so-called 'essential workers' in many parts of the world, ranging from public health to factory workers, from riders working for delivery platforms to workers in logistical warehouses and agriculture.⁴ Needless to say, many such workers are migrants whose lives are circumscribed and limited by the action of a series of borders and boundaries.

In such a complex economy of mobility and immobility that characterises the management of the pandemic, borders are tested and reorganised in multiple ways. Hygienic-sanitary border enforcements have been enacted to increase pandemic containment in many parts of the world, including Europe. Temporary suspension of asylum procedures and declarations of ports as 'unsafe' by the governments of Malta and Italy have opened up the space for the emergence of what Martina Tazzioli calls 'forms of racialized containment predicated upon health and safety'.⁵ While the governmental rhetoric behind such measures emphasises the need to protect both citizens and migrants, they actually accelerate ongoing trends in the politics of migration containment, make passage even more risky, spread conditions of quarantine and detention, and construct migrants as a threat to public health as potential vectors for the spread of the virus.⁶ As Wendy Brown notes, although the pandemic condition is a result of microbes not respecting boundaries, border closures serve 'the important political function of treating the virus as if it invaded us from the outside and acting as if we are meeting that threat with sovereign power'.⁷

Border closures and travel restrictions were some of the first measures taken by governments in the face of the coronavirus pandemic of 2020. While migrants and refugees in transit were targeted in a particularly harsh way by those measures, crossing an international border became more difficult and, in many cases, impossible for all kinds of people, including tourists, businessmen, academics, and political activists. After decades of accelerating and intensifying transnational and transcontinental mobility, we experienced an abrupt end and reversal of the trend. Borders matter again not only for migrants and poor people on the move but also for those who had become accustomed to cross them without even taking note of it. This is an experience destined to profoundly influence patterns of transnational cooperation and exchange in the near future, even after Covid-19 – and one need only look at the boom in (corporate) platforms like Zoom, or Teams, to enable working and political meetings as well as business communication.

While international borders have been tested by the pandemic and border controls have been reorganised according to a hygienic-sanitary rationale, an array of internal boundaries took on new meanings over the last months. A logic of bordering reshaped social relations at the most elementary level of keeping 'social distance' and wearing masks. Particularly during lockdowns, a logic of confinement shaped labour in several sectors where 'smart working' is impossible. This was particularly apparent in agriculture, in care and domestic labour, in logistical warehouses, in food delivery managed by platforms, and in factories, making visible and exacerbating social inequalities and the uneven distribution across society of the burden (which also means the risk) of so-called 'essential' services. The situation is not going to change as long as the pandemic stays with us. The logic of confinement inscribes new borders within the world of labour and there is a need to take stock of its implications also from the angle of labour struggles (keeping in mind that 'essential workers' have been among the protagonists of the most intense struggles in the last months). Moreover, in many parts of the world the virus disproportionately hit racialised minorities, reinforcing another specific instance of internal boundaries. This was the case in the US with blacks and *latinxs*, and the insurgence of Black Lives Matter after the murder of George Floyd must also be read against that background – as a rebellion against the bordering devices that fragment and divide social cooperation and the working class. This was also the case in Brazil with indigenous and black people, while in general the policing of slums (that is, of confined spaces) was particularly harsh there and elsewhere, for instance in India and Nigeria. Race and poverty point to another set of internal boundaries as well as to the relevance of Neo-Malthusian and Social Darwinist government schemes in the global management of the pandemic.

Home as a boundary

Any attempt to come to grips with the transformations of borders in the face of the coronavirus should combine an investigation of international borders with a detailed analysis of the multiple internal boundaries that I have just mentioned. Allow me to introduce another one, which seems crucial to me. For everyone during lockdowns, confinement was first of all confinement at 'home'. In a way, one can say that the home itself became a boundary. Needless to say, for homeless people this was a particularly difficult moment, while in general the kind of home one inhabits of course made a huge difference, reinforcing once again the essential boundary associated with money. Even beyond that, confinement at home tested the border between production and reproduction, opening up a whole set of tensions and conflicts in gender relations. While the home as a boundary was meant to be a safe place with respect to contagion, in many cases it became a nightmare and even a site of physical violence for women, as feminist movements have emphasised across the world. Confinement at home has definitely often led to the reinforcement of a disproportionate gender division of reproductive labour but also to a re-politicisation of the domestic space through feminist interventions.

Renationalisation and international cooperation

The pandemic definitely led countries and societies to look inward, potentially nurturing processes of renationalisation of politics that were already underway since the financial crisis of 2007/8 and that had become associated with the rise of old and new forces of the right, epitomised by such names as Boris Johnson, Donald Trump, Jair Bolsonaro, Narendra Modi, and the like. Such a renationalisation is closely linked to a hardening of international borders and to the internal boundaries that I have just mentioned. The spread of the coronavirus has exacerbated such trends, adding a different twist to them – which means the reinforcement of the hygienic-sanitary rationality that has always been a constitutive aspect of border regimes.[8] 'Society must be defended', one could gloss quoting the title of a famous course held by Michel Foucault in 1976,[9] and the border becomes a crucial site from this angle. Nevertheless, there is a need to stress that society can be defended in many different ways, including through the expansion of public health, the entrenchment of the universal right to healthcare, and processes of social cooperation and self-organisation. This is the reason why the struggle over public health today will also have far-reaching implications for the way in which borders will be managed and policed in the near future. The quality and nature of social relationships prevailing within a given political space are indeed crucial variables for the shape of the borders circumscribing it.

While it is definitely true that processes of renationalisation have been nurtured by the outbreak of the pandemic, its further development has given rise to different reactions and in many cases to an increasing and pronounced awareness of the need to promote and enhance international and multilateral cooperation to cope with coronavirus. These are ambivalent and even contradictory effects of the pandemic, which have clear implications for borders. In Europe, in particular, the clash between national interests and the cooperative logic of integration continues to shape negotiations regarding the so-called 'recovery fund' (or, the 'Next Generation EU' plan), although it is clear that in the next months and years national solutions to the deep economic and social crisis engendered by the virus will only be possible within a common European framework. This opens up a new battleground for social movements and forces of the left which will increasingly have to coordinate their action at the continental level and hopefully be able to combine the struggle for social justice within Europe with the struggle to 'democratise' external borders.

Breaches and contestations

Borders are not things; they cannot be equated to a wall, to barbed wire, or for that matter to a bridge. Rather, they are complex institutions, made up of social relationships and tensions between techniques of border reinforcement and practices of crossing. My point is that there is a lot to learn about borders considering them from the angle of their contestation – which also means from the angle of the subjects that contest them. It is important to remind ourselves that all the internal boundaries I mentioned above, from the confinement of labour to racial boundaries, from slums to homes, are contested borders. The struggles surrounding them, which often involve migrants, are relevant in themselves, but they also have crucial roles to play with respect to international borders. The point is indeed that a multiplication and a reinforcement of internal boundaries necessarily leads to a hardening of external borders (and vice versa). And it is safe to contend that a breach in an internal boundary at least potentially leads to a breach in external borders.

In *Border as Method*, Brett Neilson and I introduce the notion of 'border struggles'. We emphasise the fact that 'border struggles are not simply, or not only, fought at the border', opening up the space for the investigation and political acknowledgment of the multiple conflicts surrounding internal boundaries, such as the ones I just touched upon. But we also contend that 'once we investigate the multifarious practices with which migrants challenge borders on a daily basis, it becomes clear that border struggles are all too often matters of life and death'.[10] This is a materiality that immediately refers to specific international borders, where conflicts revolving around migration are particularly intense. The Mediterranean is an obvious instance of such borders, with all the complications that pertain to a maritime border.[11] Particularly the 'central Mediterranean', over the last years, has become the most lethal passage for migrants and refugees, with more than 20,000 dead women, men, and children since 2014 according to the IOM's Missing Migrants Project.[12] As mentioned above, the situation has not changed during the pandemic, when migrants' departures even increased both due to the war in Libya and the impact of the coronavirus on the economies of countries on the southern shore of the Mediterranean such as Algeria and above all Tunisia.

What is really striking under such dire conditions is the stubbornness with which migrants and refugees continue to challenge the European border regime. While we need to denounce Europe's cooperation with Turkey and Libya to contain migration, which is part of a longstanding process of externalisation of border control (and ultimately of the border itself), I think that it is even more important to take stock of such stubbornness and to understand it as part of ongoing border struggles in the Mediterranean. Far from being mere 'victims', as they have been portrayed for a long time by humanitarian discourses and actors, migrants and refugees are engaged in full-fledged border struggles. These struggles are increasingly considered a crucial point of reference by activists engaged in rescue operations at sea, who were able to build a genuine 'civil fleet' with its own communication centre, 'Alarm Phone' – a multi-sited hotline employing information and communication technologies to provide immediate assistance to migrants in distress.[13] At a time of pandemic this powerful instance of cooperation at the European level has only intensified, connecting with migrants' and refugees' struggles and making the Mediterranean a contested border space.

World-configuring borders and the expanding frontiers of capital – the logistics revolution

This contested border space must be analysed in a focused and detailed way to grasp the impact of coronavirus and its implications for border struggles. This is no less true for other borderlands, such as, looking still at Europe, the so-called Balkan route that has steadily been turned into a kind of 'vertical border'. Deployment of military forces at international borders, pushback practices and collective expulsions, fully inadequate accommodation facilities for people in transit, and wilful neglect of hygienic and sanitary standards characterise the situation there since the outbreak of the pandemic.[14] I repeat that in-depth and grounded analyses of specific border spaces are urgently needed. At the same time, it is also important to keep in mind that borders – each border, although in different ways – always perform what Étienne Balibar calls a 'world-configuring function'.[15] This is an important point for the study of borders. What Balibar means is that far from simply circumscribing and partitioning an already existing global space, borders have outstanding roles to play in its *production*. And this leads us among other things to raise the question of the relation between territorial borders and what Brett Neilson and I call the expanding 'frontiers of capital', whose production of space is inscribed in the framework of the 'world market'.[16] This is a last point I want to address here from the angle of the impact of the pandemic on borders.

In her fascinating study of the international health conferences on cholera in the second half of the nineteenth century, Valeska Huber stresses the awareness in the medical and government discourse of the link between the new pace and spatiality of cholera outbreaks and the revolution in transport and logistics. 'Diseases', she writes, 'could travel at a new speed from place to place and profit from the revolution in transport achieved by the development of steamships and railways'.[17] A sense of exposure and vulnerability emerged as the reverse side of the thrilling experience of living in a shrinking and boundless world. The Suez Canal, the most ambitious logistical endeavour of the nineteenth century and at the same time a crucial border between Europe and the 'Orient' became the privileged site for the fight against cholera within a fierce competition involving the major European colonial powers.[18] It is easy to see how this story resonates in our present. But it is even easier to add that today we are living in the wake of a much more radical revolution in transport and logistics, epitomised by shipping containers, interoperability, and digital steering of flows. And the connection between logistics and the spread of Covid-19 has been amply acknowledged by the epidemiological models that employ logistical data to trace the diffusion of the virus along transport and trade routes.[19]

The development of logistics over the last decades has indeed significantly altered how the question is posed of the articulation between territorial borders and the expanding frontiers of capital. Although modern logistics has military and colonial origins that continue to matter in the present, contemporary logistics can be seen as the main way in which capital produces its own spaces, in particular through the stretching and coordination of global supply chains that it enables. In one of the most important studies of this question, Deborah Cowen stresses that the logistical production of space is not predicated upon national borders, which often produce frictions in the 'smooth' circulation of 'stuff', but rather on what she calls 'seams'.[20] What she has in mind are zones and corridors, hubs, and 'points of entry', which in a way describe all border spatial formations but whose governmental rationality and map do not coincide with those of political borders. The expansion of logistics led to some friction and even conflicts over the last years, ultimately resulting in what Michael Hardt and Toni Negri call the existence of two spheres (the international political space and the global space of capital), which are 'increasingly out of sync'.[21]

Under such conditions, logistics, for many critical scholars and activists over the last years, has become a privileged point of entry into the analysis of the multiple tensions, frictions, and even conflicts that today characterise the relation between borders and the expanding frontiers of capital – which also means the shifting configurations of the global order and disorder. One has only to think of the ambitious Chinese project 'One Belt, One Road', (the Silk Road Economic Belt), a logistical undertaking for the global projection of China's power predicated on the negotiation of a collection of borders and boundaries, to get a sense of the issues at stake here.[22] Needless to say, the hardening of political borders makes the working of logistical 'seams' and flows less 'smooth', even threatening to obstruct them. 'Border security', Cowen writes, 'can itself be a source of insecurity for the supply chain', and this was particularly clear after 9/11, when 'trade disruption (not the twin towers) was the key casualty' in the world of logistics).[23]

We can say that the outbreak of the pandemic was a similar moment, in which the sudden rigidity and closure of borders had an impact on the mobility of 'stuff' no less than on the mobility of people. In an impressive article published in the *New York Times* in May 2020 ('What happened to the great American logistics machine?'), David Segal has very effectively described the 'bewilderment', the very astonishment in the face of the slowdown and in many cases the standstill of the logistical machinery in the US.[24] Elsewhere in the world the situation was no different. It was unquestionably a shock to logistics, which shed light on the fragility of what seemed to be a perfect machine. Nevertheless, as Brett Neilson notes, the further development of the pandemic 'has also accentuated the ways in which logistics industries are essential for capital circulation, exposing many workers, including seafarers stuck on vessels that cannot port and those active in gig economies, to vectors of infection').[25] The situation is particularly critical in logistical warehouses, and it is safe to contend that the shock of the Covid-19 outbreak has been paid for first of all by workers in terms of a hardening of discipline, increased health risk, and accelerated work pace.

Labour struggles in logistics will therefore become even more strategic in the next months and years.

The pandemic is far from over, and in the next period it will be necessary to further monitor and investigate the shifting articulation of borders and boundaries. In doing so it will be particularly important to focus on the contestation of borders and the multifarious struggles that surround them. Those border struggles have indeed prominent roles to play in the more general attempt to invent and fabricate another world within and against the pandemic.

NOTES

1. Sandro Mezzadra and Brett Neilson, *Border as Method, or, the Multiplication of Labor*, Durham, NC: Duke University Press, 2013.
2. See, for example, Jeremy Slack and Josiah Heyman, 'Asylum and mass detention at the U.S.-Mexico border during COVID-19', *Journal of Latin American Geography*, 2020, Project Muse, <doi.org/10.1353/lag.0.0144>.
3. Ranabir Samaddar (ed.), *Borders of an Epidemic. Covid-19 and Migrant Workers*, Kolkata: CRG, 2020.
4. Xiang Biao, 'Shock mobility: convulsion in human migration are having large impacts (part I)', *COMPAS Coronavirus and Mobility Forum*, 18 June 2020, at <www.compas.ox.ac.uk/2020/shock-mobility-convulsions-in-human-migration-are-having-large-impacts-part-i/>.
5. Martina Tazzioli, 'Confine to protect. Greek hotspots and the hygienic-sanitary borders of Covid-19', *Border Criminologies Blog*, 9 September 2020, <https://www.law.ox.ac.uk/research-subject-groups/centre-criminology/centreborder-criminologies/blog/2020/09/confine-protect>.
6. See Maurice Stierl and Martina Tazzioli, '"We closed the ports to protect refugees". Hygienic borders and deterrence humanitarianism during Covid-19', forthcoming in *International Political Sociology*.
7. Wendy Brown, 'A worldwide mutual pact', *The Drift*, 24 June 2020, <https://thedriftmag.com/a-worldwide-mutual-pact/>.
8. Alison Bashford (ed.), *Medicine at the Border. Disease, Globalization, and Security, 1850 to the Present*, London: Palgrave MacMillan, 2007.
9. Michel Foucault, *Society Must be Defended: Lectures at the Collège de France, 1975-76*, New York: Picador, 2003.
10. Mezzadra and Neilson, p. 18.
11. Charles Heller and Lorenzo Pezzani, 'Forensic Oceanography: Tracing Violence Within and Against the Mediterranean Frontier's Aesthetic Regime', in Krista Lynes, Geneviève Morgenstern, and Paul Allan (eds), *Moving Images: Mediating Migration as Crisis*, Bielefeld: Transcript Verlag, 2020, pp. 95-125.
12. International Organization for Migration, <https://missingmigrants.iom.int/>.
13. See Maurice Stierl, *Migrant Resistance in Contemporary Europe,* London – New York: Routledge, 2019, chapter 4; Étienne Balibar, Caterina Di Fazio, and Sandro Mezzadra,

'A joint statement on sea rescue', *Open Democracy*, 6 October 2020, <https://www.opendemocracy.net/en/can-europe-make-it/joint-statement-sea-rescue/>.

14 Border Violence Monitoring Network, *Special Report: Covid-19 and Border Violence Along the Balkan Route*, 2020, <https://www.borderviolence.eu/special-report-covid-19-and-border-violence-along-the-balkan-route/>.

15 Étienne Balibar, *Politics and the Other Scene*, London: Verso, 2002.

16 Mezzadra and Neilson, chapter 3.

17 Valeska Huber, 'The unification of the globe by disease? The international sanitary conferences on cholera, 1851-1894', *The Historical Journal* 49,2 (2006), 453-476, 455.

18 Huber, 465-68.

19 See Brett Neilson, 'Virologistics I: the virus as logistical "force majeur"', *COMPAS Coronavirus and Mobility Forum*, 18 April 2020, <https://www.compas.ox.ac.uk/2020/virologistics-i-the-virus-as-logistical-force-majeure/>; Brett Neilson, 'Virologistics II: the logistics of viral transmission'" *COMPAS Coronavirus and Mobility Forum*, 18 April 18 2020, <https://www.compas.ox.ac.uk/2020/virologistics-ii-the-logistics-of-viral-transmission/>.

20 Deborah Cowen, *The Deadly Life of Logistics: Mapping Violence in the Global Trade*, Minneapolis: University of Minnesota Press, 2014, Chapter 2.

21 Michael Hardt and Antonio Negri, 'Empire, Twenty Years On', *New Left Review* 120 (2019), 67-92, 68.

22 See, for example, William A. Callahan, 'China's "Asian Dream": The Belt Road Initiative and the New Regional Order', *Asian Journal of Comparative Politics* 1,3 (2016), 226–43.

23 Cowen, p. 78.

24 David Segal, 'What Happened to the Great American Logistics Machine?', *New York Times*, 22 May 2020, at <https://www.nytimes.com/2020/05/22/business/logistics-supply-chains.html>.

25 Neilson, 'Virilogistics I'.

Covid and the Unequal Distribution of Vulnerability

Monika Mokre

Vulnerability is, according to Judith Butler, a general human characteristic 'that arises with life itself',[1] for people are tied to other people and always at risk of losing this tie or suffering violence at the hands of these others.[2] She thus contests the notion of a sovereign, self-transparent subject, and thus a central paradigm of capitalist thinking: that people can precisely know what their individual interests are and egoistically pursue them – which according to Adam Smith leads, through the invisible hand of the market, to the wellbeing of all.[3] Subjects do indeed wish for sovereignty, but what remains is the 'primary experience of helplessness'.[4] However, capitalism, especially in its neoliberal form, understands vulnerability to be weakness. In neoliberalism, the ideal person is self-determined and self-confident and takes his or her fate in his or her own hands, without needing or asking for social security in its broadest sense. The description of a person or group of people as vulnerable thus represents a denigration to the level of paternalistic care-receivers, and in the worst case to ostracising.

While Butler rejects the bipolarity between the sovereign and the vulnerable (and therefore incomplete) subject, it is of fundamental importance for her ethical position that vulnerability is unequally distributed in the world and that this distribution is neither naturally determined nor determined by individual characteristics but through socio-political structures and decisions.[5] The particular vulnerability of social groups is in some cases recognised, in others not. For example, in the short summer of the culture of welcome in 2015, all refugees, at least in Germany and Austria, were regarded as vulnerable and thus deserving of help. This recognition of vulnerability went hand in hand with both offers of help and paternalistic attitudes as well as refusal to meet with them as equals. A short while later, a discourse developed that defined refugees as no longer being *in* danger but as *a* danger. In the best of cases, those refugees were seen as vulnerable who had specific characteristics – especially women and children. The further escalation of this discourse subsequently led to the eclipse of even this idea of vulnerability and to the idea of protecting 'us' and 'our women' from refugees.[6]

The new normality in virus times

The Covid-19 pandemic drastically changed social discourses, norms, and modes of behaviour. Instead of the sovereign subject, a subject is now invoked who submits unquestioningly to the rules of the government and lets his or her freedoms be restricted without resistance – even such central capitalist freedoms as consumption or profit. Both the fundamental vulnerability of the human body and its inseparable connection to other bodies is being recognised. Responsibility for oneself is no longer associated with the free decision of the individual but with responsibility for the social whole. Instead of the pursuit of self-interest, solidarity is being demanded, in a sense that fully corresponds to the origin of the term. 'The term *in solidum* in Roman Law indicates a duty toward the whole, joint liability, joint debt, solidary obligation. One for all, all for one. All stand for the individual who cannot pay his debt, and, inversely, he is obligated to all the others.'[7] Solidarity in this sense thus does not primarily mean supporting the weak but is a relationship among equals, in a community that solves a problem together, in the current concrete case the effects of the pandemic. This, however, does not exclude some from benefiting more from this solidarity than others; what is fundamental is that, on the one side, everyone might need solidary help and that all feel themselves to be part of the community. For example, during the first Covid-19 wave in Austria the particular threat to 'our' older fellow citizens, or the particular danger for people in system-maintaining professions, was often put forward. In this form, account was taken, to a certain extent, of the unequal distribution of vulnerability. On the other hand, other forms of unequally distributed burdens, for example due to the housing situation, were hardly considered; for example, when during the first Covid wave in Vienna, parks were in part closed, National Council President Sobotka called on people to go to their backyards. Psychological problems of insecurity and isolation also hardly received attention.

And the community that is called upon to be solidaristic is almost exclusively the national community.[8] Considering the very nature of a pandemic this seems illogical, but it only illustrates the well-known findings that the nation-state, underlaid with the construct of the nation and the feeling of nationalism, remains the most resilient identity-establishing unit, apart from the local environment. This is also – once again – seen in the EU's incapacity to develop a common, solidary approach.

The form of solidarity that is demanded of the population is a difficult one, for it requires keeping physical distance from each other while solidary feelings have much to do with corporeal closeness, as we know from marches and demonstrations. Yet social distancing is a central component of the Covid-19 measures, just as are increased hygienic measures, especially frequent hand-washing, and the greatest possible avoidance of public areas. These measures are, it is true, irksome or even painful but relatively easy to observe – for the majority of the population. That these general rules affect different population groups to different extents and in some situations cannot be implemented was, however, not taken into consideration: homeless people, for example, have no place to be other than public space and no capability to observe hygienic measures. And for people who are sheltered in confined spaces with other people social distancing is absolutely impossible.

Covid in mass facilities

In Austria, this particularly involves refugees or, more precisely, asylum seekers or already rejected asylum seekers who are in receiving or transit centres, as well as prisoners – in pre-trial detention, serving penal sentences, or in custody pending deportation. In these cases social distancing in Austria is interpreted differently from the way it is applied to the majority population – not as distance between individuals but as the isolation of the whole institution from the rest of the population. This conforms to the usual way of dealing with institutions of this sort and their inhabitants; they are confined and in this confinement excluded from society.

In the case of prisoners, this exclusion through confinement is regulated and prescribed by law. The protection of personal liberty and security, guaranteed to everyone in Art. 1, paragraph 1 of the Federal Constitution, is limited by the next article: 'Personal freedom can be denied to a person in the following cases in the manner prescribed by the law: 1) when activity that is subject to penalty results in forcible detention' (Art. 2, Paragraph 1). This is the only (severe) punishment the Constitution provides for, but other grave forms of interference in the life of prisoners follow from the practice of life in the prison institutions. 'They involve, for example, the right to family life, to healthcare, to appropriate wages for work, and adequate social security, and in many cases also political rights'.[9] The right to a family life is reduced to visitor contacts, whose duration, frequency, and form are determined by the prison administration and in practice differ widely between different institutions.

During the spring 2020 lockdown the right to family life was almost completely suspended. From 23 March to 10 May all visits were prohibited; only telephone contact and video calls were permitted. In practice, these opportunities for communication were also severely limited – in many penal institutions video-call technology is not made available and the times in which calls are allowed are so limited that longer calls cannot be made. Most prisons are equipped for visits behind a glass partition; in this case direct infection is impossible. Yet even these visits have been prohibited with the argument that the visitors could infect the personnel even though prison guards, outside their working hours, were just as much in contact with the rest of the population as the visitors were.

In addition, relaxations for penalities enacted shortly before their release were suspended and petitions to relax foot-shackling were not reviewed. This would appear irrational, as a reduction in prison staff would automatically reduce the risk of infection. For this reason prisoners in France,[10] Greece, Iran, and Afghanistan,[11] as well as Berlin[12] and New York[13] were granted early release in order to ease the situation in prisons. Turkey also adopted a similar approach,[14] which however excluded amnesty for political prisoners.[15] The only measure taken in Austria to relax the situation in prisons was to allow the newly sentenced to begin their prison terms later.

Prison terms always also punish the families of those sentenced and obstruct the maintenance of relationships; there are hardly any partnerships that survive a long prison sentence. The Covid measures were particularly harsh also for family members, especially families with small children.

Starting on 11 May visits were permitted again, although in very limited forms even during the summer – as a rule a half hour per week by appointment – and exclusively with glass partitions. Releases and other relaxations have also mostly been suspended – at a time when the rest of the population was leading a more or less normal life.

In May 2020, UNODC, WHO, UNAIDS, and OHCHR issued a common statement on Covid-19 in prisons, which emphasised the special vulnerability of prisoners.[16] Apart from the high risk of infection in shared confined quarters, the organisations also pointed out that prisoners, more frequently than in the average population, have taken drugs or been infected with HIV, tuberculosis, and hepatitis B and C, and so Covid-19 infection will likely have more severe consequences for them. In Austria, the Ludwig Boltzmann Institute for Human Rights's position on Covid in prisons emphasises that 'the privations, the fear of infection and for family members, as well as the limited communication they can have with the latter […] have negative effects on the psychological and social health of prisoners and [can] lead to acts of violence directed at themselves and at others'.[17]

The consequences of Covid-19 measures in Austrian prisons are ambivalent. Fundamental human rights and freedoms were encroached on in forms whose appropriateness is at least doubtful. It is also clear that 'secure custody' of prisoners took priority over rights such as that of health protection. On the other hand, a great deal of attention was paid to protecting the prisoners and personnel from Covid-19 infection – at the cost of other human-rights and psychosocial considerations. And this strategy was successful: an outbreak of the pandemic in Austrian prisons was in fact prevented.

Protection *from* refugees instead of protection *for* refugees

Accommodations for asylum seekers were similarly isolated from the outside world. Twice last spring, leaving and entering Austria's largest receiving centre, in Traiskirchen, was prohibited. After a stop on new acceptances was imposed, two mass accommodations in Styria were newly redeployed. After an outbreak of Covid-19 in Vienna's Erdberg facility, which has single rooms, the inhabitants were brought to the trade-fair centre Messe Wien where they were housed in two halls. The demand put forward by numerous civil-society organisations that asylum seekers be housed in smaller quarters or in private accommodations was not heeded, although many lodgings rented in 2015 have long been empty.[18]

For refugees this situation is particularly burdensome. Many of them are traumatised – by the causes of their flight, the experience while fleeing, and the prospect of an insecure future. Added to this are language difficulties and the insufficient availability of interpretation and translation, which makes comprehensive understanding of the situation much harder. The evacuation of Erdberg and transfer to the Messe, for example, was carried out by the police without any explanations; many refugees imagined they were being deported. An inhabitant described the situation: ' […] they told us that we could no longer leave the asylum home and that we had to pack our things in order to be evacuated to Messe Wien'. At the same time police cars arrived with sirens turned on.[19] And a refugee recounted the situation in Traiskirchen shortly after the lifting of the restricted access order: 'We only want to get out of here. We are afraid – afraid of being infected, afraid of going crazy, afraid of simply being thrown onto the streets.'[20]

Although deportations were not possible during the first Covid-19 wave, in April 2020 ca. 100 people were put in detention pending deportation. This is not in line with the law's purpose according to which deportation detention can only occur in order to carry out a measure terminating a residence (Fremdenpolizeigesetz, §76), and it naturally led to lodging people once again in cramped conditions. Just as with imprisonment, visits were completely prohibited; the cells were locked for the entire day. In April 2020 more than ten persons in the Rossauer Lände police detention centre went on hunger strike; some of them sewed their mouths shut.[21]

The way in which asylum seekers are dealt with bears much similarity to the treatment of prisoners: collective quarantine instead of social distancing, repression instead of easements. At the same time, this strategy has proved less successful here than in penal institutions. Even in summer there were repeated infections in Traiskirchen; in November 2020 there was a Covid-19 outbreak in the remote Bürglkopf camp in Tyrol. All of this could be expected in cramped quarters with inadequate hygiene facilities and rapid fluctuations of inhabitants, and it could have been avoided. By contrast with penal institutions, in which an outbreak of the pandemic, with its high psycho-social and human-rights costs for the prisoners, could be averted, one has the impression that here the concern is chiefly, if not exclusively, the protection of the population outside these camps.

The situation is particularly grim among refugees still outside Austria's borders. A March 2020 decree by the Minister of the Interior stipulated 'that only persons with a current health certificate may enter the country. This also obtains in cases in which an application for international protection has been filed'.[22] This unequivocally violates the Geneva Refugee Convention and makes it clear that Austrian refugee policy is concerned with protection *from* refugees, not protection *for* refugees – particularly as it would have been quite easy to protect the population only by quarantining the newly arriving asylum seekers.

However, what this decree involved was primarily a populist gesture, for at that moment, according to the Minister of the Interior's own statement, there were about 12 asylum petitions per day in all of Austria.[23] In terms of realpolitik what is much more significant here is that already before the pandemic, and still more clearly after it began, Austria had refused any form of solidarity with refugees from clearly poorer countries or solidarity with the countries in question. It is clear that Federal Chancellor Sebastian Kurz's slogan, 'I have closed the Balkan route', obviously successful with voters, has led, on the one side, to an increasing number of refugees stranded in Greece and, on the other, to the displacement of the Balkan route so that now, alongside Greece, it is Bosnia Herzegovina, one of Europe's poorest countries, that has to bear the main burden of accommodating the refugees. And even if state authorities in Greece and Bosnia are acting irresponsibly, the Austrian government is principally to blame for this untenable situation in the EU's isolationist policy.

In Greece as in Bosnia, the predicament of the refugees has been catastrophic for years now. We hear only scattered reports from Bosnia of Covid-19 cases, which is probably due to the fact that the refugees there have, for the most part, to get by without healthcare or any other support. At any rate, Covid-19 intensified resentment in the population, which had been escalating already before the pandemic. In the beginning, Bosnia's population reacted very positively to the refugees and supported them – surely in part because of their own experience with exile – and there are still many who, despite their own precarious living conditions, consistently support the refugees. However, due to the complete overstretching of the country's capacity with many refugees without lodgings the mood of the majority of the population has changed. With the onset of the pandemic, the refugees were additionally accused of having introduced the virus. The mood is becoming increasingly more hostile; many shops refuse entrance to refugees. And the general measures against Covid-19, such as the prohibition on gatherings in public space or the use of public transport, hit homeless refugees particularly hard.[24] NGOs from Bosnia and the wider region, as well as from Central and Northern Europe, are supporting the refugees; nevertheless, there is no sign that governments of EU member countries or even the European Commission will take responsibility here. The EU is not even reacting to Croatia's and Bosnia's illegal and well-known pushbacks; on the contrary, pushback from Austria and Italy has been increasing since summer 2020, which often develops into chain-reaction pushbacks reaching Bosnia.

The camp at Moria has been a symbol of the situation in Greece for several years now. The completely unsustainable conditions there were further aggravated by the Covid-19 crisis and the expectable outbreak of the pandemic in the hopelessly overfilled camp lacking any sanitary facilities. The camp was locked down from March through August. A Doctors Without Borders psychologist said:

> Before the lockdown, people, for example, had access to various psychosocial support services and to simpler activities that were, however, important for their mental health. They could buy the food that they preferred to eat. They could go for walks outside the camp. They could socialise with local people. Now they have no more access even to these simple things; in addition, there are more tensions in the camp and more violent incidents. I work principally with torture survivors. For them it is particularly difficult to experience these violent incidents. They have come to Greece, to the European Union, in search of security, and, instead of this, the camp and life in the camp repeatedly trigger memories of past traumatic experiences.'[25]

When a further lockdown was announced in the beginning of September, there was a major fire in the camp, which completely destroyed it. In a newly constructed provisional tent camp conditions are still worse than before. By the end of September, 240 new Covid cases were reported from the new camp.[26] Various EU member countries have declared their readiness to take in unaccompanied minors and families from Moria – in small numbers and not recognising the fact that this camp is also mortally dangerous for single men. Austria has refused to accept any refugees from Moria.

Which lives are more grievable?

Judith Butler asks which suffering we mourn and comes to the conclusion that dangerous populations are never grievable: 'They are represented as a threat to human life in its usual form and not as living people who need protection from illegitimate state violence, hunger, or epidemics. If such lives are lost, they are consequently not grievable, for in the tortured logic rationalising their death their disappearance is seen as necessary to protect the life of the living.'[27] Prisoners are dangerous by definition and thus neither grievable nor deserving of compassion. But in contemporary discourse it is especially immigrants and refugees who are seen as representing a fundamental danger and are thus not grievable. 'Institutionalised racism and active racism at the level of perception brings forth iconic representations of population groups that are grievable to the greatest extent and produces images of groups whose disappearance is not considered to be a loss and which are ungrievable.'[28] While all forms of limitations of personal freedoms in the Covid crisis are declared to be indispensable for saving human lives, sea rescue is seen as a form of people smuggling dressed up in humanitarian guise and as a 'pull factor' of immigration. And people who are stranded and die on the Balkan route, whether from Covid-19 or other causes, are, for the media, worthy neither of mention nor of tears. Elfriede Jelinek gets to the heart of the contemporary nexus of solidarity and exclusion in her play *Die Schutzbefohlenen*, when she has the refugees say:

> [...] we can see that people like us are supposed to be bridled, or rather, excuse us, fenced in; we savages have to be tamed so that we don't inundate you; no, no, that mustn't be; that shows how important help is and solidary cooperation against us, especially in crises, yes, in everyday life, but especially in crises, that's where we floods of people have to be stopped, that's where you are solidary with yourselves; you have to be – with whom else should you be? Yes in the first place with yourselves, and that's where you all cooperate with the neighbourhood against us overrunning you like water; that's where you're solidary [...].[29]

The virus does not differentiate between grievable human lives and others. It nests where it can. That it succeeds in doing so more or less easily and with different effects is not due to itself; it depends on social inclusion and exclusion. People – all people – are vulnerable. And they can only deal with this vulnerability together, in their deep connection to each other and fundamental mutual dependence. Whether they travel first class or in steerage – on a sinking ship passengers share the same fate.[30]

NOTES

1. Judith Butler, *Precarious life: the powers of mourning and violence,* London New York: Verso; quoted from the German edition: *Gefährdetes Leben. Politische Essays.* Frankfurt: Suhrkamp, 2005, p. 48.
2. Butler, *Precarious Life,* p. 20.
3. Adam Smith, *An Inquiry Into the Nature and Causes of the Wealth of Nations* (1776), New York: Modern Library, 1937, p. 423.
4. Judith Butler, *Giving an Account of Oneself,* New York: Fordham University Press, 2005; quoted from the German edition: *Kritik der ethischen Gewalt,* Frankfurt a.M.: Suhrkamp, 2003, p. 86.
5. Judith Butler, *The Psychic Life of Power: Theories in Subjection,* Stanford: Stanford University Press, 1997; German edition: *Psyche der Macht. Das Subjekt der Unterwerfung,* Frankfurt: Suhrkamp, 2001, p. 81.
6. Monike Mokre, '"Young Strong Men Should be Fighting": Zur Vulnerabilität geflüchteter junger Männer', in Josef Kohlbacher and Maria Six-Hohenbalken (eds), *Vulnerabilität in Fluchtkontexten,* Vienna: Verlag der Österreichischen Akademie der Wissenschaften, 2020, pp. 17-32.
7. Hauke Brunkhorst, *Solidarität. Von der Bürgerfreundschaft zur globalen Rechtsgenossenschaft,* Berlin: Suhrkamp, 2002.
8. I am aware that the concept 'national community' is problematic because of its associations with ethnic affinity. At any rate, in terms of measures to cope with the pandemic, in my view it has always been the community rather than society that has been invoked.
9. Monika Mokre and Stephan Vesco, 'Der Ausnahmezustand im Ausnahmezustand. Gefängnisse zu Zeiten von Covid-19', *juridikum* 3/2020, 292-301.
10. <https://apps.derstandard.at/privacywall/story/2000116146913/frankreich-oeffnet-in-coronakrise-gefaengnisse?ref=article&fbclid=IwAR0IdA8v0DxALkdQqgU9DL2jP7kNdn3F40U4h3CCGT0VAQjC3W4jWnGQeBE>.
11. <https://apps.derstandard.at/privacywall/story/2000116337675/zehntausende-gefangene-werden-auf-der-ganzen-welt-wegen-corona-entlassen>.
12. <https://www.bz-berlin.de/berlin/unruhen-wegen-corona-nicht-ausgeschlossen-berlin-laesst-haeftlinge-frei?fbclid=IwAR1lCZnnYmY1dEoqDknbL_K_QmDt7ErFWMpFW-1iQZGe8GEG7JO9Diy9VmE>.
13. <https://nypost.com/2020/03/18/nyc-to-begin-releasing-inmates-amid-coronavirus-outbreak/?utm_source=facebook_sitebuttons&utm_medium=site+buttons&utm_campaign=site+buttons&fbclid=IwAR0RHx-lSg_ztS5oDa-BiUk3G1vjQRjz7pVIxHAzOtbABgAwctjaIEIPqQY>.

14 <https://www.heise.de/tp/features/Tuerkei-Lebensgefahr-fuer-politische-Gefangene-4697298.html>.
15 See <https://www.umbruch.at/beitraege/monika-mokre>.
16 <https://www.who.int/news/item/13-05-2020-unodc-who-unaids-and-ohchr-joint-statement-on-covid-19-in-prisons-and-other-closed-settings>.
17 Philipp Hamedl, *Stellungnahmehinsichtlich der Situation von Insass*innen der Justizanstalten Österreichs während der COVID-19-Pandemie*, Vienna: BIM 2020, <https://bim.lbg.ac.at/sites/files/bim/attachments/stellungnahme_covid-19_haftsituation_philipp_hamedl_2.4.2020.pdf> (29.10.2020).
18 <https://www.derstandard.at/story/2000114846234/teurer-leerstand-asylheime-kosteten-bund-im-vorjahr-5-3-millionen>.
19 <https://www.progress-online.at/artikel/auf-engem-raum-gefl%C3%BCchtete-und-corona>.
20 <http://www.rueckkehrzentrenschliessen.org/>.
21 <https://www.ots.at/presseaussendung/OTS_20200417_OTS0014/sofortige-enthaftung-aller-personen-in-schubhaft-bild>.
22 <https://www.asyl.at/de/info/presseaussendungen/sachverhaltsdarstellunggegenerlassdesinnenministers/>.
23 <https://www.derstandard.at/story/2000116258887/asylantrag-nur-noch-mit-gesundheitszeugnis>.
24 <https://www.spiegel.de/politik/ausland/bosnien-verstecktes-fluechtlingselend-a-ac31a278-7046-4f87-aa6a-72c0eb8959dc>.
25 <https://www.aerzte-ohne-grenzen.at/article/lockdown-moria-jetzt-sind-wir-gefangen>.
26 <https://www.infomigrants.net/en/post/27464/more-than-240-new-covid-19-infections-among-migrants-on-lesbos>.
27 Judith Butler, *Frames of War: When Is Life Grievable?*, New York: Verso, 2009; quoted from the German edition: *Raster des Krieges. Warum wir nicht jedes Leid beklagen*, Frankfurt/ New York: Campus, 2010, p. 36.
28 Butler, *Frames of War*, German edition, p. 30.
29 Elfriede Jelinek, *Die Schutzbefohlenen*, <https://www.elfriedejelinek.com/fschutzbefohlene.htm>.
30 For this metaphor I am thankful to Robert Lachmann in his *First-Class Passengers on a Sinking Ship: Elite Politics and the Decline of the Great Powers*, London/New York: Verso, 2020.

Contemporary Forms of the Death Drive in Pandemic Capitalism

Fabian Fajnwaks

Capitalism could liquidate the planet and the human race; if anyone still doubts this, the current pandemic came to forcefully confirm this frightening prospect. There are no limits to what capital can consume in its unstoppable expansion – like a furious unchained Leviathan it can attack its creators and destroy the environment in which it has contentedly thrived. If it is still difficult to predict what the world will become after Covid once the vaccine is found, what is certain is that the pandemic will have catalysed the destructive process already underway, which humanity has ignited like an insane machinery which it cannot turn off. Born as a system allowing the generation of surplus value, according to Marx's unsurpassed analysis, capitalism has also shown itself to be an infernal mechanism that produces its own destruction if it is not reined in by a series of regulations, which have to spring up and be constantly reconfigured by the capitalist system itself. Capitalism in its contemporary neoliberal version functions exactly in the manner of a disease that generates its own immunity and feeds itself by recycling the antibodies it provokes. It is clear that the true virus today is capital itself. Whether Covid-19 was a virus that escaped from a research laboratory in China or whether it was transmitted to humans through eating certain animals – either way we see that it is by humanity's transformative acting on the environment that the current pandemic has been unleashed. That Big Pharma is already now disputing which laboratory will put its label on the vaccine, and that it is already rubbing its hands as it calculates the enormous profit it can make from this is only a spectacular demonstration of how big capital recuperates as benefits the damage it has done in the act of 'conquering' the environment.[1]

In *The Shock Doctrine: The Rise of Disaster Capitalism*, Naomi Klein was able to show the direct relation between the expansion of capital as it seeks new resources to exploit and the creation of new ecological and environmental catastrophes.² Quite simply, capitalism is in the course of destroying nature, the planet, and humanity along with it, by transforming them into commodities. There are no limits to the thirst for production and accumulation, since capitalism, as a system of production and as a discourse, is constructed on limitless expansion: Marx had already articulated this, predicting the expansion of capital to the point that it would constitute a world market, and Jacques Lacan, with his formulation of capitalist discourse, made it possible to provide its 'no-limits' dimension with a structure and logic.

We will return to this.

The return of states

In observing how numerous states on the old continent are in the midst of managing the pandemic, one might think that there was a return of the state in the political scene. Where we could have believed that triumphant neoliberalism had almost sealed the progressive disengaging of the states from the management of certain services, the eruption of the pandemic seems to have heralded the return of the states. This is true of France, where in his 12 March 2020 speech President Emmanuel Macron announced the injection by the state of billions of euros for financing corporate debt in anticipation of a plan to relaunch the economy. Suddenly everything seemed to have changed. As one journalist put it: 'Magical money has been rediscovered, the welfare state is a major asset to be preserved, financing it is no longer a matter of "costs and burdens", and the market is inefficient in areas such as food and healthcare'.³ The billions that had not existed for subsidising public hospitals reappeared. Let us recall what happened in 2008 at the time of the great subprime crisis; the US government and the European Central Bank had to inject billions of dollars and euros into the markets to prevent the crash of certain banks, as in the case of Lehman Brothers. The Nobel Prize-winner for economics Paul Krugman commented in the columns of the *New York Times*: '[…] much of Washington appears to have decided that government isn't the problem, it's the solution',⁴ contrary to the ultra-neoliberal principles of the Chicago School, which preached the thinning out of the state. Krugman recalled the Keynesian principle according to which the state intervenes to permit the markets to continue to function until 'normal' times return. Recently, a journalist recalled this golden rule of neoliberalism: 'at times of crisis, there are no longer any neoliberals'.⁵ Times of crisis lay bare the limits of the system and the true role of the state as the life insurance of the markets. All ideology is then annulled; the state comes to the aid of the markets when they fail in order to allow them to work again. The same government that sought to reduce hospital costs and battled doctors, nurses, and caregivers in the streets of Paris in November 2019 because they were protesting against budget cuts to hospitals is now singing the praises of the French healthcare system and applauding the very same caregivers. The state's insidious withdrawal in recent years from healthcare and education in France had occurred, before the implosion of Covid, with a view to reforms that would privatise certain sectors of its system, in two directions: on the one hand, the transfer of the burden of social security provision to private health insurance companies and, on the other hand, the transformation of the hospital system into profit-making entities.[6] This would certainly have to be one of the last privatisations the French government would dare undertake, seeing as the French are so attached to their social security; nevertheless, it will happen.

Keynes pointed to the importance of crises in the development of capitalism, and probably the pandemic will have constituted a fundamental crisis in the affirmation of neoliberal principles everywhere in the world. Its effects will go beyond this moment in which the state has been obliged to intervene, at least in certain countries of southern Europe, for the Anglo-Saxon countries, in line with the Social Darwinism that holds sway there, initially chose the strategy of 'herd immunity': everyone for himself. It is still impossible to know what socio-economic effects the pandemic will have, but we can foretell that capitalism will continue to advance by finding new resources for exploitation and accumulation if the governments do not decide on regulations to limit its effects and guarantee a more just distribution of wealth. Regulation is the key word in capitalism today, and it is easy to understand the thinking behind this: we cannot go backwards or exit the system, and so rather than accompany the system in a headlong rush or a mad dash toward the consumption of the capitalist system itself, we prefer to find ways of establishing regulations everywhere. There was the idea of regulating capital and financial movements with the Tobin Tax, but the task proved impossible. Conservative governments throughout the world tried to curb the free flow of imports to defend national industries by heavily taxing imported products, as the Trump Administration did, or, as with Brexit, to simply leave the common market to defend national sovereignty. Today regulation is trying to introduce into the markets what Jacques Lacan called a 'master-signifier' – an element that makes it possible to lend coherence to the ocean of capital flows, which by its structure is acephalous – a task that will probably prove impossible but which betrays the deep malaise that economists of varying stripes are beginning to notice in the recurrent crises that the markets, left to their own devices, are producing.

Neoliberal discourse seeks to make subjects responsible for their voluntary adherence to the alienation inherent in the system of production and blames those who do not conform to it and those who try to remain in the welfare system, waiting for assistance from the state. Byung-Chul Han has explored this dimension in his *Psychopolitics: Neoliberalism and New Technologies of Power*.[7] But what is missing from Han's analysis is that this projection onto the subject of responsibility for having to know what to do in the struggle for survival is the dismissal, the denial of the destructive activity that is at the very core of capitalist discourse. Capitalism blames the subjects, making them feel responsible for their own inscription into this discourse. This is precisely the way neoliberalism reintroduces the splitting of the subject by submitting them to an alienation that tends to deny the destruction in the heart of capitalism.

The pandemic: A magnifying glass of social differences

For the French philosopher Jean-Luc Nancy, the pandemic is an enormous magnifying glass that has laid bare the social gaps and cleavages that exist in our society. It has made it possible to show that all human beings are in the same boat, but that, as in all boats, there are classes and not all passengers experience the journey in the same way; it is not the same thing to travel first class, with a terrace and view of the ocean, as it is to travel fourth, in the holds of the vessel and without windows. Certainly, if the ship sinks everyone has to be able to get onto the lifeboats, but even there first-class passengers in general have the right to an access that is easier and more rapid than the lower classes. If the situation created by the pandemic has only made more palpable that we all live on the same planet it has to be said that before it implodes the more privileged will be able to live through global warming with superior means and the various toxic transformations that humanity is in the course of imprinting on the earth.

The countries that have put lockdowns in place to impede the contagion's spread have not been able to guarantee help to the sectors that have had to lay off its workers. Thus, lockdown has been easier, indeed possible, for the better-off classes, but in Latin American countries, for example, very hard hit by the virus, where a significant part of the population lives as casual workers, staying at home without working was more difficult to establish and observe. A great many shops have had to close down for months for lack of business, and in this case the states have not been able to come to the aid of the neediest. Access to testing, for which the Sécurité Sociale has taken responsibility in France, but which has to be paid by individuals in other countries like the US, and at very high costs, also functions as a magnifying glass for the social differences in countries where the state has less of a presence. We will see how the states deal with the vaccines that will emerge in a few months.

At any rate, and this is in danger of being one of the most nefarious effects of the pandemic with more than a million deaths throughout the world to this point, there is no doubt that an enormous economic crisis will follow the months of lockdown. The gap between the better-off classes and the working classes will probably widen still more and we will see a pauperisation of the middle classes, which has already been well underway before Covid. They are in danger of being among the main victims of these months. The increasing marginalisation of significant sectors of the population may lead to a 'Yellow-Vest-isation' of protest with the kind of criminalisation we saw when the Yellow Vests marched in France: a political power that becomes increasingly deaf and, without being able to hear the grievances of these marginalised sectors of the population, represses them and with them their voices which it can no longer hear.

A catalyst of biopolitics

If anything is certain it is that the pandemic will have been an enormous catalyst of what Michel Foucault called *biopolitics*. This is so not only because, in the way Foucault used the term in his course at the Collège de France starting in 1976, the principle characteristic of biopolitics is to 'live and let die' – something with which the medical services were literally familiar during the pandemic when they had to decide which sick patients could be treated and which they had to let die. But it also has to do with the fact that the massive application of digital technologies enabling the geolocation of persons and making it possible for us to know with whom we have been in physical contact – and in the event we have been in contact with someone who has been infected with Covid, to warn us[8] – this in our opinion consecrates the control of the masses that remote surveillance has already established. Bodies, as Foucault expressed it, literally become the object of bio-power and thanks to digital technology, can be followed and controlled remotely. The model of the town under a plague that Foucault analysed in his 1974-75 course at the Collège de France, *Abnormal*, as a model of the positive exercise of power, is now witnessing a new development beginning with the actual control that technology makes possible to exert over bodies. The power that Foucault describes in his model – which submitted a town to the constant control of police investigating whether any of the inhabitants of all the houses of a neighbourhood were contaminated with the plague

– today has turned into the voluntary subservience of individuals to big data through digital technology and its applications. Because of this danger, western governments have refrained from applying the technology in this way, but this is not the case in China, for example, where we know that the government can have access to this information in order to trace the activity of its citizens. This is also the case with opinions expressed in the pages of facebook or Twitter; and we have seen it more recently in the recent US elections. It was already clear in 2016 with the Cambridge Analytica affair, which the excellent documentary *The Hack* has allowed us to reconstruct.

The exemptions applied by the French government during the lockdown to allow movement outdoors is only one example of how the government can, thanks to technology, follow the movements of its citizens. Here technology is put at the service of a good cause: the care of its citizens, but we can easily imagine a misuse of this well-intentioned use for authoritarian ends, for example in the context of political demonstrations.

A fine intellectual like Giorgio Agamben has noted this inversion in which the state of exception in politics becomes a 'normal paradigm of government'.[9] Agamben has been studying this inversion in exceptional situations ever since his work *Homo sacer*, in which he investigates what Walter Benjamin called 'bare life', Political refugee camps and transitional zones such as hotels in airports where the police hold refugees who are to be expelled for lack of identity documents are examples. But, according to Agamben, the pandemic tends to generalise this state of exception to the point of giving governments rights to exercise control that go beyond the strict framework of the law. This was already seen with the Patriot Act in the US after 11 September, which permitted the stopping of US and foreign citizens, subjecting them to interrogation and even torture in defence of US interests. The war against Covid would authorise similar types of acts, with decrees quickly voted in parliaments (as happened in France) to 'protect the populations' from a health threat. It is not only that this type of paradigm of exception tends to become official in the privileges that governments permit themselves, but it is reinforced by the very figure of the leaders who, like Trump in the US and Bolsonaro in Brazil, go beyond the legal framework to impose their individual will. The contestation of the US election results with the demand for vote recounts is an example, even if the legal system has thwarted this authoritarian intent within the framework of democracy.

Toward a collective calculation?

In his last essay, *Pandemic: Covid-19 Shakes the World*,[10] Slavoj Žižek raises the possibility that a 'pragmatic communism' generated by the pandemic will follow the 'disaster capitalism' theorised by Naomi Klein. As a consequence of the state intervention that the Covid-19 explosion has caused, Žižek sees the possibility of a return to a regime in which the movement toward privatisation of the public healthcare systems, a movement that has been at work in most countries in the world, reverts to a regime in which the states intervene more widely in the management of healthcare. We clearly see this when the state requisitions hotel rooms to house the sick and accommodate healthcare workers, in order to compensate for the drastic reduction of funds allocated to public healthcare that the very same state has put in place for years, at least in France. Or when the US president orders General Motors to produce respirators, or again when Trump feels obliged to invoke the Defense Production Act to empower the federal government to ask pharmaceutical enterprises to significantly increase the production of emergency medical equipment. Here too we see that under exceptional circumstances the state can intervene and that it must do so to ensure the common good.

For Žižek these kinds of measures will gradually be established in this 'viral world' where something that occurs in one corner of it can easily have repercussions in the rest of the planet. We are certainly led to collective calculation when it is known that the actions of some risk having an effect on the others. Today's hyperconnectivity and speed of communications enables this rapid and easy virilisation; what is less certain is that this global awareness will bring about the will to share, that the 'communism' invoked by Žižek is actually possible. In fact, we have been compelled to communicate with each other not by our own will but by the exceptional circumstance of the pandemic. It is clear that the pandemic has awakened us to the fact that we cannot continue to imagine our future solely within capital's profit framework and the destruction of the planet that it even encourages. But it is also certain that we will not wake up from this to then sleep better afterward. What actions followed the subprime crisis of 2008, when nearly the same thing was seen – that the banks could not continue to feed this almost blind quest for profit? We fear that the 'social distancing' that the fencing-off gestures impose, so emblematic moreover of the distance that will from now on separate the social classes, will be intensified as the gaps grow between those who have more and the enormous mass of the population who will have exponentially much less. We would hope that new forms of cooperation evolve as a result of the realisation that capitalism is bringing humanity to self-destruction and that before it bursts it will annihilate many people along with it. The enslavement of human beings to capital, having become commodities, which all theories of reification have always emphasised, already implies a certain sacrificial and, why not, melancholy position.[11] When Lacan said in his 'Third' 1974 lecture in Rome that 'every individual is in effect a proletarian, that is to say that no discourse is at the disposal of the individual by means of which a social bond could be established', was he saying anything different?[12] The individual reduced to her status as a proletarian has no available discourse with which to establish a social bond and is thus reduced to her status as a commodity who not only sells her labour power in a market, as Marx magnificently theorised in *Capital*, but becomes herself an object. We should remember that in the regime that preceded capitalism, when the individual depended on the feudal lord or, in antiquity, when he was a slave, he was, however, inscribed into a relation to the master, a relationship which Hegel superbly described. Capitalism has definitively broken this bond and it is not possible to inscribe oneself in a production-consumption relation other than as an object; for the capitalist too becomes an object, being subjected, albeit with more resources but nevertheless subjected, to the absence of a social bond and in danger at every moment of finding himself in the position of being waste, a position which in the end every individual can occupy in the capitalist discourse.

And psychoanalysis in all this?

Jacques Lacan focused on capitalism to which he assigned the structure of a formalised discourse: 'the discourse of the capitalist'.[13] For Lacan, the notion of discourse determines a mode of social bond, and capitalism is a social bond, a paradoxical one because it tends to undo itself. The bonds of solidarity that existed above all in the working classes are seen to be dissolved through the economic competition that neoliberalism establishes. The *uberisation* of society, the increasingly global spread of the idea that everyone can become an entrepreneur and the logic of transformation from social bond to commercial ties, in which everyone can rent his or her possessions and have access to those of other people, has only accelerated the fragmentation of the social bond already underway. The pandemic will have only intensified this process by the increasing spread of *teleworking*. Eva Illouz has warned of the dangers of isolation that accompany this form of work – an isolation reinforced by a privatisation of activities which leads in a direction quite different from democracy.[14] All trade-union activity or activism by workers' organisations becomes fragmented in the face of the isolation of teleworkers.

Lacan said that although capitalist discourse is 'wackily astute' it is 'doomed to collapse'.[15] It works like a charm but it consumes itself through its entropic movement. Why? Because by contrast to the other four discourses formulated by Lacan, which constitute barriers to the presence of the death drive in civilisation, the capitalist's discourse is a formidable machine for producing enjoyment (jouissance). Enjoyment is a term that links *Eros* and *Thanatos*, the two drives identified by Freud and with which civilisation constantly has to negotiate. Lacan borrows this term from juridical discourse to give it a completely different value – that of designating that force at the core of all human activity destined to be useless. We know how much human beings specialise in cultivating the useless; thinkers following Freud have been able to identify this passion for the useless so typical of human beings. Georges Bataille wrote a splendid essay, *The Accursed Share*, which, leaning on the work of Marcel Mauss on *potlatch*, was able to identify the notion of 'unproductive expenditure', characteristic of a number of human activities, such as luxury, recreation, and, let us add to the list in order to bring up a very contemporary issue: addictions of all sorts.

Two economists, Bernard Maris and Gilles Dostaler, were able to articulate the death drive with capitalism in a delicious essay.[16] In an analysis that examines both Freud's position regarding 'Civilisation and its Discontents' and the writings of John Maynard Keynes, the authors attempt to decode capitalism's recent crises in the light of what Keynes called a morbid desire for liquidity and Freud, more abruptly, the death drive. Embedded in the heart of capitalism, this drive pushes it to destroy and self-destruct, in particular through the accumulation of capital produced by the last stage of development of capitalism – financial capitalism. After the crises of 1997 and the explosion of the 'internet bubble' at the beginning of the 2000s, this has been demonstrated by the most recent of the major banking crises, that of 2008, starting with the explosion of capitals contaminated by toxic funds – the subprimes – which the banks were not able to cope with and which have ended by polluting the banking system as a whole. Keynes had already seen in the accumulation of capital the principal symptom of capitalism, for it diverted capital from its initial destiny – investment in production – but he did not imagine the gigantic volume that cash flow was to reach nor the diversity of forms that it would assume. Hedge funds, financial instruments of all sorts – the system's imagination in creating forms of investment that depend on capital itself has seen its limits. The grand deception of neoliberal discourse for decades now is to make us believe that this capital has liberated itself from production and that it circulates freely through the world's stock exchanges, seeking – sometimes in thousandths of a second thanks to super-powerful algorithms – the best interest rates to increase the profits of its owners. This enormous mass of capital, which certainly does rest on production – if the activity of a particular industry ceases, its stock values in the exchanges plummet – constitutes, on the one hand, the powerful fuel of the financial system but, on the other hand, its most fearsome danger. Its excessive accumulation can lead to bankruptcies or to new crises if it is not reined in by regulations or given forms of investment other than those which continue to make the system inflate. Like an enormous golem without a master and without a head, this mass of capital can contaminate itself by turning against itself and those who created it, and then exploding. Curiously, Jacques Lacan's remark that exiting from capitalist discourse occurs through décharité ('non-caritas') becomes very pertinent here. This neologism, which invokes Christian charity, attempts to specify what action would be the inverse of accumulation, an expenditure that does not involve capital itself but the satisfaction associated with it: its enjoyment. It is thus an expenditure of the satisfaction of accumulation, in a movement exactly contrary to the satisfaction expressed by the famous smile of the capitalist, as Marx pinpointed it, when he allocates to himself the surplus value that was not included in the initial cost bill for producing the commodity. It is a satisfaction of the expenditure not of capital, let us be clear, but of the satisfaction associated with it.

Lacan saw in this 'non-caritas' action 'the way out of the capitalist discourse', which will constitute progress if it is not just for the few.[17]

NOTES

1   Heidi Chow, 'Beware of *Big Pharma* in rush for Covid-19 vaccine', *The Guardian*, 15 September 2020.
2   Naomi Klein, *The Shock Doctrine: The Rise of Disaster Capitalism*, New York: Metropolitan Books, 2007.
3   Romaric Godin, 'Emmanuel Macron: Saint-Paul de l'Etat providence', *Mediapart*, at <https://www.mediapart.fr/journal/france/130320/emmanuel-macron-saint-paul-de-l-etat-providence>.
4   Paul Krugman, 'Crisis endgame', *The New York Times*, 18 September 2008.
5   Romaric Godin, 'Emmanuel Macron.
6   Philippe Batifoulier, 'Réformes de la santé : une diversité de privatisations', *Journal Alternatives économiques*, 1 October 2018.
7   Byung-Chul Han, *Psychopolitics : Neoliberalism and New Technologies of Power*, London : Verso, 2017.
8   In France the telephone application Tous anti Covid launched by the Ministry of Health has only been partially successful, with only two million downloads.
9   Giorgio Agamben, 'Eclaircissements', *L' Obs*, 27 April 2020.
10   Slavoj Žižek, *Pandemic: Covid-19 Shakes the World*, New York: Polity, 2020.
11   I am indebted to my friend Pierre Sidon for giving me this idea and for the fruitful exchanges we had on this subject.

12 Jacques Lacan, 'La Troisième. "La cause du désir"', *Revue de l'Ecole de la cause freudienne* 79 (2011) (originally Jacques Lacan, 'La troisième', in *Lettres de l'Ecole freudienne de Paris* 16 (1975), 187) ; in English: Lacan, 'The Third', *The Lacanian Review* 'Get Real' Special Issue 07, Spring 2019, p. 92.

13 Jacques Lacan, lecture at the University of Milan, 12 May 1972, published in the bilingual volume *Lacan in Italia 1953- 1978*, Milan : La Salamandra, 1978, pp. 32-55.

14 Simon Blin and Eva Illouz, 'Le télétravail est un mode de fonctionnement qui s'oppose à l'activité politique et sociale', *Libération*, 9 June 2020.

15 Lacan, lecture at the University of Milan.

16 Bernard Maris and Gilles Dostaler, *Capitalisme et Pulsion de mort*, Paris: Albin Michel, 2009.

17 Jacques Lacan, 'Télévision', in *Autres Ecrits*, Paris: Éditions du Seuil, 2001, p. 520.

Exercises in Exorcism – Ways of Healing (Through) Art Education

Collective of Royal College of Art University College Union branch members, staff, and alumni, including Kevin Biderman, Eleanor Dare, Laura Gordon, Eleni Ikoniadou, Matt Lewis, Joseph Pochodzaj, Cecilia Wee, and Dylan Yamada-Rice

Enter: A Great Refusal

In the introduction to his unfinished last book, *Acid Communism*, Mark Fisher draws on a passage from Herbert Marcuse's *Eros and Civilization* (1955), pausing on the statement 'Civilization has to protect itself against the spectre of a world which could be free.'[1] For the last forty years, according to Fisher, the main objective of the neoliberal project has involved 'the exorcism' of that spectre of possible freedom. As he explains, 'Instead of seeking to overcome capital, we should focus on what capital must always obstruct: the collective capacity to produce, care and enjoy.' It is, he says, this fundamental insight about the function of capital to block the production of a 'Red Plenty' and of 'common wealth', which is necessary in overcoming the system. Crucially, for our purposes, this exorcising of the possibility of a free world has been as much a cultural, as it is a political, question. Fisher revisits Marcuse's well-known conviction that art constitutes a 'Great Refusal, the protest against that which is', and his conviction that, through art and this space of alterity enabled by the 'aesthetic dimension', a newly transformed world is possible.

The prospect of a life freed of drudgery and the grim reality of labour under neoliberal capitalism, requires a collective counter-exorcism. This is at the forefront of our concerns as academics and practitioners in the field of art education/ in Higher Education (HE) / in the UK/ in this current moment/ bearing the impact of corporate capitalism for the last forty years. As Fisher recognised and attacked head on, the institutionalisation of knowledge and its inevitable collapse into extraneous and senseless administration, is an apparently inevitable slow blood-sucking process. Knowledge and study have never been the sole privilege of academia, and, crucially – as the blood-sucking of students, academics, administrators, and technical staff continues on the part of the vampires that haunt our institutions – will soon not be done at all in universities. In *Women Who Make a Fuss*, outlining their identical experience in other European institutions, Isabelle Stengers and Vinciane Despret write:

> We knew perfectly well that we were under attack but everyone seems to have thought that if s/he was clever enough, good enough, s/he would be able to escape the worst. Now we see converted colleagues manifesting a great loyalty to the new standard, firmly shouldering the role of guard-dogs against escapist temptations. There may well be a connection between this lack of resistance to what is making us fall in line and the way in which, for several decades, universities have 'endured' what is called their democratization.[2]

The authors of this collaborative exercise in counter-exorcism are academic staff at London's Royal College of Art, who – alongside workers from other British art schools and the larger educational sector in the UK – carried out fourteen days of strike action between 20 February and 6 March 2020. Before we were struck by Covid-19, we had our own strike against four major consequences of the corporatisation of HE in general, and of the art school in particular: decreasing pay, unpaid labour, staff casualisation, and racist/ sexist pay gaps. The strike action came out of a recognition of the fact that 'we' had been quick to 'convert' and adapt to the 'new standard' and to 'fall in line'[3] for too long, and that we were willing to do this no more.

These mass events were immediately followed by the mass succumbing of the world to Covid-19, and its disastrous handling by the UK government and its overzealous converted institutions, academic or otherwise. Once more, 'we' are reminded of Thatcher's unashamed preaching that the market must be saved at any cost, including that of human lives, and asked to keep the academic show on the road. During this time, the pandemic of racism has reared its ugly head again, with the mass witnessing of the murder of African-American George Floyd by a white police officer and the subsequent Black Lives Matter protests around the globe. 'We' are forced to turn our face violently towards the spectacular failing of art schools, universities and art institutions at large, to install and assert anti-racist policies and conditions of work for black people, indigenous people and people of colour. Currently, in Britain, we are reliving the trauma of Brexit but this time implemented as xenophobic reality. 'We' are asked to prove our right to live, work, and exist in the UK, as well as having to reinvent ways of continuing to collaborate with our newly alienated 'continental' colleagues.

The above sets the stage for our present situation. One that's not unique to the UK and its art schools but the direct result of a Western, colonialist ideal, under which the notions of the single self, individual property, and possession of objects—and of objectified people – emerged and thrived. Counter-exorcising the ghosts that haunt (art) education under neoliberal capitalism requires more than resisting the latest mutation of the system. The remedy involves nothing short of time-travel. After recognising the problem, the first thing to unlearn is bowing to the authority of the methods and curricula formulated by the 'great founders' of the university, on the basis of excluding all 'others' – women, black people, migrants, working class, queer communities, and people with disabilities. To this day, our models of knowledge production, methods of assessing, and ways of conducting 'the order of things', rely on decisions made without us, yet for us, which only now are beginning to be unravelled by the rise of decolonising practices across a handful of universities. Our educational institutions were established by those who saw themselves as great individuals, enlightening and liberating other individuals. What strike action, mass protests, and the formation of subgroups and unions, outside the institutional clutch, belatedly reveal to Westerners, is what communities in the Majority World have always known: education is liberation only as a collective affair.

Black study scholars, such as Denise Ferreira da Silva, have called for the destruction and reinvention of the university rather than its mere decolonising. The latter risks being adapted as a tokenistic gesture and often demands of those who have been excluded from the archives to carry the burden of the work needed in order to rewrite it. Rather than adding a few black studies texts to the reading list to tick the box, as educators we should pursue the widespread recognition that: '1) all thought, insofar as it is genuine thinking, might best be conceived of as black thought and, consequently, 2) all research, insofar as it is genuinely critical inquiry, aspires to black studies. Blackness is theory itself, anti-blackness the resistance to theory.'[4]

This intensified nightmare of working and living under the grip of late capitalism – 'haunted by the spectre of a world that could be free' – has renewed an urgency for the (re)constitution of a collective subjectivity. As we learn from Fred Moten and Stefano Harney, this is unquestionably the case both for reproducing the university and producing fugitivity: 'The university needs teaching labor, despite itself, or as itself, self-identical with and thereby erased by it. It is not teaching that holds this social capacity, but something that produces the not visible other side of teaching, a thinking through the skin of teaching toward a collective orientation to the knowledge object as future project [...]'.[5] Learning and teaching in the art school today seems so far removed from fugitive study, if, following Moten and Harney, the latter is 'what you do with other people. It's talking and walking around with other people, working, dancing, suffering, some irreducible convergence of all three, held under the name of speculative practice [...] The point of calling it "study" is to mark that the incessant and irreversible intellectuality of these activities is already present.'[6]

World-building, caregiving, healing, and committing to the formulation of collectivities and great unions should be the foundations of the new art school. Caretaking is an activity usually falling on the shoulders of women, people of colour, the economically and socially marginalised, and one that takes its toll, leading to chronic exhaustion, sickness and early death. The intersecting barriers of gender-race-class-disability create a cycle of dispossession that seems impossible to break out of, and which requires engaging with movements such as black radical feminism and their responses to the oppression of those who are perceived as minorities. We must learn to share the responsibility of caretaking and healing, 'on the basis of mutual understanding, respect, and the old socialist edict that an injury to one (is) an injury to all.'[7] These are the art schools, higher education institutions and art institutions we must dare imagine and create, rather than merely incorporating or, worse, (the nauseating British contentment in) 'tolerating' difference.

The pages that follow are part of our wider effort to exorcise the demons that haunt the art school. By beginning to think about ways of healing (through) art education, we must choose to defy a knowledge culture founded in the European cogito and work towards bringing forth 'other' voices. A polyphonic chorus of the dispossessed, whose refusal to 'return to normal' after the pandemics of Covid-19, racism, and ecological disaster are either removed or adjusted to, is required for 'sustaining dreams of the otherwise.'[8]

Anti-viva – an institutional critique

There are questions I have, not just about the topic I was studying, but about the authority that gave me permission to study it. Who or what is testing me, giving me legitimacy as a researcher, granting consent for me to think and analyse? Am I complicit in this institution's history? Its use of living labour and what it socially reproduces? These are questions for an anti-viva.

To answer these questions fully, we need to examine the origins of my place of work and study - the Royal College of Art. In 1837, the Board of Trade started a small Government School of Design. From this beginning a larger scale National Art Training School was developed in 1853, with money from the Great Exhibition of 1851. This was a crucial point in the development of what was later to be named the Royal College of Art (RCA) because Henry Cole who founded this training school also organised the Great Exhibition. Even though the exhibition's full name was the 'Great Exhibition of the Works of Industry of All Nations' it specifically focused on the promotion of British industry and its industrial prowess. This was also a vision of Britain at the top of a hierarchy of nations based on notions of imperialism and colonialism. In the organising structure of the Great Exhibition, certain countries were seen as advanced, but more importantly certain peoples were seen as advanced. And the idea was instilled throughout the exhibition that if certain countries and people were insufficiently advanced then it was the responsibility of Britain to go into these locations, 'civilise' the people who inhabited them and obtain their raw materials for productive use.

Furthermore, this exhibition was a way of framing discourses around work at home. Karl Marx said of the Great Exhibition: 'with self-satisfied pride, it exhibits the gods which it has made for itself.'[9] At the Great Exhibition it was machinery rather than human labour which was pictured as the main driver of industry. Garments and commodities of all sorts were shown at the fair, but there was a deletion of the living labour which helped bring them into the world. The attempt here was to reform the idea of industrial production which was previously tied to the use of humans. We might posit it as a prime example of commodity fetishism. In the exhibition, all we see are products and technology holding value. There is nothing about the labourer.

This deletion of the worker didn't just come out of nowhere. Three years before the Great Exhibition in 1848 there were mass revolts around Europe, the Communist Manifesto was published and elites across the continent were becoming increasingly worried. In the midst of this, a People's Charter was signed by millions of people and delivered to parliament in London. It demanded a greater democratisation of governance.[10] This movement had been organising through labour unions, mass meetings and protests since the 1830s and included women such as Susannah Inge and Emma Matilda Miles and people of colour such as William Cuffay and Benjamin Prophitt. The march which was supposed to have accompanied the petition delivery in 1848 worried the state so much that it was eventually declared illegal. Four thousand police were positioned on bridges to stop the demonstration with seven thousand troops placed on standby.

After the state physically cracked down on Chartism, John Saville argues, there was an attempt to create a sense of amnesia around working class political engagement.[11] In part, this fuelled spectacles like the Great Exhibition which attempted to create a new frame for seeing Britain. A huge Crystal Palace made of glass was erected in Hyde Park to house the 'great' exhibits. It was visited by 6 million people and through its visual framing worked as early mass media. As Peter Bailey asserts, it dramatically magnified the 'delusional optics of capitalist modernity'.[12] Wonders from around the world could be viewed in a single location. Yet in its structural layout the audience were visually guided through an exhibition which deleted workers completely from their part in creating the products on show.

Today we work and study in the shadow of that deletion. Reared at an early age by an exhibition which obliterated the worker from social vision, the RCA continues in this tradition by ridding its halls of working-class students and those without reserves. At the RCA, home students pay £19,500 for their postgraduate Masters degree and overseas students pay £58,000. As this exceeds the amount students can get a loan for, they still need to have about £9000 to spare. Currently, fees are set to rise. Say what you want about current budgetary requirements or a lack of government funding, but the fact is, it has never been more difficult to be a working-class student at the RCA than it is today. This has effectively become a form of class cleansing and it disproportionately affects people of colour.[13]

During key moments in the RCA's history, students and staff have attempted to shift the institution toward a truly progressive and emancipatory path. Now it is our time to continue the struggle to redefine the RCA. To do this we need to build solidarity between all workers and students in the university, because only solidarity has the power to burn through the corrosion of neoliberalism. We carry within us the sparks of yesterday and today. They can illuminate our path, but it is up to us to ignite a blaze.

DIY Art School

Monday 6 July 2020, 16:12
From: Siddhi Gupta
To: Laura Gordon

Welcome to the Art School! Here we can talk art, walk art, eat art and make art. This workshop will give you a glimpse into the different manifestations of the Art School. You can borrow, steal and combine to build your own version in the classroom/studio. A lot can be learnt from the Art School by those who wish to integrate art in education, but only if what happens in an Art School does not remain in an Art School.

In July 2020, Siddhi invited me and Arzu Mistry to collectively build and run a workshop titled 'DIY Art School' with Indian educators from higher education institutions. Siddhi invited Arzu as an educator and artist practising in India, with experience of international educational contexts. She invited me because we had worked together on a project called Practice of Teaching, in which Siddhi had been developing the Kalakarm Curriculum – a resource developed in collaboration with educators in India, which acknowledges the lack of art training as an obstacle to integrating art in their lesson plans.[14] As Siddhi puts it, 'it is a resource for every educator because if any educator could be an arts educator, then every learner could be an artist'.

Due to Covid-19, Siddhi had left London and the Royal College of Art in March 2020, rushing as many students did, to be with their families before borders closed and flights stopped. She had been suspended by the college for non-payment of outstanding fees and was unsure whether she would be allowed to take part in the graduating students' show, the culmination of two years of postgraduate study. Nevertheless, when the college released a tranche of funds for events as part of the RCA2020 graduating students' show, she submitted a workshop proposal.

The three of us worked collectively in the 'flat fabric' of 2020 – a series of Zoom calls (8:30 pm Mumbai, Kolkata, New Delhi / 4:00 pm London) and Google Docs and Slides. Weaving together strands from three bodies of work – Kalakarm Curriculum, the Accordion Book Project,[15] and Elastic Octopus: Fear of Failure in Creative Education, we built a 2-hour workshop that invited the groups to dream up their own DIY Art School – from the tools and the furniture, to the space itself. The workshop was framed around the DIY Art School as a permissive space, one that does not require you to be an expert to enter, encouraging a do-it-yourself approach. We invited educators to consider the similarities and differences between the art studio and the classroom, and to explore the possibilities of integrating the arts into their classrooms.

Forty-five participants gathered together on Sunday, 26 July 2020 (4:00 pm Mumbai, Kolkata, New Delhi / 10:30 am London) in a workshop that would have been implausible only six months earlier. The three of us, working together thousands of miles apart, paid out of the RCA2020 events budget, running a workshop with Indian educators, many of whom did not use computers as part of their teaching prior to the pandemic – this could never have happened in another 2020.

Employing her unique position, Siddhi was cross-pollinating two educational systems that rarely meet, and creating new knowledge in the overlaps. This knowledge was deeply rooted in context and place – the antithesis of the flattening that can happen in institutions where people leave their lived experience at the door. This version of internationalism rejects homogeneity, leaning into the local and difference. I think here of Audre Lorde: 'Difference must be not merely tolerated, but seen as a fund of necessary polarities between which our creativity can spark like a dialectic.'

Alone together, Arzu led us in making our accordion books. We tilted our screens down, shifting the focus from our faces and words to our hands and materials. We drew objects to bring with us to our art schools, then imagined the spaces that would hold these objects. Someone asked how to get to the back of their accordion book, and Arzu suggested cutting a window or door to climb through. The physicality of the books, and the act of making together, opened up new ways of collective thinking.

We imagined a school on a beach that works with the tides, we imagined a school with a tree at the centre, we imagined schools as theatre groups that moved from one place to another. The fruits of our collective dreaming prioritised challenging the profound disconnection between formal education and the natural world. Groups spoke to the perception of the arts as separate from other subjects and forms of knowledge. Through our DIY Art Schools we shared thoughts on the purpose of education, both inside and outside the institution. We explored the balance between structure and freedom – and how some of the freedoms of this kind of DIY Art School could be beneficial to the classroom.

Between the folds of the accordion books made in Ahmedabad, Bangalore, Kolkata, London, New Delhi, and Norwich, we can catch a glimpse of what thinking bigger about the role of arts education would look like – beyond the degree show, beyond the art world and the design press, beyond time zones – and of employing the resource of the institution, while rooting the work where it wants to grow. Like many other students around the world, the Royal College of Art Visual Communication class of 2020 was pushed out too early – they had no choice but to actualise the work in whatever way they could. We will not romanticise this horrible year. We will hold close this learning about what can happen when the work lives outside of London, beyond the gallery, and expands and exceeds the institution.

*With thanks to Siddhi Gupta &Arzu Mistry

Choose Your Own Academic Adventure
Term 1: Great Academic Balls of Fire or Metrics in the End Times

You know the scenario – molten asteroids are falling from the sky in their hundreds, you are carrying (or rather juggling) a dozen or so hand-scolding projects/tasks/deadlines/marking/spreadsheets/20 thousand emails to answer (etc, complete as you see fit:_____), zigzagging across a wilderness littered with flaming Microsoft Word documents and the burnt out husks of ex-colleagues. Out of the sulphuric mist a figure emerges; kindly, decent, always evenly tempered, even as great gashes open up in the ground around him into which a dozen or so administrators and students plunge, screaming.

'I know there's never a good time for this' he says, as asteroid shrapnel rips off your left ear, 'but it's about that REF form'.[16]

Choice: stop to complete the REF form OR run as fast as you can?

❑ **Choice A:** Stop to complete the form.
❑ **Outcome**: You are swallowed by a passing National Student Survey and are never seen again.

❑ **Choice B:** Run as fast as you can.
❑ **Outcome:** Proceed to Term 2.

Term 2: Design 'Thinking'

Like many neoliberal organisations yours is in thrall to vapid yet insidious propaganda constructs and their representatives, who are called 'design consultants'. Having survived the asteroid apocalypse in term 1, you have been called in for a chat with a consultant from a firm called 'Despicable'. You ask him what he is there for and he replies (without any irony at all), 'we are here to help you think'. You immediately grasp he is a 'Design Thinker' otherwise known as the ideology which 'requires an almost absolute faith in its own universality and authority',[17] aka colonial fundamentalism.

'But I'm an academic with a lifetime of works devoted to epistemology', you protest.

'Whatever', he says.

'But I don't need any help thinking.' You check your phone and notice you have 120 thousand new unread emails, all marked URGENT.

'Everyone knows academics don't have any time to think', he replies.

❏ **Choice A:** Do what the college has demanded and tell him what you teach.
❏ **Outcome:** You have contributed to a report which recommends your college become a business school, you are made redundant three weeks later.

❏ **Choice B:** Tell him Design Thinking is a white supremacist construct perpetuating the myth of Western creative specialness and refer him to excellent papers by Irani,[18] Ansari,[19] and Buzon.[20]
❏ **Outcome:** Proceed to Term 3.

Term 3: Art School is really for Business and Computing, sucker

You are randomly called in for psychometric testing; the bad news is the bogus pseudo-scientific bullshit your college fervently believes in has decided you are too creative for art school, and what the bosses really want are 'business leaders' and right-wing 'innovators'.

❏ **Choice A:** There isn't really a choice, proceed to Convocation.
❏ **Outcome:** Teach business studies if you still want your job at the No.1 Art School in Kensington Gore. You turn out to be crap at that: Proceed to Convocation, the final chapter.

Virtual Convocation (yes, plague and the one-year super accelerated business system dressed up as a widening participation initiative has arrived)

Over the months and even years of your teaching 'career', hundreds if not thousands of students and colleagues have told you they want more from academia then successive precarious jobs and individualised markers of success; indeed, at Convocation (your college's weird word for what everyone else calls the 'graduation ceremony') you are reminded of how often students have told you they urgently want much wider, much more actively anti-racist, non-colonial, non-extractivist frames of reference and representation, but also ways of teaching and learning which support those imperatives. A 'banking' model of how students learn, one in which knowledge is poured into passive individuals by figures of epistemic authority (think of great white male *design saviours* such as Jony Ive), is irreconcilable with social justice imperatives, yet it is all the benighted Higher Education leaders can seem to imagine for their fee paying 'customers'. The move to online learning risks reinforcing that model even further if you, your colleagues, and students are not vigilant. Indeed, most senior Higher Education management and marketeers seem to be facilitating a creeping return to nineteenth-century teaching models, with software platforms which do not obviously support a relational flow of discourse between students and staff, let alone supporting practice as a break from the fixed, disembodying representation of West-centric reasoning, aka the *Cogito*. But, **it does not have to be like this because most of us do not want this**. You complete this story knowing that it has been a colonial misadventure in which all the choices given to you are bogus. You open your share drive and begin to write a new story.

A short course in saving the world

Come to the world's No.1 art institution and take part in an exclusive master class in entrepreneurial thinking! If you like white-collar boxing, favela tours or a Shoreditch hack lab, then this Executive Education short course is definitely for you! This bespoke, salon experience gives you the unique opportunity to circumvent some of the usual boring labour involved in acquiring knowledge and skills. If you thought DIY culture and participatory education was about necessity, community building and resistance, you were wrong! Fuck 'pay what you feel', you can do a course in hacking and DIY making for just £1500 for five days! This will ensure that anybody that could really benefit from the course cannot possibly join in, so you won't feel guilty about your company paying for you☺

Not only will you learn how to co-opt the ideas and methodologies of other people and groups, you'll also become a certified expert in patronising the shit out of people whilst also learning the essential skills of Othering.

SIGN UP HERE

They can't forbid me to sing

They can change nearly everything
But they can't forbid me to think
And they can't forbid my tears to flow
And they can't shut my mouth when I sing.

They can monetise nearly everything
But they can't forbid me to think
And they can't forbid the ideas from flowing
And they can't shut my mouth when I sing.

They can make one-way staff zoom meetings
But they can't forbid me to think
And they can't forbid my hand from drawing
And they can't shut my mouth when I sing.

They can brand nearly everything
But they can't forbid me to think
And they can't forbid my sense of knowing
And they can't shut my mouth when I sing.

They can spend nearly everything
To buy the buildings they want to show
But they can't forbid me to think
And they can't shut my mouth when I sing.

They can casualise nearly all staff things
But they can't forbid me to think
And they can't forbid my tears to flow
And they can't shut my mouth when I sing.

They can eat sushi and give their staff nothing
But they can't forbid me to think
And they can't forbid the paint from flowing
And they can't shut my mouth when I sing.

They can ignore their students gathering
For the answers want to know
But they can't forbid me to think
And they can't shut my mouth when I sing.

An adaptation of Sarah's Song by the women of Greenham

From Your Vice Chancellor

Our creativity will support new global innovation.
Our strategy has a digital future through international mobility.
We will continue to support our significant research output.
This year we will have higher rankings in the world.
Our specialist projects will create new opportunities for students.
Future funding will build more industry partnerships.

This is an environment for creative excellence across disciplines.
We will work to ensure a strong community, making the most
of future challenges to education.

We are now committed to more investment.
It is time to create a new framework of experience.
Our new buildings and technology will allow students to feel
free to experiment and produce remarkable results.
I am delighted that our students are at the heart
of our outstanding global position.

I would like to thank all of our staff and students for their work.

Text generated from UK Art School Vice Chancellors 'Public Statements',
2014-2019
10 published texts (8723 words) analysed on 28 January 2021.

Exit: On exorcising the marketised fascism of art school administration.

'one can't see the economy, but one can see art'.[21]

'like the society to which it has played the faithful servant, the university is bankrupt'.[22]

'the classroom remains the most radical space of possibility in the academy'.[23]

Royal College of Art's University and College Union members, 'to be an artist is to be a citizen, an inherently political position. Without the awareness, freedom and choice education should offer, the body politic fails. Within educational structures, openness, curiosity, experiment, freedom, discipline, generosity, engagement and equality breed the same. This is equally true of their insidious opposites'.[24]

The art school is bankrupt and its infrastructures are rotten to the core. We need to abolish and rebuild them. We need to exorcise the adrenaline turned sour, expunge the stress factors causing a constant uncontrollable release of cortisol that degrades our long-term health. The bodies involved in the art school body are tired and isolated. And yet, the current situation has been planned as a utopia for someone, someone like a Vice Chancellor, a Rector or a Director earning £300,000 every year. The texts in this dossier are articulations and symptoms of the diseased marketised art education system, an intentionally parasitic system that produces exhaustion, so that its hosts are both resistant to compliance and vulnerable to self-exploitation. That's the truth of the art school today. We are full of contradictions, in disagreement, too much to bear, excessive, flighty, untameable. And that's the way it is.

So, let us recite these spells and mantras together, to protect against the spread of 'total administration' within the art school!

1. **Shun the internalisation of trauma, the corporeal tax stemming from the corporatised art school.** Our adaptability as artists and designers will no longer be extracted, appropriated, and used to exploit us further. In order to grieve, repair, and heal from the operations of our violent institutions, which have come to an apotheosis with the pandemics of Covid-19, racism, and climate catastrophe, let us perform new oaths and divine collective rituals to guard against the fallacious logic of Art Academy Inc.

2. **Exorcise and abolish the instrumentalised and commodified apparatus of art education.** Renounce the lack of humanity, shame, guilt and failure that management structures consistently project onto us, as we apparently never achieve enough. Instead celebrate and rebuild, recognising the necessity of a different type of education: environments of learning that value and nurture cultural production in all of its manifestations.

3. **Reject what Paolo Freire calls the 'banking' model of education.** This approach is arguably utterly redundant for those with access to digital resources, as lessons for imparting skills are today freely available over the internet and through other means outside the art academy. Art school administrations are truly lost, 'banking' on a delusional business model that assumes art school education merely consists of tutors and technicians manufacturing and moulding – aka disciplining – thousands of minds and bodies, willingly and robotically executing the 'employability agenda' to produce model creative consumer-practitioners. A futile adherence to this myopic interpretation of the potentials of art education reproduces a heavy burden of expectation: the investment by students in six figure sums for art college degrees is of course a lie that we as art educators are forced to swallow, especially since our own experiences and relations with the administration tell us that we are valued as less than one of the many mid-century armchairs in the Senior Common Room.

4. **Expel the administration's systems of accounting, refuse the respectability politics underpinning the forced transformation of art schools into universities.** Our work is valuable in its multiplicity, alterity, abundance and resistance to being contained. If you cannot see that you need to go back to school. I suggest you pay six figure sums to learn from our work. We learn from our relations and peers – we honour the creative magic of those who have been otherwise marginalised and dispossessed by the art school system. Art education wants to build solidarity and remove the boundaries between the academy's inside and outside. As Silvia Federici says, 'no common is possible unless we refuse to base our life and our reproduction on the suffering of others, unless we refuse to see ourselves as separate from them'.[25] We learn from the multitudinous forms of creative practice that make up collective organising: we learn from banners, songs, murals, dances of strike actions, political movements, and vernacular forms that deliberately disturb the overwhelming recurrent waves of white

cis hetero ableist artistic practice. We reinsert those collective histories to rewrite the domination of patriarchal hyper-individualist 'genius' univocal narratives within Western-centric art worlds.

5. **Eject the violent assumption and relentless ongoing practice of women, disabled and neurodiverse people, working class people, queer people, Black people, indigenous and people of colour, and people from minoritised communities taking on the burden of labour – particularly the labour of pastoral care – within the academy.** The core materials of our labour are not only digital media, sounds, paints, metals, clay, texts, and textiles, but also the messy conditions of our bodily, material existence. Resist this lack of care and abusive toxicity which has pushed us into crisis and sickness, forcing so many cherished colleagues, broken, out of the academy. From the truth of black and brown women, queer and disabled scholars, such as Gail Lewis, Sarah Ahmed, adrienne maree brown and Leah Lakshmi Piepzna-Samarasinha, we learn that we who inhabit bodies that are marginalised within the art school already enact abundant creative strategies. Recognise and value this knowledge for what it is: as expertise, leadership, and wisdom.

Vice Chancellors, Rectors, Provosts, Directors, Senior Management Teams, and Strategic Management Groups – don't you know that the system of production that you supposedly manage doesn't just create product? Don't you know about the relations, knowledge, experiences, and community that make up the art school? Without such embodied knowledge, you clearly have no idea what cultural production is really about.

Go and learn your leadership. True leadership is what we are building in spite of the barriers you erect against the energies of our community. True leadership is built on relationships of generosity and trust, requiring genuine analysis of the activity you are part of, careful construction and maintenance of resources and infrastructure to achieve collective aims, and the devolving of power, based on recognition of the privilege you hold within current hierarchies. You're welcome! But first you need to exorcise yourselves to heal the rotting flesh of administration within the body politic that you are strangling.

Out!

Get out of the way!!

NOTES

1. This unfinished introduction was circulated amongst participants of the Mark Fisher Reading Group at Somerset House Studios, hosted by Laura Grace Ford and Dan Taylor between September 2018 and April 2019. All quotations are from this document, now widely available online.
2. Isabelle Stengers and Vinciane Despret, *Women Who Make a Fuss, The Unfaithful Daughters of Virginia Woolf*, Minneapolis: Univocal, 2014, p. 17
3. Stengers and Despret.
4. Jared Sexton, 'Ante-Anti-Blackness: Afterthoughts', *Theory, Lateral, Journal of the Cultural Studies Association* 1, 2012, <https://csalateral.org/issue/1/ante-anti-blackness-afterthoughts-sexton/>.
5. Fred Moten and Stefano Harney, *The Undercommons: Fugitive Planning and Black Study*, New York: Minor Compositions, 2013, pp. 26-27.
6. Moten and Harney, p, 110.
7. Keeanga-Yamahtta Taylor, 'Until Black Women Are Free, None of Us Will Be Free', *The New Yorker*, 20 July 2020, <https://www.newyorker.com/news/our-columnists/until-black-women-are-free-none-of-us-will-be-free>.
8. Saidiya Hartman, *Wayward Lives, Beautiful Experiments: Intimate Histories of Social Upheaval*, London: W. W. Norton, 2019, p. 347.
9. <https://www.marxists.org/archive/marx/works/1850/11/01.htm>.
10. Many in the Chartists movement also fought for voting rights for women, however this was not in the final 1848 Charter.
11. John Saville, *1848: The British State and the Chartist Movement*, 1987, Cambridge: Cambridge University Press, 1987.
12. Peter Bailey, 'Review of The Great Exhibition of 1851 by Jeffrey A. Auerbach', *Journal of Modern History* 73,3 (September 2001), p 675.
13. See Ash Sarkar's examination of the current economic effect of racial inequality in the UK, <https://www.independent.co.uk/voices/working-class-culture-race-not-as-white-as-you-would-like-to-think-a7903421.html>.
14. <https://www.kalakarmcurriculum.org/>.
15. <https://accordionbookproject.com/>.
16. The REF is the system for assessing the quality of research in UK higher education institutions. See <https://www.ref.ac.uk>.
17. Ahmed Ansari, 'Politics & Method: Design Thinking Arrives in Pakistan', *Medium*, 2016, <https://aansari86.medium.com/politics-method-cd4cc2c8f5e6>.
18. Lily Irani, '"Design Thinking": Defending Silicon Valley at the Apex of Global Labor Hierarchies', *Catalyst, Feminism, Theory, Technoscience* 4,1 (2018), Special Section on Illness Narratives, Networked Subjects, and Intimate Publics, <https://catalystjournal.org/index.php/catalyst/article/view/29638>.
19. Ansari.
20. Darin Buzon, 'Design Thinking is a Rebrand for White Supremacy. How the Current State of Design is Simply a Digitally Updated Status Quo',<https://dabuzon.medium.com/design-thinking-is-a-rebrand-for-white-supremacy-b3d31aa55831>.
21. Leigh Clare La Berge, *Wages Against Artwork*, Durham: Duke University Press, 2019. p.77
22. Research and Destroy, 'Communique from an Absent Future', 2009, p.1

23 Bell Hooks, *Teaching to Transgress*, London: Routledge, 1994, p.12.
24 Royal College of Art's University and College Union members, 'Reflections on Education from the Frontlines', *Art Monthly*, 435 (April 2020), 17.
25 Silvia Federici, 'Feminism And the Politics of the Commons', <https://thecommoner.org/wp-content/uploads/2020/06/federici-feminism-and-the-politics-of-commons.pdf>.

Country Reports

US Politics in Freefall

Ethan Young

US politics changed 180 degrees in a few hours on January 6, 2021. This day was marked by two decisive blows to the status of the Republican Party and its leader, former President Donald Trump. First, the results of two special runoff elections for two Senators in the state of Georgia were announced. Both seats went to Democratic candidates, a huge upset that proved Republican Trump was no longer a kingmaker after his failure to win reelection the previous November. More importantly perhaps, it gave the Democrats a decisive voting edge in the Senate, dooming the Republicans to lesser party status in the legislative branch, ending the high tide of their power in 2016.

Then came the formal counting of votes from electors from the states, which as everyone knew and expected would favour Trump's opponent and elect Joe Biden, returning the executive branch to Trump's enemies, as he charged fraud like an incorrigible brat.

That would have been enough. But the delusional sociopath who 'led' for the four years that culminated in the pandemic made things worse for himself, his loyal if equally deluded followers, and the standards of liberal democracy which have long been presented as the hallmark of US world hegemony.

This was Trump's Joseph McCarthy moment. McCarthy is remembered as a rampaging anti-Communist Senator in the 50s, who stepped over a line, and lost all backing from the establishment right who still dominated US politics. In Trump's case, there were many moments that would qualify – his sins already far exceeded Nixon's before Trump was halfway through his term in office. But nothing ever shook Washington like a sitting President calling on a rabid crowd of followers to physically threaten the Capitol and national lawmakers. And more outrages are coming to light. Now Trump loses not only his office, but faces real punishment in court, even after Republican resistance denied Democrats the necessary votes to disqualify him from public office after his second impeachment by Congress.

Understanding this turn of events requires examination of many aspects of the Trump era's social and political components. In 2016, Republican strategists recognised what their foes overlooked about Trump and US society. While Obama was still popular, enough racial backlash festered in states that could be exploited to push through one of their own through the indirect electoral scheme that empowered certain states over others, even if the overall popular vote favoured the Democrats. The ability of the Electoral College to bypass the popular vote, by utilizing winning margins in certain populous states, was used in the Republican victory that installed George W. Bush in 2000, with help from a conservative-dominated Supreme Court.

This was not anticipated by the Democratic strategists before 2016, who had run for years on the appeal of the welfare state, but watered down its actual public service with neoliberalism and liberal technocratic elitism. The strategists knew they had the edge in terms of vote count. Furthermore, they believed that the flood tide of xenophobic populism that pushed a blatant con artist into the Republican nomination for President would undo the conservatives' repeated scandals and disasters. It would appear that the Democratic consultants were oblivious to political patterns elsewhere, and watched in horror as victory was snatched from under their noses.

So much the worse for immigrants from the Global South, Latin America in particular; Muslims, stigmatised in the classic style; and working class civilians faced with a wave of murders by police. The Democratic base was increasingly radicalised as a power resembling fascism took shape in Washington before their eyes. This became evident with mass mobilisations, peaceful and violent, over women's rights, gun control, the environment, and police terror. The Bernie Sanders presidential campaign and the election of anti-neoliberal leftists to Congress challenged centrist presumptions about public fear of any candidate that could be demonised as socialist. Meanwhile the power of incumbency helped the far right to cohere into a political force with power they had not seen since the Civil War.

High-stakes gambling

This was the prelude to the current reversal of political power relations. The rightists who took over the Republican Party under Reagan made a bad calculation when they allowed the far right to share power to ensure Trump's indirect election. The centre right, which had ties to big capital, was forced out. This divided the billionaires that considered the Republicans their most reliable advocates. It brought executive power to a collection of susceptible internet gazers, religious fanatics, armed racists, and extreme anti-government laissez-faire egoists. All under the supervision of a swindler with no history of party loyalty.

The Democratic leadership made their own gamble in 2020, but played it safe, and it paid off, just barely. They lined up their best young contenders in the primaries, to see if any could win against Sanders in the run-up to nomination, and Trump in the election. None attracted the numbers to beat Sanders, so they closed down the contenders and put all their money on Biden, a dependable party warhorse who tried for the presidency repeatedly but not successfully.

Biden gathered support from the centre right, who went after Trump with everything they could muster. The left, for the most part, sided with Biden, including Sanders and newly elected young 'Berniecrats' and their supporters. This alliance of left, centre-left, centre, and centre-right against the right and far right came immediately and never really gelled, but it was enough to end the biggest mistake bourgeois democracy ever made.

Now Biden is safely in office, even though the shadow of violence still hangs over the heights of power. The far right has been deeply wounded by the failure of their pathetic putsch, Trump's disavowal of it after calling for it, with the resulting sudden disappearance of their passport to power, and the personality cult that motivated them. They are scrambling, but they have nowhere to go. In a week, they were forced back into society's outskirts. The biggest success for the far right was not the insider positions they gained – these were presented to them by Trump's advisors. The advance for the far right was their infiltration into the police, military, and judiciary, and effective exploitation of attitudes in support of the police as protectors and against the break-up of a white supremacist consensus. This is why even some Capitol rampagers caught committing crimes on video have been allowed to walk free.

The centre leans left

In this setting, another surprise: the centre is tacking left on a number of issues. The Biden Administration's priority is, naturally, the pandemic, especially since the discovery that Trump never had a proper plan. This means, among other things, that the federal budget will be set under the watchful eye of Bernie Sanders, now head of the Budget Committee in the Senate. The expanded Democratic left wing in the House includes open democratic socialists – which was unheard of until recently and is getting more media attention as it grows. The key left issues, from national health, to work programmes aimed at cutting fossil fuel use, to ending police misconduct, are no longer called out as extreme, for the time being.

Why the shift? Did the Capitol rampage put the previously presumed left threat to centrist control in a more personal perspective? The left itself is still marginal, though thanks to Sanders and the new faces, its views are being heard by more people than ever. The diffuse electoral movement in every state is mostly independent and to the left of the national party organisation, and backed by young activists who are very fast learners. Many incumbent Republicans (and Democrats) are feeling the heat. This development led to serious tension even as the 'Berniecrats' gave their support to the effort to unseat Trump. Now, however, perhaps because the threat of fascist violence came so close, what was taboo from the left has become accepted language – except on the increasingly unstable right.

The right is now trying to figure out whether it should stick with the demagogue who is, as the ex-President himself would put it, 'skyrocketing downward'. Trump may yet rise again, as he claims and as many of his party are convinced, and he is most vengeful towards ex-allies. Ties to the far right are viewed by some would-be conservatives as a lifeline, and by others as an anchor. How many of each group hold on to power depends on how far Congress and the White House pursue far rightists, including Trump, for various crimes.

Centre and left

In this setting a centre/left alliance close to the top, but with the centre in control, is more in the centre's interest than at any time since before World War II. Alone, neither the centre nor the left is in a good position to fend off a rising fascist movement, and the centre's apparent realisation of this is all to the good, even if many on all sides don't agree. Any threat to established power relations is tempered by the left's fragmentation and its political incoherence. In the current situation, that can change fast. It depends on whether the left can grow, without dropping its demands as it digs deeper into the old power structure, while still encouraging the centre's opposition to the far right as fascism continues to pervade the political atmosphere.

These challenges facing electoral activists of every stripe have real consequences for working people. Catastrophic crises are demanding immediate attention. At the same time, the changing racial demographics of the US engulf all politics. The question of power since the Civil War was seen by the rulers through the lens of race, and today that is reasserted more than ever as the once-presumed 'white Christian nation' stands exposed as raw exploitation and expropriation over centuries. This brought on a panic that peaked when Obama won a second term despite the far right's best efforts. But it also brought more and more popular forces to the left, with recognition of the pervasiveness of racism marking the reemergence. This is demonstrated by the spontaneous, internet-driven, multiracial Black Lives Matter protests that targeted police atrocities. The recent elections of openly left political figures 'of color' after the first Sanders campaign, solidified the connection between racial justice, economic and climate demands.

The symbolism of the choice of Kamala Harris as Vice Presidential candidate, after a poor showing in the primaries, is not just about race and gender. She comes from the social milieux that gave rise to a lot of the new generation of activists: students and young professionals of color, though her politics were decidedly centrist. This is an acknowledgement by the Democratic leadership that the years of chasing the elusive, and largely imagined bloc of business-minded 'white workers' ('Reagan Democrats') are over. The open rejection of New Deal Keynesianism at the highpoint of neoliberalism was the hallmark of Bill Clinton's politics, which went on to dominate the party even during the Obama years. Now the watchword is 'multicultural democracy', using the language of scholars trying to figure out how to square the circle of social solidarity with rising and sometimes colliding group demands. If this shift in stance continues, it means some leaders have concluded that neoliberalism is no longer viable, or at least needs to be critiqued if the Democratic Party is to restore its public standing as the party of labour and social movements.

Fighting the right and far right

This unexpected realignment came about through a convergence of circumstances that reached the point of no return. These include, first, the demographic shift from an overwhelmingly and definitively white-identified nation, to what the ancient promoter of racism and colonialism Lothrop Stoddard called 'the rising tide of color'. Between the descendants of African slaves, annexed Mexicans and Hawai'ians, conquered indigenous American Indians, colonised Puerto Ricans, and immigrants from everywhere, the European-descended population is seeing its supposed hegemonic status fading away. For wealthy conservatives in particular, 'the browning of America' was seen as cause for panic. The result in the broader population is a (painfully gradual) process of integration of the working class, which undercuts white nationalism, the historical standard in politics and society. The claiming of democratic rights by civilians 'of colour' stirred the racist right. The Republican Party increasingly courted nervous white voters since the Civil Rights Movement's overcoming of de jure racial discrimination in the early 1960s.

The second circumstance behind the shift was the Trump era split in the Republican Party, Wall Street's favoured twin in the two-party system. The party's far right galvanised as a political force in response to the 2008 election of Barack Obama, the first black President. The right, Reaganite leaders split as the populist Tea Party faction began to gain strength, and the once-powerful centre-right was pushed out of the party. This enabled the nomination of the sociopath, demagogue, and swindler Donald Trump. The openly racist far right joined the Trump administration as an active decision-maker in the party and government for the first time, not just as a pawn in electioneering.

Third, the rise of open socialists and anti-austerity Democrats into elected offices following the unexpected surge of support for Bernie Sanders in the 2016 and 2020 Democratic primaries set the stage for a broader opposition to the hegemonic right/far right bloc in the Republican Party and government. This was accompanied – not directly – by mass protests against sexist reaction, permissive gun laws promoted by the right, climate destruction, and police violence against civilians. Social movements for nationalised healthcare, a higher minimum wage, gun control, and immigrant rights, gained ground and became increasingly politicised.

We have come to an important juncture: Living conditions are in decline, which undercuts faith in established authority, across the population. The ruling class, which had grown torpid in the era of free market 'greed over governance', has been shaken awake by the crises and the disruption of social peace. At the same time, a new generation has grown amidst the shambles caused by neoliberalism, as the paths of activism, and in particular electoral activism, have opened to people who in previous times were locked out, or locked into machine politics.

The combination of these circumstances gave rise to a hastily organised alliance of the centre, the dominant force in the Democratic Party; the angry centre-right, reduced in electoral strength but still enjoying support from big capital; and the broad left, including labour leadership and electoral activists sharing an anti-neoliberal agenda.

A report for *Time* by Molly Ball[1] tracked the convergence of left, centre, and centre-right against Trump's administration and his leadership of the Republican Party. This rally included the AFL-CIO, the business leadership's Chamber of Commerce, and the anti-neoliberal Working Families Party. 'The handshake between business and labour', Ball wrote, 'was just one component of a vast, cross-partisan campaign to protect the election' from attacks against voting rights carried out by respectable, and less-than-respectable, white nationalists in every state. 'The pact was formalised in a terse, little-noticed joint statement of the US Chamber of Commerce and

AFL-CIO published on Election Day. Both sides would come to see it as a sort of implicit bargain – inspired by the summer's massive, sometimes destructive racial-justice protests – in which the forces of labour came together with the forces of capital to keep the peace and oppose Trump's assault on democracy.'

The terms of this pact, if Ball has it right, are open to interpretation and analysis. But the circumstances reveal a determination to isolate a fascist upsurge which opens many new chances for mass democratic political action. Business and labour were joined by the predominantly white liberal National Association of Evangelicals and the National African American Clergy Network. They wrote: 'We call on the media, the candidates and the American people to exercise patience with the process and trust in our system, even if it requires more time than usual.... [We] are united in our call for the American democratic process to proceed without violence, intimidation or any other tactic that makes us weaker as a nation.' In other words, if Trump wins, it must be after a fair count, which was, by Election Day November 3, seen as less than likely without national and local diligence (a demand long promoted by the left and centre-left). This was an acknowledgement that the Republicans were engaged in voter suppression, and an oblique recognition of the role of the far right in mobilising white enclaves in populous states (Pennsylvania, Michigan, Ohio, etc.) in allowing Trump to override the popular vote in 2016.

New polarisation

The shift in political alignment became apparent virtually overnight after the events of January 6, 2021. Seven days later, on January 13, the House of Representatives debated over a second impeachment of Donald Trump. The speeches were mostly uniform for each party. Either Trump was a seditious violator of the Constitution, or he was a victim persecuted by a conspiracy from the top and bottom of society against the middle class.

One particular statement captured the political moment. It was Cori Bush's first speech before the House. She had recently been elected to Congress from Missouri, to represent the mostly black districts that include the town of Ferguson, where mass violence broke out following the murder of Michael Brown by a police officer in 2014.

Representative Bush is a nurse, not a career politician, and her recognition as an organiser was decisive to her election victory. She has the politics of a seasoned social movement activist, openly critical of entrenched power, both corporate and white nationalist.

Bush testified: 'If we fail to remove a white supremacist President who incited a white supremacist insurrection, it's communities like Missouri's First District that suffer the most. The 117th Congress must understand that we have a mandate to legislate in defence of Black lives. The first step in that process is to root out white supremacy, starting with impeaching the white supremacist-in-chief.'

A few Republicans booed. If this had taken place anytime before the 2018 midterm elections, It would have caused a bipartisan uproar, if only on grounds of protocol and respect for the Presidency. But after Trump's elevation of ostensibly fascist politics, and the deadly brawl through the Capitol to stop the House validation of his electoral defeat, Bush's words now reflected common knowledge, a Democratic Party consensus.

Every detail of this event is telling. Representative Bush's own election is a result of the increased violence against civilians by police, and the politicisation of black, brown, and yellow eligible voters, as the racial demographic in the US shifts away from a white majority. The demographic shift prompted a national ideological nervous breakdown. Fascism as a popular movement has always been isolated in national politics, but white nationalism is an ideology that is deeply rooted in property relations, within the labour market and otherwise. White nationalism was invoked in the American Revolution, and numerous other wars, including the Civil War and the so-called wars on terror, drugs and 'crime'.

The four years under Trump were marked by open and belligerent reversals of democratic rights. Trump's constant demagogy, aimed at dehumanising black youth, Latin American immigrants, Muslims, and his political challengers, changed the tone of public discourse. He championed the hatred that has always lurked under the surface, but was previously kept in reserve, occasionally promoted to attract votes. For Trump it was less a political tactic than part of an ongoing swindle. If it worked once, he would keep it up until it stops paying off. Those who chafed at the hushing up of racist rhetoric, felt vindicated and liberated. For the far right in all its forms, Trump's stance represented the white worm finally turning, and the political movement grew in size and ambition as a direct consequence.

Trump's sociopathic tendency to operate on a hustler's instinct led him to his fascist political stance. It was easy enough to get into his inner circle, as such determined fascists as Steve Bannon and Steven Miller discovered. They bolstered the right-of-right wing of the Republican Party – Tea Party, religious right, gun collectors, nativists – with their connections to the more extreme right wing on the Internet – political lunatics, conspiracy theorists, the subcultures of the rejected that traditionally flourished only in prisons, police departments, and suburban basements. With backing from several ardent billionaires, they successfully drove out of party leadership the once-dominant moderates – educated, old-school conservative plutocrats from Harvard and Yale.

With the election of a great pretender in 2016, the US ruling class slowly came to recognise that they no longer had full control of the ship of state. Their traditional default party was commandeered by a bloc of the white establishment right and the crypto-fascist fringe, fueled by their shared terror of politicisation among the rising numbers of nonwhite Americans. The elite, rendered dull-witted by individualism and the 'greed is good' ethos of neoliberalism, were accepting of Trump's white populism at first. Trump himself fawned over the rich (except when faced with criticism) and cut their taxes to next to nothing. That gave him the same freedom enjoyed by Republican Presidents from Reagan to George W. Bush, at first.

Trump's freedom to terrorise was curtailed in his third year (until he broke loose on January 6), and the Democrats' hand strengthened, as his corruption became impossible to ignore or explain away. In particular, his disinterest in and inability to meet the challenge of the pandemic horrified the world. He continued to maintain that climate change is a hoax, against the warnings of scientists everywhere. The demand for safety from murderous police and recognition of racial injustice was spreading fast among youth across the color line. The shredding of public services was lowering living standards for the majority, with the labour movement stagnant and defeated. A semi-fascist bloc was in power, but its hegemony was waning, despite the usual advantages bestowed on incumbents in the US.

A vacuum appeared as the centre and centre-right weighed their options: whether or not to take action that would address the issues, but potentially scare the white-identified majority into submerging into Trump's bloc, and alienate funders. While trying to decide, The Sanders movement of 2015-16 re-entered the fray with an openly democratic socialist platform: socialised medicine (Medicare for All) and New Deal-style public works programmes geared to end reliance on fossil fuel (Green New Deal). In 2018 a small group of newly elected Congress members formed a mini-caucus dubbed 'the squad' – four Democrats, all women, three of them Bernie Sanders supporters ('Berniecrats'), one black (from Massachusetts), one Puerto Rican (New York), one a Muslim Somali (Minnesota), and one Palestinian (Michigan). The tiny squad, with Senator Sanders, took the lead in government in challenging the Trump-dominated Republicans and the centrist leadership of the Democratic Party.

The Democratic old guard won the 2020 primary, installing Joe Biden over Sanders, but they discovered that the public mood of their voter base was listing left. This was not new. Polling has consistently shown that single payer health care and the left's Green New Deal were popular even among hardcore supporters of centrists like Biden who called them extreme. New leftist members were elected to the House over entrenched moderates and Republicans. Trump's more desperate moves after losing a close election (rejecting the vote count and launching the putsch at the Capitol) gingerly pushed the centre to the left. This was reflected in Democratic officials' rhetoric in the weeks leading up to Trump's second impeachment on January 13, and some of the appointments to Biden's administration.

The left in the centre/left bloc

The emergence of a politicised left comes in the wake of neoliberalism's decline and the commingled crises of climate, pandemic, police violence, and austerity. Neither party offered a serious solution. The last high point for the left, the growth of social movements that confronted racism, sexism and militarism, petered out with the transition from Cold War to free-market triumphalism; but the left faced repeated violent repression since the postwar Red Scare, and were politically marginalised for decades. After the 1999 Seattle protests, a new generation moved from unfocused altermondialism to radical reformism and democratic socialist politics, with a surge of anarchism before the Occupy Wall Street protests.

The path was frustrating and demoralising. Two developments indicated a new approach to left politics, in the waning months of Obama's second term: the Bernie Sanders campaigns and the growth spurt of young activists joining Democratic Socialists of America, which joined with Sanders early in his 2016 Presidential primary campaign. Significant mass actions around women's rights, police violence, environment, voting rights and gun control increased after Trump's victory. Public demands seeded ferment, which brought new energy for electoral campaigns, mostly involving Democratic candidates embracing the Sanders platform of Medicare for all, reducing the power of 'the billionaire class' in politics, and the Green New Deal.

By 2020 the political scene showed the signs of a new alternative. A number of groups with the shared goal of electing progressives to local and national legislatures began to challenge incumbents, both Republicans and moderate Democrats. This broke through the longstanding strategy of protecting Democrats with seniority as a safeguard against Republican hegemony. The old strategy became a buttress to bureaucracy that strengthened the hand of right populists. Between 2018 and 2021 it became clear that centrism was declining in local races, and the new wave was rising.

The extraordinary double win for Democrats in Georgia's runoff Senate elections on January 5, 2021 was a victory for both the centre and left, and demonstrated the erosion of Trump's vote-getting power after the general election. Georgia is Dixie – that is, a white political empire in which the sizable black population has been disenfranchised since the suppression of postslavery Reconstruction in the 1870s. The efforts to mobilise black and other, sympathetic voters, through mail-in ballots and careful organising, while combating the active campaign to isolate and disable the anti-Trump vote, broke the historical political dominion that undergirds the far right nationally. This intersects with the regional fight between overt racist Republicans and the more muted social operators who have no home but the Democratic Party. But the party conflict is only a frame for class conflict between local capital and a population engulfed in misery.

The winners in Georgia, the state's new Senate delegation, were announced on January 6, the very morning Team Trump gathered outside the Capitol to violently overturn the Presidential vote count. Both were Democrats: a left-leaning black minister, Rev. Raphael Warnock, and Jon Ossoff, a centrist – Jewish, at that. The worst conspiracy nightmares of the far right seemed confirmed. (Anti-Semitism was not a pronounced feature of Trumpite rhetoric until the rise of the social media conspiracy craze known as QAnon.)

Mainstream media in the aftermath of the election and siege have watched Biden much more carefully than they did Clinton or Obama. The left has more pull in the consensus view of reform vs 'normalcy', at least momentarily. Challenges to neoliberalism have provoked some response from the centre, while the enormities of the whole Trump debacle and January 6 in particular have put the centre on the offensive against the right/far right. There is a view, possibly a majority view, that if the new administration limits its response to empty gestures, they will empower the right/far-right. The pundits and the party base are nervous about Saudis, air strikes, detention centres, and kid gloves for the GOP. In this freefall moment, the left's voice has more resonance.

The left in the left/centre bloc is concerned with bolstering the centre's stance against the right/far right bloc. The Democratic centrist leadership is more concerned with working with the centre-right who have been all but purged from the Republicans. The centre-right faction, whose public face before and after the election is the Lincoln Project, is small but backed by very powerful capitalists, who are actually more determined to drive the Trump bloc into the shadows than the centre seems to be. However, they want a return to Bush days, which seems to be the preferred path for the centre. The left argues that this position is ultimately untenable. The path to safety and security is through solidarity, not a return to Post-Reagan neoliberalism, and there is plenty of money to save people's lives if federal and state governments tax corporations and redistribute Pentagon funds to infrastructure and social services. This is a very precarious moment where the damage done by the Trump bloc gives the left a higher profile, which it must use constantly.

Republicans in freefall

However, the right/far-right bloc is not dying yet. All parties recognised the phenomenal voter turnout in the 2020 Presidential election. The US electorate is notoriously sleepy, but that year nearly two-thirds turned out, or a relative 7 percent increase over the 2016 vote. Biden won 81 million votes, the highest vote count in history. Trump won 72 million votes – the second highest count in history. A majority of white voters went to Trump, and an unexpected number of voters of color also went for the incumbent.

The fissures within the Republican Party are real, but Trump remained party leader in early 2021. This is due less to the electoral strength of far-right, cryptofascist organisations, than to the elected officials and party apparatchiks who believe their career, and maybe their own and their families' lives, depend on their maintaining public deference to Trump. So we saw the seemingly illogical move of the strongest elected official in the party, Senate Minority Leader Mitch McConnell. First McConnell guaranteed the Democrats would be denied a two-thirds Senate majority needed to convict Trump at the second impeachment trial. After the vote, on the same day, McConnell gave a speech indicting Trump in the same language used by the investigators who prosecuted the case against Trump regarding the January 6 siege.

This captures the cynicism behind the party's angling for power. Now Trump and McConnell are enemies, but unless and until the party unseats him, he continues to hold the whip hand in dealing with the Democratic administration's measures. This is an unstable party – its membership and voter base held together by a personality cult around an unhinged paranoid, while its financial base seems determined to keep Trump away from the reins of power for good. The anti-Trump Republicans are centre-right, with the majority of big capital on their side. The right hopes to win back the favour of funders without losing the party base. That requires regaining the upper hand in 2022 and 2024. The main means to that end is to lay waste to the voting rights of Democratic strongholds, an old tradition practiced since the Constitutional Amendment gave black men the vote in 1870.

The voting rights watchdog group Brennan Center for Justice reported:

'In a backlash to historic voter turnout in the 2020 general election, and grounded in a rash of baseless and racist allegations of voter fraud and election irregularities, legislators have introduced well over four times the number of bills to restrict voting access as compared to roughly this time last year. Thirty-three states have introduced, prefiled, or carried over 165 restrictive bills this year (as compared to 35 such bills in fifteen states on February 3, 2020). [...] These proposals primarily seek to: (1) limit mail voting access; (2) impose stricter voter ID requirements; (3) slash voter registration opportunities; and (4) enable more aggressive voter roll purges. These bills are an unmistakable response to the unfounded and dangerous lies about fraud that followed the 2020 election.'[2]

The once and future left

The future of the left is at stake in the 2020s. A concrete definition of the US left goes beyond parties or even a section of the Democratic Party. Its political effectiveness is disabled by historic fragmentation of constituencies – defined by work category, location, racial identity, ideological legacies, sectarianism, and the seemingly unlimited ability of capital to adapt and adopt opposition forces. While the right/far right bloc promote the lie that the Democratic Party is controlled by socialists, in fact the social movements have both grown in the Obama years, and moved to embrace democratic socialism, broadly defined as opposition to neoliberalism and climate destruction. They are not in control of any part of the party, nor do they set the agenda, unlike the far right in the other party.

The other decisive obstacle to a strong left is political incoherence. The left has suffered from repeated state attacks and disruptions of historical continuity. Many of the problems the left needs to face as it struggles out of the margins are addressed by its rich historical legacies, including the fight for racial justice in various forms, and the rise of the labour movement. But the institutions that were built out of those struggles have been tied to the two-party system, in part out of limited options, and in part out of a co-dependent relationship with the Democratic Party as it moved from New Deal Keynesianism to neoliberalism with a human face. After the 1950s red scare, the left was defined mainly by opposition to racism and imperialist adventures. This had a powerful impact on the direction of both parties, despite the continued dominance of the Pentagon in foreign policy and the continuation of racial profiling by police, and the disproportionate violence suffered by working people that resulted from the racially inspired 'war on crime' (and on drugs and terror).

Throughout that period to the present, the left has lacked an organised political leadership that could reach beyond the scope of one fragment or another. Social movements generate political leadership circles, but there is competition and rivalry amongst them, exacerbated by the scraps offered by private and government funders, and by sectarianism from the left and double-crossing from the right.

Bernie Sanders and 'the squad' broke the pattern by proclaiming their opposition to neoliberalism, corporate power, and the rise of police brutality. Sanders sought to prove that a self-proclaimed democratic socialist could win the support of millions with a left populist message, and succeeded beyond expectations. The squad, all Democrats, forced the party to accept anti-neoliberal (if not forthrightly socialist) politics as part of the recognised agenda. This sent the Republicans into a paranoid frenzy (with 'socialists' becoming the newest tag for the xenophobes' perennial 'spectre'). For the Democratic leadership, it offered a choice: continue to try to beat back the left in the party, or accept their support in fighting the right/far-right. They chose the latter, for the time being, recognising that (1) the left is only beginning to emerge from the margins of the political stage, still seemingly posing only a minor threat, and (2) they were more interested in currying favour with the centre-right Republicans, who are as focused on fighting the Trump camp as the left is.

The left's main dilemma, overcoming fragmentation and political incoherence, poses problems of ideology, capacity, and strategy. In the electoral arena, there are progressive-to-socialist groupings in every state, some with labour or other social movement connections, others born out of various national and local campaigns. Some are national, some strictly local. Leaderships from these groups have begun to confer and coordinate their work, below the media radar. They represent the left in the centre/left alliance that took down Trump and claimed the Senate by the narrowest of majorities. But they are still far from exercising real influence in policy direction, either in the government or in the party.

Socialist organisations, publications and intellectuals have long been divided between those who oppose Democratic campaigns and elected officials on principle, and those who see the party base as the prime political target and view the party leadership, more or less, as an ally in the fight against the reactionary right. The second position is perpetually undermined by the party leadership's role as a guardian of capital, but most socialists today are in the 'inside/outside' camp (that is, working 'inside' Democratic campaigns and sometimes in the party between elections, while supporting independents 'outside' – based on the political stakes in each case). The threat of Trump's fascist direction even drove some of the most notorious ultra-leftist groups to endorse Biden. However, the willingness and even ability of the Democratic leadership to undercut the damage done by neoliberalism, pandemic, and climate destruction is still in question. Nevertheless, the hope of a left third party in any form continues to be stymied by the electoral system, making it impossible to push ahead of either party long enough to secure a potential majority even in the best of circumstances for the left.

The rise of Democratic Socialists of America (the writer is a member) from a relative handful to a 50-state group approaching 100,000 members is significant, but also indicative of the challenges of fragmentation and incoherence facing the left as a whole. The transformation of DSA (founded 1972) came directly from the success of the Sanders campaign in 2015-16. Since DSA's emerging new generation of leadership had the foresight to join Sanders, it was the logical first step for many just finding their way to politics. Today's DSA shares some of the strengths and weaknesses of Students for a Democratic Society (SDS), which dominated the 1960s New Left. It's an inclusive, big tent group with room for experimenting and trial-and-error. But it has no clearly defined political pole in leadership, and is ridden with factions. It has developed skilled organisers, particularly adding a stronger critical note to left electoral efforts, with real success, including good relations with Ocasio-Cortez and others in the squad. Others involved in electoral work, in groups like Indivisible and Justice Democrats, have less strict procedures for their endorsements. This has isolated DSA in some left political circles, but also helps to sharpen the focus of candidates who seek DSA's support.

DSA drifted into an agnostic position on the 2020 election, which marked the group's confusion of the permanent target of capitalist politics as a whole with the immediate urgent danger posed by a second Trump term, which was recognised as crucial by Sanders and the squad. This both highlighted and aggravated DSA's isolation from the broader left.

All these problems point to the need to strengthen the left as a political force, but in the context of a complex and fast-changing array of forces and tendencies within forces. On one hand, the bottom-line positions that distinguish the left from the centre are opposition to neoliberalism, militarism at home and abroad, and corporate power and money in politics. The left and centre are closer (and more in conflict with the right) on the questions of fascism, and diversity in political representation that mirrors the prevailing politics in different constituencies (as opposed to mere tokenism). These are, roughly, the terms for conflict and cooperation between the left and centre. The left leans towards anti-militarism but it lacks a strong, consistent peace movement, for complicated reasons. The centre has long been actively hawkish, though since Vietnam, usually more in the name of 'humanitarianism' than anticommunism or Islamophobia. Overall, the demands put forward by the 'Berniecrats' have won favour with many, perhaps most Democratic voters, and many party stalwarts.

Discussions online, in publications (which include some widely read magazines that have moved left as the Cold War generation dies out), and inside socialist groups have tried to figure out how to present the left to the public as an alternative option. There is the ever-present economic programme, which was elaborated in the last decade by Ocasio-Cortez and environmentalists to revive the infrastructure development strategy of the New Deal, the most historically significant turn to pre-World War II social democracy in US history. Both the Green New Deal and Medicare for All (universal healthcare) rate high in polls, but are only glancingly acknowledged within the centre/left alliance. It is unlikely to get a renewed push until it is determined whether or not the new administration can end the pandemic. If it can, the central policy question will be what kind of 'normalcy' the US will 'return' to. If it can't, the debate will turn to radical reform, either authoritarian austerity à la *The Hunger Games* (not far from what the Republicans, still dominated by the Trump cult, advocate today); or a sharp break from neoliberalism, which would pit the government against the industrial giants that most fiercely oppose environmental protection and socialised medicine. The centre could go either way, in part depending on how much of a threat the right/far right appears to be in the eyes of the rest of big capital. This will determine the future of the centre/left alliance, and the left needs to be prepared to respond one way or the other.

The Green New Deal/Medicare for All platform does not address the question of popular political agency, especially regarding the depoliticised, socially conservative working class. One response on the left is to focus on revitalising the labour movement. This is a critical moment for unions; the movement was decimated by deindustrialisation and neoliberalism, and politically has been reduced to an appendage of centrist elected officials. The older generation of leadership is phasing out, but who will fill the vacuum is still uncertain. If the new generation identifies with the left, that still leaves the problem of politically mobilising the membership.

However, social mobilisation is on the rise, in particular on the question of democratic rights. The Republicans remain committed to eliminating abortion rights, and with the current rightist majority on the Supreme Court, the centre/left may remain on the defensive, especially if the balance in Congress shifts right again in 2022. This was why the first demonstration against Trump in power was the historic Women's March in 2017. While the left is committed to defending workers' rights, the unions tend to see the centrists as their only foothold in government, and many rank-and-file workers are sympathetic to right populism. As workers' rights are coming more to the fore, the left has a particular role to play as the social conscience of the centre/right bloc, advocating for labour, economic justice, and democratic rights when the centre tries to shift to neutral.

The most critical of democratic rights, the right to life and safety from state repression and xenophobic violence, continues to erode, and the public awaits to see what the new administration will do to restore it. This will require the state to purge organised fascist forces from both the military and law enforcement, an infiltration that has been documented, but only hinted at in the aid offered to the January 6 putschists, and in the ongoing inability to prosecute murder by police despite clear evidence in numerous cases. Here again the role of the left is distinguished from the centre, which perpetually stands between the right to survive and the right to exploit workers and amass capital, which are more and more in conflict.

The question of democracy goes beyond rights under capitalism, to the heart of the left's purpose, tasks and goals. The Cold War definitions of democracy have lost their meaning. To the West, it meant the capitalist system in place, with the US embodying it. To the East, and much of the Western left, it meant 'anti-fascism', which turned the Western version on its head. Neither definition gets anywhere near the idea of democracy spawned out of the desperation of life in the slums and favelas: rule by the populace, including whether or not corporations get to exist.

This is understood as something different, although connected, to who does or doesn't get elected. It involves the politicisation of the public in the course of their fight to survive. Just what kind of politics will be determined by the quality of the discussion as the movement creates new and different organisations. The organised left, in the narrow sense of various parties and projects, and left scholars and artists – can play a very big role, but less internal to their own parties and more to the broader, multi-tendency movement, where leaders are always in motion.

The 'movement' posited here is a united front. That is, not a laundry list of groups, but a conscious and organised alliance. It sets up the beginning coordination of work by mutually recognised parts of the political and social movement left. It fights sectarianism, turf warfare, and superficial rivalries. It also operates with democratic decision-making, which it promotes and encourages as central to collective wellbeing. This united front could be the start of a mass national opposition, one that could fight the right and the centre when necessary. It could also spark a process that could reinvent democracy by developing the components of a working class-interested, direct democratic political system.

There is no nationally recognised group in the US advocating for this direction. It develops incrementally but distinctly with the increase in politicisation of social movements, indicated by their official statements in some cases, and by the sentiment of the activists and organising bases. In part it comes when Democratic sympathisers find themselves moving left of centre, look for a coherent left, and discover the left as it is … confused, anxious, but rapidly realising there's no turning back.

NOTES

1   <https://time.com/5936036/secret-2020-election-campaign/>.
2   <https://www.brennancenter.org/our-work/research-reports/voting-laws-roundup-february-2021>

Golden Dawn:
The Rise and Fall of a Nazi Gang

Dimitris Psarras Interviewed by Haris Golemis

Haris Golemis: On 7 October 2020, Golden Dawn (GD) was declared a criminal organisation by the court which tried the murder of Pavlos Fyssas and other acts of violence committed by its members. With a history that dates back to forty years, this Nazi formation is anything but recent, though. Back in 1980, its leader Nicos Michaloliakos had published a magazine under the same title, propagating Nazi ideas; in 1983 he founded the political movement People's League; as your own investigative work has shown, in 1987 the group drew up a secret Nazi statute. Ever since, and up until 2007, when their sixth conference was held, GD members, armed with bats and knives, carried out a string of brutal attacks targeting refugees and immigrants, members of leftist organisations and youth squatters, culminating in the 1998 near successful assassination of Dimitris Kousouris. 2009 marked the expansion of their criminal activity, encouraged as they felt by the relative consolidation and the electoral breakthrough the party enjoyed both in the Greek and European Parliaments. It all led to the assassination of the young anti-fascist rapper, Pavlos Fyssas, in 2013, and the opening of legal proceedings that ended up with GD's conviction, in October 2020.

The legitimate question arises as to how the Greek authorities tolerated the lawful operation of a Nazi group and later on of a Nazi party, but in Germany and perhaps in other European countries as well, a group of this kind would have been outlawed. So, how was it finally possible for its members to be prosecuted and eventually taken to court, charged with running a criminal organisation? What changed?

Dimitris Psarras: Golden Dawn was founded in December 1980 by Nicos Michaloliakos, the life-long leader of the group. At the beginning, it was a small team operating as a closed National Socialist self-education society. Since the end of the 1980s, some propaganda actions were launched in the streets, and in the early nineties a campaign of violent attacks against anyone they classified as a 'subhuman' began; they started targeting students, left-wing youth, and anti-authoritarian movements and continued with immigrants, refugees, and, in short, anyone they thought of as 'diverse', such as people from the LGBTQ+ community for example.

For many years their actions went unpunished, but even when the crimes had multiplied and some sort of investigation was launched by the police and the judiciary, the doctrine prevailed that the Nazi perpetrators should be treated as individuals and not as agents of an organisation. This longstanding immunity was based on three elements: a) historically, GD was the outgrowth of the Greek deep state that survived the German and Italian occupations (1941-45), the Civil War (1946-49), and the dictatorship (1967-1974); b) politically, the organisation had operated for years assisting the forces of order by performing their 'dirty business' for them, that is to say clashing with demonstrators in ways the state cannot directly do; c) institutionally, the Greek Constitution, passed in 1975 in the aftermath of the abolition of the dictatorship, provides political parties with excellent protection, with no provisions whatsoever for them to be outlawed. That is why Michaloliakos, as you rightly point out, founded the People's League in 1983 and filed a relevant statement with the Supreme Court. Eleven years later, in 1994, GD ran for election for the first time. As was evident in the trial, Michaloliakos's aim in founding a 'political party' was precisely to obtain the necessary constitutional protection.

In September 2013, the Greek judiciary was called upon to rule on whether it was a criminal organisation that was operating behind the mantle of the GD, the political party. It was the first time anything of this sort had ever occurred. So the question is what happened to bring about this change. Well, I think it's because since the summer of 2013 the Golden-Dawners had been feeling so confident that they believed they could take the lead in the broader spectrum of the right, directly colliding not only with the left but also with the New Democracy (ND) party. In September 2013, within just a few days, GD carried out a series of murderous attacks, first on KKE[1] trade unionists in Piraeus, then on right-wingers in Meligalas, Peloponnese, where the annual ceremony commemorating the right-wing victims of the Civil War was held, and finally they murdered Pavlos Fyssas. The escalation of the attacks forced the Greek state to eventually intervene, following the large wave of anti-fascist reaction that had surged throughout the country. So what happened next? Simply, what should have happened years ago. All 35 pending cases regarding the illegal actions of GD members were consolidated into one, and the judicial authority undertook to determine whether such actions fell under Article 187 of the Greek Criminal Code, that is, whether a criminal organisation using the façade of a political party had orchestrated the bloody attacks, motivated by its Nazi ideology.

H.G.: You have been occupied with GD since its emergence, and your contribution to the verdict reached by the court has been crucial, mainly, though not only, because of the disclosure of the organisation's secret statute. How did this special interest of yours arise, and what difficulties has your research encountered over the years? Have you faced threats from the Golden-Dawners?

D.P.: I belong to the generation of the student anti-dictatorship movement. My relation with politics has been marked by the experience of the dictatorship (1967-1974). At the pinnacle of the anti-dictatorship resistance – in the Athens Polytechnic Uprising of November 1973 – I was a student of the School of Architecture and I was there, inside the university premises, where we had gathered. Michaloliakos, four years younger than me, was outside the Polytechnic along with the junta police forces. He was a member of the neo-fascist group '4th of August Party'[2] led by Konstantinos Plevris. He actually belonged to the most extreme part of the group, along with another man called Elias Tsiapouris; on the night the junta's tanks raided, Tsiapouris was the one who shot at the crowd of young insurgents from the roof of the Ministry of Public Order, located just a block away from the Polytechnic at the time, in the centre of Athens. It has been documented that at least two people were killed in these shootings. Tsiapouris fled abroad and escaped punishment, but until only a few years ago, at GD gatherings, Michaloliakos would emotionally narrate stories about the deeds of the 'heroic Elias'.

What I mean is that my interest in the organisation has naturally followed from my approach to politics. So when the Junta was brought down, Michaloliakos found himself involved in indiscriminate terrorist attacks performed by far-right groups, originating from the same neo-fascist organisation (the '4th of August Party'). I have been following them ever since, and along with my colleagues in the journalist researchers' collective Ios[3] we published relevant analyses that were then considered to be excessive, if not 'obsessive'.

Ever since the beginning of its activities, GD never hid its Nazi structure, and in fact it was the leadership itself that had sent us many relevant documents, including the famous 'Statute' I handed over during my three-day testimony in court. Of course, in time threats followed along with plenty of articles against me featured in the organisation's publications. As a matter of fact, in his apology Michaloliakos referred to me as being his 'personal

Javert'. However, I have been directly attacked by GD only once, in a courtroom in 2009, right after the court's announcement that the deputy leader of the organisation, Antonios Androutsopoulos, had been convicted of the attempted murder of Dimitris Kousouris. It should be understood that the targets of the organisation are not people like me or even their direct 'political' opponents. When referring to the violence used by GD, the pattern of 'split delegitimisation' suggested by Ehud Sprinzak seems appropriate to describe the particularity of far-right terrorist groups.[4] Such terrorist organisations usually avoid conflict with the authorities and they gang together on the basis of their conviction that the target they strongly oppose to is a priori delegitimised (minorities, foreigners, immigrants). The targeted people are seen as different from the community they consider themselves members of; it is said that they do not belong and therefore must be kept in a subordinate legal status, expelled, or even exterminated.

H.G.: Do you know if GD was connected to other Nazi or fascist organisations in Europe?

D.P.: Strange though it may seem, GD had kept in touch with counterparts all over Europe ever since its foundation, back in 1980. The first close contact was the neo-Nazi CEDADE (Círculo Español de Amigos de Europa – Spanish Circle of Friends of Europe) founded in Spain in 1966 and already in decline by the early 1980s. The original form of GD was modelled on CEDADE, on the model of a 'spiritual association'. *Golden Dawn* magazine not only featured analyses of CEDADE's activities but also selected exactly the same Nazi models as the Spanish organisation, namely Adolf Hitler, and others such as Alfred Rosenberg, Corneliu Codreanu, and Léon Degrelle. Actually, in April 1990, a close associate of Michaloliakos, Christos Pappas, visited Degrelle who was at the time in exile in Spain. Pappas, in the same trial also convicted of running a criminal organisation, has evaded arrest and is still in hiding. In 1994 two GD officials made contact with the neo-Nazi French group PNFE26, and in September 1995 *Golden Dawn* was being sold at the kiosk of the youth wing of Front National de la Jeunesse during the festival of the French far-right party. Michaloliakos had met Le Pen in person during an earlier visit of the French far-right leader to Athens. At that same time, GD was also especially connected with the racist South African AWB (Afrikaner Weerstandsbeweging), which violently resisted the collapse of apartheid. GD officials participated, alongside the Bosnian-Serb perpetrators, in the 1995 Srebrenica massacre, and in 1996 the organisation was invited by the leader of the Russian far-right LDPR, Vladimir Zhirinovsky, to represent Greece in the Patriotic International (Patrintern) which was then being established.

GD also had contacts in the USA. In 1991, it had already published a brochure by the American Nazi Party founder George Lincoln, while in 1998 William Luther Pierce, leader of the Neo-Nazi National Alliance and author of the infamous *Turner Diaries*, came to Thessaloniki, invited by the organisation, which later translated the *Diaries* in 2002. In fact, GD launched a campaign to support the prisoners of the terrorist organisation The Order, which had been inspired by the Turner Diaries.

Up until the prosecution, the organisation maintained close ties with the most extreme far-right parties. In the mid-2000s, GD participated in the European National Front (ENF), alongside organisations from 13 European countries. Among them were the German NPD, Romania's Noua Dreapta, and Italy's Forza Nuova. After the party's election to the Greek Parliament and the European Parliament it joined the Alliance for Peace and Freedom (APF), a pan-European party founded in 2015. Actually, with its electoral success, which was unprecedented for such an extreme and openly Nazi organisation, GD also attempted to export Nazism. It came to be a role model for many extreme political formations around the world. A very characteristic case is that of the American neo-Nazi - and of course Trump supporter - Matthew Heimbach, the founder of the Traditionalist Workers Party (TWP), who was one of the leaders of the Alt-Right movement and played a leading role in the violent incidents in Charlottesville, Virginia that resulted in the death of a woman. Heimbach himself stated on camera after the episodes that he had been guided by GD's modus operandi. There is plenty of evidence documenting his presence at GD's offices and photographs of him posing with Michaloliakos.

The organisation even kept contact with the German Nazi terrorist organisation NSU, through the NPD officials André Kapke and Thorsten Heise. In 2013, officials from Freies Netz Süd, which has already been prohibited in Germany, were photographed in the party's offices in the Greek Parliament.

H.G.: After its foundation, GD remained a small far-right organisation for many years. Throughout the period following the onset of the economic crisis in 2010, not only did it continue and intensify its criminal activities, but as a political party its vote share rose sharply from 0.29% in 2009 to 7% in May 2012, while in the next three elections its electoral strength remained steadily above 6%. What do you think were the reasons for this significant electoral increase?

D.P.: We experienced the first surge of the organisation's appeal at the onset of the crisis. It was built on its rhetoric targeted at the many immigrants in the centre of Athens. In the 2010 local elections, the organisation exceeded 5% and Michaloliakos was elected municipal counsellor in Athens. It was a rough time for Greek citizens who suffered an outright attack not only on income but also on their social and political rights. The political system of bi-partisanship (ND – Pasok[5]) collapsed, paving the way for other options. Basically, I would say that those who had not given up hope for a change in the situation turned to the left, that is, to Syriza, while those who were absolutely convinced that there was no way out, were particularly vulnerable to extreme, nationalist, xenophobic, and conspiracy groups. For many people, their vote for GD simply indicated that by making that choice they would be having their 'revenge' against the political system that had betrayed them. Contrary to what is sometimes argued, it is not primarily the anti-immigrant discourse that attracted wider social strata to the organisation. That is the reason why a similar voter turnout was evident even in areas that had not become host communities for migrants and where people's only awareness of the issue came from what they saw on television.

There was also a circumstantial reason that boosted the Nazi organisation. In November 2011, just a few months ahead of the elections, the hitherto powerful party of the far right, Laos (Popular Orthodox Rally), under Georgios Karatzaferis joined the three-party government together with ND and Pasok, under the leadership of the banker Lucas Papademos. In so doing, Laos lost its 'anti-systemic' feature, and as a result, many of its voters shifted to GD. After the 2012 double elections (May and June) GD rose to 7%, thus establishing its predominance within the far right. Its performance in these elections was higher particularly in areas where it had deployed its aggressive activism (especially in the centre of Athens) and despite its appeal in the major urban centres having been dampened by the disclosure of its criminal activity, in the following elections the party maintained the same nationwide percentages. This was possible because it had inherited the traditional far-right voting pools, mainly in Northern Greece and some prefectures of the Peloponnese. But GD had never been a parliamentary far-right party. That is why, as soon as the criminal activities of its central core became more widely known, the collapse began. It should be noted here that as early as September 2013, after the first arrests of the leadership officials, and although its appeal in the electorate still remained strong, very few people (a few dozen) took to the streets to protest.

H.G.: What was GD's relation to the police, the Church and the media? What was its influence among young people?

D.P.: I have already referred to the special relationship GD enjoyed with the so-called 'deep state' which has survived the World War II occupation, the Civil War, and the dictatorship. The term 'deep state' indicates the reactionary mechanisms within the army, the police, the judiciary, and the Church, the latter operating in Greece like a state apparatus par excellence. So this special relationship runs back to the time when the organisation was a totally marginal task force of Nazi fanatics and had no aspirations to become a parliamentary party. As regards the special relationship particularly with the police, there are official reports from the beginning of 2000 that record information about contacts with police officers and how HELAS (Hellenic Police) officers covered fugitive Golden-Dawners and provided GD officials with weapons, in exchange for their cooperation during demonstrations in the centre of Athens. In the 2012 elections it was found that 30-40% of the officers that constitute the riot police (MAT) had voted for the Nazi organisation. High-ranking military and judicial officials accepted GD's invitation to run as GD candidates even in 2014-2015, that is, after the prosecution of its leadership had begun. It is worth noting that a part of the Church leadership (seven metropolitan bishops) supported GD in the 2012 elections, despite the fact that they had plenty of evidence of its anti-Christian-pagan background. The media played a significant role in promoting GD. Perhaps not so much as in the case of Laos, which has been a television creation par excellence, but quite a significant role all the same.

In the early 1990s, the first phase of the 'Macedonian' question (that is, the outbreak of the nationalist wave in Greece, triggered by the issue of the name of the former Yugoslav Republic of Macedonia - today Northern Macedonia) coincided with the arrival of the first immigrants and refugees in Greece (following the downfall of the regimes of so-called real socialism) and the first ever establishment of private radio and television channels. In this context, extreme voices were a welcome element in the competition for higher audience ratings. In fact, after GD's success in the 2012 elections, much of the media presented the criminal activity of the Nazis as an interesting new lifestyle.

This lifestyle found resonance among the young, along with the allure of power and the cult of gyms and anabolics. Since the early 2000s Golden Dawn has been reaching out to young people through black metal bands. To add to that, a subsidiary organisation, the so-called 'Blue Army', targeted the fans who were following the progress of the National Football Team as it rose, in 2004, to the top level in Europe. Many of the core officials fall into this category. Of the seven who were sentenced to 13 years in prison as directors of the criminal organisation, two were leaders of extreme right-wing music groups (Germenis and Matthaiopoulos) and two others came from football fan organisations (Lagos and Panagiotaros).

H.G.: Did the working class constitute GD's base?

D.P.: According to the 2012 analyses on the composition of the electorate, there was a remarkably high percentage of unemployed among GD voters. But there was even more widespread appeal in petty bourgeois and rural strata, and male voters were twice as numerous as women. Interestingly enough, although GD's activity was limited to the working-class districts of Piraeus and the centre of Athens, it was substantially supported in the upper-class suburban areas of Northern Athens as well.

H.G.: In other European countries, organisations with ideological and political roots similar to Golden Dawn's – for instance in France, Italy, Austria, the Netherlands, etc. – accomplished a political turn at one or another point, renounced their past, and turned into major parties. The majority calls them right-wing populist, and a minority, a quite small one, neo-fascist. (Let me say here that the majority is not always right). Has GD tried to do the same, but without really having enough time to succeed, or was it something they were never concerned about? Had there been different trends within the organisation?

D.P.: Here lies yet another element of GD's specific character. Precisely because it is an organisation whose leadership has maintained its fanatical adherence to Nazism to the end, there has never been a real denunciation of its extremist positions. Since the early 1990s, GD has, of course, ceased using Nazi symbols openly and officially denied its connection to historical National Socialism. But we know that, within the party, Hitler and Nazism were still exalted and party officials would still take the oath to the Führer and have swastikas tattooed on their arms. When Michaloliakos was arrested in September, 2013, he claimed before the interrogators that the organisation had abandoned National Socialism since the late 1980s. But, as soon as he went out of the building, he hailed the few fans waiting for him with the cry 'Long live Victory!' (Sieg Heil!). Moreover, there are articles in the organisation's newspaper explaining that they are no longer called Nazis but nationalists, but they have not altered one comma of what they believed in all along. The court reviewed a great amount of evidence that documents the fact that until the very end the organisation remained fanatically faithful to Nazi ideology.

H.G.: At your suggestion, the day before the verdict was issued by the court the headline on the front page of the *Newspaper of the Editors* (*Efimerida ton Syntakton*) where you work, was 'The Democracy Wall'. It was illustrated with photos of the Greek Prime Minister, the heads of all parties in the Greek parliament, with the exception of the right-wing populist party Greek Solution, and with a photo of the right-wing populist New Democracy MP, Antonis Samaras, as he was the Prime Minister of Greece when the prosecution of Golden Dawn began and its members were arrested following Fyssas' murder. There was a special supplement in the newspaper with pieces written by the politicians mentioned above, where they supported GD's conviction as a criminal organisation

This initiative of yours, which I personally applauded, was met with resentment by several members of left-wing parties and organisations, who were of the view that in this way 'the right was white-washed', and above all Samaras who, they claimed, had 'paved the way' for the gang's activities. What is your answer to this left-wing discontent?

D.P.: I am convinced that the only way to confront the GD phenomenon was to insulate criminal activity from any affiliation to any party in the so-called constitutional arch. The political responsibilities of the parties for the rise of the GD phenomenon are one thing, and the need for this criminal activity to be isolated by everyone is another. Those disturbed by the front page couldn't grasp that we could not but include Samaras as the initial prosecution against the GD leadership was carried out under his government. The reason I chose this illustration was to stress that the court was not going to rule in a vacuum. Behind it stood the whole of democratic society and its political exponents. I believe that this choice has been justified. On 7 October, when the decision was announced, we were met with an unprecedented scene. Gathered outside the courthouse were tens of thousands of citizens chanting: 'They are not innocent!' Among them were representatives of all parties, including ND. Inside the court, around the emblematic figure of Magda Fyssa, the mother of Pavlos, stood the lawyers of the prosecution, who represented the broadest possible spectrum of the left. It was the only way to reach what was finally achieved – a court decision that restores law but also corrects decades of institutional errors, healing a deep wound in democracy.

H.G.: A related question: The right and the extreme centre accuse Syriza of joining hands with GD in support of the reactions to the memoranda in those years, thus classifying it, or at least having classified it so far, as one of the two extremes of the political system. On the other hand, Syriza argues that ND tolerated GD's action, with an eye to the votes of the far right. This became obvious when both ND and GD participated in the nationalist rallies for the Macedonian issue. I personally believe that neither of these two positions reflects reality. But what we are interested in here is your position.

D.P.: There is a European tradition that says that conservative and Christian Democratic parties flirt with the ideas and the leaders of the far right, while the centre-left and the social democrats open their doors to it in order to reduce the electoral appeal of the right. The same thing has happened on more than one occasion in Greece, especially in the case of the far-right Laos that preceded GD. But with the Nazi organisation, things became more difficult. And of course, in the spring of 2012, when ND realised that the polls were predicting numbers that would allow GD to enter the Parliament, it began to adopt parts of GD's tough anti-immigrant agenda, to talk about an 'invasion of illegal immigrants' and to prepare closed concentration camps for them. It was the wrong recipe because policy of this kind does not isolate extreme voices; it legitimises them. To make things worse, after the 2012 elections, ND restored hidden channels of communication with GD, through the Secretary General of the Government Panayiotis Baltakos, who was a close associate of Prime Minister Samaras. There was no alternative but to interrupt this connection in September 2013 when that same right-wing government was forced to proceed with the judicial investigation into the activities of the Nazis. For its part, Syriza had its own difficulty in dealing with the phenomenon. Even historical figures of the anti-fascist movement during wartime occupation, such as Manolis Glezos, greeted the adoption of restrictive measures against the Nazi organisation with scepticism, fearing that they might also be used against the left. In fact, when Syriza won the elections in January 2015 and formed a government, the whole issue seemed rather awkward due to the traumatic experiences of the left in Greece and its prosecution in the past. Moreover, GD's 'anti-memorandum' garb made some naïve people on the left believe at the time that it could not be excluded from the 'anti-memorandum' front. Thankfully, illusions of this sort were very soon shattered, since GD's street task forces continued their activity, setting its sights on the left itself as its prime target.

I think these developments taught everyone a lesson.

H.G.: Has GD left behind successors or has Greece broken free of gangs of this sort, and will it remain free of them for quite some time?

D.P.: Even before the court reached its verdict, GD had effectively disbanded. There only remained a core around the leader, Michaloliakos, while two more organisations appeared. One of them was led by the former trainer of GD's task forces, Elias Kasidiaris, and the second under the organisation's Member of the European Parliament, Ioannis Lagos, who had been involved in all the murderous attacks. I think that none of these three groups have any chance of staking out a serious political presence. I mean that with the conclusion of the trial, we're really done with the criminal part of the case. But that doesn't mean we have gotten over the far right at all. One can say that the extreme version of the far right represented by GD, and its Nazi and criminal character, served in a way as an effective bulwark for many people. And so far right percentages have remained relatively stagnant in Greece as compared to many European countries. The political issue today is how to deal with the ideas and rhetoric of the far right, which are unfortunately widespread in much broader political contexts in Greece. This, of course, is an issue not for the courts to resolve, but for political struggle and ideological confrontation.

H.G.: What do you think the left's attitude towards Nazi and fascist formations should be? Confront them in the streets, following the lyrics of a renowned Greek leftist song: 'Grasp fascism deeply, it won't die on its own, crush it!'? Or seek their institutional ban? And pursue the creation of broad democratic fronts or fronts on the basis of opposing the system, in line with what Horkheimer said in the 1930s: 'But whoever is not willing to talk about capitalism should also keep quiet about fascism.'[6]

D.P.: I think that today we have the dramatic historical experience of the interwar period and of the strategies of the left against mass fascist and Nazi movements. We also have the more recent post-war experience from the Years of Lead in Italy and the way dictatorships collapsed in Portugal, Greece, and Spain in the mid-1970s. This accumulated knowledge should serve us as a guide, not as a ready-made recipe. Because GD, for example, may have tried from the outset to imitate these interwar movements, but it has not been able to keep large sections of the population mobilised through to the end, as those movements did. The Greek 'raid squads' in no way exceeded a few dozen members. The same small task force acted in Piraeus, in the centre of Athens, in the Peloponnese, on the northern border of the country, in the islands of the Eastern Aegean, and in Crete. The organisation's electorate may have at some point exceeded 500,000, but those who acted as a criminal organisation were the narrow core of the initiated Nazis around the leadership group, constituted by Michaloliakos, Lagos, Kasidiaris, Pappas, and Panagiotaros. GD's strategy was mainly an attempt to replicate the action of Italy's far-right terrorist groups in the 1960s and 1970s. The purpose of the violent acts was not to 'seize the state' or 'bring down democracy', but to provoke a similar violent reaction from the other side (groups of left-wingers, anti-authoritarians, or even immigrants), in order to make the 'rescue' intervention of the deep state appear necessary, in the form of some sort of coup. Panagiotaros confessed, speaking in 2012 to BBC's Paul Mason: 'Greek society is ready – even though no one likes this – to have a fight: a new type of civil war. On the one side there will be nationalists like us, and Greeks who want our country to be as it used to be, and on the other side illegal immigrants, anarchists and all those who have destroyed Athens several times'.[7] It was also announced by Konstantinos Barbarousis, a GD MP, in the summer of 2018, inside the Greek Parliament, when he called on the army to arrest the President of the Republic and the Prime Minister, so that they wouldn't sign the historic agreement with Northern Macedonia.

It is absolutely fortunate that the challenge was not answered by the other side. No 'task forces' of the anti-fascist movement were created, nor was the theory of an informal civil war adopted. The solution was given by the fully civil mechanism of justice which investigated the crimes and issued the final verdict, ruling that, in the case of GD, the 'party' form concealed a criminal organisation and that the leadership of the former identified with the direction of the latter. This does not mean that the popular movement did not confront the Nazi organisation – quite the contrary. If the anti-fascist movement had not sprung up in the autumn of 2013, the Samaras government would not have taken GD to court. As for Horkheimer's saying, it is certainly correct. But Horkheimer nowhere claims that fascism and capitalism are synonymous. In the same small 1939 text ('The Jews and Europe'), he pinpoints the autonomy of the state from the ruling class during the pre-Nazi period: 'Liberalism contained the elements of a better society. The law still possessed a generality that also applied to the rulers. The state was not directly their instrument'.[8] So those who invoke Horkheimer to support the simplistic view that fascist organisations are simply the 'long arm of the system' are necessarily stunned that this 'system' has finally cut off its 'long arm'.

(translated by Katerina Antonakou)

NOTES

1. The Communist Party of Greece.
2. Named for the date on which the Metaxas fascist dictatorship was established in 1936.
3. Meaning 'virus' in Greek.
4. Ehud Sprinzak, 'Right-wing terrorism in a comparative perspective: The case of split delegitimization', *Terrorism and Political Violence* 7,1 (1995), 17-35.
5. The Panhellenic Socialist Movement.
6. Max Horkheimer, 'The Jews and Europe' in Stephen Eric Bronner and Douglas MacKay Kellner (eds), *Critical Theory and Society: A Reader*, London: Routledge, 1989, p. 78.
7. Paul Mason, 'Greece far-right party Golden Dawn: "We are in civil war"', <https://www.bbc.com/news/world-19976841>.
8. 'Der Liberalismus enthielt die Elemente einer besseren Gesellschaft. Das Gesetz besass noch eine Allgemeinheit, die auch die Herrschenden betraf. Der Staat war nicht unmittelbar ihr Instrument', Horkheimer, ‚The Jews and Europe', p. 92.

Something Rotten in the State of Denmark? New Lessons and Old Problems for the Movements and Political Parties

Asger Hougaard

On the surface, one might imagine that Denmark is being led by progressive politicians, securing new climate legislation backed by a historically strong parliamentarian left and a weakened far right. But on closer inspection it becomes evident that there are more than enough inherent contradictions in the ongoing coalition project backing the Social Democratic Party, and that in the process of re-mooring the Social Democratic Party in state administration, something fundamental might be lost on the left. Despite small improvements and promises in some areas, something seems rotten in the state of Denmark.

This essay outlines recent political developments in Denmark. The Danish left has entered into an alliance with the Social Democratic Party, with the promise of bringing about tangible improvements on both social and climate issues – but so far, change has been only marginal, with the coalition to a great extent maintaining a right-wing status quo.

There are five parties to the left of the Social Democratic Party (Socialdemokratiet) in parliament. The far left is represented by the Red-Green Alliance (RGA - Enhedslisten – De Rød-Grønne), a member-party of the GUE/NGL-group in the European Parliament as well as the Party of the European Left. The Socialist People's Party (Socialistisk Folkeparti), traditionally a leftist party but today more centre-left and EU-positive, sometimes finds common ground with the Social Democratic Party and the right including the Danish People's Party, as was the case with the so-called 'ghetto package', which targets immigrant communities (including the forced removal of persons and destruction of functioning housing). The Socialist People's Party is a member of the European Greens group in the European Parliament (Group of the Greens/European Free Alliance). The leftist and separatist Community of the People (Inuit Ataqatigiit), fighting for Greenland independence, present in parliament since 2001, currently holds one of Greenland's two seats in the Danish parliament. The fourth party to the left is 'The Alternative', a relatively new centre-left and green project. The Alternative promised a radically new democratic culture and a break with Danish 'bloc politics' but has now more or less disintegrated after a series of internal conflicts.

In September 2020 a new party, the Independent Greens (Frie Grønne), was founded by a group of politicians who had recently lost a power struggle within The Alternative where some had held central positions, joined by some new candidates (three out of five MPs from The Alternative now support the Independent Greens). The Independent Greens can be seen as an attempt by opportunistic professionals to cling to the positions they achieved, but can also be seen as a form of radicalisation within social liberal milieus, where anti-racist struggles and climate issues are limited by the lack of a coherent systemic critique of capitalist society at large. The new party can potentially become a challenger to the Red-Green Alliance, which might increasingly be perceived as a normalised party instead of one representing alternatives or as the guarantor of real change.

Left in its own right

The radical left Red-Green Alliance was founded in 1989 as an alliance of the Left Socialists (Venstresocialisterne), the Communist Party of Denmark (Danmarks Kommunistiske Parti), the Socialist Workers Party (Socialistisk Arbejderparti) – the Danish section of the Fourth International, and of independent leftists. The parliamentary activities of the Red-Green Alliance have, of late, tended to make it function as a junior partner to the Social Democratic Party, but the two have historically had strong ideological differences on key issues, such as the EU, NATO, and privatisations of public infrastructure. In 2015, a resolution was adopted at the Red-Green Alliance's Annual Conference, positioning the organisation in opposition to both the right and the Social Democratic Party. The resolution, 'The Red-Green Alliance Will Build the Left of the Future and Strengthen Popular Movements', was adopted after an extremely disappointing experience when the party supported the Social Democratic-led governments from 2011-2015 – a period marked by continued neoliberal austerity policies in key areas like social welfare and public infrastructure, such as the sale of shares of the public energy company Dong Energy (now Ørsted) to the investment bank Goldman Sachs. The resolution adopted at the Annual Conference stated 'We are left in our own right with our own project and our own course'.[1] Yet, despite this, the Red-Green Alliance is to this day supporting a Social Democratic Party that is continuing to enact right-wing policies in a number of key areas such as immigration and economic policy in general, but which has also made slight improvements on key issues, including a new climate law, biodiversity initiatives, and minor improvements on key social issues in the area of day-care institutions, psychiatry, and care for the elderly.

At the time of writing, the Red-Green Alliance is in the process of assuming a junior role in relation to the Social Democratic Party, more or less becoming its left flank. But this is occurring within a welfare state project that has strong exclusionary tendencies, especially towards persons designated as 'non-Western'. Not surprisingly, conflicts are evident within the Red-Green Alliance. This was especially clear in the spring of 2020, when a group split from the youth organisation connected to the Red-Green Alliance, the Socialist Youth Front (Socialistisk Ungdomsfront - SUF), to form another organisation, 'Young Red-Greens' (Rød-Grøn Ungdom - RGU), which in a number of areas is less critical than the SUF is of Red-Green Alliance policies.

At the Annual Congress of the Red-Green Alliance in October 2020, the new organisation was accepted by a majority of the delegates, which means that the Red-Green Alliance now has two affiliated youth organisations. The debates at the congress revealed a relatively divided party and widespread mistrust of the central organisation. But the conflict over youth politics cannot be isolated from other political conflicts within the Red-Green Alliance.

The 2019 'climate election'

After the 2019 elections, the Social Democratic Party entered a one-party minority government supported by the Danish Social Liberal Party (Radikale Venstre), the Socialist People's Party, and the Red-Green Alliance. In other words, the Social Democrats came to power through the support of a centre, centre-left, and far-left coalition. This coalition produced some green results, first and foremost in the form of the climate law, promising a 70% CO_2 reduction by 2030 (as compared to the 1990 level). This is a step in the right direction, and a victory for the left, but it is only a small victory. Support for the one-party government was tied to the signing of a 'memorandum of understanding'– a document open to interpretation and without legal force. The price of the climate law was a de-facto acceptance of the Social Democratic Party's policy on immigration from countries characterised as 'non-Western', or of people adhering to so called 'non-Western values', resulting in a situation in which the radical left is now supporting a government continuing far-right policies on immigration, asylum, and which single out certain minorities.

The election campaign of 2019 was described in the media as 'Denmark's first climate election'. This said, the elections of 2019 were also marked by the participation in national debates of both the alt-right party Hard Line (Stram Kurs) and the 'low-taxes and closed-borders' party New Right (Nye Borgerlige). Both are to the right of the already far-right Danish People's Party (Dansk Folkeparti) – a party using the rhetoric of 'Danish values' combined with an emphasis on social welfare and animal welfare. The elections set the far right back in the total number of seats, with the Danish People's Party dropping from 21.1 to 8.7 percent of the vote. Of the two new parties, only New Right passed the two-percent threshold. New Right is now threatening the Danish People's Party's far-right hegemony.

Climate issues played a central role in the elections, but the elections cannot be reduced to them, as evidenced by the massive attention given to the far right and the Social Democratic Party's embrace of far-right positions on immigration. Nor can the elections be understood in isolation from socio-economic issues, especially the question of retirement age, a central campaign issue for the Social Democratic Party that proffered small improvements for a selected group of workers to redwash itself before the election. Probable causes of the Danish People's Party's decreasing support are: its inability to deliver on central welfare issues after nearly twenty years of occupying a central position in Danish politics; the Social Democratic Party's promise to enact a new retirement-age reform and probably to some extent its promise to continue right-wing immigration policies; or competition from the two new far-right parties as well as the inability to prioritise climate issues.

Regarding immigration, climate, and retirement age, the government has delivered on its promises: a continuation, unfortunately, of the previous right-wing governments' exclusionary politics with, at the same time, a new climate law that can be seen as a step in the right direction (albeit based on the premises of economic growth) as well as a new early retirement reform, for certain groups – also a very small step in the right direction. A central problem with the proposed retirement age reform, however, is that it ties the right to an earlier retirement to presence in the labour market; thus social rights are in this sense not universal but linked to liberal logic. The new scheme will mean that after 41 to 44 years in the labour market you can retire one to three years before the general retirement age. The general retirement age is politically adjusted every five years according to increased life expectancy. At the time of writing the retirement age is about to be raised from 68 to 69 years (for those retiring from 2035 on). Concerning the early retirement age, there are some differences depending on the specific situation, but in general it is based on a quid-pro-quo approach to social welfare, along the lines of the old social democratic slogan of doing your duty and demanding your rights, except that nobody knew the scheme when they entered the labour market and for many different reasons might not have been able to stay in it for so long. With the three years deducted after 44 years in the labour market a person who is 30 today is set to work until the age of 70. At the same time, the early retirement-age proposal will most likely affect workers in professions characterised by early entry into the labour market, which in turn means that the scheme targets professions predominately occupied by men.

In December 2020 it was announced that the Danish state, which is the largest oil producer in the EU (after Brexit), will phase out oil and gas extraction by 2050. Furthermore, it will not provide licences to new oil and gas extraction in the North Sea, with some exceptions for existing fields. Phasing out the production is of course a good thing, but the deal made includes a de facto acceptance of extractivism for the next 30 years. A new biodiversity initiative was announced shortly afterwards. The initiative includes the creation of 13 new 'nature national parks' and 75,000 acres of so-called 'untouched' forest in what is the most intensively cultivated country in the EU. The parks and forests will function as much needed biodiversity reserves as well as create spaces for recreational activities. It is a step in the right direction, but is not nearly enough. The initiative does not involve a radical change in land use, as no private farmland will be used to become part of the new national parks.[2] Instead, the state will use areas it already manages, not challenging the ongoing destruction of habitats and mismanagement of land and resources by the agribusiness sector. It is estimated that more than 62% of the land is concentrated in the hands of less than 35,000 owners (0.6% of the population).[3] A large number of Danish farms are highly indebted, resulting in the countryside being controlled by a mix of large banks, agribusiness interests, and rich landowning families which in some cases have strong links to the right wing, both through the former governing Liberal Party, but also the far right, which was visible in recent minor protests, blown up out of proportion by the media, directed against the government for the confiscation and culling of mink following a new Covid-19 mutation (see below).

Another 'green' initiative is the cheapening of electric cars through a new taxation scheme. This will most likely prove to be more of a helping hand for the car industry than for those who are unable to afford a vehicle. At the same time, electric car batteries are still very reliant on minerals such as lithium and cobalt, which means the acceptance of continued extractivism. Changes are taking place, but they are not systemic.

Ten years after COP15: From depression to anxiety

To understand the lead up to the signing of the climate law some contextualisation is needed. In 2009, the United Nations climate conference known as COP15 was held in Copenhagen. Before 2009 it was normal for the then relatively small organised climate movement to mobilise a couple of hundred people to protest in Copenhagen, but during the COP15-conference, the main demonstration had an estimated participation of as many as 100,000 people.

The COP15 conference is remembered today as a big failure of both international climate diplomacy and of the left's and the environmental NGOs' ability to influence the outcome of the negotiations. Instead of landing a climate agreement that could succeed the Kyoto Agreement, the negotiations broke down and a decisive battle was lost. Extra-parliamentary attempts to create what we could call a 'Seattle moment' ten years after the WTO protests in 1999 were similarly unsuccessful. Speaking with radical activists who participated in 2009, one gets the impression that COP15 resulted in an overall weakening of movements, sometimes referred to as 'the climate blues', instead of the hoped-for kick-start of a reinvigorated climate movement.

In the past few years, the term 'climate anxiety' has been used to describe the mental state especially of young people in the face of the climate crisis and sometimes in the context of school strikes. In the Danish media, school strikes, inspired by Swedish activist Greta Thunberg, began to gain media and public attention in 2018. So too did the new organisation The Green Student Movement (Den Grønne Studenterbevægelse), founded in the same year. The Green Student Movement became central in public debates on climate, certainly helped by a great deal of media attention. The 'Fridays for Future' slogan spread to Denmark where school children entered into an alliance with the mainstream climate movement. So far, the recent climate demonstrations have, according to some media sources, culminated in around 30,000 to 40,000 people at the May 2019 protest, The People's Climate March in Copenhagen, where Thunberg participated as a speaker and criticised the Municipality of Copenhagen's climate plan (to make Copenhagen the first CO_2-neutral capital by 2025) for not including transportation, shopping, food, aviation, and shipping.[4] The protest was strategically timed just before both the European Parliament and Danish Parliament elections. The flags and banners of the participants evidenced the contradictions that exist within the broader climate movement, which is split along very central issues, such as the EU, nuclear power, food consumption, and the hegemonic economic system. Another factor central to the building of momentum was certainly the global protests on 15 March 2019, which were marked by nationwide activities in Denmark. The ability to sustain activities outside of Copenhagen and the capital region has doubtless been one of the major strengths of the climate movement.

A climate law has been a long-term goal for parts of the Danish environmental and climate movements. In the organisation NOAH – Friends of the Earth Denmark, one of the more radical sections of the environmental and climate movement and an organisation with historical ties to the radical left, the climate law is seen as a step in the right direction but not ambitious enough and definitely not the law NOAH fought for. Central points of criticism by the radical environmentalists are that the promised 70% reductions in emissions by 2030 are much too small, especially taking historical emissions and global inequality into consideration, and that the new law does not rest on a carbon budget specifying the future total cumulative emissions.[5]

The momentum of the school strikes and the build-up to the adoption of the climate law have not been followed by larger mobilisations. A concrete example of this failure to mobilise is the current struggle against the planned gas pipeline Baltic Pipe, set to bring natural gas from Norwegian gas fields to Poland through Danish territory. As of August 2020, the movement against the pipeline was unable to secure the 50,000 votes needed for the 'citizens proposal' that would be required to have the Danish Parliament vote on the issue. The protesters are backed by the Red-Green Alliance, and party members are active in the campaign against the pipeline. Nevertheless, instead of being a steppingstone for further action, the climate movement and the left has so far been unable to build on the momentum from the earlier climate enthusiasm to effectively stop the planned pipeline.

The ongoing environmental and climate struggles in Denmark show that, contrary to the myth that the climate movement is now surging, mass organisation has not taken place. During the ongoing pandemic and economic crisis, the left and the movements in general have seemed unprepared and unable to steer a course and organise. Local struggles have to a great extent remained local, while the climate movement seems completely dependent on media attention to function.

The struggle against the non-sustainable expansion of the city of Copenhagen into the Øresund Strait in the form of the planned new district 'Lynetteholmen', or the so-called development of the Amager Commons, a green area located close to the centre of Copenhagen, has not been able to put enough pressure on the Social Democratic-led municipality to stop the further destruction of the area. Apparently, parts of the so-called 'lungs' of Copenhagen, including a stretch of beach meadow that has not been cultivated for 5,000 years, can be sacrificed.

Wasting principles or delivering results

'Recycling is gold' is the slogan of a campaign by the Social Democratic-led Municipality of Copenhagen to encourage people to recycle more. But we need to ask: Who exactly benefits from recycling and renovation? In the summer of 2020, an agreement on waste and recycling was reached in the Danish Parliament. The agreement sheds light on some of the contradictions within radical-left politics in parliament. The agreement was a so-called 'broad agreement' and had the support of a coalition ranging from the Red-Green Alliance to right-wing parties. The tradition of signing these kinds of broad agreements is a political strategy favoured by parties in government or likely candidates for entering government. For many years the phrase 'All Parties Except the Red-Green Alliance' was relatively common in Danish politics, but this has changed over the last ten years. By participating in broad agreements, the Red-Green Alliance has entered the arena of 'compromise-seeking politics'. Even though the main argument for participating in the deal was to avoid privatisations of recycling and incineration facilities by using the political influence gained through the compromise, the deal essentially compels privatisations of municipally owned and not-for-profit companies, that is, companies that do not seek more inflows than necessary to cover expenses, with excess revenues returned to the consumers. Participating in the deal makes the Red-Green Alliance complicit in forced privatisations – something the party has adamantly fought against since the 1990s. This participation has been heavily criticised by some party members who have mounted internal opposition to the renovation deal, resulting in the party's national board criticising the deal.[6]

With both the climate law and the recycling deal, the Danish left is now in a situation in which real influence through parliament is at the mercy of the Social Democratic Party. Instead of becoming 'a left in its own right', as the 2015 resolution stated, the left has pursued a path of appeasing the Social Democratic Party. This appeasement has continued through the 2020 Covid-19 pandemic, as the Red-Green Alliance opted for a strategy of parliamentary peace, just like all other parties in parliament.

Some would say that the appeasement strategy is already working, pointing to the climate law, the new biodiversity initiatives, and some social improvements. But although these are visible improvements they are still marginal, and for now we are still waiting to see if any major results follow. At any rate, this appeasement comes in some respects at the cost of the left being able to present itself as a viable alternative rather than a left wing within the political projects of other parties, that is, essentially as part of the social democratic project of maintaining the status quo with some ecological modernisation.

Heroes of the (exclusionary) welfare state

The left is in danger of buying into a vision of the welfare state as the end goal of history, reducing politics to defensive struggles for social rights. 'The Heroes of Welfare' was even a title used in a campaign launched by the Red-Green Alliance in 2017. The campaign featured images and topics connected to public-sector workers, including social workers and educators, teachers, social and healthcare assistants, skilled workers, nurses and midwives, as well as, notably, police officers.[7] The inclusion of the latter group in the campaign was relatively controversial as many on the left do not consider Danish police officers heroes. The Heroes of Welfare campaign can certainly be seen as a tool in a struggle for better conditions for parts of the working and middle classes, as well as for benefits for the rest of society which depends on their work. But it can also be regarded as a continuation, or even a return, of older traditions that celebrate heroic workers, as nostalgia for the welfare state, or as resulting from a form of 'left populist strategy'. Perhaps it is a mixture of all this. There is, however, something strange, and disturbing, about a campaign based on the concept of heroism combined with the welfare-state project's exclusionary tendencies.

At the annual award event for the Nordic Council's prizes in 2019, two of the prize winners, the Swedish activist Greta Thunberg (who turned down the Environmental Prize) and the Danish writer Jonas Eika (who accepted the Literature Prize), both responded with criticism. Among other things, Eika pointed to what he described as the 'state racism' prevalent in Denmark, the deportation camps and militarisation of EU borders, as well as the Social Democratic Party's use of the previous right-wing governments' 'racist language and politics'. The Danish prime minister, who was present at the award show, was unable to give compelling answers to Eika's criticism, a criticism which can, in some ways, be just as well directed at the left parties supporting the governing social democratic parties.

The inability to solve existential problems might be an expression of a crisis of legitimacy for the Social Democratic Party. For now, it is relatively popular in elections and opinion polls, it and its prime minister benefitting from the Covid crisis. But the ground under it might not be so firm. This became evident after the appearance of a new mutation of Covid-19 at Danish mink farms, which led the government to order the liquidation of the mink population. Before November 2020 Denmark led the world in the production of mink furs, with an estimated yearly production of more than 12 million skins (in a country of 5.8 million people). Closing down the mink farms has long been a goal of parts of the left, and the new situation might lead to the sector, which employs more than 6,000 people, being restructured or phased out. In 2019 mink constituted 0.7 percent of total Danish exports and 3.8 percent of total agricultural exports.[8] The order to liquidate the minks was met by heavy opposition from the right, and the legal basis for the decision was challenged by parties from all over the political spectrum. In November, the government appeared somewhat weakened, and the March 2020 rally-around-the-leader mood vanished. In some respects, normality reappeared, and parliamentary political life centred around the Social Democratic Party.

It is essential that the left, if it is to partner with social democratic parties, not accommodate far-right positions on immigration and asylum and ever increasing retirement ages or accept half-baked solutions on emissions. Coalitions must be built in the fight against climate change, but the left must also identify the root causes of the problems and act accordingly.

Unfortunately, the Red-Green Alliance has not been able to produce and communicate viable alternatives, for instance, to the current government's continuation of far-right policies on immigration and asylum. In September a demonstration involving 500 empty chairs demanding that the Danish state receive at least 300 people from the Moria Camp on the island of Lesbos was organised by members of the party. But the 500 chairs were a rather small echo of the 13,000 empty chairs that had been put up in Berlin the same month, in a protest demanding the closure of immigrant camps in Greece. In a sense, the chairs are a perfect metaphor for a way of conducting politics that can be summed up as: Start small, and hope for a very small improvement, for we must not appear too radical. A month before, in August, the Danish government had announced that it would only accept 200 out of a planned 500 refugees indicated by the United Nations quota. Tailoring demands to minor openings in the system is possible, but it risks reducing political discussion to very small improvements while not moving the whole context to the left.

For now, the minor social improvements and green transitions have to a large extent been planned in accordance with big capital. The inability to deliver a better climate deal and a just retirement-age reform, the celebration of the heroic workers, and the exclusion of immigrants and asylum seekers are all connected through nostalgic visions of a welfare state that must be preserved and protected from outside attacks while carrying out forms of cosy and green modernisation. Instead of establishing a left flank of administrators within the current system, the left should upscale its criticism and connect everyday struggles to visions of a radically different world for everyone, not settle for improved conditions for the urban middle classes which are looking forward to their next trip to the new nature parks in their electric cars.

NOTES

1   Enhedslisten, 'Politisk udtalelse på Enhedslistens årsmøde 2015: Enhedslisten vil opbygge fremtidens venstrefløj og styrke folkelige bevægelser', September, 2015 <https://org.enhedslisten.dk/files/politisk_udtalelse._enhedslisten_vil_opbygge_fremtidens_venstrefloej_og_styrke_folkelige_bevaegelser_0.pdf>.
2   Agnete Finnemann Scheel, '"Nu batter det!" 888 millioner til naturnationalparker og urørt skov vækker jubel', <dr.dk>, 5 December 2020.
3   Kjeld Hansen, 'Dansk landbrug er en elendig forretning', *Gylle.dk*, 20 September 2020.
4   Thea Deleuran Müller, 'Thunberg kritiserer Københavns klimamål: 'Gør mere skade end gavn'', <dr.dk>, 25 May 2019.
5   Palle Bendsen, 'Den nye klimalov er alt for svag', <NOAH.dk>, 23 January 2020.
6   Simon Halskov, 'Uenighed om affaldsaftale', *Rød+Grøn*, August 2020, <https://rg.enhedslisten.dk/blade/august-2020/>.
7   'Velfærdens helte (temaer)', *Enhedslisten.dk*, <https://enhedslisten.dk/temaer/velfaerdens-helte>.
8   Peter Keiding, 'Stor fyringsrunde på vej hos Kopenhagen Fur', *Fagbladet* 3F, 5 November 2020; Thomas Søbirk Petersen and Peter Mollerup, 'Det er løgn og latin, når folk siger, at minkindustrien er en god forretning', *Gylle.dk*, 8 November 2020.

Corbynism's Demise: A Warning from the Brexit Moment

Michael Chessum

The defeat of Jeremy Corbyn and Bernie Sanders is a devastating setback for progressive forces across Europe and the world, and marks the end of an improbable moment in which the Anglosphere carried the hopes of the left. Despite the mass movements they mobilised and the transformation of British and American domestic politics that Corbyn and Sanders wrought, in the end it was not close. After a promising start, Sanders crashed out of the Democratic primaries in April. And despite confounding the political establishment on multiple occasions and coming close to winning power in 2017, Corbyn's defeat in December 2019 was, in terms of seats won, Labour's worst result since 1935.

But if the men have in common an improbable rise, an anti-climactic end, grey hair and an appeal to the young, they were defeated in the end by very different forces. Bernie Sanders failed for the second time to overcome the conservatism of the Democratic selectorate and the strength of the party establishment still clinging to unreconstructed neoliberalism. Corbyn was defeated by the new nativist right - an insurgent populism married to large chunks of the pre-existing centre-right establishment and committed to a mixture of right-wing economic policy and a politics of migrant-bashing. In Britain, the project around which this coalition has coalesced is Brexit, and its victory in the 2016 EU referendum was, though many on the British left did not recognise it at the time, the moment when the window of possibility began to close for us.

Prior to the summer of 2015, the socialist left was regarded as a fringe curiosity in UK politics. The Labour Party ran in the 2015 election on a platform consistent with its position as a degenerating European social democratic party, that is to say continued and deeper austerity, and a vague but menacing promise to be 'tough on immigration'. Its membership stood at around 190,000, and the internal life of the party was anaemic. Had the left not won the leadership of Labour, it could easily have gone the way of its withered continental counterparts.

By the time of the 2019 election, membership of Labour had roughly tripled to 590,000 making it the biggest left-of-centre party in Europe. Its manifesto promised a £10 minimum wage; the nationalisation of rail, water, electricity, and the postal service; free higher education; a massive expansion of state housing; the extension of the franchise to seven million migrants; and the biggest expansion of public spending in Britain's peacetime history. Though in historic terms these might represent a modest social democratic programme, they represented a major political shift. Jeremy Corbyn and his chief shadow economic minister John McDonnell shattered the neoliberal consensus, inside and outside the party.

One must be sober, however, about the legacy of the Corbyn leadership. This was a period in which industrial struggle and social movements collapsed in the UK, as hundreds of thousands of young activists threw themselves into party meetings rather than onto picket lines. In 2017, the number of working days lost to strike action was lower than at any time since records began in 1893. The leadership relied heavily on trade-union bureaucracies, and the left failed to organise on a rank-and-file basis for democracy and militancy in the unions. Corbynism failed to democratise the Labour Party; the parliamentary party is barely accountable to members, and policy is still ultimately set by the leadership rather than conference. Much of the new mass politics took the form of cheerleading Corbyn rather than building a serious new left movement with activists who think for themselves.

The new Labour left has now suffered a double-defeat. Following the general election, the leadership election of 2020 saw Corbyn's anointed successor, Rebecca Long Bailey, secure just 28% of the vote. The party is now in the hands of Keir Starmer, who won with the support of many members who had backed the Corbyn leadership. Starmer is not the kind of neoliberal politician that once dominated Labour – he is a social democrat who promised to honour the policy agenda of the old leadership – but the Labour left is now beginning to come to terms with the fact that Corbynism's fan base was never transformed into a politically coherent socialist movement. His victory also pointed towards another difficult subject: he won over so many left-wing members in large part because he was perceived to have argued for Labour to take a firmer line against Brexit, an issue on which Jeremy Corbyn's office found itself at odds with the mass of Labour members.

The British left is now in a deep strategic crisis. Corbynism was an upside-down project, which seized the leadership of Labour before it had a movement underneath it. Its one strategy – win an election and form a government – has failed. It has nowhere to go outside of Labour in electoral terms because the voting system does not allow it. Having done very little to build social movements or wider struggles, it seems set on spending its time as an internal opposition within Starmer's Labour. Above all, it is divided on who to blame for Corbyn's defeat, and on what to do about the spectre of right-wing nationalism. To some extent, everyone agrees that Brexit destroyed Corbynism. But how?

The Labour left's Brexit problem

The outcome of the 2016 EU referendum was both decisive and ambiguous. The British people – driven by overwhelming support among men, Conservative Party voters, and the over 50s – had voted to leave the EU. But one of the core reasons that this had happened was that Leave meant different things to different people. Libertarian millionaires who believed in open borders and open markets found themselves on the same side as retired miners living on council estates who wanted to kick the establishment, and far-right activists campaigning to repatriate immigrants. There was a majority in favour of the concept of Brexit, but no majority support for any particular form of it – either in the country or in parliament. With the political class in deadlock, especially after the Conservatives lost their parliamentary majority in 2017, and the country more deeply divided than it had been on any issue, it was inevitable that Brexit would dominate British politics for many years. It was, after all, a project aimed at completely reshaping the country – the most ambitious attempt to deregulate the economy in British history and the biggest expansion of border controls in recent years.

The Leave vote and the prominence of the Brexit issue put Labour on a collision course with its electoral base and highlighted a series of political tensions within the project of Corbynism itself. Two-thirds of Labour voters had voted to stay in the EU, while two-thirds of the parliamentary seats its MPs represented had voted to leave it. For Labour's members, more than 80% of whom had voted Remain, and for its politicians, the referendum was a bruising and emotional experience. The result was a shock to many, and the campaign was marked by escalating racist rhetoric, and a real sense of physical danger. Just a week before the vote, a Labour member of parliament, Jo Cox, was murdered in broad daylight by a far-right activist while in her constituency.

In contrast to the overwhelming views of the Labour members and voters, the attitude of the leadership was more ambivalent. Jeremy Corbyn and his allies in parliament argued for Remain, but they did not regard it as a priority. They handed ownership of Labour's presence in the referendum to the right wing of the party, who delivered a boring, status quo-ist campaign. Corbyn's closest advisors were even less enthusiastic about winning the referendum. Head of communications Seamas Milne and senior advisor Andrew Murray both came from in or around the Moscow-aligned Communist Party tradition and were open supporters of Leave.[1] Len McCluskey, the general secretary of Unite the Union, was also a Eurosceptic. Along with Karie Murphy, Corbyn's chief of staff and a close ally of the Unite machine, Milne, Murray, and McCluskey became known as 'the four Ms'. Their domination of Corbyn's inner circle was a determining factor in the development of Labour's Brexit policy after the 2016 referendum.

The tradition of supporting a Left Exit (or Lexit) from the EU has a long history on the British left. It was championed by Tony Benn and others in Britain's last referendum on EU membership in 1975. The Communist Party of Britain and its newspaper *The Morning Star* are avid opponents of EU membership. The far left is divided on Europe, but the two largest Trotskyist organisations, the Socialist Workers Party and the Socialist Party, campaigned for Leave in 2016. Throughout the referendum and beyond it, the experience of Greece at the hands of the Troika was wheeled out, often without much understanding of the position of the Greek left itself or the distinction between EU and Eurogroup membership and. Lexiters also made the case against the Posted Workers Directive and argued that state aid rules and the European courts would act against any socialist government in the UK. These arguments had merit, but had little traction amongst the vast bulk of left activists and progressive voters in a referendum that was essentially about immigration, Altantacism, and British imperial nostalgia. It seems surreal given the rampaging deregulation now underway in the UK to look back at analysis from the Lexit perspective which hailed the result as 'a revolt against austerity and the Tory millionaire government'.[2]

Lexit ideas had slightly more purchase in the internal discourse of the left after the referendum, especially in the minds of activists who had voted Remain but were now keen to rationalise support for the implementation of Brexit. But, as a policy proposal, it was a fantasy. To satisfy it, Labour would have had to argue for the hardest Brexit imaginable, leaving the Customs Union, the Single Market, and any international treaty which enshrined the EU's state aid rules, while at the same time arguing for more open borders with the world and more economic regulation. This policy would have alienated Labour's overwhelmingly anti-Brexit voter base while also alienating the vast majority of Leave voters, who were right-wing on both economic and social questions. As a result, Lexit was never openly or honestly advocated by its adherents within the Corbyn project, even if their instincts informed what the leadership did. And so, rather than seeking to explain the evolution of Corbyn's policy in terms of Lexit versus Remain one must instead understand it as a mesh of electoral calculation and – ironically, given Corbyn's defining role as an isolated but principled politician – a conventional centrist politics of triangulation.

Corbynism was built and maintained under siege. Immediately after the referendum, the Labour right launched a coup against Corbyn's leadership, using their overwhelming majority in the parliamentary party and their control over the party machine to great effect. They failed and Corbyn was re-elected as Labour leader in September 2016 with an increased mandate – but the coup set the tone for the coming years. The only distinctive policy of Corbyn's challenger, Owen Smith, had been to support a second referendum on Europe, and much of the right wing of the party had supported him in this not because they believed in it but because they thought it would resonate with the membership.[3] The Labour right were happy to use Brexit as a 'wedge' with which they could, despite being very unpopular in terms of their wider policy, champion the wishes of members on the key issue of the day. The attempted coup against Corbyn in the wake of the referendum hardened the outlook of the leadership and its supporters against any attempt to oppose Brexit or meaningfully soften it – not on a political basis, but as a matter of loyalty. This was to prove a devastating error.

A strategy of triangulation

Looking back at Labour's policy on Brexit after 2016, one sees not a coherent strategy but a constantly moving series of zigzags. The leadership began, quite understandably, by promising to honour the referendum result and the triggering of Article 50. For the entire period preceding the 2017 election, it refused to define, other than in vague terms, what kind of Brexit deal it wanted – and repeatedly insisted that it would not support membership in the Single Market, or a Norway-style settlement. The Corbyn leadership actively abandoned free movement, explicitly stating in its 2017 manifesto that it would end. By early 2018, it announced that it would support membership in the Customs Union, and later in 2018 – after a substantial campaign by members – adopted a complex position which kept 'all options on the table' and explicitly did not rule out a second referendum. After the party's annihilation in the 2019 European elections, it switched to supporting a second referendum outright, but resisted any attempt to say which outcome it preferred. At the 2019 general election, the position was that Labour would negotiate its own Brexit deal and put it back to the people, alongside an option to Remain. Jeremy Corbyn, when pressed on the campaign trail, stated that he would remain neutral in this referendum.

There was no guiding principle to Labour's strategy. Brexit was treated as a morally and politically empty issue, despite the fact that it was the main project of the nationalist right and contained several policy areas which ought to have been ethical red lines. The leadership's acceptance that free movement would end, an acceptance of the biggest expansion of border controls in Britain's recent history, was greeted with dismay by the rank and file of the party. This situation was only overturned at the 2019 party conference, after a lengthy internal campaign. The public witnessed Jeremy Corbyn – a man whose popularity rested on his reputation as a principled, consistent champion of radical politics – be evasive on Brexit and repeatedly argue for contradictory positions, often in dry technocratic language. He was one of the most consistent advocates for migrants' rights in British politics but found himself being outflanked on his left by Blairites and Liberal Democrats on the question of immigration. Still worse, the situation meant that Labour had no means of winning a public argument about its policy, whatever that policy was. By the time of the 2019 election, Labour supported a second referendum but had spent years arguing publicly against one. No attempt was made to popularise the policy, no attempt was made to use the mass base of Corbynism to campaign on council estates or in towns in the north of England to change people's minds – in large part because this mass base had spent years being told that the concept of a second referendum was a plot by the right wing of the party to undermine Corbyn.

The other mass movement

The reality was that the movement against Brexit after 2016 was far bigger and more complex than its detractors would admit. As the Brexit project unravelled under Theresa May's premiership, support for a second referendum grew exponentially. From early 2018, pro-Europeans on both the centre and left switched from lobbying for a softer Brexit to fighting against it outright. With Labour having thus far supported neither a soft Brexit nor a second referendum, the leadership of the official anti-Brexit movement – known as the People's Vote campaign – was dominated by figures from the Liberal Democrats and the right wing of the Labour Party. Other organisations – like Best for Britain, European Movement, and Britain for Europe – existed without much active political identity but generally put forward socially progressive ideas on immigration and internationalism. My organisation, Another Europe is Possible, has been dedicated to fighting

Brexit with an independent left-wing perspective since 2016. After initially campaigning for a softer Brexit, it later led the campaign for Labour to adopt policy in favour of freedom of movement and a second referendum. Affiliated to it were the Green Party, the British affiliate of the European Left Party, and two Trotskyist organisations including the British section of the Fourth International. Its supporters in Labour are overwhelmingly of the left. For us, pushing the Labour leadership on Brexit and immigration was about saving the project of Corbynism, not undermining it.

By late 2018, it was clear that the demand for a second referendum had mass appeal. In October of that year, around a million people marched through London to demand a public vote – the biggest protest in the UK since the Iraq War period. They mobilised in huge numbers again in March and October 2019. Because the official Labour left was absent, the official rallies of these protests were dominated by liberal establishment politicians and celebrities. But the mass of people attending them, like the mass of people who had voted Remain, were amenable to a more radical message. Another Europe is Possible organised 'left blocs' on the marches which heard speeches from migrants, trade unionists involved in disputes, and a caucus of anti-Brexit Corbynite MPs. One left bloc ended by occupying a nearby pro-Brexit hedge fund which had funded the Conservative Party, draping a gigantic banner across its balcony bearing the slogan 'Brexit = disaster capitalism'. Tens of thousands carried placards with slogans such as 'Remain, Reform, Revolt', 'Free movement for all', and 'Stop climate chaos'. When polled as early as January 2018, 78% of Labour members supported a second referendum.[4] Among the population as a whole, there was a consistent majority in favour of Remain from June 2017 onwards.[5] The anti-Brexit half of the population had hardened and grown.

The other side had polarised, too. With Boris Johnson elected as Conservative Party leader in the summer of 2019, the government switched to pursuing a much more openly populist and confrontational strategy. In late August, it provoked a constitutional crisis by illegally suspending the sitting of parliament. By September, 73% of Leave voters supported No Deal[6] and less than a quarter regarded a softer Brexit as an acceptable compromise.[7] In the postmortem debate currently being conducted on the British left, it is common to hear the argument that Corbyn's best hope of winning an election would have been to take a position in favour of a soft Brexit which both Leavers and Remainers could have lived with. This might have been true had Labour adopted such a position in 2016 or 2017 and fought to unite the country around a Norway-style settlement, but this was rejected by the leadership at the time. By the time of the 2019 election, such a policy was utterly untenable, and would have resulted in the collapse of Labour's vote to the Liberal Democrats, as was the case in the European elections in May. As a result, Labour moved. Corbyn's Eurosceptic inner circle of advisers (the 'four Ms' mentioned above) were defeated behind closed doors, as John McDonnell and other close allies convinced Corbyn to shift Labour to supporting a second referendum. But it was too late: Labour was smashed to pieces in December 2019, despite probably the biggest grassroots campaign in British history, losing 1.9 million Remain voters, 1.8 million Leave ones, and around a million mostly younger voters who had not voted in the 2016 referendum.[8]

A warning from Brexit

Brexit was not the only thing that killed Corbynism. The 2019 election witnessed an extraordinary coalition of forces and underhand tactics come together to prevent the breakthrough of a radical social democratic government. The UK provides especially hostile terrain for left electoral projects. Most of the print media is owned by right-wing billionaires, and almost all of it supports the Conservative Party and backed Leave in the 2016 referendum. There is a revolving door between the BBC's political desk and the communications staff of Conservative leaders. An LSE study found that 75% of media coverage misrepresented Jeremy Corbyn during the 2019 election.[9] The first-past-the -post electoral system is designed to give decisive majorities to parties on a minority of the public vote. With the anti-Brexit and anti-Tory vote fragmented, Boris Johnson secured 56% of seats with just 43% of the vote.

Brexit and Corbynism are at once both peculiarly British and part of a wider European moment. It is impossible to imagine, say, Germany revelling in exactly the same mix of imperial nostalgia, Altantacism, and populist rhetoric, while at the same time electing a Prime Minister, Boris Johnson, who is the walking embodiment of privilege and the old moneyed class. And yet right-wing nationalism and the new far right are everywhere in Europe, and almost everywhere the fragmentation of the European project is one of their central aims. There is something deeply English about Jeremy Corbyn's appeal – a reserved grandfatherly figure with an awkward public speaking style who makes jam and tends an allotment. The movement he led was conditioned by the weakness of the organised far left in Britain, the historic absence of a mass Communist Party, and the fact that the UK's voting system had forced trade unions, centrists, and leftists of all kinds into the same political party. And yet the new Labour left, an insurgent alternative to mainstream social democracy, is a project that has common ground with others across the continent. The experience of the new Labour left can provide some invaluable lessons for the wider European left in terms of how it deals with the questions of European fragmentation, borders, and nationalism.

Firstly, Labour's mistakes on Brexit were not the result of intellectual or ideological differences, though these did exist. Rather, they stemmed from two recurring problems of electoralist projects: a lack of internal democracy and a politics defined by triangulation. Had the membership been allowed to determine the party's policy, Labour would have committed to supporting either a Norway-style arrangement or a second referendum very early after 2016 and the movement might have had the necessary time and clarity to campaign for the policy and convince the voters it needed to convince. Instead, policy was made by a cabal of advisors and Westminster insiders, many of whom held diametrically opposing views to the bulk of Labour members and adopted a bunker mentality when it came to grassroots pressure on the subject of Brexit. There was no means of bottom-up redress for this situation: although local parties could submit motions to conference, these motions were subject to a process of compositing, in which party staff and trade union officials can effectively manipulate the text so that it becomes meaningless. This is what happened in 2018, when, after Another Europe is Possible and its allies organised the largest number of motion submissions in Labour's history, the text that went to conference floor contained a position so vague that it was voted through unanimously. The power of the trade union leaderships at conference and on party committees, whose modus operandi is almost always one of cutting deals rather than having debates out in the open, provided another roadblock. Momentum, the left's organised faction, might have provided a space for the rank and file of the left to debate and push Labour's Brexit policy, but its internal democracy was shut down as early as 2017 with the support of the leader's office. Ultimately, despite the promise to do politics differently, Corbyn's Labour retained the traditional model of decision-making handed down to it by the New Labour era. Grassroots pressure on the leadership did have some effect, but it was filtered through so many layers of processes and advisors that Labour's Brexit policy lagged around a year behind the political landscape.

Throughout the post-2016 period, there was a lot of noise and mental gymnastics emanating from the new Labour left which aimed to unpick the progressive aspects of EU membership – such as migrants' rights – on the supposedly radical basis that they were, in themselves, exclusionary or Eurocentric. What this masked was another recurring problem of electoralism: a straightforward rightward triangulation on the questions of immigration and nationalism. At no point did the leadership's abandonment of European free movement go hand in hand with a comprehensive and principled policy to open Britain's borders or increase the rights of migrants from other countries. This would have defeated the point, which was to appeal to Leave voters who blamed Polish immigrants for driving down wages. When, in September 2017, the leadership organised to ensure that motions in favour of free movement and Single Market membership were not debated at party conference, they were using traditional party management methods to defend a traditional Labour Party practice of sacrificing the rights of migrants in the name of electoral expediency.

The debate on the Single Market was conducted in a similar way. Lexit arguments about state aid and European deregulation gave left cover to the leadership when it was tempted to support a Brexit settlement not so different from the one being pursued by the Conservative government. But Labour had no intention of ever implementing Lexit; Corbynism had, in historical perspective, a relatively modest social democratic programme, and all of its spending plans and policies were within EU rules and norms. The rationale for not developing a serious alternative to the Tories' Brexit agenda early on in the process was not based on a principled political position or an alternative programme for the future of UK-EU relations, but on acquiescence to the populist frame of 'the will of the people' and a calculation about where the leadership thought public opinion was. Despite having built an entire political project in opposition to the politics of triangulation and centrism that had dominated Labour for decades, Jeremy Corbyn deployed a remarkably familiar strategy of compromise on the main issue that faced him.

The entire point of triangulation on immigration and nationalism is that it is supposed to win elections. The lesson from the UK is that it plainly does not. In refusing to combat the Conservatives' Brexit agenda as a priority, all that Labour did was give them more time and space to control the narrative. Corbynism attempted to overcome the divisions in the working class with a crude appeal to economic interests. It promised to throw money and public resources at communities which had been devastated by neoliberalism and de-industrialisation. What it failed to understand was that the alienation and disenchantment of the past forty years needed more than material investment: it needed a narrative, a sense of belonging and meaning. The tabloid press and the nationalist right had been providing that narrative for decades, and to a great extent it had already sunk in. Without challenging this ideology directly, Labour stood no chance.

Some on the British left dismissed the question of Brexit as a 'culture-war' distraction from real class politics.[10] But the fragmentation of Europe on terms set by the far right, and the raising of its borders, is a fundamental attack on the working classes of Europe – on their transnational unity, on the limited regulatory frameworks that guarantee their rights, and on many millions of migrant workers. There was a political tendency within Corbynism – and I am sure that it exists in every mass left movement in Europe – which regards the 'real' working class as white men over the age of fifty who speak with regional accents. Any serious attempt to build a socialist movement in the 21st century must reject this from the start. The working class is composed of the young, the precarious, women, ethnic minorities and migrants, at least as much as it is composed of older people living in post-industrial towns – many of whom have, in the UK, been drawn to anti-migrant and nationalist narratives since the collapse of the labour movement in the 1980s.

The overriding ruling-class narrative of our age is that migrants are to blame for the falling wages and crumbling public services of the neoliberal era. When socialists refuse to fight this narrative head on – or if they lend their weight to the idea that the primary task is the accrual of national sovereignty against foreign powers, rather than a struggle against capital whichever flag it bears – they undermine the very class consciousness from which the left draws its strength. This was true of Corbyn's triangulation on free movement and Brexit, just as it is true of Sahra Wagenknecht's attempt to persuade Die Linke to drop its support for open borders, or Jean-Luc Mélenchon's infamous statement that posted workers were 'stealing bread from the mouths'[11] of French workers. Brexit planted a bomb under Corbynism, which it lacked the intellectual courage and political confidence to diffuse. If we are to take anything from its demise, it should be that our only road to victory is to stake out class politics as the explicit alternative to the nationalist narratives of the new far right.

NOTES

1 Milne and Murray were both involved with Straight Left, which agitated against the development of Eurocommunism in the Communist Party of Great Britain prior to its 1984 split. In 2012, they were co-authors of a pamphlet entitled *Building an Economy for the People*, published by Manifesto Press, which made the case for leaving the EU. Murray remained in the Communist Party even after Corbyn was elected as Labour leader, and only joined Labour in 2016 after he was appointed by the leadership as an advisor.
2 Peter Taafe, 'Referendum revolt: Capitalist establishment shattered' for the Socialist Party website, 27 June 2016.
3 Their opportunism was stark: prominent Blairite Chuka Ummuna was, as late as

September 2016, arguing that Labour should not only support implementing Brexit but oppose the free movement of people – see 'Chuka Umunna: We Should Be Prepared To Sacrifice Single Market Membership To Axe Freedom Of Movement' in *Huffington Post,* 22 September 2016.
4   Tim Bale, Paul Webb, and Monica Poletti, *Grassroots: Britain's party members: who they are, what they think, and what they do,* Mile End Institute, Queen Mary University of London, January 2018 <https://www.qmul.ac.uk/media/qmul/media/publications/Grassroots,-Britain%27s-Party-Members.pdf>.
5   'What Britain Thinks' polltracker.
6   BMG, Ipsos Mori, Yougov and ComRes data, July/August 2019. Calculated by Professor John Curtice.
7   Yougov data, August 2019.
8   Research by Datapraxis, June 2020.
9   <https://www.lse.ac.uk/media-and-communications/research/research-projects/representations-of-jeremy-corbyn>.
10   See for instance Ronan Burtenshaw, 'Hold the Line', *Tribune*, 27 May 2019.
11   See 'Travailleurs détachés: les curieux propos de Mélenchon', *Le Monde*, 13 July 2016.

Anniversaries

2021: 100 Years From the Founding of the Italian Communist Party – Ten Years After the Passing of Lucio Magri

Luciana Castellina

If today, on the centenary of the Italian Communist Party (PCI), I am asked why I continue to call myself a 'communist' – today at the age of 92 and 74 years since I joined the party – and particularly now, 30 years after it has ceased to exist – I would answer: because of the history of Italian communism. The fifteen years of the party's existence in which I was part of *Il Manifesto* but not in the party (1969 to 1984) is also part of that history, and not a contradiction but an enrichment. This year – 2021 – is, moreover, the anniversary of the death of Lucio Magri, whose life and work had so much to do with the history of the PCI and the potential solutions to its dilemma during its final years.

Certainly, I realise that mine is an answer that speaks of the past and not of any current project – because now I do not have a political programme aimed at achieving a society that can be called communist. Which, moreover, can be said of everyone else who, like me, continues to call themselves a communist. And yet, there is one commitment we can preserve: to not relinquish the attempt to reconcile liberty and equality, which is ultimately the essence of the communist project, two goals that no political project has been able to combine, neither the French Revolution, which brought us very close to the first but in no way to the second, nor the Russian Revolution, because in its attempt to guarantee the second it ended by suppressing the first.

If, in reaffirming this commitment to attempt a coupling of the two goals, I refer to the history of Italian communism it is because I see it, with all its darker sides and weaknesses, as the most significant historical attempt yet made to set out on the path to achieving both of them.

Palmiro Togliatti, who was intelligent as well as witty, liked to define the party whose unquestionable leader he was as a 'giraffe', that odd animal with an uncommonly and extravagantly long neck, a diplomatic way of expressing his displeasure at almost all the other parties called 'fraternal', including their progenitor the Soviet party – with which he nevertheless, even though he thought the worst of it, never broke – even conscious of the turn things took in the Kremlin with the successive liquidation of almost the entire original leadership of the CPSU. He was so aware of this that, when hospitalised in Moscow for the after-effects of an accident in the early 1950s, he dared to challenge Stalin, by refusing his proposal to head the revamped Cominform, in order not to risk being held in Moscow. Stalin's proposal came despite Togliatti's having pursued a line in Italy that had little in common with the thinking in the Kremlin and which marginalised the philo-Soviet old guard when it was officially theorised at the party's Eighth Congress in 1957 as the 'Italian road to socialism'

For this Togliatti was accused of duplicity and ambiguity. But it was not about that; it was about a 'double truth': although convinced that the 'Italian road to socialism' (an expression he actually coined) could not be more different from the orthodox path, he was also conscious that in those post-war decades a reference to the USSR was essential for keeping open the perspectives of a different society, the symbol of an otherness that was indispensable for avoiding a bland compatibility of the PCI with the capitalist system. And, in the international context of the period, at the peak of the Cold War, this was an essential issue.

Moreover, it would have been emotionally difficult to operate a break of this sort. The 1917 Revolution had had an extraordinary and profound propulsive effect on the popular masses, a feeling that was only reinforced during the hard years of fascism and war. Rereading the history of the period from today's perspective, as we are celebrating the centenary of PCI's birth, which took place in Teatro San Marco in Leghorn where the communist wing came together after having abandoned the congress of the Socialist Party at Teatro Goldoni, one is struck by the incomprehension of what was happening even on the part of the most estimable figures within the reformist wing – for example, Turati, who completely underestimated the enthusiasm stirred up by the unprecedented storming of the heavens in Russia. An incomprehension which was justified, other than by the serious divergence in political lines, by the very decision to split, a move that has been called into question by many today and considered a grave error. As Gramsci always commented afterwards (his presence at the congress was very marginal and Togliatti was not even in town), the break 'was necessary, yet it was also a disaster'.

It is discussible whether this double truth about the split – as not only necessary but disastrous – was something that Togliatti kept to himself for too long, and I think this is the case, even though when the 1956 Khrushchev report was made known the distance Togliatti took from it was not due to any factual dissent from its condemnation of Stalin on his part but rather only concerned – as he then explained in a historic interview in the journal *Nuovi Argomenti* – the superficial way in which it interpreted Stalinism as a 'cult of personality', which, he felt, evaded deeper problems.

When the PCI, under Berlinguer, finally broke with Moscow in 1980 it was too late. When we who had launched *Il Manifesto* had proposed this in 1968, after the entry of Soviet tanks in Prague (and were expelled from the party for it), the left was on the rise throughout the world, and the relation of forces had changed. This was a result of the wave of workers' and students' struggles and the entry onto the world political stage of the third-world countries that had just been decolonised. In that context the criticism of the USSR had the meaning of a criticism of so-called 'real' socialism made in the name of another, a more 'true' socialism; ten years later, when the conservative counter-offensive was in full swing, the meaning shifted, and criticism sounded as if 'socialism can no longer happen'. And that, in fact, was how the break was understood by the very epigones of Berlinguer who hastened to liquidate all of communist history, including the October Revolution; while Berlinguer had only said that it had 'ceased to perform a propulsive function', not that it would have been better had it not occurred.

As we now know, this was the prelude to the dissolution of the PCI – or, as many came to say, its suicide. Its authors were those who had gradually recanted everything, based, however, on two opposed and equally absurd interpretations: the idea that the PCI had been a simple expression of Moscow's power and that it had, on the contrary, only been social democracy in disguise. In both cases, according to the liquidators, the PCI should have publicly made amends and changed its name.

As everybody knows, the name was then changed several times, invoking all manner of plant varieties (oak, carnation, olive tree), as was its own political line and social location.

Among the merits of many Lucio Magri, who together with Rossana Rossanda founded the journal *Il Manifesto*,[1] is that his history of Italian communism – *The Tailor of Ulm*[2] – was one of the few to have avoided two contrasting errors: denying that there ever was a close connection between the PCI and the international communist movement, and thus with the CPSU, maintaining that the PCI was always so different that it always had little to do with Moscow, which was not true – or the inverse: that the relationship was very close and profoundly negative and that this necessitated the erasure of all trace of it, even by changing the name of the party. Magri's admirable achievement is perhaps due to his having written one of the very rare histories of the PCI that, though not written by an outside observer but by one of its protagonists, is not an autobiography but an objective collection of facts – which enable a critical reflection, something indispensable for all communists but which no organised force, even when calling for it, has really undertaken. (This could and ought to be a task undertaken by the Party of the European Left, which also contains non-communist forces but whose history is nevertheless interwoven in diverse ways with communist history.)

This critical reflection is needed not only to settle accounts with the past but because the generic reference to common 'values' to which the definition of our identity is nowadays entrusted is completely inadequate for producing the cohesion required for any kind of organisation that intends what Marx expressed in a very simple and thoroughly ideological word: 'Aufhebung', 'the removal of the present state of things'. All the more so today, at a time in which the social base that we claim to represent no longer has the homogeneity of interests and culture of the old twentieth-century working class, now fragmented by globalisation and post-Fordism. The terms of the old debate that coursed through the European communist movement, opposing spontaneism to consciousness, seem dated today. Because today – this is a point on which Magri always insisted in the heated debate on these questions that opened up within the PCI and also within the new left – political unity is continually less the result of the immediacy of needs, as it once was. Instead, this unity increasingly requires an overarching political mediation that makes it possible to identify with a common strategic project with a culture strong enough to stand up to the continually heavier and more insidious impact of the dominant culture, capable as it is of oppression and strangulation as never before by means of its powerful and insidious media machine.

This, of course, does not mean that we should seek refuge in a sterile identitarianism drawn from a historical context that by now no longer exists, which becomes a cage without relation to the real historic processes. However, while eschewing this identitarianism we cannot give up the attempt to equip ourselves with a common vision of the world and a project able to find common ground through which it could be possible to give voice, and a solution, to the new contradictions that have ripened in recent years and which, albeit rooted in the fundamental capital/labour contradiction – that is, in the capitalist system – are expressed via diverse subjects, and thus diverse movements: the gender contradiction above all, the contradiction that arises from the consciousness of ecological disaster, as well as the ethnic/racial contradiction.

It is precisely in terms of this level of problems that the PCI's most serious lag occurred in the last decades of its existence. On the other hand, the new alternative movements, which – for fear of being suffocated by the old parties of the left – have ended by taking refuge in the exaltation of 'difference', have finished by abandoning the goal of reconstructing a common universalism. (This universalism is naturally something other than an imposition of one's own (Western) culture on the world, passing it off as a point of arrival in the march of civilisation.) And, above all, they have proven incapable of giving birth to a more stable organisational presence on the ground.

What the PCI really was

There is a phrase of Jean-Paul Sartre's which I think is more helpful than any other for understanding what the PCI was, at least up to the mid-1960s. The great French intellectual often came to Italy towards the end of the 1950s to participate in one or another cultural conference and was curious about the Italian communists who immediately appeared to him so different from the rigidity of their French counterparts; then he got to know Togliatti (on whose death he wrote a page-long in memoriam. 'To My Friend Togliatti' in *l'Unità*), and then one day he wrote: 'I have finally understood what the PCI is: it is Italy'. He meant that this party reflected the country; that it was not a body extraneous to it nor a marginal structure; that – ultimately – in the veins of those two million members, which the party had at the time, ran the same blood of the country where it operated; that they reflected its features; that it was not a vanguard but a big popular organisation.

If you read Pier Paolo Pasolini's novels, many of which describe the working-class suburbs (borgate) of Rome, the hero – a sub-proletarian and sometime also a petty thief out of necessity – has one thing that he holds on to: being a member of the PCI, the precious membership card, always in his jacket pocket. At one point in one of the most beautiful plays by the great Ascanio Celestini, the characters speak of the old mother who is about to go out and vote, and she goes to the dresser drawer where she has her most important things: an image of the Madonna, her identity card, the ballot form, and her PCI card. Even in the comedies of the glorious period of Italian neorealist cinema the hero is almost always a PCI member. And it really was that way: it wasn't 'the' people, it was a people that felt redeemed from misery because they were proudly communist. A people not subjected but subjects (this difference needs to be pointed out to many who are discovering populism).

As a girl I spent a lot of time in the Roman borgate where the local PCI federation sent us to do political work with the women of the area, popolane[3] whom I watched gradually grow to become protagonists of the life of their region. So that even when they had to struggle to get the public water fountain on the corner to work they did not feel like poor unfortunates up against the degradation of the slums but part of a large international movement that was changing the world. Because in the neighbourhood PCI section they too were involved in the political discussion (and they were taught how to read through *l'Unità*), a widespread experience that enabled them to resist when during the hardest years of the Cold War an unprecedented clerical assault rained down on them that even had recourse to the medieval weapon of excommunication.

Much of this character was due to the very courageous choice made by Togliatti as soon as he disembarked in Naples in February 1944, coming from Moscow. He understood that he could not entrust the party to the comrades, however heroic, who had spent many years in prison, confinement, or exile but who were exactly for this reason out of their element. He irreverently put the party and the newspaper in the hands of youngsters who in the 1930s had been in GUF (Fascist University Groups) and who had distinguished themselves in the Littoriali, the only literary competitions which then existed. A group that was to become prominent in the party came right out of the Cinecittà school of cinematography: Ingrao, Alicata, Lizzani, Visconti and others. For all of them their graduation exam was the Resistance in whose ranks in the mountains they had discovered communism for the first time. And the workers. Those extraordinary proletarian nuclei that had defied the Nazi occupation, blocking the factories with the strike wave of 1943-44.

The PCI, the Italian constitution, and the consolidation of democracy

Togliatti was also courageous in his choice – and there are still those who scold him for it now – to not embark on a revolutionary adventure for which Italian society, just emerging from twenty years of fascism, was not even minimally prepared, with a party that had suddenly enlarged to reach two million members but about which Luigi Longo himself, Togliatti's vice chair, returning in 1946 from an exploratory expedition throughout the country, said: 'I didn't find a party, I found a crowd.'

What was needed – this was Togliatti's idea – was to first construct a subject, without spending energy on questions such as the provisional acceptance of the monarchy or a clash with the Catholic church, which was less important in comparison with the consolidation, still anything but guaranteed in that phase, of a democratic system, requiring alliances and the maturation of a people used to protest by burning down city halls.

The result was the 'miracle' of the Italian Constitution, approved in 1946, Europe's most advanced charter, not so much because of the rights recognised in it (they also figure in the other major post-war European constitutions) but above all because it set a precise limit on the 'terrible right of property'. (When, in 1957, the first European nucleus was formed, the Common Market, Germany's economic minister asked that Italy be excluded precisely because of its 'socialist' constitution.[4])

In reality, it was really this choice that allowed the PCI to handle the difficult social conflict that was triggered after the rupture of the anti-fascist alliance and the – very harsh – beginning of the Cold War. The dreaded police force under Mario Scelba, the hated Christian Democratic (DC) Minister of the Interior, was responsible for veritable massacres perpetrated against workers who had been laid off en masse for political reasons or had protested the severe capitalist restructuring of industry that had already begun. And against day labourers who occupied fields and planted red flags in them.

At the time, the country was divided into two separate societies, one DC, entrusted to the parishes, the other communist, congregated around the Case del Popolo[5] built with voluntary manual labour, through which people responded to the need for solidarity, culture, and recreation for the excluded.

This rut, this Cold War context, helped the DC in its project of appearing to be democracy's indispensable bulwark against the menace of a looming communist danger. It was a scenario that led, on the one hand, to recourse to every possible weapon (police brutality but also provocations by the secret services, above all the famous Gladio, steered by the CIA), and, on the other, to the temptation on the part of the PCI's base to always respond with an insurrectional uprising.

The most important of these uprisings flared up when the bitter electoral defeat of 18 April 1948, in part the result of the ferocious contestation produced by the Cold War, was followed by the assassination attempt against Togliatti two months later. The entire country exploded in an unprecedented popular uprising. (FIAT's president, Vittorio Valletta, was held prisoner by workers in the Mirafiori plant; the Tuscan-Emilian sharecroppers were penned by the owners inside fenced camps pending something even worse. There were thousands of arrests (mine too, the first of a long series, fortunately always for brief periods).

The framework that resulted from the political line adopted by Togliatti posed not a few problems. As Magri wrote in *The Tailor of Ulm*: 'the democratic path [...] did not appear to be easier than the revolutionary path'. It was time to make a new choice, and Togliatti decided to put a halt to the anger, sending a famous message from his hospital bed, where he was recovering in serious condition: 'remain calm'.

The party, though embittered, obeyed. In Turin, inside the factory they put Valletta in a car and sent him out.

This choice was followed by another intended to further legitimate the PCI's attention to democratic principles: the major campaign against what was called the 'Scam Law' (legge truffa), a new electoral regulation – awarding a superbonus of two-thirds of Chamber of Deputies seats for a party that obtains at-large an absolute majority of votes – imposed by the DC for the 1953 elections. The battle was won – the quorum was not reached that would have given the DC an absolute majority, a result that was uncertain for days because there were doubtless those in the DC who were contemplating altering the vote count. But the prestige and weight that the PCI had by then achieved in the country made the conservative majority fearful of deploying undemocratic practices.

The PCI and the diversifying Catholic world

However, it is also true that these were years in which a significant fault line opened up in the Catholic world, and in the DC itself; no less than two presidents of the powerful youth group of Azione Cattolica resigned in protest against the reactionary clerical wing that dominated the Vatican in those years and became missionaries in Africa; in the DC, under the leadership of Fanfani, which had made the clear-cut decision to place itself at the head of the new unbridled capitalism, the exodus began of many of its youth cadres, many of whom, some sooner, some later, landed in the PCI.

Among them was Lucio Magri, who was not a believer but had grown up in Bergamo, a 'white' zone, that is, DC par excellence, where the only available political choice for a boy was between the right and left wings of Christian Democracy. (Precisely this experience led him to take relations with the Catholic world seriously – one of the themes to which Gramsci, as is known, had paid attention – considering the popular and above all rural masses to be socially closer to the communist *folk* base than they were to the enlightened bourgeois strata of the urban liberal world. It was, moreover, Magri himself who inspired those drafting the theses for the PCI's Ninth Congress to insert a passage that later was always strongly emphasised: 'A faith that is authentically felt can be an important contributor to an anti-capitalist critique.' (Today we could add: 'as the preaching of Pope Francis shows'.)

Also important in this phase was the extraordinary success in Italy of the campaign against nuclear rearmament: in Italy, the appeal, which in other European countries was almost always signed by a squad of famous intellectuals, became a mass campaign signed by 16 million people. (Being assigned to follow it, I remember the astonishment of all the participants in the Salle Pleyel in Paris, where in 1949 the first historic congress of peace activists was held, at the Italian delegation – mixed in with a few leading intellectuals was a large group of popolane who were surprised but quite disappointed that there was no pasta in France.)

Among the signatories of the Appeal were also numerous top representatives of the Catholic world and of the DC in which a minority left wing had remained – with people like Giovanni Gronchi, the future president of the republic, and Giorgio La Pira, the mayor of Florence.

All of this created a fabric of relationships and alignments that gradually increasingly connected the PCI to Italian society as a whole.

The 'Italian miracle' – catch-up Fordism and the development of neo-capitalism

But the 1950s were also the years which saw the beginnings and then increasingly significant development of the 'Italian miracle', the name given to the economic boom because it had little to do with the acceleration of a growth stimulated by post-war reconstruction as in all the other European countries. In Italy, still characterised by the backwardness of its productive apparatus, what was involved was a genuine leap making it possible to climb the steps of development in very little time, where elsewhere the process was much more gradual. The GDP had growth rates that we would today call 'Chinese', 5 to 6%, greater than that of Germany's high rate; average income rose from 350,000 lire in 1953 to 571,000 in 1964, creating deep social transformations also through massive urbanisation. At the same time there was a dramatic discrepancy between wage growth – no more than 6% after 10 years – and productivity growth, which was 50%.

In those years the PCI tried to understand the extent of the new economic, social, and also cultural phenomena. And it was on this terrain – the transformation of the factory and of the culture of the new generations that on the left had just come out of the protected cage of the Case del Popolo and rural isolation and, on the right, of the parishes – that both communist and clerical hegemony began to crack. The young were less marked by the harsh repression suffered by the preceding generation, and industrial development brought near full employment, giving the young working class greater bargaining clout. The kids who entered factories through the recommendations of the parish priest immediately mixed with those who had at first suffered discrimination but then also ended by achieving the industrial employment they had sought. Both groups, impatient with the caution of the union, brought protest, which finally became something joyful, to the streets. The urban centres began to fill with protests that came to be called the 'kids with whistles', a ferment that surprised the union itself. It was especially the electromechanics, the new 'white' sector, the white of refrigerators and washing machines, with whom students – for the first time – united in Turin and Milan.

And in this phase above all the Communist Youth Federation began to change – it no longer had 400,000 members as it did up to 1957-58 but it was healthily unruly. Older people distrusted them because they liked coca cola more than the native drink, wine; and because they wore blue jeans and striped t-shirts – all of this being signs of 'Americanisation'. However, they were the ones who overwhelmed the older leaders and animated the big revolt against the last gasp of the centre-right: the DC Tambroni government which, in 1960, dared to rely on the vote of the small fascist squad that had entered parliament using the name Movimento Sociale (MSI) as cover.

They were the ones who planned, or rather spontaneously made themselves protagonists of, the days of protest that started in Genoa, the gold medal Resistance city,[6] where the MSI dared to convene its congress. The protest marches spread as far as Sicily, attacked by police forces that had never before been so violent. The balance sheet was 10 young people killed and hundreds wounded. Tambroni was forced to resign, his being Italy's last centre-right government.

Workers' struggles and the communist left

I do not want to dwell too long on this period, which would inevitably involve some autobiographical indulgence since in the late 50s and early 60s I was director of the weekly put out by the Communist Youth Federation, *Nuova Generazione*, and every Monday I was called to the party central to answer – to Giorgio Napolitano, who represented the commission charged with following union matters, to Mario Alicata of the cultural commission, or to Gian Carlo Pajetta of the international commission – for various mistakes made by the newspaper. Perhaps because we had criticised a peaceful coexistence between the two great powers that threatened to paralyse the peoples of the third world struggling for their independence (chief among them Algeria) or because we had given too much space to unorthodox writers, or else because we had criticised the approach of one or another union leader. It was no accident that the first serious incident that led to my dismissal from the managing board of *Nuova Generazione* (which I then rejoined for another year) arose from the attack we published on the agreement signed by Luciano Lama, secretary of the powerful FIOM (Federation of Metal Workers of the CGIL – Italian General Confederation of Labour), subsequently general secretary of the CGIL, with the Genoa firm Italsider. This involved accepting the modification requested by the company's board: 'job evaluation'[7] (or paghe di posto[8]) to substitute the old system of pay based on skill and qualifications.

This may seem a small detail but it involved a question that then became central in the 1968-69 struggles. Essentially, it was about the introduction of an American method of evaluation, which – contrary to salary based on the worker's 'career', that is, his accumulated qualifications and length of time in his profession – in which the subjectivity of the worker, his skills or even prowess is brought to bear – based the wage level only on the worker's objective positioning within the productive process – for instance on the assembly line or within the production process, say, as windshield-wiper controller – decided entirely and arbitrarily by the line manager. In substance, it involved an aspect of the Fordist reorganisation of production that was making its first strides in Italy in the large factories as automation came in.

I am concentrating on this change because it is indicative of the debate that arose in the PCI at the beginning of the 1960s, that which for the first time rather explicitly pitted a left current, named after Pietro Ingrao, one of the party's most eminent leaders – out of which *Il Manifesto* arose in 1969, first only as a journal, then as a political group, a daily newspaper, and also a party, the PdUP (Party of Proletarian Unity) with a parliamentary presence – against a conservative current based on the right wing of Giorgio Amendola and Giorgio Napolitano.

I am saying left 'current' of thought, not organised tendency – for it would never have occurred to any of us to create the latter, as we were too strongly rooted in a sense of discipline. It was only after the Soviet invasion of Prague, when the conflict deepened and extended to other issues, that a part of the Ingrao group decided to go beyond the limits within which dissent had to be kept.

Thus, the issue against which the communist left measured itself at the beginning of the 1960s in the area of immediate operational decisions was the new character and the different kind of importance that had to be assigned to workers' struggles. While Togliatti, and the majority of the leadership group of the party, tended to maintain workers' struggles as just one of the many and equivalent components of a broad front of popular struggles, the Ingrao area held that we had to make the workers' struggles into the axis of a new mass activism, arguing that capitalism, precisely because it was developing, had to be attacked at its nerve centres.

The strategic debate

The polemical confrontation had as its point of departure a different analysis of the phase we were in, a judgement about neo-capitalism and thus of the role of workers' struggles that were developing, starting from the new large factories that had grown with the economic boom. Was Italian society already an integral part of mature capitalism or was it still marked by backwardness? The answers to this question (which I am conveying here somewhat crudely though it deserves fuller treatment because this was a very rich discussion) naturally led to two different strategies. For the left, the large Fordist factory and the new working class it produced could have a decisive role to play and required a new political response if we wanted to look ahead to the long-run tendencies that were going to prevail. It would therefore be a disaster to remain enclosed in a context that was by then being transcended. Our argument was that we should not limit ourselves to pressure through generic demands but instead propose a real plan, an alternative model that would make a dent in and modify the type of development underway, through 'structural reforms' able to cut into the existing model – alternative because the model would involve reforms in the very structure of the system. Thus a plan based on significant public intervention that would accentuate the mixed character of the economy – state and private – accompanied by forms of direct workers' control. In addition, the plan envisaged a drastic shift of consumption from individual to collective.

The party's right wing was fearful of a line that would put the central focus on a class conflict so harsh that it could damage the shrewd politics of social alliances built up by the PCI over the years and very centred on the relation to the 'middle strata'. In those years, many of the same communist ex-workers had become, thanks to the boom, small entrepreneurs and there was much talk about them in the party. (An example was the famous speech made by Togliatti in Reggio Emilia 'The Middle Strata and Red Emilia'.) The party also feared that the axis of conflict would move too far outside parliament where thanks precisely to the pressure of more generic demands significant gains could be made. In the lingo of the ongoing debate the confrontation became: 'a different model of development' vs. 'protest in a thousand rivulets'.

On this Magri wrote: 'Certainly it was not a matter of a short-lived battle. But didn't it perhaps represent the horizon of the democratic road to socialism that was the PCI's emblem? Could it not be the possible basis for a left government? Perhaps it should have provided for more steps and hypothesise a slower process. But the project was not unrealistic – it envisaged structural, not corrective, reforms; a different development model, not more rapid growth; a different modernity, not the continuation of the current one.'

The first event at which this argument came to the fore was, in 1962, a Gramsci Institute conference on the 'tendencies of neo-capitalism': on the one side Amendola, on the other the report by Bruno Trentin, the general sSecretary of the FIOM who was to play a very important role in the CGIL and finally become its general secretary. But it was Lucio Magri's intervention that took the political sense of the debate to its most extreme consequences, which drew the very harsh excommunication by Amendola who decided to have it out with this very young, still unknown second-tier leader. And yet this attack on Magri is interesting to read. Jean-Paul Sartre was so enthusiastic about Magri's intervention that he wrote him the following note (which was accidentally found in one of Lucio's books, as he was little inclined to preserve mementos) after having asked his permission to publish it in *Les Temps Modernes*, the monthly he directed, where it came out the following month in a much enlarged version:

> My dear Magri, yesterday I found your article and read it all in one breath. I want to convey to you my enthusiasm and my admiration. Your article is the best of all those that we will publish, the only one that goes to the heart of the problem that has a philosophical dimension. In you I have found the central ideas of an introduction that I had written for this issue of the journal, but better expressed than I could have done. [...] 27 July 1962.

These thematic points, which were attacked as 'workerism', were then at the centre of the Workers' Conference promoted by the PCI at Genoa in March 1965, the first time that the conflict between the Amendolans and the Ingraoans came into the open. At the same time the content of this workers' struggle was taking on the character of a claim to power, not just for better redistribution; that is, there was the attempt to wrest for workers the power to discuss work organisation, environmental conditions, etc.. The idea was to move beyond a line based on demands, which always remained generally wage-based and aimed at forcing a sector-wide national contract, to a collective bargaining that would confront the bulk of the elements constituting the condition of the working class that otherwise remained beyond any control. And beyond control by a narrow trade-union leadership to which the management of struggles had been entrusted. The watchwords 'negotiate the entire wage and the entire condition of the worker', 'bring the workers' struggle into the factories', were two distinguishing elements at the beginning of 1960, those which, thanks to a major push from the base, most shaped the overall practice of the workers' movement after 1968.

The debate over this question was not, moreover, just an Italian peculiarity. These were the years in which there was much discussion abroad as well on neo-capitalism and the social and cultural phenomena it generated. It was, for the young Italian left, also the period of reading non-Italian literature, the deprovincialisation of our Italian culture. Thus we discovered the English *New Left Review*, which began publication in 1960, but also the analyses that came from Paris, the studies on the working class by Mallet and the early ecologism of André Gorz. Not to mention the literature of the older Frankfurt School, which began to appear in Italy. It was also the time of discovering a less orthodox and crude Marxism than that transmitted by the labour movement, that is, the rediscovery of the Marx of *Capital*, polemically reintroduced against the PCI's historicist culture by intellectuals like Galvano della Volpe and Lucio Colletti who were then party activists. It was the Turin journal *Quaderni rossi*, directed by the anomalous left-wing socialist Renato Panzieri, that brought us closer to workerism, a current of thought that aroused much suspicion in the PCI of that time. In a certain sense, the PCI, which in those years remained the political point of reference for young people who had a left orientation, was reinforced, but the new arrivals came through paths that were culturally unorthodox and through mobilisations that often did not follow the union's line.

'The extraordinary 60s.' It is an oft-repeated phrase, and in fact they were extraordinary, a time of openings and high-level debates, but also of enormously important social upheavals that suggested a very different Italy, that of the epic migration from the South to the North, of the abandonment of the countryside and the massive entry into the new factories, of mass education with the introduction of the unified middle school, of the first proletarian tremors – it is the July 1960 workers' revolt that led to the very violent confrontations at Piazza dello Statuto in Turin. And there was a profound turning point in the Catholic world with the pontificate of John XXIII and the extraordinary opening promulgated by the Second Vatican Council. Not to mention the impulse that came from the victorious advance of the movements of national liberation – Vietnam, Algeria, Africa, Cuba – viewed with a certain unease by the orthodox supporters of a peaceful coexistence between the two great powers whose equilibrium they threatened.

It is not true that '68 was born spontaneously; in reality, it was an educated movement, the fruit of a rich process of cultural and political accumulation in those exceptional years.

The new left within the PCI

It was in Milan – a city marked in those years by the first worker demonstrations, which after a long hiatus returned to the streets, headed by the very young workers of the electromechanics sector – that the movement, we could say, began to form the first embryo of the new left within the PCI. And it was in this city that the first outlines began to appear of a group that would develop a common thinking, which included Magri, who landed in the Secretariat of the Lombard Regional Committee, Rossana Rossanda, member of the Milanese secretariat and director of the prestigious Casa della Cultura, Aniello Coppola, director of the Milan edition of *L'Unità*, Luca Cafiero, later the leader of the student movement of the state universities, along with a group of the city's Communist Youth Federation, among them Achille Occhetto, Michelangelo Notarianni, and Lia Cigarini (who later became one of the main protagonists of the Italian feminist movement and first woman secretary of the city's Communist Youth Federation), with whom I was in frequent connection as director of the weekly, coming from Rome.

By contrast, added to these issues in the mid-1960s was the question of PCI-PSI (Italian Socialist Party) unification, a proposal put on the table by Giorgio Amendola, 'improvidently' – as he himself had to subsequently admit – which was connected to the appearance of the first centre-left government, of the DC and PSI in 1963, and to the ensuing split of the PSI's left wing (which founded the PSIUP – the Italian Socialist Party of Proletarian Unity) which opposed the coalition. Around this, opinion was split in the PCI, some being in favour of an ambiguous reformism, others who thought the socialists' break with those on the left and their concession to the DC was a fatal blow to the possibility of a real alternative. As a result there was both antipathy to and sympathy for the small PSIUP split, which at the time represented positions in many respects more radical than those of the PCI. And in fact not a few (including many '68ers) looked favourably at that party in those years.

It was starting at this point that the connection to Ingrao became closer and the left network consolidated. When the unitary party proposed by Amendola was discussed in the Central Committee, Luigi Pintor, and

Milani (later the only secretary of a PCI federation who officially supported *Il Manifesto*), voted against it, as did also Coppola and Occhetto. The confrontation became harsher in all offices of the party and union, while the Youth Federation lined up completely with the left. The relationship with Ingrao and Alfredo Reichlin, in particular involving Magri, Rossanda, and Trentin and another important union leader, Sergio Garavini (who was to become the first secretary of Rifondazione Comunista) became almost daily, even if no attempt at a split was made, since party discipline, as I have said, was so deeply rooted in us that it would never have occurred to anyone to create organisational forms that could strengthen ties to the left that was emerging everywhere in the regional federations. But in the Youth Federation too Ingrao had by then become the most respected leader.

1966: The inner-party conflict becomes explicit

The conflict became less subterranean, and at the Eleventh Congress in February 1966 it exploded. The tension was already high as people arrived, also because it was the first congress without Togliatti and therefore without the authority that everyone had recognised and that could have led to a mediation. The two lines came out into the open, and the censorial climate thickened. So much so that on the eve, the Youth Federation, intimidated, ended by distancing itself from the left, and the defection of Occhetto, who in 1966 had already been its secretary for some years, necessarily carried weight. And the trade unionists too stepped back a bit, their responsibilities being too important to put their role at risk.

Magri remained very close to Ingrao who by now was more radicalised, and in fact he collaborated with Ingrao in drafting his intervention in the congress, that famous moment in which he publicly said, in the solemn context of a congress: 'I would not be sincere if I told you that Comrade Longo [who had then succeeded Togliatti after the latter's death in 1964] has persuaded me'; and, against the criticisms of the party secretary, he went on to recommend the advantages of a free internal debate as being much more useful to substantive unity than reticent discipline.

Ingrao's speech was met with a standing ovation, but afterwards he was always in the habit of saying, self-ironically: 'Let's hope that they don't applaud Pietro'. Because although he was much applauded by the base he promptly suffered a defeat.

The worst defeat was that of the Eleventh Congress, which closed with the elimination from the Central Committee of two representatives of the left (who were subsequently among the founders of *Il Manifesto*) : Ninetta Zandigiacomi, a trade-unionist from the Veneto, and Eliseo Milani, secretary of the Bergamo federation. Pintor and Rossanda remained members of the CC but were both relieved of their previous functions: Pintor from the vice-directorship of *L'Unità* to become regional vice-secretary for Sardinia, and Rossanda from supervision of the cultural commission to become simply a parliamentarian and not even re-elected in 1968. More serious still was the downgrading of Ingrao who was entrusted with the prestigious post of president of the parliamentary group in the Chamber of Deputies, a full-time task making it impossible for him to stay in the secretariat and thus cutting him off from the real leadership of the party.

Those who were not members of the CC were distanced from their interaction with the party central in Rome. This is what happened, for example, to Filippo Maone, who then opened a bookshop in Naples, and to myself, moved from the central women's section to a non-party function, the presidency of the Union of Italian Women, a position which though prestigious was wrested for me with difficulty from Nilde Jotti against the more hardline Alicata and Napolitano who clearly wanted to get me out of the way.

The approach to Magri was different. Immediately removed from the delicate Commissione di Massa (which dealt with the trade unions), Amendola wanted to keep him in a marginal position within party headquarters. He feared his influence could have gathered support on the left if he were moved to a regional federation. He was even denied the post of vice-secretary of the federation of a small city in the Veneto – Rovigo – which Magri would have preferred. It was precisely after this that Magri rejected Amendola's proposal, preferring to be a simple party member rather than remain in a demeaning bureaucratic position in party headquarters.

The PCI in the face of the 1968 movement

For three years, up to the founding of *Il Manifesto*, he remained a simple member. He lived by stretching out his 30,000 lire severance pay and translating political texts from English – as if they were in Latin for he didn't know English – which Luca Trevisani, a professional translator who also had left *l'Unità*, gave him. (Luca then became editor in chief of the daily *Il Manifesto*.) In summer he stayed at the homes of people who were away on holidays, in winter at the country houses of those who had them.

It was by no means a wasted vacation. Lucio, who led a hermit's life, read intensively and certainly those years of study provided him with much of the material he used in laying out *Il Manifesto*'s Theses. He often carved out time at Sant'Elia, a small port at the edge of Cagliari where Pintor, also almost a hermit, had gone to live.

When he arrived at the Twelfth Congress, in Bologna in February 1969, much had already occurred: the explosive beginnings of Italy's long '68; the invasion of Prague by Warsaw Pact troops; the renewal of struggles in the country's principal factories. The PCI was by then no longer the only place where the left expressed itself; new and diverse arenas had been opened, each one of us felt the totalising weight of the PCI less than previously when the very thought of being distanced from it had always been equated to suicide. We all found more courage, we felt more extraneous to the organisation in which we had so long been active; but at the same time, whether for generational reasons or through culture and habit, '68 was also not our home. At the Twelfth Congress, however, we were more resolved to take risks, even though Ingrao and the trade-unionists had told us that they would not go along with us. This made the hostility we faced all the stronger. In the Congress, among the members of the Central Committee who took the floor were Rossana and Pintor, but also Aldo Natoli and Massimo Caprara with whom we had since met even if they were not among the Ingraoans.

Their interventions were all scheduled for 8:30 in the morning, at the day's opening session when, as everyone knew, few of the delegates would have been present. But the anticipation of the confrontation by now expected as imminent resulted in a hall packed with journalists but also with delegates, even at that 'predawn' hour.

It was in this climate of isolation, cut off from the older and more authoritative leaders, that what had remained of the left now really became an organised entity. It was founded in Bologna, at Hotel Orologio, where Lucio, who was not even a delegate, made clear what the proposal and the concrete first steps should be. One could say that *Il Manifesto* – we still did not know that this is what we would call it – was born in the very simple parlour of the hotel next to San Petronio. Later the owner – I don't know if he is still the proprietor of today's rather more elegant and expensive Orologio – remained proud of this.

After two months of delay, with Magri and Rossanda as directors, the first issue of *Il Manifesto* was published. After many tries, Lucio, Luigi, and I hit on the name while we were seated on a wall in Via San Valentino, opposite the apartment where Rossana then lived. I don't remember who of us three came up with the immodest idea; at any rate, we were all immediately enthusiastic because it accentuated the call to action, not theoretical efforts – another of our concerns, which Lucio later somewhat regretted.

The matter came on the agenda of the CC after a declaration by the Political Office that condemned the initiative and a very harsh article by

Paolo Bufalini on 30-31 July, after two numbers of the journal had already been published and many attempts at mediation had failed. This was followed by expulsion (but of a less severe type, which did not include moral condemnation nor rule out re-entry) on the basis of a document written by Alessandro Natta, against which only three voted: the philosopher Luporini, Chiarante, like Lucio coming out of the rebellious Christian Democratic youth of the early 1950s, and Fabio Mussi, the youngest member of the CC (today in Sinistra Italiana after having left the PD). The first to be expelled were the members of the CC – Rossanda, Pintor, Natoli – then Magri in his capacity as director of the journal. The others subsequently suffered the same fate, as soon as they wrote for *Il Manifesto*.

But at this point we were in the midst of the explosion of '68, a movement the PCI had not anticipated; on the contrary, it didn't understand it. With the exception of Luigi Longo, still the party's secretary, who was committed to attempting a discussion with the movement's leaders, but who was by then too old and ill to insist and force the hand of a party that remained closed.

Italy's '68 was, however, different from France's. As in France, the movement in Italy immediately sought contact with the workers and although here too the union was at first hostile to student intrusion it was significantly more open than its French counterpart. The CGIL was already marked by the debate precisely on the political role of workers' struggles that had coursed through the PCI for the whole previous decade, in which many of the young trade-unionists were protagonists. With FIAT, the country's largest factory, Turin became the epicentre of the movement. And there the creation of the factory councils resulting from worker pressure and the stimulus provided by the student movement, brought back memories of *Ordine Nuovo*, the weekly socialist journal and group established in May 1919 by Gramsci, Angelo Tasca, Umberto Terracini, and Togliatti, that had, like the new movements, theorised the councils during the Red Biennium of 1919-21, based on the council theories of the early Lenin and then of Rosa Luxemburg: as organs that are not purely trade-unionist but political, an embryo of organisms of direct democracy indispensable for making parties less self-referential. It was a subject already reintroduced in the 1960s by Magri in various texts, and finally, though with a thousand limitations, lived through the concrete class conflict. The councils lasted almost a decade, but in the end the movement was defeated – the first signal of the reactionary Thatcher-Reagan counteroffensive of the 1980s. At the last act of the workers' defeat at FIAT, in the 1980s, Enrico Berlinguer put in an appearance at the Mirafiori plant besieged by workers in the struggle and responded to a worker with a megaphone in the crowd who asked him 'if we occupy the factory what will your party do?': 'It will stand with the workers.'

The compromesso storico and Berlinguer's turn

The question exhibited the mistrust that grew due to the inattention with which the PCI followed the conflict, and the party secretary's response declared a break of sorts with the right wing of his party, which in fact was not to forgive him for this, isolating him within the organisation, even though he was its secretary.

Shortly before, Berlinguer had accomplished a self-critical turnaround in respect to his choice of the historic compromise – the support, though without participation, of DC governments. He had launched it after 1976, when the PCI had reached the highest electoral result of its history – 34% of votes. But with the first major world economic crisis already having exploded in 1973 a dangerous phase had begun. The coup in Chile was the first of several dramatic signals; and it was precisely a long essay in *Rinascita* reflecting on the Allende government that first aired the new strategy. Faced with this difficult phase it was necessary to create an alliance that would save democracy because even where it was possible to conquer 51% of votes, such a majority was not enough to govern. All very true as far as it goes, except that in Italy it was all the less possible to think that such an alliance could be made with all of the DC, with what that party, by now deeply intertwined with a corrupt power, had become. To think that it was possible, as Berlinguer wrote, 'to help it to change', and that the task before the PCI was to 'force it to do it', was purely illusory. But this was the choice of the entire PCI; I still remember the paradoxical atmosphere in the hall of the Chamber of Deputies on that 9 August 1976 when Lucio Magri took the floor in the name of a band of new '68 left deputies united in the Democrazia Proletaria list (three from PdUP, one from Lotta Continua, and two from Avanguardia Operaia) to announce his vote against a government that, thanks to the decisive support of communist votes received a majority never before seen. 'I find myself', he said, 'fulfilling a curious, embarrassing role verging on the ridiculous although emblematic of what many think. Indeed I am speaking in the name of a group of just six deputies out of 630 and at the same time as leader of the opposition.' The – highly ambivalent – majority had never been so overwhelming!

We must keep in mind that the left in those 1976 elections (the PCI, the PSI and the small groups), attained 48% of votes; and above all in that same moment it had, despite limits and mistakes, accumulated a great political potential within society, and so an alteration in the balance of forces was evident, precisely because of that movement which the PCI had ignored. In judging that tragic experiment with 'compromise', Magri, in *The Tailor of Ulm*, remembers the keen observation of Ramsay MacDonald, the British prime minister who led a coalition government in the 1930s. After that not brilliant experience MacDonald responded ironically to an American journalist who asked him how it had gone: 'I had learned how frustrating it was to be long excluded from government, but then I understood that there was something yet worse: going to government and seeing that you can do almost nothing.' What is more, the PCI was not even allowed into the executive; it supported it while it remained excluded – the exclusionary taboo still remained in force!

These were sad days. In this period in which the PCI was in 'half-government' it did not add any significant conquest; it had wrested all of its conquests when it was in opposition, made strong by great popular pressure on which it broadly exercised its own hegemony, a hegemony which, despite its 34% of votes, it began to increasingly lose. It thus called for a series of dangerous reactions against a deluded movement, vulnerable to the lure of terrorist groups which took the stage in those years culminating in the sensational assassination of Aldo Moro. Disenchanted, many retreated to private life, many turned to drugs. The new left groups were dissolved, except for Democrazia Proletaria, which however was not able to pass the threshold and in the 1979 elections remained outside parliament in which, in a climate of disorientation and distrust, only the PdUP per il Comunismo entered. Our idea – that of *Il Manifesto* – which was always reaffirmed despite the irony with which it was received by other groups – that is, that our goal was not to substitute for the PCI but to work for its refounding, since we had always said we considered ourselves a 'provisional' party – appeared to have definitively failed.

But at the end of 1979 a very large area of southern Italy, Irpinia, was struck by a tremendous earthquake, which aside from its physical damage also upset politics: the DC's corrupt power was exposed as well as a large part of Bettino Craxi's PSI, which at first seemed able to profit from the crisis of its government partner, the DC, by preparing itself for the presidency of the Council. But it in turn was crushed to the point that Craxi felt compelled to seek refuge in Tunisia to escape a jail sentence.

A courageous Enrico Berlinguer acknowledged the need to abandon his strategy and declare it unfeasible in the face of a DC that had by then proved unsalvageable. In a very tense CC session held in Salerno, at the edge of the earthquake zone, Berlinguer decided, and the CC agreed, to say 'basta' and ask for a return to the commitment to a left alternative. This was to be known as the 'second turn of Salerno' because it was there that Togliatti, right after arriving in Italy in February 1944, had articulated the contours of the new post-war PCI.

It was alas too late. The PSI was by now firmly set on another path, the movement lacked strength after the workers' defeat at FIAT, and the post-Fordist reorganisation of the process of production and atomisation of the working class was fully underway. All this was accompanied by a reactionary counteroffensive in Europe and the world.

The most serious thing, however, was that Berlinguer's turn left him isolated in his own party, with the right convinced that it could, that it had to, follow the Craxi pattern. Accompanied by a violent anti-communist campaign, transmitted by a 'modernist' propaganda that presented Berlinguer's interview on corruption as an outburst of conformist respectability rather than what it was: the denunciation of a dangerous crisis of our democratic model; that accused him of bigotry for his denunciation of consumerism prompted by an early ecological awareness; isolated him because of his support for the peace movement that had grown throughout the 1980s in opposition to the installation of US and Soviet missiles; and, finally, isolated him because of his request for a referendum to cancel the law with which the Craxi government had abolished the sliding wage scale ('scala mobile'), that is, the automatic adjustment of wages to the cost of living, a historic conquest of the labour movement.

Re-entry of the PdUP and the liquidation of the PCI

Under these conditions, we of the PdUP did not – I think correctly – feel we could run in the elections, which would have required us too to attack Berlinguer's PCI. And so in 1983 we accepted the offer to present our candidacy in alliance with the Communist lists (in which, incidentally, the PdUP candidates received an avalanche of votes because we were freed from the blackmail of wasted votes, many now voting for us who would had never dared to do so before). And, finally, in March 1984: Berlinguer, present at our National Congress in Milan, and having heard Magri's address, went up to him and asked: 'But why don't you come back into the PCI now that the differences that divided us have been overcome?' We had been a very small party but strong with about a thousand cadre with a lot of experience, and Berlinguer certainly thought we would have been useful in changing the balance of forces within the PCI. We accepted the offer, after having discussed it in a special congress. But Berlinguer died unexpectedly during an assembly in Padua. Without him the wager was impossible. Indeed, after a few years the PCI was dissolved.

When we re-entered – Natta had succeeded Berlinguer – there was a fine declaration, perhaps the first time in which a communist party welcomed back heretics and honoured them: 'Sometimes', the declaration said, 'breaks are useful for everyone.'

And so we returned after 15 years of absence, but we immediately understood that the PCI was no longer the party we had left. There was a lot of trendy 'newist' ('nuovista') vocabulary whose substance was a shift of social and political location pulling the party quite a bit to the right of European social democratic parties. Curiously, after the fall of the Berlin Wall when the name change was proposed, we found ourselves on the same side as Alessandro Natta who had pronounced the closing argument for our expulsion.

The name-change proposal really concealed a substantive change, as the US attack on Iraq was showing at the same time and around which the Communist parliamentary group split from the beginning, in August 1990, due to the ambiguous official position taken by the party. The slow, contradictory process came to a head that had been sparked in the 1960s and then accelerated by worldwide transformations – globalisation, the liberalist counteroffensive against the social gains of the 1960s and 70s (with the famous declaration of the Trilateral Commission: 'an excess of democracy' has spread throughout the world, the system cannot permit it), but also the atomisation, with the advent of post-Fordism, of that working class whose political representation had for more than a century legitimated the proletarian parties.

The abandonment of the term 'communist' occurred in two stages: a congress, the Nineteenth, in Bologna, where in March 1989, the proposal was formalised; another, the Twentieth, in Rimini, in January-February 1991, when it was accepted. At this last, decisive, meeting, the 'NO' to Occhetto, unlike what had happened in the previous congress, was concentrated in a single unified motion, despite the diverse political-cultural provenances that had always been typical of its components: motion 2, composed both of the ex-Ingraoan area, a significant part of the Belinguer leadership (Natta, to be precise, Tortorella, Chiarante et al.) and of the area around Armando Cossutta, which was more conservative and tied to the Soviet Union. Nevertheless, a positive harmony was achieved, so much so that at the last seminar organised by the motion to once more articulate its own position, a short while before the conclusive congress, the report representing everyone was entrusted to Magri.

The seminar was held at Arco di Trento, where we presented ourselves in the name of 33% of the party. Which was no small proportion. Unfortunately, between the two congresses a good 400,000 members had left out of discomfort. With the change of name their spinal cord had been broken; it meant that we had to be ashamed of our history. The anger of the first weeks after Occhetto's announcement gave way, after a few months, to resignation.

With his report at Arco representing the second motion, Magri was in reality putting forward a complete project of party renewal, emphasising that a break in continuity was certainly indispensable but in the opposite direction of what the PDS (Party of the Democratic Left, the successor to the PCI, which then became the Democrats of the Left – DS – and then, no longer even left, the Democratic Party – PD) had done.

In Arco, unfortunately, the NO was in the end divided on the immediate choices to be made in the face of Occhetto's by now evident victory: Ingrao said that he would remain in the 'river' (that is, in the mainstream), while Cossutta said that he would go. And that is how it went: on 1 February 1991, in a rainy Rimini, the split was completed, and it was a defeat for everyone. If that 33% had remained unified it could have had the substance to wage an internal battle in the new party, even if, in the end, to create a new, but non-minority, party.

A group left the Communist Youth to go with Cossutta, among them Vendola; with Ingrao we of the ex-PdUP went, reluctantly. There was a great deal of emotion, crying, and embraces. But there was no enthusiasm, not even among the Occhetto majority that won.

Both options were aimed at saving the PCI, but precisely because of the division, they both proved inadequate: we of the ex-PdUP, like many others, needed only a few weeks to understand that we could not be in the PDS, and we left silently, many of us going into Rifondazione Comunista, which had in the meantime been founded by Cossutta, Vendola, and others; Ingrao also left the PDS. Rifondazione Comunista? There needs to be a serious reflection on this experience, something that not yet occurred. But that is another story; suffice it to say here that it certainly had its moments of glory but that a refounding of communism nevertheless was essentially never seriously attempted.

This year we have been celebrating the birth of the PCI 100 years ago, but it was a life that lasted only 70 years. And yet one thing must be said: This PCI has to such an extent remained the flesh and blood of Italy that what happened a century ago at the Teatro San Marco in Leghorn is remembered today by everyone, friends and foes, all the TV and radio networks, the newspapers, the journals; and then the conferences, debates, symposia ... I ask myself: For what other party could so much have happened and been done, and for a party that never was even in government!

NOTES

1   The daily newspaper *Il Manifesto* has been published continually from 1971 to the present. Eighteen issues of the irregularly appearing monthly journal *Il Manifesto* were published from 23 June 1969 to 28 April 1971.
2   Lucio Magri, *The Tailor of Ulm: Communism in the Twentieth Century*, London: Verso, 2011.
3   'Women of the people', 'of the popular classes'.
4   To which Berlusconi was later to refer as 'that soviet constitution'.
5   Some of these Houses of the People (Cdps), that is, neighbourhood clubs, were the successors of the historical Mutual Aid Societies of the pre-fascist era, but mainly they were built by the voluntary labour of Communists to provide places in villages or urban centres to relax, watch films, dance, follow cultural and social activities, as well as to hold normal political meetings. From the beginning of the 1950s these activities were organised by the new national organisation (formally founded in 1956) created by Communists as well as Socialists – ARCI (Italian Recreational and Cultural Association). It remains strong to this day with nearly 1 million members and almost 5,000 clubs, most of them no longer in the old Cdps, unfortunately sold after the dissolution of the PCI.

    Understanding the very asymmetrical presence of the Socialists and Communists in the Cdps requires mention of the complex relationship between the PCI and the PSI. The two parties were linked by a united action pact, which even led them to run in the same electoral list after the war – as the Fronte Popolare in 1948. In the first post-war years the PCI and PSI had a common youth organisation: first the Fronte della Gioventù and then Avanguardie Garibaldine. Even later, although each party had reclaimed its own electoral identity, and even from 1956 on, when the unity pact was broken and the PCI and PSI found themselves on opposite sides with the advent of the centre-left government (made up of the Christian Democrats and the PSI, along with other small secular parties), the two parties nevertheless remained together within the large mass organisations – in the first place in the CGIL (the powerful trade-union central), and in ARCI, UISP (Unione Italiana Sport Popolare), the Cooperatives League, etc. All these organisations very often had offices in the Case del Popolo even if the building was owned by the PCI, which it normally was. But in all these organisations the Communists were immensely more numerous than the Socialists.
6   After Liberation, the Italian state and armed forces awarded gold medals to individuals and cities that made particular sacrifices in the anti-fascist Resistance.
7   The English phrase was used.
8   Payment based on placement within the production chain.

The Constitution and Class Struggle: On the 100th Anniversary of Austria's Federal Constitutional Law[1]

Walter Baier

I am neither a historian nor a jurist. I am also not concerned with *the beauty of the constitution* or with historical commemoration here; my intervention deals with the interpretation of the constitution from a current, political science perspective and, if you will, that of revolutionary theory. The pandemic, the ecological crisis, the recession, digitalisation, and the state policies tackling all these challenges posed to the capitalist system – these are the questions I am concerned with.

The present recession had already set in before the corona virus pandemic, and the pandemic did not initiated but rather boosted the current restructurings of companies and technological quantum leap.

The Venezuelan economist Carlotta Pérez, a neo-Schumpeterian, shows that all the technological paradigm shifts capitalism has undergone in the past 250 years have occurred in two phases: An 'installation phase' during which the new paradigm is concretised through trial and error. The high risks of investments and laissez-faire policy in this phase means that economic leadership rests with financial capital. The result is growing inequality and financial bubbles , culminating in an economic crisis like the one we experienced in 2007/2008. The following, second phase consists in the generalised implementation of the new paradigm ('deployment phase'). This occurs under the leadership of real capital. However, since the exit from the crisis and transition to the new path of development requires, according to Pérez, state intervention, it could, also through the impact of social struggles, usher in a phase of prosperity and rising income.[2]

If this is right, the current state interventionism, which contrasts with the reactions at the beginning of the last financial crisis, would be the 'new normal'. Of course, we still need to ask whether the European Recovery

Plan and the European Commission's so lauded Green Deal meet the requirements of a transformation of European economies at all or merely suffice to reduce the technological lag behind the digital super-powers, China and the US.

But in any case, the question of the state is coming back into focus, though not in the form of a debate on whether state intervention in market processes is desirable – as in the confrontation over neoliberalism – but now in terms of the goals and methods with which state intervention ought to occur. This is the economic framework in which right-wing populists, conservatives, and liberals are fighting over a new hegemony.

My argument is: if socialists are to be more than a left wing within liberalism, this will only happen if they talk about socialism again, and not presenting it as the Promised Land but as a process of transformation.

Equilibrium of class forces?

I have a special interest in Austro-Marxism and the reflections of Otto Bauer, Karl Renner, Max Adler, Käthe Leichter, Therese Schlesinger, and Hélène Bauer, and their debates especially with Hans Kelsen, not only because they involve the Austrian Federal Constitution, but because they posed the strategic problems of a democratic socialism differentiated both from Bernsteinian reformism and Lenin's and Trotsky's Bolshevism at a theoretical level that has never since been equalled.

This was due not only to the qualities of these theorists, who ranked among the most important social scientists of their day, but by the sheer size of the Social Democratic Party in Austria, unparalleled by any party then and ever since, which in the 1920s represented the overwhelming majority of the working class.

By contrast with most of the nation-states newly founded in 1918, in which the long sought independence covered over the existing social antagonisms, the *passive revolution* in Austria, which overthrew the existing order in the interest of the bourgeoisie, intensified the class antagonisms and pressed towards a social revolution.

Otto Bauer's book *The Austrian Revolution* describes the period between 1918 and 1922, in which the adoption of the Federal Constitutional Law also occurred. There was a rapid alternation of political constellations: The *original hegemony of the socialist labour movement*, in which the establishment of a council (soviet) government would have been possible (but which in Bauer's conception could only be an episode), was followed by an *equilibrium of class forces* which was to lead to the ascendancy of bourgeois forces and – under external, economic, and military pressure – to a complete restoration of bourgeois rule.

To describe political conditions under the hegemony of the labour movement, Bauer coined the term *functional democracy*.³ Max Adler retrospectively describes this system as an idiosyncratic 'modification of parliamentary state life in which the political decision-making process no longer occurs merely through parliamentary resolutions but in which the agreement of the organisations of the major economic sectors has to be sought, above all that of the workers and employees'.⁴

For Bauer this meant 'an expansion of the idea of democracy as government with the consent of the governed', in which 'First, the constant efforts in the assemblies of party delegates and trade-union representatives, in the workers' and soldiers' councils, in the factory and barracks assemblies, [...] had to be worked out day after day in hard struggle'. He emphatically writes of 'a complete revolution in the relation of the masses to the state'.⁵ In a research proposal attributed to Käthe Leichter and written after the February 1934 defeat for the Frankfurter Institut für Sozialforschung – entitled *Autoritätsprobleme in der österreichischen Arbeiterbewegung* (Problems of Authority in the Austrian Labour Movement), this situation is described considerably more soberly as a 'suasion system' whose key figure is the 'party representative, the SPÖ's most important type of person, neither an extreme authoritarian nor revolutionary type'. 'One is almost tempted to point to the, not consistent, parallels to feudalism, which constructed a pyramid of authority with a continuous conferment chain of authority titles.'⁶

The revolutionising of the working class thus took the form of a 'statification' of the workers' party, which tried, through 'suasion', to talk the class out of revolution.

This condition was then followed by what Bauer called the 'equilibrium of class forces'. In terms of actual politics, this was about the struggle of the Christian Socials and the Social Democrats within the coalition government, in which the relations of power did not allow either party to wrest a decisive victory, thus forcing them to seek compromise.

That is why Kelsen is not wrong when he deconstructs Bauer's concept of 'equilibrium of class forces' as an attempt to reconcile Social Democracy's 1919/1920 coalition policy with Marx's and Engels's theory that the state is nothing more than an instrument of oppression in the hands of the ruling class.

This theory gets into trouble, he writes, because 'the proletariat – not least thanks to a democratic constitution⁷ – has become a political power, which directly confronts its party with the possibility, if not necessity, either alone or together with bourgeois parties, to take over the government of that state which was, in the proletariat's theory, rejected as an organisation of exploiters destined to "wither away"'.[8]

In parentheses: The concept of equilibrium of class forces had a Renaissance in the mid- to late 1970s when the Italian and French communist parties believed they had arrived in the anteroom of power and attempted conceptually to understand the problem posed by the transition to a democratic socialism – and this partly because Austro-Marxism provided a vocabulary that enabled a rapprochement with the left tendencies of Social Democracy.[9]

But back to Kelsen's observation, which as correct and keen as it was, underestimated the profundity of Bauer's analyses, above all in its socio-political aspects. For example, Bauer writes about the two successive coalition governments (1919/1920 and 1920), both of them led by a Social Democrat, Karl Renner, but with a crucial difference:

> At the time the first coalition government was formed, the sharpest clash within the government was between the peasant and Viennese branches of the Christian Socials. This antagonism was overcome as the 'home-comers' became peasants again, the peasant movement lost the strong democratic features it had in the time of upheaval, and it turned continuously more one-sidedly against the working class. The Viennese Klerikalen gradually succeeded in bringing the peasant deputies under their leadership. [...] Thus, the Christian Social Party was far stronger in the second coalition than it was in the first. The first coalition was a class alliance of the workers with the peasants. The second was a banal party coalition of Social Democrats and Christian Socials [...] with the section of the bourgeoisie represented by the urban Christian Socials, which now once again commanded the peasant vote.[10]

Here we find everything: Lenin, Gramsci, and Poulantzas.

But also Bauer's wishful thinking: 'Thus, the Republic was neither a bourgeois nor a proletarian republic; it was [...not] an instrument of the class domination of the proletariat over the bourgeoisie. In this phase it was the result of a compromise between the classes, a result of the equilibrium of class forces.'[11]

The assumption of a class-neutral state and democratic constitution is also Hans Kelsen's position, which he continually defended against both the left and the right.

Allow me the following digression: In his essay *Democracy and Socialism*, published in the US in 1955, at the height of the Cold War, Kelsen opposed Friedrich Hayek's *The Road to Serfdom* in the following terms: 'The results of the foregoing analysis is that the attempts at showing an essential connection between freedom and property, as all other attempts at establishing a closer relationship of democracy with capitalism than with socialism, or even the exclusive compatibility of democracy with capitalism, have failed. Hence our thesis stands that democracy as a political system is not necessarily attached to a definite economic system.'[12]

Class Neutrality of the State?

Kelsen intervened in the debate on state theory conducted in the mid-1920s within Austrian and German Social Democracy with an interesting essay entitled *Marx oder Lassalle*. In it, he took Bauer's theory of equilibrium at its word: Since every state is a compromise struck on the basis of the relations of force between the classes, 'it is only a difference of degree that separates the current state from 'a future one – a social construct that completely corresponds to the socialist ideal – a difference of degree consisting of purposeful reform, which cannot be elided by revolution.'[13]

This levelling of difference is something Bauer for ideological reasons did not want to accept. But his insistence on a qualitative difference between a socialist and bourgeois state comes across as weak. The precariousness of his *functional democracy* argument, which he thought made all the difference, has already been mentioned.

Yet, most of all it is the experiences of the socialisation policy he conducted that show us something completely different from a neutral state. 'Socialisation', Bauer wrote in the brochure *Der Weg zum Sozialismus (The Road to Socialism)*, should not take 'the form of brutal confiscation of capitalist property but of compensation'.[14] When the attempt was made to socialise the Alpine-Montan Mining Company, the largest industrial complex in the country, in a 'not brutal' way, it turned out that a Viennese speculator, Richard Kola, had – significantly enough, in agreement with the minister of finance, Joseph A. Schumpeter – bought up the shares of the company and re-sold them to an Italian financial group, behind which stood one of the War's victorious powers. The entire socialisation plan was thus shipwrecked.

What is interesting here is not only the *what* – 'it's the economy' – but the *how*, which Poulantzas called the *strategic selectivity of the state*, a system of filter mechanisms and prioritisations within the state – which privileges certain practices and excludes others – for instance, socialisation moves decided at top state levels – and whose ultimate cause is the social division of labour and the relations of production.

In the words of Max Adler: 'It should, incidentally, be noted that this is the reason why even a so-called workers' government, even consisting only of Social Democrats and even if based on a Social Democratic majority, can never be a socialist government as long as the proletariat is not strong enough to wrest the economic power in the state to itself. From this arises the historic tragedy of every workers' government, which certain domestic situations can make necessary, the tragedy that it too can only be a manager of the bourgeois state, even though with very radical protections and support for workers' interests. For it will at the same time be called upon to represent 'state necessities', which are still the necessities of the class state of the possessors, of the capitalist economic order.'[15] It is impossible not to think of many historical and contemporary examples that confirm this.

More realistic than the assumption of a class neutrality of the democratic state is the critique developed by the socialist-oriented German constitutional law scholar, Otto Kirchheimer, of the Weimar Constitution, which, also as an expression of a class compromise, stipulated a social obligation of property, and even allowed for the possibility of expropriations. But nevertheless, he observes, 'The great and ever-present weight of what pre-exists, in this case, private property, is even further strengthened [...] by the fact that the constitution does not pronounce on what economic system ought to prevail.'[16]

Karl Renner, who in his 1929 *Wege der Verwirklichung (Paths of Realisation)* once more raised the question of socialisation, was able to claim on the basis of empirical arguments and not only from the Austrian experience, that socialisation through the state is unthinkable as long as one does not really and permanently dominate it. This would mean that politics is at a dead end: That state is bourgeois as long as capitalist property prevails, and capitalist property cannot be socialised as long as the state is bourgeois.

Renner contrasted to what he called Otto Bauer's *Politismus (politism)* the concept of a 'socialisation through self-empowerment',[17] i.e., the idea of an *economic democracy* realised through works councils, trade unions, producer and consumer co-operatives and numerous other forms of the working class's democratic self-organisation. This '*new economy* can be prepared *as a means of free organisation*, a means of a *purely economic nature*, a means of transforming the economy from inside, *already in the womb of the old economy*'.

This argument has relevance for the present situation, for example, when the paradigm of innovation based on the idea of commons, initiated by the free and open-source software movement, is headed to become the dominant paradigm even within capitalism and has by now also been integrated by the big players such as Microsoft and Google into their business models. But what do such absorptions of non-market logic mean in the wake of technological change for the strategy of social transformation?[18]

Does Marxist state theory have to go back to the orthodox-Marxist, and in equal measure anarchist, position that socialist transformation can only be achieved from outside – against the state and the constitution? Or does democratic socialism rather consist of connecting the strategies of socialist parties aimed at political power with the construction by civil society of economic and social power in enterprises, municipalities, cooperatives?

Poulantzas rejects the simple alternative between a war of position and a war of manoeuvre à la Gramsci, because it too is based on the idea of the state as a fortress which has to be occupied and seized from the outside. 'Yet', he writes, 'the long process of coming to power through a democratic path to socialism essentially consists in opening up, strengthening, coordinating, and directing the nests of resistance scattered within the networks of the state as well as in creating and developing new centres', so that they become effective centres of power.[19]

Remarks on the socialist state

As I have said, I am convinced that if socialists are not to turn into more or less radical left liberals, they have to talk about socialism again. But at the same time, we also have to give up the idea of imagining socialism as a society of unlimited material possibilities. This is unthinkable simply due to the ecological limits of civilisation. And it is unsatisfactory, from a theoretical point-of-view, to sum up all the progressive agendas – ecology, feminism, democracy, social justice etc. – in one *grand narrative* and then call it *socialism*. The challenge does not consist in proclaiming ideals but in finding methods to put them into practice, to realise them.

In a manuscript written ca. 1927, referring to Engels's phrase about *humanity's leap from the realm of necessity into the realm of freedom*, Karl Polanyi defines socialism as that economic system whose property regime and political democracy enables humans to shape their interaction with each other and with nature – consciously, that is, freely.[20]

The way in which people live their freedom is another question, which also applies to democratic socialism. In individuating one's own ideas a comparison with the view of critical outsiders is sometimes helpful. Joseph Schumpeter, already mentioned in another context, held the, for bourgeois economists, eccentric view that socialism is the necessary consequence of capitalist decadence, and understood socialism as a societal mode of operation that is culturally indeterminate.[21] This means that socialism would be compatible with different cultural and value orientations.

This secularisation of the socialist ideal seems to me, at least from a social scientific point of view, to be worthy of consideration. Seen this way, one could distinguish between socialism as an economic *mode of operation* of society and socialism as a *moral-cultural project*, which assumes a concrete form in time and space and, above all, is imprinted by the social and political movement which puts it into practice. In that sense, the socialism we are fighting for is a democratic, an ecological, an internationalist, and a feminist project. Through the competition of ideas we would have to prove that – and show how – it can form the material basis for the realisation of those values which we want to establish as the socially leading ones in the particular historical moment in which we live.

This is how I understand Polanyi when he writes, 'Humanity will not be free until it knows the cost of its ideals. […] For only when the connection between the sacrifices to be made and the progress we hope to achieve along the path to the realisation of our ideals becomes visible in a direct, verifiable form, quantifiable down to the smallest details, can we as humans develop the drive to walk the upward path undeterred.'[22]

NOTES

1   The Federal Constitutional Law was adopted by the Constituent National Assembly of German-Austria on 1 October 1 1920. This Assembly was the outcome of the first democratic elections. The greater part of the draft was written by the philosopher of law and state theorist Hans Kelsen, the author of *Pure Theory of Law*.

2   See Carlota Pérez, 'Using the history of Technological Revolutions to help us understand the present & shape the future', 2020, <https://www.youtube.com/watchv=zKDkI3yohTc&feature=youtu.be>.

3   Otto Bauer, *Die österreichische Revolution*, (1923), Vienna: Caesarpress, 2015, p. 192; Otto Bauer, The Austrian Revolution, edited by Walter Baier and Eric Canepa, Chicago: Haymarket, 2021, p. 257.

4   Max Adler, *Politische oder soziale Demokratie* [Political or Social Democracy], Berlin: E. Laub'sche Verlagsbuchhandlung, 1926. Adler, as if he had been able to foresee the institutionalised system of social partnership practiced decades later with the participation of the Austrian Social Democratic Party, warned about the following misunderstanding of what functional democracy is: 'It has nothing to do with the wholly erroneous notion […] that it is about producing a harmony of functions within today's society so as to create a "healthy organism" out of it […] In its very nature it is a revolutionary means and can thus only fulfil its purpose, its "function", if these masses are revolution-minded and organisationally combat-ready' (pp. 151 and 154).

5   Bauer, *The Austrian Revolution*, p. 256.

6   Käthe Leichter (undated, probably 1937 and 1938), 'Vorschlag für eine Untersuchung über die Autoritätsprobleme der österreichischen Arbeiterbewegung' [Proposal for an Investigation into the Austrian Labour Movement's Problems of Authority], in Archive of the Frankfurt Institute of Social Research, *Studien zu Autorität und Familie* [Studies on Authority and Family), F 1/V Box 70

7   The Federal Constitutional Law, the major part of which Kelsen drafted.
8   Hans Kelsen, 'Marx oder Lassalle. Wandlungen in der politischen Theorie des Marxismus' [Marx or Lassalle. Changes in the Political Theory of Marxism] (1924), in *Hans Kelsen: Ausgewählte Aufsätze*, ed. and with an introduction by Norbert Leser, Vienna: Verlag der Wiener Volksbuchhandlung, 1967, p. 145.
9   See Detlev Albers, Josef Hindels, and Lucio Lombardo Radice (eds), *Otto Bauer und der 'dritte Weg': Die Wiederendeckung des Austromarxismus durch Linkssozialisten und Eurokommunisten*, Frankfurt a.M. and New York: Campus Verlag Frankfurt/New York, 1979; und Detlev Albers, Josef Cap, Pietro Ingrao, and Didier Montchane (eds), *Perspektiven der Eurolinken*, Frankfurt and New York: Campus Verlag, 1981.
10 Bauer, *The Austrian Revolution*, pp. 318-19.
11 Bauer, *The Austrian Revolution*, p. 354.
12 Hans Kelsen, 'Democracy and Socialism', The Law School of the University of Chicago: Conference on Jurisprudence and Politics, 30 April 1954, pp. 63–87
13 Kelsen, 'Marx oder Lasalle', p.160.
14 Otto Bauer, *Der Weg zum Sozialismus* [The Road to Socialism], 1921, p. 32.
15 Adler, *Politische oder soziale Demokratie*, p. 125.
16 Otto Kirchheimer, 'Weimar – und was dann? Analyse einer Verfassung' [Weimar – and What Next? Analysis of a Constitution] (1930), in Otto Kirchheimer, *Politik und Verfassung* [Politics and the Constitution], Frankfurt a.M.: Suhrkamp, 1964, p. 159.
17 Karl Renner, *Wege der Verwirklichung. Betrachtungen über politische Demokratie, Wirtschaftsdemokratie und Sozialismus* [Paths of Realisation. Reflections on Political Democracy, Economic Democracy and Socialism], Berlin: Verlag von J.H.W Dietz Nfg., 1929, p. 35
18 Marco Berlinguer, 'Experiments at the Frontier of Technological Revolution Commons, Markets and Public Policies', transform! europe e-paper, 2020, <https://www.transform-network.net/publications/issue/commons-markets-and-public-policy/>.
19 Nicos Poulantzas, *Staatstheorie. Politischer Überbau, Ideologie, Autoritärer Etatismus* [State Theory: Political Superstructure, Ideology, Authoritarian Statism], Hamburg: VSA Verlag, 2002, p. 286
20 Karl Polanyi, 'On Freedom', in Michael Brie and Claus Thomasberger (eds), *Karl Polanyi's Vision of a Socialist Transformation,* Montreal: Black Rose Books, 2018, p. 306., pp. 137-172.
21 Joseph A. Schumpeter, *Capitalism, Socialism and Democracy* (1942), , New York: Harper & Row, third edition 1950, pp. 170-71. 'In fact, according to our definition as well as to most others, a society may be fully and truly socialist and yet be led by an absolute ruler or be organized in the most democratic of all possible ways; it may be aristocratic or proletarian; it may be a theocracy and hierarchic or atheist or indifferent as to religion; it may be much more strictly disciplined than men are in a modern army or completely lacking in discipline; it may be ascetic or eudemonist in spirit; energetic or slack; thinking only of the future or only of the day; warlike and nationalist or peaceful and internationalist; equalitarian or the opposite; it may have the ethics of lords or the ethics of slaves; its art may be subjective or objective; its forms of life individualistic or standardized.'
22 Karl Polanyi 'Sozialistische Rechnungslegung' [Socialist Accounting] (1922), in *Chronik der großen Transformation. Artikel und Aufsätze (1920-1947)* p. 109.

Histories of the Greek Revolution – The Political Framing of a National Anniversary

Dimitris Kousouris and Milena Gegios

It was November 2019 when Prime Minister Kyriakos Mitsotakis delivered a speech in the Greek parliament in light of the upcoming bicentennial anniversary of the Greek War of Independence commemorated each year on 25 March. Given the special occasion, he took the opportunity to explain his understanding of this crucial event in Greek history and its relevance not only for the Greek people but also for his own administration.[1] Since taking office in 2019 he has repeatedly proclaimed the advent of a new era for Greece. The path towards this era features an obsessive focus on the real-estate sector, as projects such as Elliniko[2] and further urban prestige projects in the city of Athens have proven. But its central idea is a rupture with the notorious recent past in order to renew faith in what is to come.[3] Following that reading, the ethnic upheaval of 1821 with its dynamic character was the starting point for what 2021 is to become: the springboard to a European and globally oriented future – understood as the fourth industrial revolution.[4] Accordingly, the main pillars of the 'Greece 2021' Committee, as Mitsotakis presented them, are: the fourth industrial revolution, climate change, sustainable growth, the exploration of space, and peace and international collaboration. Acting as the state's coordinating body, the Committee has made headlines on multiple occasions: the resignation of appointed members, its rather cliché-driven media campaign,[5] or the lack of historic sensitivity when mentioning Greek political leaders on its own website.[6] While the goals of the Committee's action plan are set out very precisely, it remains unclear how they can be seriously pursued through a cultural agenda. Given the multiple crises that the Greek government is facing at the moment – economic recovery, migration, the escalating maritime border dispute with Turkey, and the pandemic – it is tempting for the government to adopt a shallow approach to the ever-growing complexity of daily life. But at what cost?

Modern Greek ideology and the national master narrative

As mentioned above, the political decision to create the 1821 bicentenary celebration committee was one of the first taken by the Nea Dimokratia (New Democracy) government in the summer of 2019. Among those invited to participate in its broader steering 'assembly', officially composed of 'no less than 24, no more than 45 persons', were some of the most prominent Greek historians and international scholars specialising in Modern Greek Studies, academic programme managers, political scientists, sociologists, a couple of artists, and a representative of the Church of Greece – and along with them several businessmen and CEOs who incarnate the country's potential for growth through the development of private initiatives with an entrepreneurial spirit.

The core ideas underlying the project address the actual situation of the country sometimes with a kind of belated apology, sometimes with a sort of rebranded 'megaloideatismos'[7] in the name of an undifferentiated 'we'. Thus, on the one hand, the goals are to 'highlight the achievements, remember the struggles and sufferings [...] while, at the same time, admit to our faults and shortcomings'. On the other hand, the President of the Republic's letter presenting the Committee is dangerously close to Ioannis Kolettis's brief description of the historical mission of Hellenism in 1844:[8]

> The landmark bicentennial anniversary of the Revolution is our opportunity [...] to show what Greece truly is: a modern state, democratic and contemporary, a country that imposes no discriminations or exclusions, an integral part of the Europe that we always illuminated and by which we were illuminated in return.[9]

Emblematic of the Committee is the song it chose to represent the whole project: 'May the Dances Never Stop' by Dionysis Savvopoulos, which marked the beginning of this ex-leftist troubadour's neo-orthodox identitarian turn. Written in the early 1980s at the time of the country's accession to the EU, its symbolisms are underpinned by an utterly nationalist re-appropriation of the old idea of 'the enduring course of Hellenism from antiquity to the present day'.[10] A joyful theme full of references to the modern Greek national popular tradition, explicit depoliticisation, religious identity, and conservative re-appropriation of cultural resistance in a video-clip filmed in the Stadium of the first Olympic Games, it represents almost every conceivable aspect of a neoliberal hodgepodge intended to justify the current state of the country and to propose a vision for its future described as 'a positive momentum within the Greek society'.[11]

It is hardly surprising that Gianna Aggelopoulou-Daskalaki, former president of the National Olympic Committee organising the 2004 Olympic Games held in Athens, was appointed head of the Greece 2021 campaign. For she can thus be the political incarnation of an age remote from the crisis-stricken realities Greek society has been experiencing since 2010, but even more, for the political elite and the liberal-conservative Nea Dimokratia party, she seems the perfect fit for the kind of revival intended by the current government. This is seen as an opportunity to escape from daily life but also for Greece to become known again as a modern, democratic, and European country ready to set its own goals for the future. The so-called 'window to the future', which serves as the Committee's credo,[12] is key to this narrative of a new forward-looking national self-esteem with the aim of re-representing Greece to the world.[13] The overall project concretises the 'we' through the individual contribution of remembrances and/or knowledge in a sort of crowd-sourcing project mediated and managed by the Committee. Thus, with the purpose of 'reintroducing Greece, from the beginning of contemporary history to today, in this course of 200 years', the goal set is 'to draw as many organizations as possible into the project Greece 2021 to "show respect to our history, honor our people, explore and highlight our country and plan our future"'.[14]

The endeavour gravitates around four pillars. The first two are quite obvious, 'Greece' then, in 1821, and today; the third, Greeks with international renown of various kinds 'who left their mark in the world'; the fourth, the future, with sublabels like 'fourth industrial revolution', 'sustainable growth', 'peace and international cooperation', 'exploration of space'.

However ambitious the projected goals sound, the priorities set seem quite limited or, to be more precise, of a rather procedural character: defining the calendar of (local and national) commemorative activities, the collection, evaluation, and selection of proposals submitted, the fundraising proposal, etc. Obviously, these are hastily created web pages, as can be seen by a list of names alphabetised partly by first names, partly by surnames, but also by several almost empty sections, with nothing more than an introductory thumbnail. Symptomatically, one of the pages with the most extensive contents is the Famous Greeks page, with texts containing short biographies of Nobel Prize and Academy Award laureates and a 200-year timeline of major artistic, scientific, and cultural events that looks more or less like a slide presentation for an introductory course in Modern Greek Studies, still open to contributions by the public for the whole of 2021.

Among the principal aims enunciated in first draft of the law creating the 1821 Committee was the promotion of a 'national narrative' with the purpose of creating a 'unified image and identity of the country and its representatives'. After receiving fierce criticism from the opposition for promoting a uniform idea of the nation, omitting the complexity and multiplicity of the past, the government withdrew this wording, substituting it with a vague mention of the 'branding' of the country's image abroad.[15] In sum, as is clear from the persons appointed, the aims and priorities publicly declared, and the Committee's first acts, the bicentenary is seen by the government as an opportunity to boost Greek self-esteem through a ritual reaffirmation of a collective 'belonging to the West'.[16] The creation of a consensus of 'positive' momentum is underlined by the emphasis on the future and integration into the 'civilised West'. Despite all kinds of rhetorical precautions to avoid various sorts of rigid and uniform nationalist discourse, the hallowed 'march towards the West' radiates at the core of the Committee's aims and principles. What counts, what matters, what is worth recounting through a 200-year-long national history are the moments, the persons, the events, and processes that exemplify how the doctrine of Greece abstracted from current and past realities can be unanimously reaffirmed and rebranded as attributes and assets of this collective belonging.

The past lasts a long time

The way people perceive and represent major historical events usually says more about them and their present than about the past events themselves. That the answers given by Greeks in a recently conducted survey on perceptions of the 1821 Greek Revolution were dominated by the famous heroes of the Revolution and combatants in the War of Independence,[17] confirms that the historical imagination of contemporary Greeks remains haunted by a heroic nationalist narrative. As expected, school textbooks generally reproduce the mainstream nationalist interpretation that the Greek Revolution of 1821 was a liberal exception to the reactionary conjuncture of post-Napoleonic Europe, a revolutionary spark in an otherwise dark Restoration era. This fits perfectly with the supra-historical conception of the nation and its continuity through the ages, as it was formed in the nineteenth century, gradually integrating classical antiquity and Byzantine Greece into the history of the Greek (alias: Hellenic) nation. However, in the fifty years since the 150th anniversary of the Greek Revolution, academic historical research has made considerable progress not only in exploring new historical evidence but also in developing conceptual tools that permit a critical stance to established mainstream and official narratives, opening the way to new hypotheses and interpretations.

For instance, we know today that the Greek revolt of 1821 was not an exceptional event against the historical tide; on the contrary, the revolt of the Greeks who managed to control almost all of the region of Morea in 1821 was quite in tune with the internal contradictions accumulated within the Ottoman Empire during the 'age of the Ayan'[18] but also with the liberal-constitutional revolutionary upheavals against absolutism throughout the old continent. On the one hand, research has shed light on the relative weakening of the Sultan's grip on the Ottoman provinces in the Balkans as in Anatolia, where a series of local revolts were triggered during the decades preceding the Greek Revolution, usually around issues of taxation and tax collection led by local notables – of which Ali Pasha Tepelenli was probably the most prominent figure. On the other hand, the Greek revolt was one of a series of revolts against the old regime after the Congress of Vienna. Thus, the Greek revolt against the Ottomans has begun to be explored as one of the four major revolutionary events of Europe in the 1820s together with the constitutional revolts against the Bourbon rulers of Southern Italy and Spain as well as the Decembrist insurrection of 1825 in Russia.[19] Historical research has begun systematically to explore the legacy in Restoration Europe of the military mobilisation of the Napoleonic period, the role of former military officers, as well as the patterns and networks of mobilisation of an informal 'liberal International' that reached its peak in the Springtime of the Peoples in 1848.[20] Furthermore, the European 'long nineteenth century' (1789-1914) has been studied as a long struggle between the elites and structures of the old regime and the revolutionary politics of the liberal bourgeoisie and the working classes.[21]

The changing paradigm in contemporary Ottoman, European, and Mediterranean studies has of course not left the historiography of the Greek Revolution untouched. After a period of construction and institutionalisation of the national master narrative, the debate has, since the centenary of 1821, been centred on the nationalist versus Marxist approaches, that is a 'national' versus a 'bourgeois' revolution. In these debates, the historical continuity of the Greek nation has not been seriously challenged.

Instead, in place of the state ideology of a continuous 'Hellenism' or 'Greek-Christian civilisation', identified mainly with the ruling elites and the church hierarchy, Marxists and liberals, after 1922, opposed the study of *Romiosini*, that is, the collective ethnic identity of Christian Greek-speaking subjects of the Byzantine Empire, thus constructing an alternative continuity rather than deconstructing the nationalist myth.

In fact, the major anniversaries of 1821 – in the 1870s, 1920s, 1970s, and 2020s – have coincided with a major realignment/re-adaptation of the country within a changing international context. And, as it happens, historiography often tells us more about the present than it does about the past. In the 1870s, the Oriental Crisis and the emergence of rival national Balkan States called for the consolidation of national history; in the 1920s, the end of the irredentist Great Idea and the interwar crisis called for new articulations between the political and the social components of the nation. If the Greek state emerged as a new frontier between the Civilised West and the Orient, the tension between the Eastern and the Western components of modern Greek history and collective identity took on new shapes and configurations after the Greek Civil War and all through the Cold War era, when Greece became a 'frontline state' of the 'Free World' against Communist totalitarianism. More recently, in the 1980s and 1990s marked by the entry of the country into the EU in 1980 and the collapse of the communist regimes in 1989-1991, although the commonplace of national history was the focus of historians, anthropologists, and political scientists, in reality the pattern of the 'march towards the West' was being consolidated at the core of the new national narrative. Even more so, the entry of the country into core of the Economic and Monetary Union of the EU in 2002, highlighted by the Athens Olympics and the Greek victory in the European football championship of 2004, seemed to mark a triumphant end of the road, the fulfilment of a collective hope, the realisation of a dream that guaranteed a future of political stability and economic prosperity.

Little did they (we) know. After the outbreak of the international capitalist crisis, the December 2008 revolt in Greece was a prelude to the Greek crisis and to the revolts of a new era. The international financial control imposed on the country and the austerity measures that pauperised large segments of the population triggered the collective fear of a return (or relegation) to the periphery of the continent, a feeling that had multiple effects in the political system during the 2010s. The collective disillusionment fuelled the electoral collapse of Pasok, the rise of Syriza, the entry of the neo-Nazi Golden Dawn in the Greek Parliament as well as the gradual polarisation between pro- and anti-Grexit sentiments that culminated in the referendum of July 2015.[22]

What Greece would most need in terms of collective momentum is a restoration of its dignity after being subjected to the harshest austerity measures in the history of the European Union and, moreover, singled out as an admonitory example by its own European partners, resulting in the near bankruptcy of the Greek state. The Greek debt/GDP ratio was 180% in

2019 and it is projected to rise to reach 200% for 2020-2021.²³ Given that a large part of the crisis is still ahead of us, those limits to national sovereignty will remain unaffected. The pandemic hit Greek private households and companies after a ten-year crisis, at the very moment when they were trying to gather their strength so that they could contribute to or be part of the so often predicted economic recovery. The cause for concern is that, today, instead of focusing on investment in public health, education, digital technology, innovation, and sustainable sources of income – beyond tourism – Greek employees and small-to-medium-size businesses are forced, once again, to fight for survival.

The Greek economy will continue to be extremely fragile in 2021, and it will once more have to deal with its precarious position. The damaging signs of the Covid-19 inspired shutdown have become visible not only in key sectors (tourism and shipping), but gradually in other areas as well. Consequently, the current government promulgated a range of fiscal measures to protect the Greek economy from the worst effects of the crisis, but it was clear from the beginning that real financial alleviation would not come without an EU engagement such as the 'Next Generation EU' recovery package comprised of grants and loans. This stirred up toxic memories of the bailout era with its austerity policies and intrusive monitoring by the European lenders. The first reactions of the Mitsotakis government were therefore quite lukewarm, also given that the Prime Minister's first inaugural visits were mainly about restoring trust in the chilled intergovernmental relations with Germany and the Netherlands. The highly ambivalent image of Greece that dominated in the years of the crisis needed to be rebranded through the same old 'positive associations': hospitality, the sea, the sun, the islands, and gastronomy. And so the Greek summer became the 'state of mind' of a highly risky political and economic gamble in times of the pandemic.

The reawakening of Orientalist and Balkanist discourses about the lazy and corrupt southerners, Brexit, the multiple divisions within the EU, the rise of xenophobic far-right parties, the new tensions between Greece and Turkey in the Eastern Mediterranean – these are all effects of the underlying circumstances that call into question the country's position within the 21st-century world order. As mentioned above, scholarly research of the last half century has in various ways explored the emergence of modern Greece as a process related to the region's balance of power and variable geography, a process far more complex and interesting than a heroic narrative of integration into the 'civilised West' that retrospectively justifies the present state and position of the country within the international system. From this point of view, it is paradoxical that a committee charged with organising the commemoration of a major historical event adopts a posture overtly directed towards the future and turns a blind eye to the findings of scholarly research, thus completely ignoring the opportunity to build infrastructures for further research. Nevertheless, a series of lectures by historians of modern Greece – members of the Committee – to be mainly held online due to the pandemic, may provide a window on academic research for the general public, but it still does not provide much in terms of the development of our historical knowledge or the possibility of building and maintaining research infrastructure in this area for generations to come.

Although they always coincided with times of crisis, all major anniversaries of the Greek Revolution were marked by the creation of different forms of research infrastructure for this historical event, going from the collection and publication of the combatants' memoirs, to the organisation and indexing of the relevant records at the central and/or regional level. This time, the official commission's priorities include no such plans. However, a series of research projects in the last few years aimed at a digital mapping of historical evidence regarding the event or the monuments memorialising the Revolution,[24] indicate opportunities that exist for building digital and archival infrastructures that are bridges between scholars and researchers working in different settings and specialising in different fields. Meanwhile, the research programmes organised and the publications announced in view of the bicentenary bring to light a potential for historical research that has up to now remained unexploited, especially regarding historical evidence previously inaccessible to researchers. Thus, a series of books has been announced updating the historical knowledge of a broader educated public by disseminating the findings of recent scholarly research, mainly studies on key personalities of the War of Independence or narrative reconstructions of the events.[25] Not unexpectedly, what is distinctive about the new studies to appear in 2021-2022 is, first of all, their focus on the transnational dimension of the Greek Revolution – its international links and its ideological and political impact across and outside of the Ottoman Empire. This certainly involves already familiar themes such as philhellenism or international relations, but also less studied aspects such as global perceptions in Europe, North America, and beyond. A second distinctive feature of the new research on 1821 is the thorough consideration of the Ottoman context of the Greek uprising to include the politics and ideology not only of the insurgents but also of the 'others': the Ottoman administration, the Muslim subjects, or the intermediary ethno-religious groups.[26]

All things considered, the past of modern Greece, like the human past in general, will continue to be explored, revised, and reinterpreted on the basis of the questions posed by the present. The 2021 Committee created by the Greek government to organise the celebration of the bicentenary of the outbreak of the Greek Revolution is a typical example of Public Private Partnership in our neoliberal times. In this instance, the state adopts the role of a strategic investor that transfers its responsibility for scientific research and national memory to private partners (mainly funds and cultural institutes), which are the main financiers of the project. Thus, historical knowledge is of little importance. When it comes to national memory, the present or past reality also matters little; instead what counts most is rebranding it and selling it at a better price to the country's strategic partners. Nevertheless, both historical research and collective memory persist in doing the work of revising and deepening our understanding of the past and present, beyond or despite the ideological uses of the past to justify the present.

NOTES

1   See <https://primeminister.gr/2019/11/07/22493>.
2   See <https://mohegangaming.com/2019/10/08/mohegan-gaming-entertainment-unveils-the-concept-behind-inspire-athens-a-landmark-integrated-resort-and-casino-development-for-the-hellinikon-project/>.
3   See <https://primeminister.gr/2019/11/07/22493>.
4   <https://primeminister.gr/2019/11/07/22493>.
5   Romanos Gerodimos, "To ethniko afigima kai i Epitropi "Ellada 2021"" [The National Narrative and the 'Greece 2021' Committee], <https://www.athensvoice.gr/politics/687890_ethniko-afigima-kai-i-epitropi-ellada-2021>.
6   See <https://thepressproject.gr/i-angelopoulou-yperaspizete-tin-syberilipsi-diktatoron-ke-dosilogon-apo-tin-ellada-2021/>.
7   Great Idea, the ideology of Greek irredentism from the 1840s until 1922, in various versions according to which the Greek state should become the hegemonic regional power by 'liberating' the Greeks of the Ottoman Empire and Eastern Mediterranean.
8   According to the first formulation by Prime Minister Ioannis Kolettis in 1844: 'Greece is the center of Europe; positioned thus, and having to its right the East, and to its left the West, it has been destined, on the one hand, by falling, to enlighten the West and, on the other, by being reborn, to enlighten the East.' See Balázs Trencsényi and Michal Kopeček (eds), *National Romanticism: The Formation of National Movements: Discourses of Collective Identity in Central and Southeast Europe 1770–1945*, volume II, Budapest: Central European University Press, 2007, p. 247-248.
9   See <https://www.greece2021.gr/en/letter-of-president.html>.
10 <https://www.greece2021.gr/en/may-the-dances-never-stop.html>.
11 <https://www.greece2021.gr/en/committee-greece-2021/the-objective-of-the-committee.html>.
12 <https://www.greece2021.gr/en/letter-of-president.html>.
13 Official YouTube Channel of Greece 2021, <https://www.youtube.com/watch?v=1ATUYvlHFuk>.

14 <https://www.greece2021.gr/en/communication/faq/1698-which-are-the-main-priorities.html>.

15 TVXS (2019), <https://tvxs.gr/news/ellada/ta-pairnei-piso-i-kybernisi-gia-ethniko-afigima-toy-ellada-2021>; *Efimerida ton Syntakton* (2019), <https://www.efsyn.gr/politiki/boyli/206319_ethniko-afigima-toy-ellada-2021-kai-oi-antirriseis-boytsi-dritsa>.

16 Center for Liberal Studies – Markos Dragoumis/KEFiM (2020), <https://www.kefim.org/en/how-do-greeks-see-the-revolution-of 1821/>.

17 Theodoros Kolokotronis, Georgios Karaiskakis, and Laskarina Bouboulina, *Panelladiki Erevna KEFiM*, 2019, <https://www.kefim.org/wp-content/uploads/2020/07/Apotelesmata_Pos-vlepoun-oi-Ellhnes-to-1821_FINAL.pdf>, p. 17.

18 Bruce McGowan, 'The Age of the Ayans, 1699-1812', in Halil İnalcık and Donald Quataert (eds), *An Economic and Social History of the Ottoman Empire*, Cambridge: Cambridge University Press, 1992, vol. 2, pp. 637-758.

19 Perhaps the most characteristic recent comparative study of the revolts of the 1820s is the posthumous book by Richard Stites, *The Four Horsemen. Riding to Liberty in Post-Napoleonic Europe*, Oxford: Oxford University Press, 2014.

20 See, for example, Maurizio Isabella and Konstantina Zanou (eds), *Mediterranean Diasporas. Politics and Ideas in the Long 19th Century*, London-New Delhi-New York-Sydney: Bloomsbury, 2016; and an older debate in Marion S. Miller, 'A "Liberal International"? Perspectives on Comparative Approaches to the Revolutions in Spain, Italy, and Greece in the 1820s', *Mediterranean Studies* 2 (1990), 61-67.

21 See Arno J. Mayer, *The Dynamics of Counterrevolution in Europe, 1870-1956. An Analytic Framework*, (New York: Harper & Row, 1971; and Arno J. Mayer, *The Persistence of the Old Regime: Europe to the Great War*. New York: Pantheon. 1981.

22 See Dimtris Dalakoglou, '"From the Bottom of the Aegean Sea" to Golden Dawn: Security, Xenophobia, and the Politics of Hate in Greece', *Studies in Ethnicity and Nationalism* 13, 3 (2013), 514-522.

23 See IMF (2020), *Country Data Greece*, <https://www.imf.org/en/Countries/GRC>.

24 See, for example, the initiative of the Research Centre for the Humanities, <https://www.rchumanities.gr/en/1821digitalarchive/> and the programme of the Research Centre for Modern History of Panteion University, <https://keni.panteion.gr/index.php/el/topoi-mnimis-gia-tin-epanastasi>.

25 Thanos Veremis and Iakovos Michailidis, *Ioannis Kapodistrias. O amnos tis paligenesias ton Ellinon*, Athens, 2020; Athanasios Syroplakis, *Petrobeis Mavromichalis*, Athens, 2020; Lena Divani, *'To pikro potiri: O Kapodistrias, i Roxandra kai i Ellada*, Athens, 2020; Athina Kakouri, *1821 i arhi pou den* oloklirothike, Athens, 2020.

26 For an introduction to recent scholarly research on the Ottoman context of the Greek Revolution see Dimitris Dimitropoulos, Christos Loukos, and Panagiotis Michailaris (eds), *Opseis tis Epanastais tou 1821. Conference Proceedings, Athens,* 12 -13 June 2015, Athens, 2018. Along with a series of studies on Ottoman narratives and perceptions (see Leonidas Moiras, *I Elliniki Epanastasi mesa apo ta matia ton Othomanon* and Marinos Sariyannis and Sophia Laiou, *Othomanikes afighiseis gia tin Elliniki* Epanastasi, both published in Athens, 2020), see the various contributions in the Research Programme of the Hellenic Parliament Foundation and the Hellenic Open University '200 years from the Greek Revolution' that will soon appear in a collective volume.

The Marxist-Christian Dialogue

Catholics and the Economy: Pope Francis's Narrative and the Challenges for Today's Economy

Bernhard Callebaut

Ever since the 4 October 2020 publication of the last encyclical, *Fratelli tutti*,[1] analysts have been trying to interpret what is happening in the Catholic Church, and with Pope Francis in particular. Everyone is looking for elements that help in understanding the present period. A recent video interview was entitled: 'Not all comrades but brothers. A post-communist Pope?'[2]

What is happening? Is the Pope reaching out to everyone, including the political left? The encyclical letter points explicitly to the example of the fraternal relationship with a major representative of the Islamic world.[3] Is it legitimate to think that not even the left's well-known difficulty with religion impedes the Pope from building bridges in that direction? What does Ermis Segatti, the famous Italian theologian, mean to say when he stresses that in this period of history the Pope prefers the formula 'brothers' and not 'comrades'! Perhaps Francis of Assisi's vocabulary is needed because the left's language has exhausted its power of attraction – with the Pope the new leader and point of reference in the long road of the poor towards universal social justice?

In the framework of a 'Catholic' article in a journal like the *transform! yearbook* the question arises of whether something is hidden behind Segatti's phrase. A banal confirmation that the Berlin Wall has definitively fallen and that now another rhetoric is supplying substance in times of Covid? That the rhetoric of brotherhood, interpreted in a Catholic way by the Pope, is now providing the narrative that is to resolve the world's problems? Perhaps this was the intention behind the title. But I would like to suggest another, broader interpretation. I begin with the fact that for some time now it has no longer been so obvious that the left narrative on religion has remained unchanged (and entangled) in the 'toolbox of key concepts', in this case the 'opium of the peoples' – which in my readings does not even correspond to Marx's thinking, more nuanced and refined as it is than what later vulgar versions passed off as Marxism. And, in parallel, the Catholic Church's discourse has not remained the same in 130 years of cultivating its social doctrine.

Moving within a transversal dialogue

For decades now, things have been changing on this level. But where are we now? I would like to begin with an account published in a recent book[4] arising from a dialogue initiative between European leftists and Catholics, academics, and activists – called Dialop – supported by the interest of the Pope in it and that of Vatican officials. In 2014, on the occasion of a private audience with representatives of the Party of the European Left, among them the future Greek prime minister Alexis Tsipras and the then coordinator of transform!europe Walter Baier, Pope Francis expressed his conviction that in the face of the challenges of wars, poverty in the world, the environmental crisis, and migration, these enormous problems could not be solved by a single force, not even by the Church. He thus expressed his belief that only a transversal dialogue among people of good will could indicate the path to be travelled. All brothers already, one might think. An isolated event? A great leap forward by a Pope in search of allies in developing his ecological programme, right after having published *Laudato si'*? The great war reporter Ryszard Kapuściński wrote: 'Every time a man meets another man, he has always had three possibilities to choose from: wage war on him, isolate oneself behind a wall, or establish a dialogue.'[5] As a style of life, Pope Francis has chosen the third possibility.

A note: Throughout his pontificate, there have been occasional accusations that Bergoglio is a communist. This is what Segatti – or whoever wrote the title 'a post-communist Pope' – was alluding to. Still today, the accusation is readily levelled by a certain section of the media, even when the pope is only referring to a social issue peripherally. Those who still remember history know that the same was said of good Pope John XXIII (Pope from 1958 to 1963), and even Pope Pius XII (1939-1958), both of them light years away from being philo-communists in the epoch of the Stalinist model of communism. On occasion even the Fathers of the Church have used strong words, Augustine of Hippo maintaining that 'the overabundant wealth of the rich is the life necessity of the poor. Possessing overabundant wealth means possessing things that belong to others'.[6] In a very recent address to the Roman Curia on 21 December 2020, Pope Francis recalled: 'I think of what that saintly Brazilian bishop used to say: "When I am concerned for the poor, they call me a saint; but when I keep asking why such great poverty exists, they call me a communist".[7]

The Pope has shown himself to be attentive to what is helpful in opening up an approach more marked by a sense of social justice going in the direction of activism and preference to be given the poor in economic activity.[8] Also well known is his attention to popular movements, whose existence he regards as necessary[9] and whose representatives he has invited to the Vatican.[10] Recently, there has been prominent coverage of his dialogue dating back to 2016 with representative figures from a certain number of large enterprises who are seeking a relationship to him and aim to develop a more inclusive capitalism. Above all a stir was caused by the summer 2019 statement by some 200 US companies who declared that only increasing profits for stockholders, and subordinating all else to this goal, is a mistake. In the document they disown the mantra that has long guided company policies. To create value, according to the statement, attention has also to paid to ecological impact, to respecting the customers, and 'to dignified conditions for employees'.[11] These are interesting signs coming from large corporations, which need to be followed even if it is not easy to judge their real impact.

Things thus seem to be moving in a leftward direction, even in corporations that are not completely entangled in neoliberalism! I recall an expression used by the economist Stefano Zamagni regarding the economic sphere when he quotes the founder of the initiative Economy of Communion, Chiara Lubich:[12] 'I well understood that however much villainy there is, man is not capable of absolute evil.'[13] In this regard I also remember a conversation with the theologian and ecologist Leonardo Boff in September 1988 in Petropolis (province of Rio de Janeiro) when he told me that Liberation Theology and the Base Ecclesial Communities movement were not able to have more impact on social injustice in Brazil because they had not succeeded in interesting the middle classes in their struggle.[14] In a certain sense, the Pope speaks with everyone, that is, without excluding anyone a priori, which certainly does not prevent him from stating clearly and strongly the line of march he wants to take, starting with a strong critique of the present. And he encourages those who say they would like to move in the sense of the common good, whether from the right or the left. This recalls Pope John XXIII who said he did not ask where people came from but where they wanted to go!

The pre-condition: Recuperating the prophetic voice – some history

But what is happening? Why are the inheritors of the socialist tradition with its thousands of currents considered brothers by Pope Bergoglio, that is, credible interlocutors for confronting the evils of our time? A critical attitude towards the current world situation is not a monopoly of the socialist left, even if that camp can boast of a great tradition. In truth, the role of 'prophet' of social friendship, of social love that Segatti attributes to Pope Bergoglio is accompanied by his strong words against the reigning system. The question arises: Can a Pope express himself to this extent? The issue requires historical perspective, and we see that it is not an absolute novelty in the history of Christianity.

The authors – and first among them Karl Jaspers[15] – who have studied the so-called Axial Age mean by this term the nearly simultaneous irruption in five different areas in Eurasia of prophets, philosophers, and wise men: Confucius and Lao Tzu in China, the Upanishads and Buddha in India, Zarathustra in Iran, the prophets of Israel in the Middle East, Homer, the philosophers, and the tragedians in the West. Scholars note that these religions and currents of thought arose within societies precisely when they were characterised by the traditional fusion between political power and local religions of cities or tribes. Looking at a more evolved society, in Pharaonic Egypt the Pharoah was both a political and a religious figure, a king and the son of gods. In the pre-Axial period there was indeed no concept of dichotomy between religion and politics.[16] The Axial Age introduces – and we can perhaps better understand this when we look at the role of the prophets who oppose the kings in the history of Israel – 'higher' principles that spark the birth of a dialectic between politics and religion that was to increasingly determine the course of history. If Pope Bergoglio today admonishes the dominant economic system, introducing higher principles, he is aligning himself with this ancient tradition of 'social' criticism. Christianity has passed through different periods, following this tradition with greater or lesser vigour, a tradition which we could define – at least in the field of social justice – as a work of mediation between the poor of society and the powerful. But the Church, or at least important figures within it, has in every epoch played a prophetic role in favour of the poor and in general of the less affluent classes.

In broader historical perspective, we ought to remember that in its first centuries Christianity clearly developed concrete action for the poor – the widows, orphans, the sick, the elderly – that inspired admiration in the pagan world.[17] Then, after the collapse of the ancient world, and having to revive a European society in tatters, it was given the task of building the necessary cadres for the new ruling classes and in so doing lost in (great) part its prophetic vocation of social criticism.

The importance of its public role diminished in recent centuries. With the French Revolution the Church has been pushed out of this public role to end up confined to the private sphere at the hands of the liberal bourgeoisie – with its noted anti-clericalism – and then of socialism and communism, clearly anti- or at least a-religious. Where it maintained a cultural impact the Church attempted a third path, allying itself more, however, with the political right than with the left,[18] and this most likely not so much out of visceral sympathy for liberal conservatism but more – if not only – due to the militant atheism that was fully expressed, starting with the Soviet revolution, in the twentieth century.

Today the reality is no longer exactly the same. Two or three emerging elements show that the situation has fundamentally changed. At present, when the Catholic Church – and a fortiori all the other churches – no longer is a political weight in the sense of a party, measurable in elected parliamentarians, it is, at least in part, recuperating its more prophetic role as humanity's critical consciousness. In addition, in its recent concrete history, the evolution of the Latin American church has its own specific weight, with its preferential option for the poor as a course of action adopted since 1968. And then there was the turn represented by the Second Vatican Council, the result of which was a Church becoming (much) less conditioned by a political right that legitimated its appeal in support of the Church because the left could be characterised as atheist and anti-clerical.[19] All this lets us understand why the left too has begun to consider religion as not necessarily a negative factor for social progress but quite the opposite.

A less anti-clerical and atheist left and Catholics less conditioned by those who would maintain the status quo

But is a meeting between Catholics and people of the left, who have historically been enemies or at least strong antagonists based on their respective theoretical traditions and critiques of reality, to construct a transversal dialogue between people of good will really possible? We would admittedly have to show that bridges also existed in the past, and probably more numerous than have been supposed. But today there is a third element emphasised by the Pope: the world crisis situation.

To start from the assumption that we are people of good will, actually 'brothers' as Pope Bergoglio would say, indicates that we have something to give each other reciprocally in this historical period. Yes, the history of past antagonisms is a factor. But recent history has also shown that both traditions have taken some steps forward and have learned from the past. Moreover, an awareness has emerged that in the face of the immense problems we cannot allow ourselves to presuppose agreement on everything before we start to move together and that we can already start to move when we have some solid elements in common.[20] And, as often happens, it is the presence of a third element, the global climate and economic crisis and the phenomenon of migrations, which makes the idea of greater collaboration inescapable. Thus, even if we know that on certain issues our positions are very distant, this does not suffice to stop the transversal dialogue, as Pope Francis has defined it. He explains for anyone who cares to understand it that we have to set processes in motion, not occupy positions. But is it true that we have things to give each other? Critical social theory, as expressed in the well-known piece by Walter Benjamin on capitalism as religion,[21] is fascinating to a Catholic such as myself. And I have never under-valued the Biblical roots – and thus the link to the prophetic tradition of the Old Testament – that underlie Marx's vision. But, because I am more familiar with it, I would prefer to expand on something that is moving within Catholic sensibility.

If we do not agree on everything are we in agreement on nothing? Differentiated consent

Supporting the Pope's vision, according to which we need to set processes in motion rather than occupy spaces, I can report an experience that is bearing fruit also in the field of conflict and disagreement management and the transformation of disagreement into acceptable diversity. It involves the still existing separation between the evangelical churches and the Catholic church. The process through which – after a 500-year dispute that has dramatically divided Christian Europe – Protestants and Catholics have managed to mend the tear and at least make peace over a central issue of their original dispute – justification through works or only through faith? – is now being called the differentiated consensus approach, a term coined by Harding Meyer[22] between 1987 and 1995 and adopted in the Joint Declaration of Augsburg in 1999 of the World Lutheran Federation and the Catholic Church.

> What is involved is a 'consensus that is differentiated within itself' that always contains two consensual affirmations in relation to the doctrinal question under discussion: a declaration of agreement on what is collectively considered the fundamental and essential point in the doctrinal question. And a common declaration that explains why in the doctrinal problem the remaining differences can be considered admissible and legitimate and not threatening to the fundamental or essential agreement.

'In Harding Meyer', Franz Kronreif writes,[23] 'differentiated consensus is both (and most importantly) the result and the path that leads to the result. After Meyer, differentiated consensus has been much discussed, criticised, and further developed by others.' It is obvious that our context will itself undergo still other changes, simply because what is involved is more than two churches in dialogue; and thus we might find a more appropriate name for the approach. However, the result, in my opinion, corresponds more or less to what was said above. But is the Catholic Church truly a good partner for this process? Does it understand something of the mechanisms of economic life?

The Church has never had its own theory of the economy: Has something begun to move in 'Catholic' thinking? 'The Economy of Francesco'

'It is the first time in the history of the Church that an event has been organised whose exclusive theme is the economy.'[24] We are not speaking of Leo XIII's 1891 encyclical *Rerum novarum* but of the meeting of 2000 young economists and entrepreneurs, an event held in November 2020 in Assisi, called The Economy of Francesco. The quotation is from one of the organisers of the event, Stefano Zamagni, professor of political economy in Bologna and current chair of the Pontifical Academy of Social Sciences in the Vatican. And he insists that 'we can say that in terms of the economy as such nothing like this has ever occurred'!

In fact, since 1891 the Church essentially has taken up reflections on ethical and social aspects of the Industrial Revolution but not on the economy as such, as the French sociologist Émile Poulat pointed out at the end of the 1980s.[25] In his research on the Church's cultural reaction in the face of economic thought, Poulat expressed the belief that economics 'always was, on the terrain of the social, the Achille's heel of the Catholic Church. Today we see that the Church has provided social thinking but never real economic thinking. […] [Catholics] have lived randomly, without worrying about gathering their experience with a view to a specific doctrinal development'.

Poulat explained the reasons for this[26] and, considering the span of time from the Middle Ages up to the present, he observed a triple separation: in the first place, between the social teachings of the Catholic magisterium and the reality lived by the Christian people; in the second place, a separation between the economy and religion – 'it is as with the sciences: they formed outside the Church and they only requested of themselves the principle of their development'. And in the third place, the separation between economy and the social: '[…] as if there were a division of labour: for the entrepreneurs the economy, for the workers the social. Their antinomy, throwing the Church back on the side of the social, reinforced the two preceding effects.'[27] And staying with the French sociologist's acute analysis:[28] 'All began in the long conflict between holy poverty [the Catholic approach, symbolised by Saint Francis] and holy enrichment [Calvin and the bourgeois of Geneva], where pastors and theologians moved in their own territory. With sanctity gone, two naked forces confronted each other directly. The question for Catholic thinking then remains to work out what role it can and should play here.'[29]

Meanwhile, in the years after Poulat wrote, the Church has begun to think more systematically about the economy, among other places in the well-known 1986 letter of the US episcopate *Economic Justice for All*[30] (published in Italian in 1987). In any case, the question remains whether in 2021, after 33 years, the Catholic world has overcome its difficulty in thinking about the economy. In 1991 the initiative Economy of Communion certainly contributed to make the Catholic world think in new channels to interpret the economy starting with a vital initiative within the economy itself, putting pressure on entrepreneurs[31] and appealing to their talent for producing wealth, inviting them 1) to invest profits in aid to the poor, 2) promote a culture of sharing, and 3) to reinvest in their own company. The initiative also breathed new life into theoretical reflection,[32] which has in recent decades in fact rediscovered strands of economic thought that had existed for centuries but were marginalised by mainstream economic thinking. I am referring to the *civil economy*,[33] a line of economic thinking that, having appeared in the late 1990s, is re-emerging, also through economic phenomena that are not completely explainable through the lenses of the more traditional economy, offering categories that are able to explain more inclusive forms of economy. There is a passage in the encyclical *Caritas in veritate* (2009) by Benedict XVI that quite well synthesises where the reflection on civil economy had arrived:

> *Economic life* undoubtedly requires *contracts*, in order to regulate relations of exchange between goods of equivalent value. But it also needs *just laws* and *forms of redistribution* governed by politics, and what is more, it needs works redolent of the *spirit of gift*. The economy in the global era seems to privilege the former logic, that of contractual exchange, but directly or indirectly it also demonstrates its need for the other two: political logic, and the logic of the unconditional gift.[34]

In 2020, all of this led to the initiative named *The Economy of Francesco*.[35]

It is impossible not to think that in 2020 – with a Pope who, on the basis of the 1968 Medellin statement's preferential option for the poor, has given this sensibility a worldwide audience – fundamental steps forward are being taken in the Catholic Church. Perhaps we are really at the beginning of a new season when the Church is becoming the mediator between strong powers and the poor, but this time emphasising prophetic discourses suited to our globalised world, undergirded by a more credible economic analysis of the situation. The Church does not, at any rate, want to do this alone; there is need of people of good will everywhere to succeed in this endeavour, and this explains the Pope's – and not only his – behaviour based on 'transversal' opening.

The Economy of Francesco – we need a transformation, not a reform: five proposals

A deeper understanding of why Pope Bergoglio has inserted into the Catholic world's narrative very strong expressions that communicate his criticism of the world economic situation would require a more dedicated study. I will mention two of the strongest phrases: 'such an economy kills' and creates 'a "throw away" culture'.[36] The terms used are harsh, and more than one observer has noted an apocalyptic tone in the papal analysis.[37] It is then understandable why the Catholic world is by now not amazed when a well respected economist like Zamagni, in front of the audience of the Economy of Francesco platform, defines the situation no longer in terms of 'reform' but of the need for 'transformation'. These analyses press towards more concrete steps. To give an example, I summarise Zamagni's five proposals here, which give a rather clear idea of how positions on the economic and ecological crises are being formulated every day in the Catholic world.[38]

In Zamagni's view, we need to prioritise the problem of finance, which now seems to dominate the economy and which has become self-referential and functional only for itself, or for very few. And we also need to prioritise the rules that govern globalisation, which have remained those of Bretton Woods (1944), which were laid down by the leading industrialised countries of the Western world. It is essential to confront the endemic and systemic increase of inequalities (of income, wealth, and opportunity) between genders, different ethnicities, and other categories. Equally urgent is the environmental question and vast public policies on the abolition of combustible fossil fuels and the use of plastic, to give just two examples. We need to promote energy transition on the model of the circular economy, as a substitute for linear energies. At the same time we must work to preserve free spaces in the face of artificial intelligence (AI) with algorithms and robots that make decisions. Do we have a transversal programme here?

The inversion: the means have become the ends! The need to rethink: produce and distribute – the stimulus of the civil economy

It appears that on the terrain of fundamental reflection there is ample space to find material for a dialogue and therefore find elements to build the hoped for transversal ethic. With Pope Bergoglio, the basic criterion increasingly appears clear, that is: Does the action chosen help activate the preferential option for the poor? The idea of transforming our economic policies, measuring them according to this criterion, clearly connects to the basic sensibility of the diverse socialist family. Therefore, we can probably always continue to work more on this.

Between economy and politics the means seem to have become the ends. The relationship between the economic and political spheres seems to have been inverted: the reign of means – the economic sphere – has become the end (which would be the field reserved for politics per se). In the world of schools and of high culture, it is the economic sphere that dictates the line, no longer the democratic exchange of opinions.

Adam Smith might have helped us understand how to increase wealth (the issue of production) but today we need to look with more critical eyes inside those growth mechanisms and re-orient them. Among a thousand possible authors, I quote Edgar Morin, a thinker with stimulating ideas at this level, with the perspective of 'substituting the hegemony of quantity with the hegemony of quality, the obsession of more with the obsession of better'. He proposes, moreover, that we rethink by adopting more sensible criteria for production,[39] and for this he has more concrete proposals. The Italian school of civil economy also has valuable lessons to help us orient ourselves. But we can also enrich our approach to welfare in terms of wealth distribution, taking account of the persistent poverty in the rich north but above all the continually more alarming imbalance between the world's north and south, and in the worlds of the south among the few rich and the impoverished middle and working classes and the discarded masses excluded from development. If the option has to be to transform the economic model, what does it mean to say: begin with a preferential option for the poor?

Good practices, leading figures, specific emerging theories: The Global Compact on Education

It is not only Morin who sees that we need to find 'a progressive path' of change.[40] There are a plethora of proposals. Are there good practices to study and propose together with broader platforms? Bottom-up actions to carry out? Considering how 'economic oligarchies orient the decisions of a power guided by the neoliberal creed – they parasitise and paralyse the state, dictate laws and directives to it, blocking beneficial laws; they dominate and control industrial and agricultural production, vast sectors of the service economies, the digital economy' – we ask ourselves how we can react and not submit? Are there already good practices on this terrain?

What power does the consumer have, for instance? The words quoted above are not those of Pope Francis but Edgar Morin.[41] It would certainly be useful to study the possibilities that arise from the power of the consumer: '[…] consumer society that makes the consumer dependent on the producer can give the consumer, if he emancipates himself, a power over the producer'.[42] What can a common transversal critical sensibility offer here? What examples can non-violent struggles in this field offer for current issues like the arms race, the green deal, etc.?

I am also thinking of another side of a cultural education in the transversal ethic. There are historic figures who are seen as examples, particularly if they have combined inspiration and the ethic of religious or spiritual or humanistic conviction with social commitment. We have already had the experience in the Dialop initiative of unforgettable moments when such figures have been evoked, which a leftist friend called 'our saints in common'.[43]

And to expand the volume of cultural and academic contributions that complement left critical theoretical writings and those of the Christian world, and not just Catholic, we certainly find stimulating and transversal thinking in the studies on the gift paradigm, on dialogue and its bases and preconditions, conviviality, leadership in a complex world, and the preferential option for the poor. And there is a vast field of urgent concrete issues on which to work transversally – we need only think of hunger in the world, the arms race ('swords to ploughshares'), the urgent environmental questions, the example of Amazonia, the intercultural question within the broader issue of migrations, etc.

We have to bear in mind that every process of change requires an educational process. Dialop has always been convinced of this, and it was in this sense that it organised a first summer school in September 2018 in Syros, Greece, with 40 young scholars and activists from both sensibilities. In his discourse on the need for a new Global Compact on Education,[44] the Pope quoted Michel de Certeau, who speaks of the transformative power of education: 'To educate is to take a risk and to hold out to the present a hope that can shatter the determinism and fatalism that the selfishness of the strong, the conformism of the weak and the ideology of the utopians would convince us is the only way forward.' 'To educate', Francis continues, 'is always an act of hope, one that calls for cooperation in turning a barren and paralyzing indifference into another way of thinking that recognizes our interdependence.' It is certainly not only the Pope who feels the need for a new global education pact; for several years now European left figures and committed Catholic activists and academics, with respect for each other's different histories, have been building a fraternal dialogue – Dialop. They certainly feel close to Pope Francis's conviction that there needs to be education for change: '[…] the whole world is deeply interconnected, and […] we need to find other ways, based on a sound anthropology, of envisioning economics, politics, growth and progress'.[45]

NOTES

1. Encyclical Letter *Fratelli tutti* of the Holy Father Francis on Fraternity and Social Friendship, at <http://www.vatican.va/content/francesco/en/encyclicals/documents/papa-francesco_20201003_enciclica-fratelli-tutti.html>.
2. See interview with Ermis Segatti at <https://www.youtube.com/watch?v=xSfqIXc1QqI>.
3. *Fratelli tutti*, §§ 5 and 285.
4. 'On September 18, 2014, I witnessed the conversation between Pope Francis, the future Greek Prime Minister, Alexis Tsipras and Walter Baier. The pontiff declared that war, poverty, environmental crisis and the consequent migratory flows were too serious issues to be resolved by a single force, including the Catholic Church. He considered transversal dialogue between people of goodwill as the only way forward, crossing the fences of their respective vision of the world', Walter Baier, Cornelia Hildebrandt, and Franz Kronreif (eds), *Europe as a Common. Exploring Transversal Social Ethics,* Münster: LIT, 2020, p. 24.
5. Quoted in Raniero Regni, 'La grande pedagogia delle civiltà', in Karl Jaspers, *Origine e senso della storia*, Milan: Mimesis, 2014, p. xiv.
6. Augustine, *Ennarationes in psalmos* CXLII, 12: 'Caetera quae superflua jacent, aliorum sunt necessaria. Superflua divitum, necessaria sunt pauperum. Res alienae possidentur cum superflua possidentur' <https://www.augustinus.it/latino/esposizioni_salmi/index2.htm>.
7. <http://www.vatican.va/content/francesco/en/speeches/2020/december/documents/papa-francesco_20201221_curia-romana.html>, §10.
8. An example: 'In my Encyclical *Laudato Si'*, I invited everyone to cooperate in caring for our common home and to confront together the challenges that we face. […] Now, a few years later, I renew my invitation to dialogue on how we are shaping the future of our planet and the need to employ the talents of all, since all change requires an educational process aimed at developing a new universal solidarity and a more welcoming society.' *Message of His Holiness Pope Francis for the Launch of the Global Compact on Education*, 12 September 2019, <https://www.vatican.va/content/francesco/en/messages/pont-messages/2019/documents/papa-francesco_20190912_messaggio-patto-educativo.html>.
9. For example, see *Fratelli tutti*, §169.

10 See Papa Francesco, *Terra, casa, lavoro. Discorsi ai movimenti popolari,* (Alessandro Santagata, ed.), Florence: Ponte alle Grazie, 2017.
11 See <http://www.vita.it/it/article/2019/08/19/prima-gli-azionisti-non-piu/152417/> and <http://www.vatican.va/content/francesco/en/speeches/2019/november/documents/papa-francesco_20191111_consiglio-capitalismo-inclusivo.html>.
12 <https://www.edc-online.org/en/>. For an academic presentation see the article on 'Economia di Comunione' in Giuseppe Argiolas, Luigino Bruni, and Stefano Zamagni (eds), *Dizionario di economia civile,* Rome: Città Nuova, 2009, pp. 332-45.
13 Quoted in Stefano Zamagni, 'Un'economia per il mondo', in Maurizio Gentilini, Anna Maria Rossi, and Giuliano Ruzzier, *Chiara Lubich. Città Mondo, catalogo della mostra,* Rome: Città Nuova, 2019, p. 169.
14 Bernhard Callebaut, 'The reception of CST and the "Movimenti" Phenomenon in the Latin American Context: a Critical View', *Journal of Catholic Social Thought* X,2 (2013), 413-419, see 416.
15 Karl Jaspers, *Vom Ursprung und Ziel der Geschichte,* Munich: Piper, 1983 (1949).
16 In the Preface to the Italian edition of Jaspers' book, Raniero Regni reminds us: 'Another lasting heritage of the Axial Age connected with the fracture it produced within societies and their cultures between the sedentary and those who set out on a path animated by a new prophecy, is the spread of social criticism.' And 'the pre-Axial societies saw political power as the incarnation of a cosmic order that coincided with the social order and vice versa'. Regni, pp. viii and xiii.
17 Rodney Stark, *The Rise of Christianity: A Sociologist Reconsiders History,* Princeton: Princeton University Press, 1996.
18 The French sociologist Émile Poulat has dedicated part of his work to the triangular dynamic between the Church, liberalism, and socialism and how in different conjunctures liberal Catholics, social Catholics, and intransigent Catholics appear, ally with, or fight among themselves or with the right and the left. Émile Poulat, *Le catholicisme sous observation. Entretiens avec G. Lafon,* Paris: Le centurion, 1983.
19 Donal Dorr offers a fine analysis of this shift; see Donal Dorr, *Option for the Poor. A Hundred Years of Catholic Social Teaching,* New York: Maryknoll, 1992, in particular pp. 137-142. 'Probably the most important effect of the encyclical [*Mater et Magistra,* 1961], seen as an intervention in the continuing debate about social issues, was that it began the process of breaking the long alliance between Roman Catholicism and socially conservative forces' (p. 138). '[…] The social teaching of Pope John was a major step towards the prevention of such an ideological use of Church teaching and towards the recovery of its original purpose' (142).
20 Pope Francis, *Evangelii Gaudum* (Apostolic Exhortation *Evangelli Gaudium* of the Holy Father Francis to the Bishops, Clergy, Consecrated Persons and the Lay Faithful on the Proclamation of the Gospel in Today's World), <http://www.vatican.va/content/francesco/en/apost_exhortations/documents/papa-francesco_esortazione-ap_20131124_evangelii-gaudium.html>, §223.
21 Walter Benjamin, 'Kapitalismus als Religion', in *Gesammelte Schriften,* vol. VI, Frankfurt a.M.: Suhrkamp, 1991, pp. 100–103; Walter Benjamin, 'Capitalism as Religion [Fragment 74]', *Religion as Critique: The Frankfurt School's Critique of Religion,* edited by Eduardo Mendieta, New York: Routledge, 2005), pp. 259-262. 'Capitalism is a religion, that is to say, capitalism essentially serves to satisfy the same worries, anguish,

and disquiet formerly answered by so-called religion. [...] Capitalism itself developed parasitically on Christianity in the West.' For an important comment see Michael Brie, *Warum Kapitalismus keine Religion ist. Verteidigung der Religion gegen die Kapitalismuskritiker unter ihren Verächtern,* soon to be published.

22 Harding Meyer, 'Die Prägung einer Formel. Ursprung und Intention', in Harald Wagner and Harding Meyer (eds), *Einheit - aber wie? Zur Tragfähigkeit der ökumenischen Formel vom 'differenzierten Konsens',* Quaestiones disputatae, vol. 184, Freiburg: Herder Verlag 2000, p. 55.

23 'Drawing inspiration from the *Differentiated Consensus,* which formed the basis of the rapprochement of the Catholic Church and the Lutheran World Federation, allowing the formulation of the *Joint Declaration on Justification,* signed in Augsburg in 1999, the social ethics is also expected to undergo an analogous experiment despite completely different conditions and to achieve a shared transversal social ethics. Although we are exploring a completely new realm, the experience made so far gives us hope with reason.' Baier et al., *Europe as a Common,* pp. 25-26.

24 M. Michela Nicolais, 'The Economy of Francesco. Zamagni: "ci vuole una trasformazione, non solo una riforma" [we need a transformation, not just a reform]', SIR, 19 novembre 2020, <https://www.agensir.it/chiesa/2020/11/19/the-economy-of-francesco-zamagni-ci-vuole-una-trasformazione-non-solo-una-riforma/>.

25 Émile Poulat, 'Pensée chrétienne et vie économique', *Les Cahiers de l'Unité* 16 (1988), 37-58.

26 In a discussion on Catholic integralism and its intention to bring to Christ all of human life, Poulat notes, starting with the Middle Ages : 'In the ethical debate that opposes the Church and business, their mutual incomprehension conceals the mental mutation that operates here: money no longer has the same purpose; in other times one lent to the poor, now one lends to the rich. We are at the point of bifurcation of economic behaviour. The moralists did not continue with this ; they were never again to board the train, which in the meanwhile was to greatly accelerate its speed. Enrichment would pose all manner of problems of modern capitalism, of the industrial development of the international economy. There should be no illusions: Catholic integralism concentrated itself where it had means – on the social, because it had no hold on the economic where liberalism reigned supreme. There its integralism came up against one of its most serious limits.' Poulat, *Le catholicisme sous observation,* p. 105.

27 Poulat, *Pensée chrétienne et vie économique,* p. 54.

28 The concept of Holy Poverty is very well known and associated with Saint Francis of Assisi. On the other side, Poulat links the concept of holy enrichment to Calvin and the Reformation. There is an interesting paradox to observe here: at the end of the Middle Ages there emerged a new relationship to luxury and money not in northern Europe but principally in the south: '[...] the magnificence of Rome and Italy that were also the fruit of the wealth created by a new and positive attitude toward luxury and money during the XIV and XV centuries. Luther was deeply impressed and shocked by the mundane and market-based society he met in Italy that he considered far from the original message of austerity and poverty of the gospel. The strong reaction of Lutheran and later Calvinist Reformation was against not only the theology of the Roman Church, but also against the style of living of [the] Italian renaissance [...]. Therefore, the protestant cultural program was also a reestablishment of a more authentic and less money-oriented society, but, paradoxically, due to the elimination of the hierarchical

mediation of the church, the protestant culture created an environment much more adapt[ed] to develop the capitalist economy.' Luigino Bruni, Paul Oslington, and Stefano Zamagni, 'Economics and theology special issue: introduction', *International Review of Economics* 63,1 (March 2016), 3-4.

29 Poulat, *Pensée chrétienne et vie économique,* p. 55. Today, research on the relation between economic theory and theology applies new approaches in highlighting the role of the Reformation and Counter-Reformation: 'Most of the present-day differences in labor culture, public debt and public ethics, in welfare states, individual rights, and the idea of market lay in the two different ways that Europe took after Reform and Controriforma era. The Cinquecento and Seicento were therefore a return to Middle Age (Aquinas) as far as economic ethics is concerned. The modernization and openness to market of Quattrocento, with the key role of figures such as Bernardino di Siena or Leon Battista Alberti, were not able to fully flourish in Italy and Southern Europe. Second, the age of Controriforma was – with few exceptions, such as Menochio – a praise of agriculture and rural life and a criticism to urban and civic activities (i.e. commerce). As a consequence, starting with the second half of XVI century, Latin Europe knew a re-feudalization of society and a centrality of rent over profit of merchant and salary of workers […].' Bruni, Oslington, and Zamagni, 3-4.

30 <https://www.usccb.org/upload/economic_justice_for_all.pdf>.

31 For a sociological analysis of the project see Bennie Callebaut, 'L'Economia di Comunione, un percorso oltre l'alternativa 'santa povertà' o 'santo arricchimento'? Indagine sociologica sulle sorti di una ispirazione carismatica contemporanea in campo economico e sociale', *Nuova Umanità* XXXII,6 (2010), 192, 681-701. English translation: Bernhard Callebaut, 'Economy of Communion. A Sociologial Inquiry on a Contemporary Charismatic Inspiration in Economic and Social Life', *Claritas: Journal for Dialogue and Culture* I. 1 (2012), 71-82 <https://docs.lib.purdue.edu/claritas/vol1/iss1/8/>.

32 Zamagni synthetically defines this contribution as '[…] bringing into the agora, in addition to the issues themes of justice and liberty, that of fraternity, and inserting it into the economic sphere of reciprocity as a gratuity'. Zamagni, *Un'economia per il mondo*, p. 170.

33 Two quotations can help convey what civil economy is: 'From the market efficiency is required and thus the creation of wealth, the enlarging of the "pie". Solidarity, on the other hand, begins precisely where the market ends, providing criteria for political action to divide up the pie, assigning "slices" to individuals, or, alternatively, solidarity intervenes in those folds of society still not reached by the market.' 'The challenge of civil economy is to find the ways – which certainly exist – to let all three mentioned regulative principles coexist within the same social system. Indeed, we certainly need efficiency but also equity and also – let us dare to say it – above all reciprocity.' Luigino Bruni and Stefano Zamagni, *Economica civile. Efficienza, equità, felicità pubblica*, Bologna: Il Mulino, 2004, pp. 17 and 23.

For Zamagni, '[…] it is at Assisi that the, typically Italian, paradigm of civil economy began. In 1753, the University of Naples created the world's first chair in economics, as an academic science, and it was truly a civil economy chair. It was the point of arrival of a process of Franciscan thinking. It was the Franciscans who invented not market, which had always existed, but market economy as a ways of organising social life. Political economy, which arose with Adam Smith, had considerable merits but it has nothing to

say today – it tells us how to increase wealth but not how to redistribute it. Today there is a return to origins' (from the interview conducted by M. Michela Nicolais, 'The Economy of Francesco' <https://www.agensir.it/chiesa/2020/11/19/the-economy-of-francesco-zamagni-ci-vuole-una-trasformazione-non-solo-una-riforma/>.
Bruni and Zamagni, in their introduction to the *Dizionario di economia*, define it as follows: '[…] civil economy is being posed today as an alternative contrasting with the Smithian traditional economy that sees the market as the only institution that is truly necessary for democracy and liberty; civil economy reminds us that a good society is certainly the fruit of the market and liberty but that there are needs, reducible to the principle of fraternity, that cannot be sidestepped nor shifted only to the private sphere or to philanthropy. […] Civil economy proposes a multi-dimensional humanism in which the market is not fought against or 'controlled' but is seen as a civil location equal to others, as an element of the public sphere that, if conceived and experienced as a place open also to the principles of reciprocity and gratuitousness, can build the city' (Luigino Bruni and Stefano Zamagni (eds), *Dizionario di economia civile*, Rome: Città Nuova 2009, pp. 13-14).

34   Benedict XVI, Encyclical Letter *Caritas in veritate* of the Supreme Pontiff Benedict XVI to the Bishops, Priests and Deacons, Men and Women Religious, the Lay Faithful, and All People of Good Will on Integral Human Development in Charity and Truth, 29 June 2009, <http://www.vatican.va/content/benedict-xvi/en/encyclicals/documents/hf_ben-xvi_enc_20090629_caritas-in-veritate.html>, §37.

35   From 19 to 21 November, 2000 young 'under 35' economists and entrepreneurs met, coming from all corners of the world. The objective was the common search for the paradigm of a new economy, with explorations of 12 specific issues with the help of Nobel Prize winners, economists, scientists, entrepreneurs, and world famous experts. See the official site: <https://francescoeconomy.org/it/>.

36   Pope Francis, *Evangelii gaudium*, §53.

37   In his analysis we sense a great affinity with the critical discourses of figures like Edgar Morin, to give just one example: 'At high levels, policy is emptied of any content in order to trail after the economy. Politics has bowed down to neoliberalism and to the calculation that quantifies and dehumanises what it treats, and ignores the improbable and the unforeseen.' (Edgar Morin, *Changeons de voie, Les Leçons du coronavirus*, Paris: Denoël, 2020, p. 62.

38   It would be interesting to do a more thorough study of the affinities with the analysis of an independent thinker whose background is nevertheless clearly left wing, like Edgar Morin: 'Will it be possible, if not to regulate the world economy, to reduce the force of hypercapitalism, reform the bank systems, control stock-exchange speculation, and impede tax evasion? Will we find the principles of an economy based on a New Deal of ecological relaunching and social reform that will turn back hypercapitalism and reduce inequalities?' Morin, *Changeons de voie*, pp. 60-61.

39   Morin, *Changeons de voie*, p. 93.

40   'We have said that we need to abandon the idea of a violent devolution that "would make a tabula rasa of the past" and upturn a bad society to erect a good one' Morin, p. 82.

41   Morin, p. 76.

42   Morin, p. 77.

43   In this case the reference was to Dorothy Day.

44 <http://www.vita.it/it/article/2020/10/16/un-patto-educativo-nella-catastrofe-educativa/157018/> On 15 October 2020 Pope Francis launched a Global Compact on Education against the education catastrophe in times of the pandemic. Among the seven proposals at the conclusion of his address, the sixth shows a strong affinity with the work pursued by Dialop: Sixth, to be committed to finding new ways of understanding the economy, politics, growth and progress that can truly stand at the service of the human person and the entire human family, within the context of an integral ecology, <http://www.vatican.va/content/francesco/en/messages/pont-messages/2020/documents/papa-francesco_20201015_videomessaggio-global-compact.html>.

45 Pope Francis, *Message of His Holiness Pope Francis for the Launch of the Global Compact on Education*, 12 September 2019, <https://www.vatican.va/content/francesco/en/messages/pont-messages/2019/documents/papa-francesco_20190912_messaggio-patto-educativo.html>.

To Differ and Learn From Each Other – A Marxist Voice on the Social Encyclical 'Fratelli tutti'

Karl-Helmut Lechner

Dialogue only works when both sides are interested in each other and want to learn from each other. When Christians and Marxists meet now in 2020 and 2021 fortunately they are no longer interested in continuing 200-year-old battles by reiterating statements such as: 'We harvest our crops without God and sunshine'[1] or Pope John XXIII's 1959 decree: 'Catholics are not allowed to vote for parties or candidates that show an inclination to cooperate with communism, even if its official principles do not contradict Catholic teachings.'[2] Nevertheless, dialogue still means making clear how the two sides differ.

Certainly the Pope is no communist. But for him the yearning for complete justice on earth is a highly charged religious and theological conception shared with many of his Catholic co-believers.

Marxism is not a religion, even if this is sometimes assumed of it. Marxism seeks to understand historical and social contexts from a secular point of view that is free of religion and then to work out possibilities for emancipatory action – knowing full well that there are unsolved questions about life. Marxists know that the relation between reason and morality is complicated. Under no circumstances may ethical questions be exempt from the need for rational grounding.

These two tenets are important in the history of Christians and Marxists but they are unfortunately often confounded. There were and still are misrepresentations, spillovers, and absorption. Convergences in dialogue can only succeed if we learn to differentiate ourselves and then formulate common goals, act in accordance with them, and then succeed in realising these goals.

It is not easy nowadays for a secular person without great religious feelings to pay attention to the Catholic Church and its Pope because the Church is knee deep in scandals; hypocrisy and a know-it-all attitude that prompts a self-defensive stance in matters of sexual abuse of children, youth, and nuns. The suffering from the spread of AIDS, especially in Africa, is a consequence, among other things, of the Catholic Church's unremorseful holding on to its antiquated ethic of marriage, which permits sexuality only for the purpose of bringing children into the world and therefore disallows the use of condoms. In the matter of the Church's and Vatican's financial management, the bishop of Limburg with his golden bathtub is only the tip of the iceberg. In its catechism, the Catholic Church has summarised the doctrine and dogma that believers should know and believe. But it ought to critically ask itself whether the statement – 'those who are able to resign themselves to fundamentalist non-thinking will, to put it crudely, be left behind' – does not also apply to itself.[3]

And yet – this is only half the truth. A keen Marxist eye sees that, just as in every hierarchically built organisation, there is also in the Church not only 'those on top', that is, the cardinals and clergy, who are the first to be seen in the media, but also 'those below', those Christians who believe in and stand by the Bible's message and for whom the Church is the space of their religious life. There are not only the princes of the Church, who act dogmatically, while abusing their power, financially benefitting from the existing relations, and enjoying their privileges. No, there are typically also the many 'from below', at the base, who want to help bring about justice in the world, and for whom the Gospel of Jesus is more than dogma, domination, power, influence, and money. For example, at present there are the Focolare Movement[4] and the Mary 2.0 Movement.[5] These are people who seek by way of democratic and synodal structures to change the hierarchy of the Church with its top-down principle of obedience.[6] Thus women are demanding that they finally be allowed to assume consecrated functions and be able to celebrate the Eucharist as priests of a parish. 'It is not the consecration of women that has to be explained but their exclusion!', as they formulate it. There are also liberation theologians who in their thinking and spiritual actions stand with the poor and disenfranchised of the world. Former Popes have literally forbidden them to speak. It is indeed not only in Germany but in the worldwide Church that we see how people, driven by their belief, have stood up for democratic participation, the conservation of nature as God's Creation, and for emancipatory values and human rights. There is consequently great curiosity and interest both on the part of 'religiously tone-deaf' observers, who are fighting for similar if not identical issues in the movement of secular left people, as well as the 'actually pious' when both of these groups now hold a Papal text like *Fratelli tutti* in their hands, in which the head of the Church is propagating new ideas.

A functional relationship

The perspective of secular observers who consider the Encyclicals of a Pope and explanations by Church officials is, at the beginning, purely functional. This means that it is less the contents, certainly not the theological-religious rationales and derivations of these explanations that peaks their curiosity; their attention, rather, is to the social and political functions that these explanations have in each political context for individual people and groups who are in conflict around nature, justice, and human rights. The 'functional' question is: Do these explanations open up a possibility for people to act more freely within the space of the churches than previously? Do they create more openness in speaking and acting, in short, do they 'connect' with common concrete projects for the non-religious too? Or do these Papal utterances once again work to limit, intimidate, and frustrate people of 'good will' in the fold of the Church and beyond?

Experience teaches how important it is not to stand alone within an organisation and its conflicts. Opposing injustice and standing up for change always also means forging structural social and political plans and putting them into practice. From this point of view it is gratifying that the Pope published his document with an aim to solving such problems, which allows many people to now invoke it.

'What good can still come out of Rome?'

Many sceptically ask, turning around a familiar Biblical quotation, 'What good can still come out of Rome?', even when they read these new encyclicals.[7] The long tradition of Papal encyclicals that hampered and slowed progress has been etched deeply in people's memory.

In the 1891 Encyclical *Rerum novarum*, Pope Leo XIII described the condition of workers and warned that it was the duty of employers 'not to look upon their work people as their bondsmen, but to respect in every man his dignity as a person ennobled by Christian character'. However, the same encyclical also strongly states:

> To remedy these wrongs the socialists, working on the poor man's envy of the rich, are striving to do away with private property, and contend that individual possessions should become the common property of all, to be administered by the State or by municipal bodies. They hold that by thus transferring property from private individuals to the community, the present

mischievous state of things will be set to rights, inasmuch as each citizen will then get his fair share of whatever there is to enjoy. But their contentions are so clearly powerless to end the controversy that were they carried into effect the working man himself would be among the first to suffer. They are, moreover, emphatically unjust, for they would rob the lawful possessor, distort the functions of the State, and create utter confusion in the community.'[8]

Pope Paul VI, in his 1968 encyclical, *Humanae vitae*,[9] on the regulation of birth, permanently estranged many engaged Christians from the Church and in so doing fortified its conservative members in their reactionary fundamentalist ideology up to the present day.

Pope John Paul II continued this tendency in his May 1994 Apostolic Letter: '[…] in order that all doubt may be removed regarding a matter of great importance, a matter which pertains to the Church's divine constitution itself, in virtue of my ministry of confirming the brethren (cf. Lk 22:32) I declare that the Church has no authority whatsoever to confer priestly ordination on women and that this judgment is to be definitively held by all the Church's faithful.'[10] With this statement the Pope wanted to end the persistent discussion on priestly ordination for women in the Catholic Church. Even Pope Francis has unfortunately affirmed this statement with the striking formulation: 'This door is closed.'[11]

Just recently Pope Francis rejected all Church reform 'according to democratic standards alone', holding that the existence of the Church draws its meaning from its rootedness in Christ. What is indispensable, he stresses, is listening to the teachings of the apostles, brotherly and sisterly community, the celebration of the sacraments, and prayer. Everything that sprouts in the Church beyond these cornerstones is, he maintains, without foundation and 'built on sand'. 'It is God who makes the Church, not the clamour about deeds',[12] the Pope says. He characterises as misguided initiatives that, though based on good intentions, would want to organise the Church like a party with democratic procedure or a 'synodal path'.[13] 'I ask myself, "where is the Holy Ghost? Where is prayer? Where is love in the community?, Where is the Eucharist?" Without these four coordinates the Church becomes a human society.'' If the Holy Ghost is not there, he explains, the community of the faithful can indeed be 'a beautiful humanitarian, beneficent association' but not Church. Francis went on to say that sermons and instruction in the faith remind us of Jesus's words and deeds; the constant search for the ecclesiastical community protects us from egoism and factions; the 'breaking of the bread' in the Eucharist makes Jesus present and prayer opens space for dialogue with God. 'God bestows love and asks for love. That is the mystical root of a life of faith.'[14]

Thus there are plenty of reasons for the great scepticism which greets every Pope's declarations. Experience shows that they are written in the conservative tradition of the Church and characterised by conservative morality. They were and still are determined by the wish to stabilise the relations of domination and through its social doctrine to – very concretely – tie the labour movement to capitalism and maintain masculine privileges. The present Pope, Francis, often moves within this ecclesiastical tradition.

In his public appearances, however, he shows himself to be accessible and concerned with all believers regardless of origin or gender. Warm-heartedly he moves close to churchgoers in order – like all public figures – to make his religious and political statements in symbolically powerful ways. Moreover, already with his choice of name, which every Pope has to undertake when he takes office, he decided deliberately on Francis, the saint that stands, and not only among Catholics, for a life in poverty and brotherhood. None of his 265 predecessors in the history of the Church ever hit upon the idea of declaring the goals of the founder of the mendicant order (1182-1226) to be his model.

The emulation of Christ in poverty is the programmatic statement associated with this founder of an order. 'Francis is the "troubadour of God": The fundamental feature of his piety is a strong, overflowing feeling of joy that often becomes rapture and is ignited in particular by contemplating the suffering and poverty of Christ but also nature.' This is how the church historian Karl Heussi describes Francis who was sanctified in 1128.[15] Is the present Pope with the same name then a completely different sort from his professorially ossified predecessor Ratzinger? Pope Francis does not want to be the resplendent representative of a palatial church as symbolised by the Vatican City State, the mighty Saint Peter's in Rome, and magnificent vestments and regalia. His subject is the 'poor' and Christian poverty. But what exactly does he mean by this?

Property and human rights

If we enquire about the possibility that secular emancipatory praxis might 'connect' to the Church's proclamations, we should first look at two remarkable ideas expressed in the new encyclical *Fratelli tutti* of 3 October 2020.

First: The Pope declares the property question to no longer be absolute and unalterable. Under the rubric 'Re-Envisaging the Social Role of Property' he writes in §120:

For my part, I would observe that 'the Christian tradition has never recognized the right to private property as absolute or inviolable, and has stressed the social purpose of all forms of private property'. The principle of the common use of created goods is the 'first principle of the whole ethical and social order'; it is a natural and inherent right that takes priority over others. All other rights having to do with the goods necessary for the integral fulfilment of persons, including that of private property or any other type of property, should – in the words of Saint Paul VI – 'in no way hinder [this right] but should actively facilitate its implementation'. The right to private property can only be considered a secondary natural right, derived from the principle of the universal destination of created goods. This has concrete consequences that ought to be reflected in the workings of society.[16]

These words were very well understood by the representatives of capital, for instance in the Federal Republic of Germany. It is thus no accident that on 11 October 2020, shortly after the publication of the Encyclical, the *Frankfurter Allgemeine Zeitung* ran the title: 'Leave the Church? The Pope's Criticism of Capitalism Would be a Reason to Do So!'[17] For the first time a Papal proclamation has made it clear that it is no longer based on a demonisation of the socialist conception of private property.

Second: The Pope takes a position on the question of human rights and, in that context, on equality for women. In doing so he points in his Encyclical to his 2019 joint declaration with the Grand Imam Ahmad Al-Yayyeb. That document begins: 'In the name of God who has created all human beings equal in rights, duties and dignity, and who has called them to live together as brothers and sisters, to fill the earth and make known the values of goodness, love and peace.'[18]

If this is the common position of the Pope and Grand Imam it means that major progress has occurred. Previously, the Imam's Declaration on Human Rights differed significantly from the Universal Declaration of Human Rights. Article 6 of the 1990 Cairo Declaration on Human Rights in Islam does accord, it is true, equal value to women but not the same rights as men. 'Woman is equal to man in human dignity, and has her own rights to enjoy as well as duties to perform [...].'[19]

The joint Catholic-Islamic text of the Dubai Declaration quoted in the Encyclical no longer draws this distinction between the genders. For the first time, in their dialogue, it is no longer a matter that both theologically pray to the same God, but they speak of the 'same rights' for women and men in public and secular social space. This is progress in terms of religious dialogue.

Catholic women, however, reacted sceptically to the Pope's good words in the Encyclical. They immediately complained that in the title itself, *Fratelli tutti* (to all 'brothers'), only masculine Catholics were present and that they were not addressed as 'sisters'. They felt that 'The discrepancies between the Pope's words and Catholic reality [...] intrude too much – while on paper the Pope strongly advocates rights for women, women are discriminated in the Catholic Church and, moreover, made linguistically invisible by the problematic choice of the Encyclical's title' – they are paternalistically told that they should nevertheless feel that they are meant to be included too.[20] In the German translation the problem is glossed over by translating the world 'fratelli' with 'Geschwisterlichkeit'.[21]

A pity! Wouldn't the publication of this Encyclical have been the perfect moment for the Vatican to sign the UN's 1948 Universal Declaration of Human Rights, being thus the last state to do so? And the lack of equal rights remains – the admission of women to the priesthood is still denied. The suffering of Catholic women is increasing precisely because they take Jesus's words seriously, loving their Church and professing their faith in it!

'Option for the poor'

Ever since there have been written texts there have been 'interpretations' of them. This goes for the Bible, the Church Fathers, as well as for texts by Marx and Engels. To achieve a common access to this Encyclical it is thus important to interpretatively clarify what is meant by 'option for the poor'. In §234 the Pope quotes the bishops of Latin America: 'The option for the poor should lead us to friendship with the poor.'[22]

From the general secular point of view it would appear clear what is meant by 'poverty' and 'poor'. Germany's Federal Ministry for Economic Cooperation provides this definition: 'Absolute poverty is defined by a condition in which a person cannot afford to satisfy his/her basic needs. Relative poverty indicates poverty in relation to the particular environment of a person.'[23] Thus in the social and political arena, for people and their institutions, poverty indicates a lack that needs to be abolished on a worldwide basis. On the other hand, in Biblical-theological usage 'poor' is a very luminous concept that can be filled in both negatively and positively. This also applies to representatives of the Catholic Church, including its Popes, who have used the word in diverse ways throughout its history and up to the present day.

Among the manifold models of its theological interpretation we may here distinguish five forms of 'poverty':

First: In the Sermon on the Mount as given in Matthew 5: 'Blessed are the poor in spirit, for theirs is the kingdom of heaven.' Here the attention to the 'poor' is linked to the consolation of a heaven beyond. It is well known how great a role this vision has played in the course of history, not only in the Catholic Church. The pious poor person should be content with his social lot and hope for improvement in the world beyond. Those suffering from poverty and those who consider poverty an affliction that needs to be removed can hardly agree with this. Among Marxists this conception is clearly one of the targets of the classical critique of religion.

Second: In the same sentence in Matthew 5 another theological vision of poverty can be discovered. 'Poor in spirit' cannot mean those who have nothing to eat. Here 'poverty' is used as a metaphor for another, a 'spiritual' condition. The *Bibel in gerechter Sprache*[24] explicates this passage as follows: 'Poor in spirit means to be comprehensively impoverished – not only in the material sense but also in relation to God.'[25] Thus the powerful and rich King David repeatedly sings in the Psalms: 'I am poor and miserable [...].'[26] 'Poor' means far from God, a meaningless and alienated life. It is precisely materially rich people who see themselves as described and addressed theologically here. Is this really what the Pope means by 'option for the poor'? Seen from the secular angle, this metaphor is politically unsuitable, and not only for Marxists.

Third: In the Bible too there is a fundamental criticism of those who possess worldly wealth. In the eye of God, those who 'always want to have more' have a false security. The following applies to them: 'Thus will it be for the one who stores up treasure for himself but is not rich in what matters to God.'[27] An emphatically ascetic way of life has been directed against this, one that consciously wants to be 'poor'. 'Poor' is understood as an individual, spiritual, personal form of life. It is characterised by personal renunciation; one must not be ruled by 'greed'. Jesus sends his disciples out with the words: 'Without cost you have received; without cost you are to give. Do not take gold or silver or copper for your belts; no sack for the journey, or a second tunic, or sandals, or walking stick.'[28] The poverty movement, from medieval nuns and monks in the Middle Ages to today's alternative ways of life follows this model. Their concept of life occurs by no means only among religiously oriented people but is often found in the secular arena. There have always been people and groups that have wanted to consciously renounce wealth, escape consumerist compulsion, and lead a simple, self-determined life. Such individual ways of life have a thoroughly positive society-wide effect, for instance when the conservation of nature and the environment is at stake.

Fourth: Nothing is seen as more typical of Christianity than the love for one's neighbour that Jesus asked for. This attitude begins with a solidaristic feeling for the poor, and this kind of compassion is clearly expressed by

Pope Francis in his Encyclical: 'The word "neighbour", in the society of Jesus' time, usually meant those nearest us. It was felt that help should be given primarily to those of one's own group and race. [...] [Jesus] asks us not to decide who is close enough to be our neighbour, but rather that we ourselves become neighbours to all.'[29] 'The Latin American Bishops have observed that "only the closeness that makes us friends can enable us to appreciate deeply the values of the poor today, their legitimate desires, and their own manner of living the faith. The option for the poor should lead us to friendship with the poor."'[30] 'Normal' people who act in a politically conscious way are also familiar with this option. As a Marxist one does well not to live in a rich neighbourhood but among the working population.

Fifth: If consistent this attitude of closeness to the poor leads to action against poverty. The believer and his or her Church become socially active and actively help. Diakonie in Germany and Caritas have been institutional expressions of this up to the present day.[31] The Pope sees this not as an act of individual aid but above all as a social and political task – which is presumably what prompted the above-cited criticism from capitalist circles. Under the rubric 'Political Love' he unambiguously develops this position:

> There is a kind of love that is "elicited": its acts proceed directly from the virtue of charity and are directed to individuals and peoples. There is also a "commanded" love, expressed in those acts of charity that spur people to create more sound institutions, more just regulations, more supportive structures. It follows that "it is an equally indispensable act of love to strive to organize and structure society so that one's neighbour will not find himself in poverty". It is an act of charity to assist someone suffering, but it is also an act of charity, even if we do not know that person, to work to change the social conditions that caused his or her suffering.[32]

In saying this he – finally – confirms the activity carried out by the Christian liberation movements throughout the world, which had been unequivocally defamed by his predecessors. For people active in these liberation movements, and above all also for Marxists, this outlook is easy to connect to. However, the Pope goes even further and argues in a way that has never before been heard in the Church hierarchy:

> In some closed and monochrome economic[33] approaches, for example, there seems to be no place for popular movements that unite the unemployed, temporary and informal workers and many others who do not easily find a place in existing structures. Yet those movements manage[34] various forms of

popular economy and of community production. What is needed is a model of social, political and economic participation 'that can include popular movements and invigorate local, national and international governing structures with that torrent of moral energy that springs from including the excluded in the building of a common destiny', while also ensuring that 'these experiences of solidarity which grow up from below, from the subsoil of the planet – can come together, be more coordinated, keep on meeting one another'. This, however, must happen in a way that will not betray their distinctive way of acting as 'sowers of change, promoters of a process involving millions of actions, great and small, creatively intertwined like words in a poem'. In that sense, such movements are 'social poets' that, in their own way, work, propose, promote and liberate. They help make possible an integral human development that goes beyond 'the idea of social policies being a policy *for* the poor, but never *with* the poor and never *of* the poor, much less part of a project that reunites peoples'.³⁵

The survival of humanity

No wonder then that the Latin American Catholic 'liberation theologian' Leonardo Boff – whom Cardinal Ratzinger as prefect of the Congregation for the Doctrine of the Faith had condemned to silence within the Church and may no longer be a priest – is enthusiastic about the Encyclical. He had already said in a 2016 interview: 'The Pope has made liberation theology into the common property of the Church. […] For him a poor person is not intrinsically a pauper but an impoverished person: one is not poor, one is made poor.'

This Papal encyclical is no longer just about the reform of the Church. In fact, with its ideas this declaration steps outside the inner-Church framework and inaugurates a worldwide cooperation. Boff is right when he says of Pope Francis: 'You know, as far as I can understand him, the centre of his interest is no longer the Church, and certainly not the inside business of the Church, but the survival of humanity, the future of the earth. Both are in danger, and one has to ask whether Christianity can make a contribution to the overcoming of this great crisis, which threatens to put an end to the human species.'³⁶

To argue out and resolve the theological contradictions that have emerged as a result of the Encyclical is a matter for the believers who stand by their Church. But they need to know that they are not alone. There are many statements in this Encyclical by Pope Francis that make possible a dialogue between progressive-minded Christians, the many non-religious socially engaged people, and all those who see themselves as Marxists. They can learn from one another, cooperate, and struggle together. Thus the existence of this Encyclical is a good thing.

NOTES

1. 'Ohne Gott und Sonnenschein fahren wir die Ernte ein.'
2. <http://www.kathpedia.com/index.php?title=Dekret_vom_4._April_1958> and <https://www.domradio.de/themen/kirche-und-politik/2019-07-01/als-der-heilige-stuhl-wahlverbote-aussprach-70-jahre-anti-kommunismus-dekret-des-vatikan>.
3. Hubertus Halbfas, 'Kann ein Christ Atheist sein? Kann ein Atheist Christ sein?', *Ostfiltern* 2020, 65.
4. <https://www.fokolar-bewegung.de/> and <https://www.focolare.org/en/>.
5. <https://www.mariazweipunktnull.de/> and <http://womensordinationcampaign.org/blog-working-for-womens-equality-and-ordination-in-the-catholic-church/2020/1/22/maria-20-germany>.
6. The *synodal path* is a form of developing democratic structures in conformity with the Church [and a concrete project in Germany based on this principle]. The synodal path is not a format defined in the Code of Canon Law but a sui generis one. All those who officially participate in it take responsibility for the outcomes [?] of this path. Giving its decisions binding force is the role of the Holy See and/or the local bishop, depending on the issue involved. Article 1 of the Synodal Path's bylaws frame the task in this way: 'The Synodal Path of the Catholic Church in Germany serves the common search for steps to strengthen Christian witness. The aim is to clarify central issues and fields of action: "Power and separation of powers in the Church - Joint participation and involvement in the mission", "Priestly existence today", "Women in ministries and offices in the Church", "Life in succeeding relationships - Living love in sexuality and partnership", at <https://www.synodalerweg.de/fileadmin/Synodalerweg/Dokumente_Reden_Beitraege/2019_Satzung-des-Synodalen-Weges-englisch.pdf>.
7. 'Nazareth! Can anything good come from there?', John 1,46.
8. *Rerum novarum*, Encyclical of Pope Leo XIII on Capital and Labor, 15 May 189, §§ 20 and 4, at <http://www.vatican.va/content/leo-xiii/en/encyclicals/documents/hf_l-xiii_enc_15051891_rerum-novarum.html>. See also 'Text zur katholischen Soziallehre', in Bundesverband der Katholischen Arbeitnehmer-Bewegung Deutschlands (ed.), *Die sozialen Rundschreiben der Päpste und andere kirchliche Dokumente*, Kevelaer: KAB, 1992.
9. *Humanae Vitae*, 25 July 1968), at <http://www.vatican.va/content/paul-vi/en/encyclicals/documents/hf_p-vi_enc_25071968_humanae-vitae.html>.
10. Apostolic Letter *Ordinatio sacerdotalis* of John Paul II to the Bishops of the Catholic Church on Reserving Priestly Ordination to Men Alone, at <http://www.vatican.va/content/john-paul-ii/en/apost_letters/1994/documents/hf_jp-ii_apl_19940522_ordinatio-sacerdotalis.html>.
11. Pope Francis, 'Diese Tür ist zu', <https://www.domradio.de/themen/vatikan/2019-05-22/johannes-paul-ii-hat-frauen-debatte-nicht-beendet-papstschreiben-zum-ausschluss-des-frauen>.
12. In the Pope's Italian: 'clamore delle opere', at <https://www.domradio.de/video/papst-kirche-verwurzelt-christus>.

13 In German 'Gegen den synodalen Weg'; it has not been possible to hear or locate the Pope's original words in Italian.
<https://www.domradio.de/themen/papst-franziskus/2020-11-25/papst-kein-freund-von-synodalen-wegen-franziskus-gegen-zu-viel-demokratie-der-kirche>; see also the 25 November 2020 video message
at <https://www.domradio.de/video/papst-kirche-verwurzelt-christus>.
14 KNA, 25 November 2020, at <https://www.domradio.de/themen/vatikan/2019-05-22/johannes-paul-ii-hat-frauen-debatte-nicht-beendet-papstschreiben-zum-ausschluss-des-frauen>.
15 Karl Heussi, *Kompendium der Kirchengeschichte*, Tübingen: Mohr, 1988, p. 221.
16 Encyclical Letter *Fratelli tutti* of the Holy Father Francis on Fraternity and Social Friendship, at <http://www.vatican.va/content/francesco/en/encyclicals/documents/papa-francesco_20201003_enciclica-fratelli-tutti.html>.
17 <https://rainer-hank.de/faz-kolumne/hanks-welt/aus-der-kirche-austreten/>.
18 <http://www.vatican.va/content/francesco/en/travels/2019/outside/documents/papa-francesco_20190204_documento-fratellanza-umana.html>; *Fratelli tutti*, §5.
19 <http://hrlibrary.umn.edu/instree/cairodeclaration.html>.
20 See *Zeit-Online*, 16 October 2020: '"Fratelli tutti" Hat dieser Papst mir noch was zu sagen?', at <https://www.zeit.de/2020/43/fratelli-tutti-frauen-papst-franziskus-neue-enzyklika-katholische-kirche>.
21 Which is genderless, indicating both fraternity and sorority.
22 Fratelli tutti, §234.
23 <https://www.bmz.de/de/service/glossar/A/armut.html>.
24 'The Bible in a Just Language'. The editors of the *Bibel in gerechter Sprache* formulate their concept as follows: To translate the Bible means to do justice to the source text and thus use an understandable language to serve people in their search for God. This process is open-ended. The website <www.bibel-in-gerechter-sprache.de> documents and accompanies the disputes around the *Bibel in gerechter Sprache*.
25 <https://www.bibel-in-gerechter-sprache.de/die-bibel/bigs-online/?Mt/5/1>.
26 See Psalm 40, 18 und Psalm 70, 6.
27 Luke 12, 21.
28 Matthew 10, 8 – 10.
29 *Fratelli tutti*, §80.
30 *Fratelli tutti*, §234.
31 Diakonie is the welfare association of the Protestant churches in Germany and Caritas that of the Catholic Church throughout the world. In Germany alone, Diakonie and Caritas together have 1.3 million employees.
32 *Fratelli tutti*, §186.
33 In Italian 'economicistiche', that is, economistic.
34 In Italian 'danno vita a', that is, are creating, are giving birth to.
35 *Fratelli tutti*, §169.
36 <http://www.fr.de/kultur/interview-arm-ist-man-nicht-arm-wird-man-gemacht-a-734522>.

Authors and Editors

David Adler is a political economist and General Coordinator of the Progressive International. He is the co-founder of the Green New Deal for Europe campaign, and previously served as policy coordinator of the Democracy in Europe Movement. His research and writing have been featured in the *New York Times*, *Washington Post*, and the *Guardian*, among others.

Walter Baier, an economist in Vienna, was National Chairman of the Communist Party of Austria (KPÖ) from 1994 to 2006. He was an editor of the Austrian weekly *Volksstimme* and from 2007 has been Coordinator of the network *transform! europe*. His latest books are *Linker Aufbruch in Europa?* (2015) and *Unentwegte – Österreichs Kommunist_innen 1918-2018* (2018).

Joanna Bourke is Professor of History at Birkbeck, University of London, and a Fellow of the British Academy. She is the Principal Investigator of the project 'SHaME' (Sexual Harms and Medical Encounters and the author of many books, which have appeared in several languages, among them *Rape: A History from the 1860s to the Present* and the forthcoming *Sexual Violence: A Global History from the 1830s to #MeToo* (Princeton University Press).

Bernhard Callebaut holds the Chair of Sociology at the Sophia University Institute of Loppiano (Florence, Italy). He has taught at the universities of Antwerp, Rome, and Lublin and published in the field of the sociology of cultural and religious processes and is a founding member of the international Research Group *Social One*, of the Interreligious Research Group *Wings of Unity*, and the DIALOP – Transversal Dialogue Project.

Eric Canepa is a music historian. From 2001 to 2006 he was the Coordinator of the Socialist Scholars Conference/Left Forum in New York and from 2008 to 2012 Co-coordinator of the Rosa Luxemburg Foundation's project North-Atlantic Left Dialogue.

Luciana Castellina is a founder of the Italian newspaper *Il Manifesto* and of the Partito di Unità Proletaria, a past Member of the European Parliament, where she was president of its Culture and Education and Foreign Economic Relations committees, several times a Deputy to the Italian Chamber of Deputies, former president of Italy's academy of motion pictures Italcinema, author of numerous books and one of the leading figures of Italy's left continuously from the 1970s to the present day. Her latest books are *Manuale antiretorico dell'UE* (2017) and *Amori comunisti* (2018).

Nadja Charaby is a Senior Advisor for International Climate Policy and Director of the International Politics and North America Unit at the Rosa Luxemburg Stiftung. Having directly experienced the impact of the climate crisis when working and living in Southeast Asia from 2006 to 2015, she began working in the field of climate justice in 2015 and has closely observed the UN Climate Summits ever since.

Michael Chessum is a socialist activist and writer based in London. He is the National Organiser for the left-wing internationalist group Another Europe is Possible, which provided a radical anti-Brexit voice independent of the political establishment. In 2016 and 2017, he was a member of the Steering Committee of Momentum, and worked as a press officer and speech writer on Jeremy Corbyn's second campaign for the Labour leadership. He was, and remains, active in a wide variety of social movements around austerity, education and migration.

Collective of the Royal College of Art University College Union branch members, staff, and alumni – including Kevin Biderman, Eleanor Dare, Laura Gordon, Eleni Ikoniadou, Matt Lewis, Joseph Pochodzaj, Cecilia Wee, and Dylan Yamada-Rice – are artists, designers, cultural workers, writers, and union organisers working with multiple creative disciplines, writing from their critical perspectives and exploring possibilities for refusal, healing, and equity within global systems of marketised art schools and art worlds.

Teppo Eskelinen is Senior Lecturer in development studies at the University of Jyväskylä, Finland, and docent in political philosophy at the University of Tampere, Finland. He has also been director of Left Forum Finland, a transform! board member, and chairperson of the international affairs working group of Left Alliance Finland. His (co-)edited books include *The Revival of Political Imagination – Utopias as Methodology* (Zed Books 2020), and *The Politics of Ecosocialism* (Routledge 2015).

Fabian Fajnwaks is a psychoanalyst practicing in Paris, an associate professor at the Département de psychanalyse – Université de Paris 8 - Vincennes - Saint-Denis, and member of the École de la cause freudienne and the World

Association of Psychoanalysis. He is co-author of *Subversion lacanienne des études du genre* (Michele, 2015).

John Bellamy Foster is the editor of *Monthly Review*, one of the world's leading figures in Marxian ecological theory and author of numerous books, including *The Vulnerable Planet*, *Marx's Ecology*, *Ecology Against Capitalism*, *The Ecological Revolution: Making Peace With the Planet*, and *The Theory of Monopoly Capitalism*, along with several co-authored volumes.

Milena Jana Gegios is a political scientist whose research draws on a critical studies of development policy and practices, and models of political communication. More broadly, she is interested in transitional justice, the politics of remembrance, and the region of Southeast Europe (the Western Balkans and Greece).

Haris Golemis is a Greek economist who worked at the Research Department of the Bank of Greece, was scientific advisor to the Federation of Greek Bank Employees, and consultant to the United Nations Centre on Transnational Corporations. From 1999 to 2017 director of the Nicos Poulantzas Institute, he is now a member of the Editorial Committee of the Greek newspaper *Epohi*, Scientific and Strategic Advisor to the Board of transform! europe, and co-editor of the *transform! europe* yearbook.

Adoración Guamán Hernández is Professor of Law at the University of Valencia. She has been a visiting professor and associate researcher at the University of Nanterre, the Homa – International Human Rights and Business Centre, the Libre University in Colombia and the Joaquín Herrera Flores Human Rights Institute. Currently coordinating the CLACSO Working Group 'Lex Mercatoria, Human Rights and Democracy', she actively collaborates with several social movements and trade unions.

Asger Hougaard is a historian and PhD Fellow at the University of Bergen in Norway. He has previously worked as an organisational consultant for the trade and student union The Danish National Association of Pedagogical Students and has written on the history of the Danish radical left and the environmental and the climate movements. He is co-editor of *Miljøbevægelsens rødder* (The Roots of the Environmental Movement) on the environmental organisation NOAH - Friends of the Earth Denmark.

Ursula Huws is the director of Analytica Social and Economic Research and the editor of the interdisciplinary journal *Work Organisation, Labour and Globalisation*. Her most recent books are *Labour in Contemporary Capitalism: What Next?* (Palgrave Macmillan, 2019) and *Reinventing the Welfare State: Online Platforms and Public Policies* (Pluto, 2020).

Eleni Ikoniadou and the **C**ollective of the Royal College of Art University College Union branch members, staff, and alumni – including Kevin Biderman, Eleanor Dare, Laura Gordon, Matt Lewis, Joseph Pochodzaj, Cecilia Wee, and Dylan Yamada-Rice – are artists, designers, cultural workers, writers, and union organisers working with multiple creative disciplines, writing from their critical perspectives and exploring possibilities for refusal, healing, and equity within global systems of marketised art schools and art worlds.

Maria Karamessini is a Professor of Labour and Welfare State Economics at Panteion University. From 2015 to 2019 she was the President and Governor of the Greek Public Employment Agency. She is member of Syriza-Progressive Coalition, its Central Committee for Renovation, the coordination team of its Labour Policy Section, and the secretariat of its Feminist Policy and Gender Section. She is also on the boards of the Nicos Poulantzas Institute and the Steering Committee of the EuroMemo Group.

Kateřina Konečná, a member of the Communist Party of Bohemia and Moravia, is a former Deputy to the Parliament of the Czech Republic. As a Member of the European Paliament (GUE/NGL/The Left) she sits on the Committee on the Environment, Public Health and Food Safety, the Committee on Transport and Tourism, and the Committee on the Internal Market and Consumer Protection, in which capacity she has authored several reports, including on palm oil and the destruction of rainforests.

Dimitris Kousouris is Assistant Professor in the Department of Byzantine and Modern Greek Studies, University of Vienna. He received his Ph.D. in history from the EHESS (Paris) and has worked in several universities in Europe and North America. His current research involves a study of religious minorities and population movements in the Greek Archipelago during the Greek War of Independence (1821-1830).

Roland Kulke is transform! europe representative to the EU institutions in Brussels. He is the facilitator of transform! europe for the area 'productive transformation', with socio-ecological transformation the principal focus of his work.

Karl-Helmut Lechner, the son of missionaries in Papua New Guinea, was a Lutheran pastor in Noderstedt, Germany, left the church in 1975, and was, until 2006, a metal worker, trade-unionist, and works council chair. A member of the League of West German Communists (BWK), of Die LINKE in Schleswig-Holstein and active in the LINKE working group 'Communist Politics from Below' (KPvu), he is co-editor of *Politische Berichte – Zeitschrift* *für linke Politik* and has published widely on the critique of religion and the church.

Birgit Mahnkopf is retired professor of European Politics at the Berlin School of Economics and Law. She is the author of numerous books, including, with Elmar Altvater, *Die Ökonomie eines friedlichen Europas. Ziele – Hindernisse – Weg* (The Economy of a Peaceful Europe: Goals – Impediments – Path) (Agenda, 2000) and *Globalisierung der Unsicherheit: Arbeit im Schatten, schmutziges Geld und informelle Politik* (Westfälisches Dampfboot, 2002) and many articles on the economic, social and, and ecological dimensions of globalisation, European integration, and industrial relations.

Amelia Martínez-Lobo, a feminist activist with extensive experience in institutional politics and social activism, received her degree in journalism from the Complutense University of Madrid. She has worked in the European Parliament, through the GUE/NGL group, specialising in migration policy, as well as in security and defence. A founder of the MeToo movement in Brussels, she is responsible for the areas of migration, the struggle against the extreme right, antifascism, and feminism at the Rosa Luxemburg Stiftung office in Madrid.

Sandro Mezzadra teaches political theory at the University of Bologna. In the last decade his work has particularly centred on the relations between globalisation, migration, and political processes, on contemporary capitalism, as well as on postcolonial criticism. With Brett Neilson he is the author of *Border as Method, or, the Multiplication of Labor* (Duke University Press, 2013) and of *The Politics of Operations. Excavating Contemporary Capitalism* (Duke University Press, 2019).

Monika Mokre is a political scientist and Senior Researcher at the Institute of Culture Studies and Theatre History of the Austrian Academy of Sciences. Her research fields are migration and asylum, theory and practice of democracy, cultural politics, and gender studies. She is politically active in the fields of migration, asylum and prison. Her most recent publication is, with Niki Kubaczek, *Die Stadt als Stätte der Solidarität* (transversal, 2021).

Guillermo Murcia López holds degrees in Political Science and in Labour Health and is the author of author of articles on politics and economics as well as the translator of Andrew Kliman's *Reclaiming Marx's Capital*, published by El Viejo Topo. He is currently a PhD candidate at the University of Valencia researching labour precarity, theories of the transformation of work, and Spanish labour law reforms.

Andrea Peniche was born and lives in Portugal. An editor by profession, she studied philosophy and gender studies at the University of Porto. She is an activist in the feminist collective A Coletiva, one of the organisers of the International Feminist Strike in Portugal, a member of the Bloco de Esquerda, and participates in several collective projects, writing about feminism, identities, and political philosophy.

Dimitris Psarras was co-editor, from 1983 to 1990, of the Greek radical left journal *Scholiastis*. From 1990 to 2012 he was a member of the journalist association *Ios* in the newspaper *Eleftherotypia* and today is a columnist for *Efimerida ton Syntakton*. The author of many books on the contemporary extreme right, the revival of anti-Semitism, and neo-Nazism in Greece, his book on Golden Dawn has appeared in French (*Aube dorée. Le livre noir du parti nazi grec*, Syllepse, 2014) and German (*Neofaschisten in Griechenland – Die Partei Chrysi Avgi*, Laika, 2014).

José Miguel Sánchez Ocaña is a researcher at the department of labour law and social security at the Faculty of Law of the University of Valencia and holds degrees in law, labour relations, and business law. He has been a university researcher in the field of platform economics. His current studies are focused on the labour aspects of public-sector contracts with private companies.

Ingar Solty is Senior Research Fellow in Foreign, Peace and Security Polity at the Rosa Luxemburg Stiftung's Institute for Critical Social Analysis. His most recent book publications, all published in German, are *On the Shoulders of Karl Marx* (2021), *The Coming War against China: The U.S.-China Conflict and its Industrial and Climate Policy Consequences* (2020), and *Literature in the New Class Society* (2020).

Oguz Turkyilmaz is a member of the Left Party (Sol Parti), Turkey, and an industrial engineer dealing with energy issues. Chair of the Energy Commission of the Chamber of Mechanical Engineers (CME), he has presented at numerous national and international congresses, conferences and authored and co-authored several CME reports on natural gas and energy resources and policies. His articles have appeared in the newspaper *BirGün*, and several journals.

Katja Voigt is Project Manager for International Climate Policy, International Politics and North America at the Rosa Luxemburg Stiftung. She studied geography with a focus on climate change from a scientific as well as political perspective and began her involvement with the UN Climate Conferences in 2009, dealing more extensively with them since the Paris conference in 2015.

Paweł Wargan is the Coordinator of the Secretariat of the Progressive International. Previously, he co-founded the Green New Deal for Europe campaign.

Ethan Young is a writer/editor and political activist based in Brooklyn. He works with the social media project Portside.org, where he moderates the news feature Global Left Midweek. His political experience runs through all the organising sectors of the US left, from, in the late 1960s, Students for a Democratic Society to, in the 2010s, Democratic Socialists of America. His pamphlet, *Mapping the Resistance: Insurgence and Polarization Between 2016 and 2020* can be accessed on the site of the Rosa Luxemburg Stiftung-New York City.

transform! european network for alternative thinking and political dialogue

office@transform-network.net
Gusshausstraße 14/3
1040 Vienna, Austria

Austria

Institute of Intercultural Research and Cooperation – IIRC★
www.latautonomy.com

transform!at
www.transform.or.at

Cyprus

Research Institute PROMITHEAS★
www.inep.org.cy

Czechia

The Institute of the Czech Left (Institut české levice)★
www.institutcl.cz

Society for European Dialogue – SPED
e-mail: malek_j@cbox.cz

Denmark

transform!danmark
www.transformdanmark.dk

Finland

Left Forum
www.vasemmistofoorumi.fi

Democratic Civic Association - DSL
www.desili.fi

France

Espaces Marx
www.espaces-marx.fr

Foundation Copernic★
www.fondation-copernic.org

Foundation Gabriel Péri★
www.gabrielperi.fr

Institut la Boétie★
institutlaboetie.fr

Germany

Journal Sozialismus
www.sozialismus.de

Rosa Luxemburg Foundation – RLF
www.rosalux.de

Institute for Social, Ecological and Economic Studies – isw
www.isw-muenchen.de

Greece

Nicos Poulantzas Institute – NPI
www.poulantzas.gr

Hungary

transform!hungary★
www.balmix.hu

Italy

transform! italia
www.transform-italia.it

Cultural Association Punto Rosso (Associazione Culturale Punto Rosso)
www.puntorosso.it

Fondazione Claudio Sabattini★
www.fondazionesabattini.it

Lithuania
DEMOS. Institute of Critical Thought★
www.demos.lt
demos@inbox.lt

Luxembourg
Transform! Luxembourg

Moldova
Transform! Moldova★
e-mail: transformoldova@gmail.com

Norway
Manifesto Foundation★
www.manifestanalyse.no

Poland
Foundation Forward / Naprzód
www.fundacja-naprzod.pl

Portugal
Cultures of Labour and Socialism – CUL:TRA
e-mail: info@cultra.pt

Romania
Association for the Development of the Romanian Social Forum★
e-mail: pedroxma@yahoo.com

Serbia
Center for Politics of Emancipation – CPE★
www.pe.org.rs

Slovenia
Institute for Labour Studies – IDS★
www.delavske-studije.si

Spain
Alternative Foundation (Catalonia)
www.fundacioalternativa.cat

Europe of Citizens Foundation – FEC
www.lafec.org

Foundation for Marxist Studies – FIM
www.fim.org.es

Instituto 25M★
www.instituto25m.info

Iratzar Foundation (Basque Country)★
www.iratzar.eus

Sweden

Center for Marxist Social Studies
www.cmsmarx.org

Turkey

R-komplex★
www.r-komplex.org

Social Investigations and Cultural Development Foundation – TAKSAV★
www.taksav.org

UK

The World Transformed – TWT★
www.theworldtransformed.org

Transform! UK – A Journal of the Radical Left
www.prruk.org

★*Observers*